PROTECTIONISM

An Annotated Bibliography with Analytical Introductions

RESOURCES ON CONTEMPORARY ISSUES

RESOURCES ON CONTEMPORARY ISSUES

Richard A. Gray
Series Editor

Entirely devoted to topics that address important social, economic, and political concerns, RESOURCES ON CONTEMPORARY ISSUES is a new bibliographic series that guides the reader to the most significant literature available on these subjects. Every book in this series is designed for use in school, academic, and public libraries. Librarians, teachers and students will find them useful not only as a means of organizing the literature of the topic, but also as a framework for understanding the complexity of the issue.

RESOURCES ON CONTEMPORARY ISSUES is one of the few bibliographic series to consistently provide analytical introductions--background text which explains the significance of the topic and provides a context in which to understand the citations assigned to each chapter. Each volume contains 800 to 1,000 annotated citations, a glossary, a chronology of events, and author and title indexes.

Other volumes in this series:

Previously Published
The American Farm Crisis

Forthcoming
Endangered Species
Sandinista Nicaragua
South Africa

This Series is Available on Standing Order.

PROTECTIONISM

An Annotated Bibliography with
Analytical Introductions

by

James M. Lutz

Associate Professor, Department of Political Science
Indiana University/Purdue University at Fort Wayne

RESOURCES ON CONTEMPORARY ISSUES

Pierian Press
Ann Arbor, Michigan

1988

Library of Congress Cataloging-in-Publication Data

Lutz, James M.
    Protectionism : an annotated bibliography with analytical introductions.

    (Resources on contemporary issues)
    Bibliography: p.
    Includes index.
    1. Tariff--Bibliography. 2. Free trade and protection--Protection--
Bibliography. I. Title. II. Series.
Z7164.T2L88   1988   [HF1713]   016.3362'6   88-15273
ISBN 0-87650-249-4

Table of Contents

Chapter 4:

International Regimes, Hegemony, and Trade Liberalization 39

The international trading system's overall level of openness may be a consequence of the distribution of political power among the major countries. A key question has been whether the presence or absence of a dominant state has had an influence on the general level of protectionism in place.

Chapter 5:

International Organizations, Disputes, and Negotiations 45

The General Agreement on Tariffs and Trade (GATT) has been the most important international organization concerned with trade issues. Its framework of rules and principles has been very important in structuring much of the discussions dealing with trade and protectionism. Multilateral negotiations under GATT's auspices were very important in reducing barriers to trade after World War II.

Chapter 6: The Rise of Protectionism in the United States 63

The United States has played a central role in facilitating or hindering free trade. It has held a key position in the international economy because of the size of its domestic market and its leadership in GATT after World War II. The sharp rise of protectionist sentiment in the United States has become a matter of grave concern to advocates of free trade.

Chapter 7: Protectionism and the Other Industrialized States

Protectionism has increased in virtually all other developed countries, just as it has in the United States. The justifications for the increased use of obstacles to imports in these countries are similar to those that are invoked in the United States. In Europe and Japan, pressure from interest groups for relief from economic distress has usually been effective and governments have responded with increased measures of protection.

Chapter 8:

The Developing Countries Adrift in a Protectionist Sea

The developing countries have faced some special difficulties in the world economy as a result of the rise of the new protectionism. Some of these problems have resulted from neo-mercantile policies in the developed states while other difficulties have been a consequence of their own domestic protectionist policies. The NICs of Asia and Latin America have been targets for much of the protectionist response from other countries.

Chapter 9: Agriculture: The Continuation of Protectionism

Unlike trade in other commodities, protectionism in food products does not reflect an increase but simply a continuation of previous practices. Liberalization of agricultural trade was largely excluded from the initial GATT arrangements or later multilateral negotiations.

Chapter 10:

Customs Unions, Free Trade Areas, and Trading Blocs

Customs unions and free trade areas can have a major protectionist effect on trade patterns. The European Community (EC) is the prime example of such a customs union, but there are or have been a number of other important regional groupings. There is also a possibility that such regional economic organizations could be the forerunners of a global trading community that is increasingly regionalized.

Chapter 11: Radical Views on the

International Economy and Protectionism

The issue of protectionism can be interpreted from a more radical perspective and in the context of a broad view of the international economic system. Much of this critical concern focuses on the developing countries and their possible exploitation by the industrialized nations or capitalist classes.

Chronology

Glossary

Indexes

CHAPTER 1

THE RISE OF PROTECTIONISM

After World War II, free trade became a guiding principle for the international economic system. By the mid-1970s, rising levels of unemployment and inflation began to lead to direct public pressures for the protection of national industries and jobs. The result of a global recession has been a general movement away from the previously accepted norm of free trade.

"The term *Free trade*, like *Virginity*, refers to one condition only, whereas *Protection* covers a multitude, as does *Sin*."[1] Thus Jonathan Pincus begins his book on the domestic politics of tariff formation in the United States prior to the Civil War. His study is just one of many documenting that not only does protectionism have a long history in the international economy but that it can also take a variety of forms.

Tariff wars and economic conflicts have indeed been present in many places and times. The Opium Wars and U.S. naval demonstrations opened China and Japan respectively to foreign imports. Austria-Hungary and Serbia engaged in tariff wars in the years preceding World War I as part of a broader political conflict. The global economic problems that appeared in the late 1920s and the 1930s were exacerbated by the protectionist policies of the major trading countries as each sought to expand exports and limit imports as two means of stimulating production, easing unemployment, and reviving their domestic economies. The resulting "beggar-thy-neighbor" policies are often considered to have extended the effects of the Great Depression, to have advanced the rise of Fascism in Germany and elsewhere in the world, and to have contributed to the outbreak of World War II.[2] More recently, the United States and France have engaged in tariff wars and retaliation against each other's imports in agricultural products.

Post-World War II Developments

After World War II, however, free trade became a guiding principle for the international economic system, with the notable exception of the Soviet bloc countries in Eastern Europe. The General Agreement on Tariffs and Trade (GATT) was instituted to provide a framework for liberalizing trade, removing barriers to imports, and providing procedures under which exceptions to the established general principles could occur. The dominant free trade orientation in the countries of the West was even reflected in the relative lack of attention that scholars gave to protectionist issues in the immediate post-war era, although they continued their interest in tariff theory. Protectionist measures that were adopted were generally seen as short-term policies necessary for economic recovery in specific countries. An exception to this lack of attention was the literature on the consequences of protection in the inter-war years. These studies often reinforced the existing free trade orientation by providing evidence of the negative effects that protectionism had had on economic stability in various countries and in the overall international political system.

The New Protectionism

In the mid-1970s, there was a shift in attitudes about the value of free trade in many countries. With the rise of the welfare policies of the industrialized nations, many non-trade policies and programs began to have indirect, but important effects on trade. In addition, large increases in the prices of petroleum products and the subsequent onset of a global economic recession led to economic difficulties in most countries of the world. Some of the resulting domestic recovery programs that were attempted conflicted with the free trade ideal, either directly or indirectly, and priority was given to the domestic scene.

Higher levels of unemployment and inflation began to lead to direct public pressures for the protection of national industries and jobs. The export oriented growth of the newly industrializing countries (NICs), such as Hong Kong, Korea, Taiwan, Singapore, and Brazil, also began at this time, introducing new competitors into the world market, particularly for some manufactured products that were still being produced in developed states. The successes of the NICs in exporting, conjoined with world recession, generated additional pressures for protecting domestic markets and jobs from foreign and "unfair" competition. Barriers to trade increased as the adoption of limitations on imports in one state almost inevitably led to similar policies in other countries. Protectionism had begun to feed upon itself as it spread to new product areas and new countries. The result of these economic difficulties, and of later ones, has been a general movement away from the previous accepted international norms that favored free trade in

principle and increased liberalization of international trade in practice.

The shift towards increasing interference with the flow of trade has been significant enough to lead many commentators to talk about either the "new protectionism" or the appearance of neo-mercantilist policies. Both of these terms refer not only to a variety of new practices that have been more and more frequently used by many countries to attempt to gain economic advantages, but to the re-appearance of economic nationalism. Neo-mercantilism, in fact, is the view that a nation's foreign economic policy should be directly related to the national economic policy, and that state gains should be maximized and supported, while international principles of free trade are minimized.[3] The re-appearance and continuation of these attitudes have changed the international economy from a condition of relative openness to international trade to one in which restraints are more likely. There has even been concern that the world had begun to slip back into the patterns of the 1930s, which had such negative consequences for so many countries and for the international economy in general.[4]

Disputes about the advantages of free trade and protection have again surfaced in the context of the world's economic problems. Free trade frequently has been considered to have played a key role in the economic recovery that occurred after World War II. Much of the economic growth in countries in the 1950s and 1960s was fueled in part by the liberal trading system that had been established. Because many of those studying the effects of protectionism have concluded that free trade is still generally the better course, they have deplored the rise of the new protectionism. Free trade, or at least freer trade, is seen as being the best interest of all the participants in the international economic system. It will permit each nation to benefit from the utilization of their comparative advantages in the production of different goods. Each state will produce those items for which it has the greatest relative levels of productivity. Specialization in production, the international division of labor, and the subsequent exchange of these goods will increase the overall degree of global efficiency and benefit all the traders.

Protectionism, on the other hand, will lead to global inefficiency, economic losses, and higher costs for consumers in many countries. Further it encourages inefficient industries to continue the production of the same items and makes it difficult for them to adjust to the changing economic conditions that surround them. While there is often a recognition that some obstacles to free trade may be necessary for such purposes as developing new industries or permitting domestic economic adjustments in times of difficulties, the more frequent conclusion has been that in the final analysis protection leads to costs that far outweigh any benefits that may accrue.

The studies of protectionism that are included in this and following chapters clearly reflect a global increase in obstacles to trade. The very volume of the literature on the subject in itself indicates the level of concern that has developed. Further, the works that have been included are ones that deal only with the creation of barriers to trade in the pursuit of economic objectives or advantages. Trade embargoes and economic sanctions have been used in efforts to attain political goals in the past and continue to be so used today. These actions, however, are not principally directed toward protecting domestic economic interests. Even though they may have important economic side effects, their primary purpose is to bring about changes in the political policies of other countries. As a consequence, works that study these types of actions have not been included in the present volume.

Organization of the Volume

The items included at the end of the first chapter are works that have considered the reappearance of protectionism in the international economy from a general perspective. The annotations are divided into two groups. The "General Works" section contains studies that deal with the recent appearance of protectionist practices or ones that consider a number of the more specific topics covered in later chapters rather than concentrate on only one or a few topics. The second section contains those works that have focused on the debate over the respective virtues and vices of free trade and protection from a general perspective. Obviously, many of the works in the later chapters also consider this issue, but the ones chosen for inclusion here provide an overview of the arguments that are used. Many of the studies in the other chapters also comment on this issue of course, but in the context of the discussion of a particular subject or country. The choice of which items to include in which chapters reflects the main thrust or thesis of an article or book. Thus, individual items in one chapter will often contain insights for the topics discussed in the other chapters. Each of the chapters contains subheadings that help organize the material being discussed. With the exception of Chapters 4 and 11, which contain only a limited number of annotations, the citations and their annotations are then grouped according to the same headings, except that there is also a general section that includes items dealing with the chapter topic in broad detail or comparing materials grouped under the subsection topics. Sub-headings have been used to pinpoint particular topics. It should be remembered that other works under different headings will frequently be useful as well.

Chapter 2 considers tariffs, the traditional form of protection offered to domestic producers. The theory of tariffs has been particularly well developed over time as a consequence of its presence through history. Many of the works in this chapter are models of how tariffs operate rather than studies of their actual implementation and observed effects.

Chapter 3 considers the wide variety of non-tariff barriers (NTBs) that hinder trade and that are used to present obstacles to imports. These barriers have been of increasing importance in recent years, and many of them are directly associated with the new protectionism. The works contained in both of these chapters are general discussions or theoretical analyses of tariffs or these other obstacles. Studies dealing with the practices of particular countries in using these forms of protection are usually included in the later chapters.

Chapter 4 contains a relatively limited group of annotations that focus on the international system's overall level of openness that may be a consequence of the distribution of political power among the major countries. A key question has been whether the presence or absence of a dominant state has had an influence on the general level of protectionism in place. In the past the presence of such a major state has often been associated with greater levels of free trade. These studies thus suggest the possibility that political relationships may have an effect upon economic relationships and arrangements.

Chapter 5 considers other frequently occurring facets of international interactions. GATT has been the most important international organization concerned with trade issues. Its framework of rules and principles has been very important in structuring much of the discussions dealing with trade and protectionism. Multilateral negotiations under GATT's auspices were very important in reducing barriers to trade after World War II, and the organization remains as a focus for many efforts at trade liberalization or at limiting the impacts of protection. There have been some suggestions that the shortcomings and weaknesses of GATT have contributed to the rise of the new protectionism. More recently, diplomatic activities concerned with trade in the international arena have occurred increasingly outside of the GATT framework, and bilateral agreements have become more common in the place of the multilateralism that is associated with GATT.

Chapter 6 concentrates on the role that the United States has played in facilitating or hindering free trade. The United States has had a key position in the international economy because of the size of its domestic market and its leadership in GATT after World War II. The volume of literature specifically dealing with U.S. trade policy reflects these facts and necessitates the separate chapter. General U.S. trade policy and the advocacy of trade liberalization, interactions among the different components of the government, and the rise of protectionist sentiment in the general public are some of the key areas dealt with in this literature. Works concentrating on the U.S. tariff schedule and on various non-tariff obstacles are also included in this chapter.

Chapter 7 considers the activities and policies of the other industrialized nations in the world. Studies of general policy approaches in different countries, the special problems of the developed states in general and ones that compare different industrialized states, including comparisons of the United States with other nations, are also found in this chapter.

Chapter 8 focuses on the developing world. Developing countries have faced some special difficulties in the world economy as a result of the rise of the new protectionism. Some of these problems have resulted from neo-mercantile policies in the developed states while other difficulties have been a consequence of their own domestic protectionist policies. The NICs of Asia and Latin America have been targets for much of the protectionist response in the world since their exporting activities have been threatening industries in the developed countries with increasing import competition.

Chapter 9 is devoted to protectionism in the trade of agricultural products. Unlike trade in other commodities, protectionism in food products does not reflect an increase but simply a continuation of previous practices. Liberalization of agricultural trade was largely excluded from the initial GATT arrangements or later multilateral negotiations. Virtually all the industrialized nations have either opposed meaningful trade liberalization in this area or have been selective in supporting it in their own self-interest. Thus, agricultural protectionism has been more deeply imbedded in the structures of the national economies of these states.

Chapter 10 is concerned with customs unions and free trade areas. These economic arrangements can have a major impact on trade patterns, and they can also have a protectionist effect. The European Community (EC) is the prime example of such a customs union, but there are or have been a number of other important regional groupings. There is also a possibility that such regional economic organizations could be the forerunners of a global trading community that is increasingly regionalized.

Chapter 11, a relatively short chapter, concentrates on the issue of protectionism from a more radical perspective and in the context of a broad view of the international economic system. Much of this critical concern focuses on the developing countries and their possible exploitation by the industrialized nations or capitalist classes.

A Note on the Studies Selected for Inclusion

A number of considerations determined the works chosen for inclusion in this book. Since it would be impossible to include all the relevant works in major foreign languages, all works are in English. This decision of course does not mean that there are no important works in other languages. A reader with a knowledge of French, German, or some other language will find it quite profitable to consult foreign journals or books to gain more insight on attitudes towards protection in other countries. There is also a decided bias towards materials published in the 1970s and 1980s. Although some earlier classic works are included, the overwhelming majority of the citations are more recent. The newer articles, chapters, and books cite their predecessors in notes and bibliographies. They have also built upon the earlier studies and incorporated their major contributions.

The more recent studies also have the advantage of containing updates or re-analyses of earlier efforts in the light of new information, practices, or theories. They also concentrate in many cases on analyzing the new protectionism or new protectionist practices that have appeared. In the case of the journals that were consulted, review articles, comments on earlier articles, and rejoinders were not included. While these types of publications may add useful insights, they are generally more limited in the information that they contribute. Comments on previous articles, along with rejoinders, usually appear within six months of the original article in cases where one might care to follow up on the reaction to a particular study.

Some other studies that would otherwise have been included are not present. On occasion, a particular author who has published widely on protectionism and related topics will have his or her shorter works and articles compiled in book form. When the book has been included in the annotations because the majority of the articles deal with protection or free trade, the individual articles or chapters are not duplicated. The book is a more convenient reference form than a dozen articles in different journals. The compilation will also include pieces that would be more difficult to locate in some cases. In a few cases, an author will occasionally have substantially the same material published in two different forums (an article in a journal and a book chapter, or an article in a foreign journal and one in a U.S. journal). When such has been the case, only one of the studies has been included. The choice has usually been to include the one that is more likely to be accessible.

While there are numerous works included in the various chapters, they are hardly all the studies that have dealt with protectionism or even the new protectionism, even when the language, date of publication, and other limitations mentioned above are taken into account. Many additional studies have dealt with protectionism only in passing while considering other aspects of domestic or international economics or politics. Not all of the possible journals were surveyed. The major ones in economics, business, political science, international business, and interdisciplinary areas were all included since they are the ones more readily available in libraries. Other journals are likely to have occasional articles dealing with protectionism, and there will be other books on the subject. Thus, this bibliography, however extensive, cannot be considered all inclusive or a source for all information on the subject. With this caveat in mind, however, the items included in the various chapters do provide a solid collection of the literature available dealing with protectionism in the international system.

End Notes

1. Pincus, Jonathan J. *Pressure Groups and Politics in Antebellum Tariffs*. New York: Columbia University Press, 1977. p.1

2. Spero, Joan Edelman. *The Politics of International Economic Relations*. 3rd ed. New York: St. Martin's, 1985. p.27
    and
    Gourevitch, Peter A. "Making Choices in France: Industrial Structure and the Politics of Economic Policy." In: *France in the Troubled World Economy*, edited by Stephen S. Cohen and Peter A. Gourevitch. London: Butterworth Scientific, 1982. p.1.

3. Blake, David H. and Robert S. Walters. *The Politics of Global Economic Relations*, 3rd ed. Englewood Cliffs, N.J.: Prentice-Hall, 1987. p.18.

4. Vandenbroucke, Frank. "Conflicts in International Economic Policy and the World Recession: A Theoretical Analysis." *Cambridge Journal of Economics* 9:1 (March 1985):15

Chapter 1: Annotated Bibliography

General Works

* 1.1 *
Balassa, Bela. *Change and Challenge in the World Economy*. New York: St. Martin's, 1985. ISBN 0-313-12854-1.

Balassa considers the effects of protectionism, including structural adjustment problems, trade policies in developed and developing countries and centrally planned economies, and international issues affecting all countries.

* 1.2 *
Baldwin, Robert E. "The Political Economy of Protectionism." In: *Import Competition and Response*, edited by Jagdish N. Bhagwati. Chicago: University of Chicago Press, 1982. ISBN 0-226-04538-2.

Baldwin reviews many of the political pressures for protectionism and analyzes the ways in which interaction of various factors makes it difficult to predict whether protectionism will occur, in what forms, and at what levels. He also notes a variety of reasons why income adjustment assistance programs are not likely to work well. The work is issued as a Conference report of the National Bureau of Economic Research.

* 1.3 *
Bergsten, C. Fred. "Let's Avoid a Trade War." *Foreign Policy* 23 (Summer 1976): 24-31.

Greater protectionism in 1974 and 1975 was avoided because import barriers would have fueled inflation, the problem of greatest concern in the developed states. Failure of the GATT multilateral trade negotiations, however, has left the door open for increases in such barriers.

* 1.4 *
Easton, Stephen T., and Herbert G. Grubel. "The Costs and Benefits of Protection in a Growing World." *Kyklos* 36:2 (1983): 213-230.

The costs of protection increase as world trade expands. Since world trade has grown faster than output since World War II, the present costs of protection are very large.

* 1.5 *
Gilpin, Robert. "Economic Interdependence and National Security in Historical Perspective." In: *Economic Issues and National Security*, edited by Klaus Knorr and Frank N. Trager. Lawrence: Regents Press of Kansas, 1977. ISBN 0-7006-167-8.

Gilpin provides a useful historical summary of the linkages between international political relations and the international economy. He considers mercantilism in the eighteenth century, the periods of hegemony, the trade conflicts and economic nationalism after World War I, and the more recent appearance of protectionism among other issues.

* 1.6 *
Gilpin, Robert. "Three Models of the Future." In: *World Politics and International Economics*, edited by C. Fred Bergsten and Lawrence B. Krause. Washington, DC: Brookings Institution, 1975. ISBN 0-317-20637-0.

Gilpin compares and contrasts three models of the international economy--a dependency situation, one where multinational corporations are more important than states, and mercantilism. Mercantilism assumes that a nation will seek its own economic good through measures such as protectionism and the formation of economic and trading blocs.

* 1.7 *
Heuser, Heinrich. *Control of International Trade.* London: George Routledge & Sons, 1939. LC 40-1928.

Heuser discusses the various forms of protectionism present prior to World War II, including tariffs, quotas, and bilateral arrangements. He concludes that tariffs are generally a preferable form of protection than other measures.

* 1.8 *
Johnson, Harry G. "An Economic Theory of Protectionism, Tariff Bargaining, and the Formation of Customs Unions." *Journal of Political Economy* 73:3 (June 1965): 256-283.

Johnson provides a framework for viewing free trade and protectionism from the perspective of collective policies of the state rather than the perspective of private consumption. He includes domestic political interest groups and bargaining concepts with more traditional economic approaches.

* 1.9 *
Johnson, Harry G. "Mercantilism: Past, Present, Future." In: *The New Mercantilism: Some Problems in International Trade, Money, and Investment*, edited by Harry G. Johnson. New York: St. Martin's Press, 1974. ISBN 0-312-56840-1.

Johnson analyzes the various forms that mercantilism has taken in the past and present; he notes that the international trading system may be slipping into new forms of mercantilism incrementally. Two characteristics of the new mercantilism have been the use of subsidies instead of tariffs or quotas and the pursuit of protectionist goals through the formation of trading blocs.

* 1.10 *
Meier, Gerald M. *Problems of Trade Policy.* Oxford: Oxford University Press, 1973. ISBN 0-19-501608-4.

Meier offers background information, excerpts from key documents, and analyses of three international trade issues related to protectionism. The issues covered are trade liberalization during the Kennedy Round of tariff negotiations, the appearance of neo-mercantilism in the textile trade, and the effects of the formation of the EC on international trade and individual countries.

* 1.11 *
Meyer, F.B. *International Trade Policy.* New York: St. Martin's Press, 1978. ISBN 0-312-42357-8.

Meyer discusses many aspects of protection in his study of international trade, including U.S. trade policy, GATT, and economic integration. He also notes that efforts at free trade must include the agricultural sector to gain the full benefits of trade liberalization.

* 1.12 *
Ostry, Sylvia. "The World Economy in 1983: Marking Time." *Foreign Affairs* 62:3 (1983): 533-560.

Ostry's review of the world economy in 1983 reveals that a variety of protectionist measures were undertaken, including an important "Orderly Marketing Arrangement" limiting some Japanese exports to the EC. The movement to "managed" trade evident in earlier years was continuing.

* 1.13 *
Patterson, Gardner. *Discrimination in International Trade: The Policy Issues, 1945-1965.* Princeton: Princeton University Press, 1966. ISBN 0-691-04119-9.

Patterson provides an overview of the discriminatory policies used in the twenty years after World War II. He considers balance of payments problems, monetary issues, the formation of free trade areas and customs unions, the presence of the GATT framework, and the appearance of Japan as a major exporter.

* 1.14 *
Rangarajan, L. "The Politics of International Trade." In: *Paths to International Political Economy*, edited by Susan Strange. London: George Allen & Unwin, 1984. ISBN 0-04-382041-7.

The author reviews the rise of non-tariff barriers and other types of protectionism. The GATT system is flawed in that it favors trade liberalization in manufactures, helpful to industrialized states, but not trade in primary products that would help developing countries. The industrialized countries also face domestic pressures for protection that hurt the developing countries in particular.

* 1.15 *
Rom, Michael. *The Role of Tariff Quotas in Commercial Policy.* New York: Homes & Meier, 1978. ISBN 0-8418-0350-6.

Rom provides a detailed discussion of conventional tariffs and their consequences. His chapters deal with custom unions, the General Agreement on Trade and Tariffs, the Generalized System of Preferences issue, as well as tariff structures in a variety of countries.

* 1.16 *
Samuelson, Paul A. "Summing Up on the Australian Case for Protectionism." *Quarterly Journal of Economics* 96:1 (February 1981): 147-160.

Samuelson presents a useful summary of arguments made in a 1929 official report on the need for protection in Australia. The summary provides an interesting counterpoise to more current arguments for protection.

* 1.17 *
Spero, Joan Edelman. *The Politics of International Economic Relations.* 3d ed. New York: St. Martin's Press, 1985. ISBN 0-312-62706-8.

Spero offers an excellent introduction to the political aspects of international economic relations. Protectionist issues such as tariffs and non-tariff barriers, GATT, international negotiations, and the idea of preferences for developing states are all covered in various parts of the volume, often within the context of a broader framework of economic ties between states.

* 1.18 *
Vandenbroucke, Frank. "Conflicts in International Economic Policy and the World Recession: A Theoretical Analysis." *Cambridge Journal of Economics* 9:1 (March 1985): 15-42.

The economic problems in the West, including the rise of neo-mercantilism, result from a lack of co-ordinated leadership, similar to that which occurred in the 1930s. Policy approaches as well as goals need to be co-ordinated among the industrialized countries.

* 1.19 *
Whalley, John. *Trade Liberalization among Major World Trading Areas.* Cambridge, MA: MIT Press, 1985. ISBN 0-262-23120-4.

The author offers a model for estimating the effects of a wide variety of policies on trade among various regions of the world. He considers tariffs, multilateral negotiations to reduce tariffs, a variety of non-tariff barriers, customs unions,

trade wars, and other factors. He notes that while trade liberalization may aid many countries, domestic policies, especially in the developing states, often have greater impacts on trade flows than trade policies.

Free Trade Versus Protectionism

* 1.20 *
Blackhurst, Richard, Nicolas Marian, and Jan Tumlir. *Trade Liberalization, Protectionism and Interdependence.* GATT Studies in International Trade, no. 5. Geneva: General Agreement on Tariffs and Trade, 1977.

The authors argue in favor of trade liberalization and against protectionism. They note that protection interferes with necessary economic adjustments in states and reduces benefits received from trade. When domestic pressures are successful in gaining protection for one industry, it encourages other industries to seek protection as well.

* 1.21 *
Brander, James A. "Rationales for Strategic Trade and Industrial Policy." In: *Strategic Trade Policy and the New International Economics*, edited by Paul R. Krugman. Cambridge, MA: MIT Press, 1987. ISBN 0-262-11112-8.

Brander presents some economic rationales for protection as part of national trade policy. In essence, the elements supporting the ideas of free trade and comparative advantage are often not met. Lack of competition or monopoly, infant industry problems, predatory foreign pricing, and government-to-government interactions are among the considerations discussed.

* 1.22 *
Gray, H. Peter. *Free Trade or Protection: A Pragmatic Analysis.* New York: St. Martin's Press, 1985. ISBN 0-312-30374-2.

Gray analyzes the idea of free trade in a rapidly changing world economic system. While he does not argue against the merits of free trade as such, he suggests that protection can and should be used as a short-term transitional measure to help phase out production in industries that are no longer competitive in given countries.

* 1.23 *
Greenaway, David, and Christopher Milner. *Protectionism Again...?: Causes and Consequences of a Retreat from Freer Trade to Economic Nationalism.* Hobart Paper 84. London: Institute of Economic Affairs, 1979.

The authors analyze the new arguments put forward to justify protectionism, drawing some parallels with protectionism in the 1930s, and conclude that the arguments are largely faulty. They also favorably consider future benefits of trade liberalization and comment on the barriers that have to be overcome.

* 1.24 *
Jones, R. J. Barry. *Conflict and Control in the World Economy: Contemporary Economic Realism and Neo-Mercantilism.* Brighton, England: Wheatsheaf Books, 1986. ISBN 0-7450-0044-1.

Jones surveys the rise of neo-mercantilism, using both a general overview approach and case studies. Neo-mercantilistic practices have added to the economic well-being of countries, and some of them are essential for achieving the objectives of domestic policies.

* 1.25 *
Krauss, Melvyn B. *The New Protectionism: The Welfare State and International Trade.* New York: New York University Press, 1978. ISBN 0-8147-4570-9.

Krauss provides a readable introduction to the free trade versus protectionism argument and to the many forms that protectionism can take. He also notes the linkages between policies present in the welfare state and the appearance of new protectionist practices. Krauss does digress at various points to a more generalized critique of the welfare state.

* 1.26 *
Krugman, Paul. "Trade in Differentiated Products and the Political Economy of Trade Liberalization." In: *Import Competition and Response*, edited by Jagdish N. Bhagwati. Chicago: University of Chicago Press, 1982. ISBN 0-226-04538-2.

Krugman develops a model to explain why some industries favor protectionism while producers in other industries favor reciprocal tariff reductions. Trade liberalization will lead to mutual trade gains in countries where neither has too great a comparative advantage. The resulting trade is largely intra-industry, a pattern seen widely in the international economy today.

* 1.27 *
Miles, Caroline M. "International Trade and Structural Adaptation--Problems and Policies." In: *The New Mercantilism: Some Problems in International Trade, Money, and Investment*, edited by Harry G. Johnson. New York: St. Martin's, 1974. ISBN 0-312-56840-1.

Trade liberalization in the past did not have the adverse consequences on domestic economies that were often predicted. Adjustment assistance for industries affected by imports may mitigate adverse effects, but it will be difficult to formalize

its use by international convention given the differences in domestic economies. There is also the danger that temporary protectionist measures, permitted under GATT rules, will become permanent.

* 1.28 *
Pagoulatos, Emilio, and Robert Sorenson. "Industrial Policy and Firm Behavior in an International Context." In: *Western Economies in Transition: Structural Change and Adjustment Policies in Industrial Countries*, edited by Irving Leveson and Jimmy W. Wheeler. Boulder, CO: Westview, 1980. ISBN 0-89158-589-3.

Industrial policies and non-tariff discrimination are a disguised form of protectionism and have reduced the gains from trade liberalization. Such protection encourages domestic monopolies that may in fact import more and export less. Trade liberalization will encourage intra-industry specialization and the shift of resources into new product lines within threatened industries to the overall advantage of the global economy.

* 1.29 *
Stolper, Wolfgang F., and Paul A. Samuelson. "Protection and Real Wages." *Review of Economic Studies* 9:1 (November 1941): 58-73.

The authors consider the possibility that protection is necessary to maintain the wage levels of workers in the face of cheap foreign labor. They conclude that except in unusual circumstances such protection is not necessary in the developed states.

* 1.30 *
Strange, Susan. "Protectionism and World Politics." *International Organization* 39:2 (Spring 1985): 233-259.

Strange argues that the furor over protectionism is misguided in as much as its restrictive effect on trade has been relatively minor. The developing countries continue to export, although perhaps at a lower level than would otherwise be possible. She also argues, more generally, that fears about protectionism result from the belief of many that free trade is always advantageous.

* 1.31 *
Travis, William Penfield. *The Theory of Trade and Protection.* Harvard Economic Studies, v. 121. Cambridge: Harvard University Press, 1964. ISBN 0-674-88305-5.

Travis analyzes the effects of relative factor endowments (capital, labor, etc.) and protection on trade flows, finding that protection must be included to explain trade patterns. Protection in the developed countries has hindered industrialization in the developing countries as have protective policies in the developing countries themselves.

* 1.32 *
Willett, Thomas D. "Major Challenges to the International Economic System." In: *Challenges to a Liberal International Economic Order: A Conference Sponsored by the American Enterprise Institute*, edited by Ryan C. Amacher, Gottfried Haberler, and Thomas D. Willett. Washington, DC: American Enterprise Institute for Public Policy Research, 1979. ISBN 0-8447-2152-2.

Willet highlights some of the major challenges to an open international economic system, including domestic protectionist forces in the United States, protectionism abroad that requires a response, and the demands of the developing countries for trading preferences. He contends that trade wars and the collapse of international economic cooperation, while possible, are exaggerated dangers. The real problem is the increase of special exemptions from competing in a more open international economy and a decrease in support for the idea of free trade.

CHAPTER 2

TARIFFS

Because the tariff has been a traditional form of protection offered to domestic producers, its theory has been particularly well developed over time. Many of the works in this chapter are models of how tariffs operate rather than studies of their actual implementation and observed effects.

Tariffs have been a traditional measure used for protecting domestic producers and have been a factor in international trade for centuries. Much of the domestic and international conflict over trade in the eighteenth and nineteenth centuries involved tariff issues. Debate over the protection of new industry as opposed to the availability of cheap imports of manufactures was one major source of economic contention in the United States between the North and South prior to the Civil War. Britain consistently sought to reduce tariffs elsewhere in the world in the late eighteenth and early nineteenth centuries since such tariffs usually limited imports of British goods. Tariffs were also a major instrument used by many countries during the Great Depression in efforts to preserve domestic jobs and deal with balance of payments difficulties. While tariffs have become less important as protectionist measures with the appearance of other measures that limit imports, they still remain a widely used government policy for the protection of domestic producers. They have also been one of the most widely analyzed protectionist measures.

Tariffs are a very transparent impediment to trade in most cases since they constitute an obvious, direct cost that is borne at the border of the state. While tariffs can be seen simply as a surcharge on imports that enter a country, their actual operation sometimes has more complex economic effects on domestic economies and on the amount of protection that is actually provided. The form that a tariff takes and its application can provide greater barriers to trade in some cases. The effects on imports can also vary depending on the administration of the tariffs, the method of valuation used, and the complexity of the tariff schedule in use.

Revenue Tariffs

In some instances a basic purpose of a tariff, one that is not primarily protectionist in intent, is to raise revenue. Such tariffs or customs duties have become very minor sources of revenue in the developed states of the world and thus are of decreasing importance. For many developing states, however, they constitute an important source of government funds. The tariff serves basically as a tax that is relatively easy to collect compared to other possible sources of government funds. If the tariffs are levied on luxury goods, they can even provide a means of taxing portions of the population that otherwise are capable of avoiding many other taxes. Ideally, revenue tariffs are placed on imports that lack domestic competition within the country or on products that will be imported even with a surcharge. Under these circumstances, distortions in the local economy are likely to be fewer and the consequences for trade minimal.

Even so, adverse trade consequences could appear if the imported goods are used as inputs in economic sectors that produce exports for international markets. Export industries can also be injured when there are close substitutes available for an import that has a higher cost due to the tariff. The use of the now cheaper substitute will lead to higher costs in production that will then be carried over into the final price of the exports. In either of these situations, the tariff can thus become a hidden tax on exports; it can even limit trade by reducing exports, although in the situations described, tariffs can hardly be viewed as protectionist measures.

Tariffs as Protectionist Measures

Tariffs can be used in a variety of ways as protectionist devices. The highest level of protection a tariff can provide is attained in a rate that is prohibitive of import possibilities. The cost of the potential imports will be so high that they cannot offer any competition to domestic producers of the same items. Such tariffs will, of course, constitute a limit on trade, and they will also raise prices charged domestic consumers since the domestic producers will of necessity be passing along the higher costs of production. If domestic production is concentrated in the form of a monopoly or oligopoly, the domestic costs could be even higher since a prohibitive tariff provides no price competition. Such tariffs could also have negative effects on exports if the materials in question are an important component for the production of possible exports. While all tariffs can have wider effects in the domestic economy on savings, interest rates, and consumption, with a corresponding impact on fiscal policy, the effects of prohibitive tariffs are potentially greater.

Most tariffs have historically been imposed at less than prohibitive levels. While all tariffs tend to raise costs to local consumers, most provide only partial protection to domestic producers. The degree of protection actually provided will depend upon the tariff rate and the resulting differential in the price of the import and the price of the domestic product. With this type of tariff, there will be a limit to the prices that domestic producers can charge, a limit effectively set by the level of the tariff, even in a situation with a domestic monopoly or oligopoly. Such tariffs will also permit imports, albeit at a higher cost, when domestic production is insufficient to meet the local demand. Variable tariffs or tariff quotas can also be used to fulfill some of the same protectionist objectives. With a variable tariff, the surcharge changes with the level of imports. For example, the tariff may be 5 percent on the first 500 units imported, 7.5 percent on the second 500, 10 percent on the next thousand, and 25 percent on any additional units.[1] Such tariffs can provide for very real protection for domestic industries by effectively guaranteeing them a share of the domestic market.

More recently, studies of tariffs have come to distinguish between nominal and effective tariff rates with respect to the protection provided. Nominal tariffs are the posted rates that are levied on particular products. Effective tariffs, however, take into account the overall level of protection provided by a national tariff schedule. Calculations of effective rates attempt to take into account the costs of inputs into the production processes when tariffs affect their final prices.[2] The determination of the effective tariff rates for different products is very difficult in complex economies with many goods or when there are tariffs on intermediate goods that can affect the costs for many items as opposed to raw materials. If a key imported input, particularly an intermediate good, has a high rate of tariff protection, then the costs of many products may rise. The level of effective protection provided may also vary substantially depending upon the stage of processing the materials in question.[3] The availability of substitute inputs into the production process can also affect the effective level of protection. High effective levels of protection can clearly limit import trade, reduce the competitiveness of some exports, and lead to higher costs for consumers to a greater extent than might be obvious from a comparison of nominal tariff rates.

Costs of Tariffs

Economists have been particularly active in analyzing the effects of tariffs on levels of trade, the composition of trade, and the costs to the countries with tariffs. Their mathematical models, sometimes highly involved and intricate, have attempted to measure the relative costs and benefits of tariffs on trade. Generally, they have concluded that tariffs do raise domestic costs, which is an almost unavoidable consequence of their presence. Total benefits to the importing country have often been found to be higher under conditions of free trade than under conditions of restricted trade. The costs of tariffs have often been found to be even higher in situations in which there is limited domestic competition. There have also been a number of comparisons of tariffs with other forms of protectionism to determine if the level of protection offered is greater and whether the tariff or the other measure will better achieve the policies of the government. The general conclusion has been that tariffs work better, or at least no worse, than the other approaches in most circumstances. Tariffs have the additional advantage of being more convenient to administer, and they do not require re-negotiation or re-passage as is often the case with other protectionist devices. An *ad valorem* tariff also will automatically respond to changes in price and value for imports, whereas other protectionist measures may become less useful or even dysfunctional as the economic situation changes.

Tariffs and Other Policy Objectives

Tariffs have been justified as serving a number of government policy objectives. Their role in raising revenue in a convenient fashion has already been noted. Tariffs, as well as other forms of protection, have often been justified as an appropriate means to foster and protect infant or new industries. Such infant industries must be given time to develop so that they will be competitive with imports in the future. Governments, responding to domestic pressures, have also used tariffs to try to protect declining industries. While the levying of such tariffs can be partially explained by these political pressures, analyses have indicated that the effect is likely only to slow the industry decline rather than to arrest or reverse it.[4]. Tariffs have also been one mechanism used to deal with balance of trade problems.

Generally, tariffs alone are not a sufficient measure since the protection offered is often difficult to remove once the trade imbalance disappears. Since tariffs are highly visible, they often invite retaliation by countries whose exports are adversely affected. Thus, while tariffs can play a role in redressing trade imbalances and in reducing balance of payments difficulties, they usually work best when used in conjunction with other policy instruments.

Tariff Schedules and Complexity

The classification systems that are used with tariffs can also provide a measure of protection. Whether tariffs have a specific duty or are based on a percentage of the value of the import can be important. Specific duties or tariffs are a fixed charge on particular imports. The percentage of value, or *ad valorem* method, is based on the stated cost of the import and thus will rise or fall depending on relative price levels for the import. The specific duties can provide a greater level of protection for products that have declining prices. The relative cost of the tariff goes up as the price of the import declines. Thus, price declines in an economic sector that could otherwise lead to greater competition from the imports if *ad valorem* tariffs were used may not appear for specific tariffs. Another procedural decision that affects the protection provided is whether the tariff surcharge is levied on the total costs of the import, including transportation charges. If transportation costs are included in the tariff, it will raise costs from some sources and redirect trade patterns for the imports.[5]

The additional surcharge for transportation costs also raises the level of real protection afforded to local producers. The inclusion of a particular import in one tariff category rather than another is an additional factor that can also significantly raise the level of the surcharge. For many industrialized states such classification schedules have become very complex and present difficulties of interpretation. Intricate classifications and rules of procedure might inhibit a firm from considering the use of imported goods. In addition, many developed countries have higher tariffs on semi-processed raw materials than they do on unprocessed raw materials. Thus, if a product is classified as semi-processed, the protection that will be provided to domestic producers is greater.

Tariffs and Domestic Political Activity

More recently efforts have also been made to incorporate the consequences of domestic political activity into tariff models. Such political activities directly affect tariff issues and can be more important than economic concerns, whether there are net costs or benefits to the nation as a whole. In fact, it is quite unlikely that free trade as a policy will be possible in a pluralist democracy with such political activity and competition for voter support.[6]

Politicians and parties can be incorporated into models as economic actors that will consider the political costs and benefits of supporting a tariff, particularly when elections are close at hand. Political pressures for tariffs, for example, will often be successful since the higher prices that result from the tariffs are broadly diffused among the population of consumers while groups that will gain from the tariffs will receive more concentrated, and therefore more valuable, benefits.

The results of many of these economic models have shown that free trade is preferable to the presence of tariffs for almost any country and that lower tariffs are preferable to higher ones. Tariffs, however, may be useful for developing countries since they constitute an important source of government revenue, and they may help infant industries to develop. Although tariffs have been a traditional protectionist device used by virtually all countries on behalf of domestic groups, their prevalence in the international economic system has been declining. International negotiations have successfully focused on reducing many tariff barriers, at least in the most important trading countries. As a result of these reductions in tariff levels, other forms of protectionism have become increasingly important, particularly the non-tariff barriers that will be discussed in the next chapter.

End Notes

1. Walter, Ingo. "Barriers to International Competition: The Nature of Nontariff Distortions," in: *The United States and International Markets: Commercial Policy Options in an Age of Controls*, edited by Robert G. Hawkins and Ingo Walter. Lexington, MA: Lexington Books, 1972. p.77

2. Hawkins, Robert G. "Tariffs and Tariff Structures: An International Comparison," in: *Hawkins and Walter*. op, cit. p.46

3. Bell, Harry H. "Trade Relations with the Third World: Preferential Aspects of Protective Structures," in: *Hawkins and Walter*. op. cit. pp.303-304.

4. Cassing, James H. and Arye L. Hillman, "Shifting Comparative Advantage and Senescent Industry Collapse." *American Economic Review* 76:3 (June 1986):516-523,
    and
   Hillman, Arye L. "Declining Industries and Political-Support Protectionist Motives." *American Economic Review* 72:5 (December 1982):1180-1187.

5. Waters, G. W. II, "Transport Costs and the Static Welfare Costs of Tariffs." *American Economic Review* 64:4 (September 1974):730-733.

6. Findlay, Ronald and Stanislaw Wellisz, "Endogenous Tariffs, the Political Economy of Trade Restrictions, and Welfare," in: *Import Competition and Response: A Conference Report*, National Bureau of Economic Research, ed. Jagdish Bhagwati. Chicago: University of Chicago Press, 1982. pp. 223-234.

Chapter 2: Annotated Bibliography

General Works

* 2.1 *
Hagaki, Takao. "Multinational Firms and the Theory of Effective Protection." *Oxford Economic Papers* n.s.35:3 (November 1983): 447-462.

Multinational firms can change the effective protection gained from tariffs through location decisions and intra-firm transfers. Free trade may not be in the best interest of a host country, particularly if the multinational firm is an international monopolist.

* 2.2 *
Hagaki, Takao. "Optimal Tariffs for a Large and a Small Country under Uncertain Terms of Trade." *Oxford Economic Papers* n.s.37:2 (June 1985): 292-297.

For a small country, free trade remains an optimum policy even with uncertainty over the terms of trade. The optimal tariff for large countries seeking to avoid risk can be higher or lower than that of a large country that is neutral to risk, dependent upon other factors present for the countries in question.

* 2.3 *
Jabara, Cathy L., and Robert L. Thompson. "The Optimal Tariff for a Small Country under International Price Uncertainty." *Oxford Economic Papers* n.s.34:2 (July 1982): 326-331.

For a small country, an optimal tariff will increase the cost of imports. The higher cost is necessitated by risks associated with terms of trade decline, because a small country will have little control over terms of trade.

* 2.4 *
Kuga, Koyoshi. "Tariff Retaliation and Policy Equilibrium." *Journal of International Economics* 3:4 (November 1973): 351-366.

Kuga provides a model of the origin of tariff wars. Tariff changes by one country may lead to changes by other states, either by reciprocating tariff reductions or retaliating increases. It is possible for a series of tariff changes to reach a situation where free trade results.

Revenue Tariffs

* 2.5 *
Bhagwati, Jagdish N., and T. N. Srinivasan. "Revenue Seeking: A Generalization of the Theory of Tariffs." *Journal of Political Economy* 88:6 (December 1980): 1069-1087.

A formal analysis details the effects of tariffs and import quotas on the generation of revenues. Either one could generate more revenue in the protected state, depending upon circumstances, and in some circumstances following the policy that seeks the most revenue may also increase total welfare.

* 2.6 *
Cassing, James H., and Arye L. Hillman. "Political Influence Motives and the Choice Between Tariffs and Quotas." *Journal of International Economics* 19:3-4 (November 1985): 279-290.

The levels of domestic political strength influence government actions. If the government is secure, there will be a preference for tariffs over quotas except when concern over revenues is present. If the government is seeking revenue as well as political support, either a tariff or a quota might be used.

* 2.7 *
Dasgupta, Partha, and Joseph Stiglitz. "Tariffs vs. Quotas as Revenue Raising Devices under Uncertainty." *American Economic Review* 67:5 (December 1977): 979-981.

With uncertainty present, a pure optimum tariff will generate a greater consumer surplus than a pure optimum quota with the right to import auctioned off. The presence of uncertainty and imperfect information are important aspects of more general classes of trade policies.

* 2.8 *
Ethier, Wilfred J. "Protection and Real Incomes Once Again." *Quarterly Journal of Economics* 99: 1 (February 1984): 193-200.

Ethier's model assumes that tariff revenues are distributed in the same proportions as other forms of income. As a result, a revenue raising optimal tariff might increase the total income available in a nation.

* 2.9 *
Rousslang, Donald J. "The Opportunity Cost of Import Tariffs." *Kyklos* 40:1 (1987):88-102.

Any consideration of the effects of tariffs on general welfare should balance the costs of imposing alternate domestic taxes to raise the same amount of revenue. While comparisons are difficult, data from the United States suggest that in some cases the tariffs are the best alternative.

Tariffs as Protectionist Measures

* 2.10 *
Bertrand, Trent J., and Jaroslav Vanek. "The Theory of Tariffs, Taxes, and Subsidies: Some Aspects of the Second Best." *American Economic Review* 61:5 (December 1971): 925-931.

Extreme distortions resulting from government efforts at protection, in whatever form, need to be eliminated. The effective rate of distortion rather than the nominal one needs to be taken into account.

* 2.11 *
Bhagwati, Jagdish N., and T. N. Srinivasan. "The General Equilibrium Theory of Effective Protection and Resource Allocation." *Journal of International Economics* 3:3 (August 1973): 259-281.

The authors find that calculating effective rates of protection is quite difficult for a variety of reasons. Since effective rates and nominal rates are highly associated, use of nominal rates may be justified since complex calculations are not required.

* 2.12 *
Bruno, M. "Protection and Tariff Change under General Equilibrium." *Journal of International Economics* 3:3 (August 1973):205-225.

Bruno's models indicate that substitution effects do not present a major problem for the idea of effective protection. The inability to rank economic sectors by the level of protection received, however, is a more difficult problem.

* 2.13 *
Cohen, Benjamin I. "The Use of Effective Tariffs." *Journal of Political Economy* 79:1 (January/February 1971): 128-141.

An analysis of the nominal and effective tariff rates of 26 nations in the late 1950s or 1960s finds that both rates are highly correlated. Given the difficulties of computing an actual effective tariff rate, nominal rates are useful in ranking countries according to the level of tariff protection present.

* 2.14 *

Das, Satya P. "Optimum Tariffs and Intermediate Goods." *International Economic Review* 24:2 (June 1983): 493-508.

The author considers a model in which both intermediate and final goods are traded between two countries. With the possibility of manipulating the terms of trade in two areas with two types of goods, the optimum tariff on the final product is often less than would be the case if only the final product were being traded.

* 2.15 *

Deardorff, Alan V., and Robert M. Stern. "The Effects of the Tokyo Round on the Structure of Protection." In: *The Structure and Evolution of Recent U.S. Trade Policy*, edited by Robert E. Baldwin and Anne O. Krueger. Chicago: University of Chicago Press, 1984. ISBN 0-226-03604-9.

The authors compare the protection offered by tariffs and non-tariff barriers in 34 countries in 29 economic sectors after the Tokyo Round of multilateral tariff reductions. Their estimates of protection rates are lower than either nominal tariffs or effective tariffs as normally calculated. The protection offered to various industries is also ranked differently in their calculations.

* 2.16 *

Driscoll, M. J., and J. L. Ford. "Protection and Optimal Trade-Restricting Policies under Uncertainty." *Manchester School of Economic and Social Studies* 51:1 (March 1983): 21-32.

The authors provide a mathematical model that demonstrates that when considering one commodity, a specific tariff will optimize net domestic surplus rather than the use of a quota. In some circumstances a quota will be equivalent in its effect to a tariff.

* 2.17 *

Eldor, Rafael. "On the Risk-Adjusted Effective Protection Rate." *Review of Economics and Statistics* 66:2 (May 1984): 235-241.

The level of effective protection increases if the tariff level is above average for traded production inputs in an industry with a higher rather than a lower risk. The high-risk industry facing greater competition derives greater advantage proportionately than does the low-risk industry.

* 2.18 *

Falvey, Robert E. "Protection and Import-Competing Product Selection in a Multi-Product Industry." *International Economic Review* 24:3 (October 1983): 737-747.

The author finds government subsidies to be a better form of government assistance to a multi-

product industry than tariffs, barring foreign retaliation. A quota or specific tariff is also seen as having fewer welfare costs than a general tariff, which may adversely affect some of the products in the industry.

* 2.19 *

Falvey, Rodney. "Protection and Substitution: A Geometric Treatment." *Oxford Economic Papers* n.s.29:2 (July 1977): 312-318.

Falvey develops a model to estimate the effective rate of protection a tariff may offer. He notes that excessive protection can even lead to negative value added results.

* 2.20 *

Hawkins, Robert G. "Tariffs and Tariff Structures: An International Comparison." In: *The United States and International Markets: Commercial Policy Options in an Age of Controls*, edited by Robert G. Hawkins and Ingo Walter. Lexington, MA: Lexington Books, 1972. ISBN 0-669-84020-3.

Hawkins compares the nominal and effective tariff rates for ten industrialized countries. The United States and United Kingdom have relatively unique tariff structures, while the European Community and Japan have quite similar tariff schedules. Effective rates of protection for the United States, United Kingdom, EC, and Japan are higher than nominal tariff rates.

* 2.21 *

Hay, George A. "Import Controls on Foreign Oil: Tariff or Quota." *American Economic Review* 61:4 (September 1971): 688-691.

Hay argues that tariffs are preferable to import quotas in the case of petroleum. Quotas provide greater incentives for price increases and may facilitate side payments or bribes to government officials. Hay also notes that the cost of protection through either measure may be quite high.

* 2.22 *

Helpman, Elhanan, and Assaf Razin. "Efficient Protection under Uncertainty." *American Economic Review* 70:4 (September 1980): 716-731.

The authors compare the relative efficiencies of subsidies, tariffs, and quotas based on the idea of expected utility that will be provided. Subsidies are found to be the best policy overall, while the desirability of a tariff compared to a quota can vary.

* 2.23 *

Holden, Merle, and Paul Holden. "Effective Tariff Protection and Resource Allocation: A Non-Parametric Approach." *Review of Economics and Statistics* 60:2 (May 1978): 294-300.

Effective tariff rates in South Africa were found to be related to shifts in resources among industries. Effective tariff rates are, moreover, of greater use than nominal rates for detecting these shifts.

* 2.24 *
Kreinin, Mordechai, James B. Ramsey, and Jan Kmenta. "Factor Substitution and Effective Protection Reconsidered." *American Economic Review* 61:5 (December 1971): 891-900.

The authors find that the idea of effective protection rates are not generally useful in some situations. Profit maximization efforts by firms in response to changes in tariff structures will lead to unpredicted results.

* 2.25 *
Leith, J. Clark. "The Effect of Tariffs on Production, Consumption, and Trade: A Revised Analysis." *American Economic Review* 61:1 (March 1971): 74-81.

The author develops a model that includes production and use effects of goods subject to effective protection. The protection offered will lead to the substitution of elements having a competitive edge in the production process. These substitution effects are significant.

* 2.26 *
Panagariya, Arvind. "Import Objective, Distortions, and Optimal Tax Structure: A Generalization." *Quarterly Journal of Economics* 98:3 (August 1983): 515-524.

Uniform tariffs fail to achieve the desired level of imports if any trade distortions, such as monopoly power or smuggling, are present. If the distortions are domestic, tariffs cannot be used to achieve an optimum level of imports.

* 2.27 *
Sampson, Gary P. "On Factor Substitution and Effective Tariff Rates." *Review of Economic Studies* 41 (April 1974): 293-296.

Failure to include the possibility of factor substitutions in industries can bias the calculation of effective tariff rates. Various industries have either a different probability of such substitutions or may have greater sensitivity to such substitutions.

* 2.28 *
Yeats, Alexander J. "An Analysis of the Effect of Production Process Changes on Effective Protection Estimates." *Review of Economics and Statistics* 58:1 (February 1976): 81-85.

Calculation of effective protection rates based on outdated information on U.S. production inputs induces great biases into estimates of effective protection rates. Use of more current estimates for the value added in the production processes will yield a better measure of the level of effective protection.

* 2.29 *
Yeats, Alexander J. "A Sensitivity Analysis of the Effective Protection Estimate." *Journal of Development Economics* 3:4 (December 1976): 367-376.

Effective protection rates need to be calculated carefully for developing countries where the value added in production is highly variable. The actual level of protection offered in developing countries is thus quite volatile.

* 2.30 *
Young, Leslie. "Tariffs vs. Quotas under Uncertainty: An Extension." *American Economic Review* 70:3 (June 1980): 522-527.

Young analyzes the effects of tariffs and quotas in times of economic uncertainty. He finds, contrary to some previous work, that a quota will be superior to a tariff in many cases. Only if the tariff is small relative to the level of price uncertainty in the model is a tariff superior to a quota.

Costs of Tariffs

* 2.31 *
Batra, Raveendra N. "Nontraded Goods, Factor Market Distortions, and the Gains from Trade." *American Economic Review* 63:4 (September 1973): 706-713.

Batra presents a model suggesting that in some circumstances a higher tariff may increase total welfare. Tariffs may even be preferable to free trade. The presence of non-traded goods in the economy and differences in industry wage levels are factors that could lead to these results.

* 2.32 *
Batra, Raveendra N., and Rama Ramachandran. "Multinational Firms and the Theory of International Trade and Investment." *American Economic Review* 70:3 (June 1980): 278-290.

The authors' model, which incorporates multinational corporations, indicates that tariffs will increase the output of import-competing industries not only in the protected country but also in those abroad. Multinational corporations have increased the levels of interdependence in national economies.

* 2.33 *
Berglas, Eitan, and Assaf Razin. "Effective Protection and Decreasing Returns to Scale." *American Economic Review* 63:4 (September 1973): 733-737.

If an industry has decreasing returns from scale, or diseconomies of scale, an increase in the effective protection rate could actually lead to a decline in total domestic output. The rise in marginal cost for additional items produced with protection could exceed the average price.

* 2.34 *

Berglas, Eitan, and Assaf Razin. "Protection and Real Profits." *Canadian Journal of Economics* 7: 4 (November 1974): 655-664.

The authors' model suggests that in the short run protection will lead to an increase in profits for the protected firms. Situations will exist in which both labor and investors will have an interest in seeking protection. No long-term trend on profitability, however, appears with the model.

* 2.35 *

Burgess, David F. "Protection, Real Wages, and the Neoclassical Ambiguity with Interindustry Flows." *Journal of Political Economy* 88:4 (August 1980): 783-802.

Burgess proposes a mathematical formulation to determine if protection will raise the real wage level of labor, whether capital owners will gain or lose, and whether employment will shift to unprotected sectors from the protected ones. Due to the influence of technology and the fact that protected industries may still receive inputs from unprotected industries, Burgess concludes that answers to his questions are indeterminate.

* 2.36 *

Das, Satya P., and Yoshio Niho. "A Dynamic Analysis of Protection, Market Structure, and Welfare." *International Economic Review* 27:2 (June 1986): 513-523.

Tariffs will not normally lead to an increased concentration of firms in an industry since the protection encourages new entrants. When domestic concentration already exists, the effects of the tariff are not likely to be optimal for national welfare.

* 2.37 *

Findlay, Ronald. "Comparative Advantage, Effective Protection and Domestic Resource Cost of Foreign Exchange." *Journal of International Economics* 1:2 (May 1971): 189-204.

Industries will be ranked differently if the cost of foreign exchange, the level of effective protection, or comparative advantage is used as the indicator. Effective protection, whether by tariff, quota, or a mixture of the two, does not lead to comparative advantages in most cases.

* 2.38 *

Horst, Thomas. "The Theory of the Multinational Firm: Optimal Behavior under Different Tariff and Tax Rates." *Journal of Political Economy* 79:5 (September/October 1971): 1059-1072.

High tariff structures may be counter-productive in encouraging a multinational firm to locate production facilities inside one country. A formal model displays greater gains under conditions of free trade.

* 2.39 *

Itoh, Motoshige, and Yoshiyasu Ono. "Tariffs, Quotas, and Market Structure." *Quarterly Journal of Economics* 97:2 (May 1982): 295-305.

With a restricted number of domestic firms, quotas may lead to either prices higher than, or the same as, tariffs. Quotas are more likely than tariffs to provide a domestic producer with monopoly power.

* 2.40 *

Kimbrough, Kent P. "Tariffs, Quotas and Welfare in a Monetary Economy." *Journal of International Economics* 19:3-4 (November 1985): 257-277.

While both tariffs and quotas will improve a balance of payments situation, adjustment occurs more quickly with a tariff. Trade liberalization, however, would lead to benefits for the nation.

* 2.41 *

Lloyd, P. J. "Intra-Industry-Trade, Lowering Trade Barriers and Gains from Trade." In: *On the Economics of Intra-Industry Trade: Symposium 1978*, edited by Herbert Giersch. Tubingen: J.C.B. Mohr, 1978. ISBN 0-89563-548-8.

Lloyd's model of trade found that lower tariffs increased both intra-industry trade and inter-industry trade. The significant gains found in previous studies of trade increases resulted from the removal of the past distortions that existed with the previous tariff levels.

* 2.42 *

McKenzie, George. "A Problem in Measuring the Cost of Protection." *Manchester School of Economic and Social Studies* 53:1 (March 1985): 45-54.

McKenzie argues that the concept of "net consumer surplus" that is often used in measuring the effects of protectionism is virtually impossible to derive in an acceptable fashion. He suggests that other measures of the costs and benefits resulting from tariffs are consequently the preferable ones to use.

* 2.43 *

Mutti, John. "Aspects of Unilateral Trade Policy and Factor Adjustment Costs." *Review of Economics and Statistics* 60:1 (February 1978): 102-110.

Using U.S. industry data, Mutti finds that the removal of tariffs will only infrequently result in a net welfare loss for the country. Phased reductions will have even greater benefits for the country that lowers tariffs.

* 2.44 *

Panagariya, Arvind. "Tariff Policy under Monopoly in General Equilibrium." *International Economic Review* 23:1 (February 1982): 143-156.

The author offers a model that analyzes the effects of a tariff in an import-competing industry when the domestic producer has a monopoly. The terms of trade may worsen, and output may not respond correctly. It is not possible to rank tariffs in relation to protection or revenue production. Such a tariff with a monopoly present may not expand output or employment and will have welfare costs.

* 2.45 *

Sjaastad, Larry A. "Commercial Policy, 'True' Tariffs and Relative Prices." In: *Current Issues in Commercial Policy and Diplomacy*, edited by John Black and Brian Hindley. New York: St. Martin's Press, 1980. ISBN 0-312-17926-X.

Protective tariffs in one economic sector will damage other sectors, and import duties can hurt the export sector when the imported goods and domestic goods are close substitutes. Export subsidies can serve to offset some of the costs of the protection.

Tariffs and Other Policy Objectives

* 2.46 *

Anderson, James E., and Leslie Young. "The Optimality of Tariff Quotas under Uncertainty." *Journal of International Economics* 13:3-4 (November 1982): 337-351.

A tariff quota with its increasing duty is a useful mechanism when there is uncertainty about foreign supply. Tariff quotas can provide sufficient flexibility to meet a variety of policy objectives.

* 2.47 *

Cassing, James H., and Arye L. Hillman. "Shifting Comparative Advantage and Senescent Industry Collapse." *American Economic Review* 76:3 (June 1986): 616-523.

U.S. industries that no longer have a comparative advantage have not followed any one pattern in their decline and collapse. By incorporating lobbying activities for protectionism in tariff models, the authors provide at least a partial explanation for the particular pattern or course of decline a senescent industry may have taken.

* 2.48 *

Corden, W. M. "Protection and Growth." In: *International Economics and Development: Essays in Honor of Raul Prebisch*, edited by Luis Eugenio di Marco. New York: Academic Press, 1972. ISBN 0-12-216450-4.

Protection will normally lead to a decline in domestic savings and investment. Subsidies to savings or investment, direct taxes, or subsidies to production are preferable to tariffs, even tariffs protecting industries with a high propensity to save. Protection may be useful for infant industries or those with a high learning curve and therefore with applications elsewhere in the domestic economy in some circumstances.

* 2.49 *

Hillman, Arye L. "Declining Industries and Political-Support Protectionist Motives." *American Economic Review* 72:5 (December 1982): 1180-1187.

The author examines the idea that protection may be applied to help a declining industry when political authorities desire to maximize political support. The model developed indicates that tariffs will slow but not reverse the industry's decline.

* 2.50 *

Lucas, R. F. "Tariffs, Nontraded Goods, and the Optimal Stabilization Policy." *American Economic Review* 70:4 (September 1980): 611-625.

Given the limited information that is available, tariffs can play a role in domestic stabilization policies. Although tariffs are often a second-best alternative in some theoretical constructs, they create fewer divergences from the ideal approach than many other policies.

* 2.51 *

Mayer, Wolfgang. "The National Defense Tariff Argument Reconsidered." *Journal of International Economics* 7:4 (November 1977): 363-377.

It has been argued that national defense considerations may require the use of a tariff to maintain domestic production. Given the possibility of embargoes of certain imports, Mayer argues that such tariffs are economically useful, independent of national defense considerations.

* 2.52 *

McCulloch, Rachel. "When Are a Tariff and a Quota Equivalent." *Canadian Journal of Economics* 6:4 (November 1973): 503-511.

An import quota is a less costly measure to use when the policy goal is to fix the domestic price and perhaps to control profits as well. A tariff is a less costly device to expand domestic output or limit imports.

* 2.53 *
McCulloch, Rachel, and Harry G. Johnson. "A Note on Proportionally Distributed Quotas." *American Economic Review* 63:4 (September 1973): 726-732.

Quotas on imports that are distributed as a proportion of imports to domestic production are the optimum means of meeting government policy objectives. Replacement of a tariff or auctioned quota by such proportional quotas will lead, however, to a revenue loss for the government.

* 2.54 *
Melvin, James R. "The Regional Impact of Tariffs." In: *Canada-United States Free Trade*, edited by John Whalley with Roderick Hill. Toronto: University of Toronto Press, 1985. ISBN 0820-7253-4.

Melvin analyzes the regional effects that tariffs can have. Tariffs not only create additional costs to consumers directly but may cause additional losses in the form of inter-regional transportation costs. Small regions may lose by tariff reductions due to their inability to achieve economies of scale.

* 2.55 *
Murphy, Robert G. "Tariffs, Non-Traded Goods and Fiscal Policy." *International Trade Journal* 1:2 (Winter 1983): 193-211.

Tariffs, in addition to providing protection, will also affect domestic interest rates, consumption, and savings. Governments, as a result, should take tariffs into account in planning fiscal policies.

* 2.56 *
Pomfret, Richard. "Intra-Industry Trade in Intraregional and International Trade." In: *On the Economics of Intra-Industry Trade: Symposium 1978*, edited by Herbert Giersch. Tubingen: J.C.B. Mohr, 1978. ISBN 0-89563-548-8.

Actual tariff reductions seemed to have been biased in favor of intra-industry trade. Governments appear to have avoided changes in levels of protection that would have eliminated some industries in efforts to maintain a diversified industrial base.

* 2.57 *
Sauernheimer, Karlhans. "Tariffs, Imported Inputs and Employment." *Economica* 53 (August 1986): 393-399.

With flexible exchange rates, a tariff is likely to lead to reduced levels of employment in many circumstances. Its negative effects are likely to occur even without foreign retaliation.

* 2.58 *
Sundararajan, V. "The Impact of the Tariff on Some Selected Products of the U.S. Iron and Steel Industry, 1870-1914." *Quarterly Journal of Economics* 84:4 (November 1970): 590-610.

U.S. tariffs did permit an infant steel industry to become competitive with foreign producers in at least some product areas. Producers actually became competitive sooner than government tariff laws assumed because effective tariff rates were low, even though the nominal tariffs were designed to provide protection.

* 2.59 *
Young, Leslie, and James E. Anderson. "The Optimal Policies for Protecting Trade under Uncertainty." *Review of Economic Studies* 46 (October 1980): 927-932.

With price uncertainty for imports, a tariff is an optimum policy. A specific tariff is best for maintaining a ceiling on the volume of imports while an *ad valorum* tariff is best for limiting the expenditure of foreign exchange.

Tariff Schedules and Complexity

* 2.60 *
Feller, Peter Buck. "An Introduction to Tariff Classification." *Law and Policy in International Business* 8:4 (1976): 991-1004.

Feller provides details on the classification of imports used in U.S. tariffs and the rules of interpretation that govern it. Classification of imports is often very important given the different tariff rates that apply to different categories. It is also very complex.

* 2.61 *
Greenhut, M. L., and George Norman. "Spatial Pricing with a General Cost Function: The Effects of Tariffs on Imports." *International Economic Review* 27:3 (October 1986): 761-776.

Specific tariffs, much like transportation costs, will be absorbed by the exporters if necessary. *Ad valorum* tariffs are less likely to be absorbed by the exporter and thus are more likely to provide protection against imports.

* 2.62 *
Ray, Edward John. "The Optimum Commodity Tariff and Tariff Rates in Developed and Less Developed Countries." *Review of Economics and Statistics* 56:3 (August 1974): 369-377.

Rising tariff rates as the level of processing increases are a phenomenon present in the tariff structures of both developed and developing countries. Tariff structures tend to be similar for countries at the same general level of development. Political influences also affect the level of tariff protection.

* 2.63 *
Waters, W.G.,II. "Transport Costs and the Static Welfare Costs of Tariffs." *American Economic Review* 64:4 (September 1974): 730-733.

In addition to the usual costs, a tariff that is levied on the total valuation of imports, including transport costs, can lead to shifts in the source of imports after protection. The imports may now come from other than the lowest cost supplier.

* 2.64 *
Waverman, Leonard. "The Preventive Tariff and the Dual in Linear Programming." *American Economic Review* 62:4 (September 1972): 620-629.

The author presents a model that takes into account geography and distance for formulating tariff policy. In cases where transport costs are an important component of the final price of a goods, policy cannot assume that either production or consumption will occur at one fixed point in a country as opposed to multiple points.

Tariffs and Domestic Political Activity

* 2.65 *
Brock, William A., and Stephen P. Magee. "The Economics of Special Interest Politics: The Case of the Tariff." *American Economic Review* 68:2 (May 1978): 246-250.

Brock and Magee incorporate the idea of special interest groups and lobbies into the models used for analyzing tariff structures. They see politicians as calculating the costs and benefits of supporting tariffs when the latter are running for re-election.

* 2.66 *
Brock, William A., and Stephen P. Magee. "Tariff Formation in a Democracy." In: *Current Issues in Commercial Policy and Diplomacy*, edited by John Black and Brian Hindley. New York: St. Martin's, 1980. ISBN 0-312-17926-x.

The authors formulate a tariff model that incorporates political parties, their attitudes on protection, and the activities of interest groups. Tariffs are seen as reflecting the terms of trade between organized groups favoring protection and less well organized consumer groups.

* 2.67 *
Feenstra, Robert C., and Jagdish N. Bhagwati. "Tariff Seeking and the Efficient Tariff." In: *Import Competition and Response*, edited by Jagdish N. Bhagwati. Chicago: University of Chicago Press, 1982. ISBN 0-226-04538-2.

The authors' model assumes that import competition leads to lobbying by labor for tariff pro-

tection. In a small country the government may use the revenues from the tariff as a source of funds from which to meet the demands of labor.

* 2.68 *
Findlay, Ronald, and Stanislaw Wellisz. "Endogenous Tariffs, the Political Economy of Trade Restrictions, and Welfare." In: *Import Competition and Response*, edited by Jagdish Bhagwati. Chicago: University of Chicago Press, 1982. ISBN 0-226-04538-2.

The authors develop a model of the process of tariff formation that results from a clash of competing interest groups. They find that welfare loss does not increase one for one with the increase in tariff rates. They also note that free trade is unlikely to occur in a pluralist democracy with checks and balances among competing interest groups such as the United States.

* 2.69 *
Mayer, Wolfgang. "Endogenous Tariff Formation." *American Economic Review* 74:5 (December 1974): 970-985.

Mayer develops a general equilibrium model to determine the effects of political activities on tariff structures. He proposes that additional research be undertaken on important issues such as vote trading, policy formation in a democracy, and the effects of a multi-party system.

* 2.70 *
McKeown, Timothy J. "Firms and Tariff Regime Change: Explaining the Demand for Protection." *World Politics* 36:2 (January 1984): 215-233.

McKeown presents two theories on protectionism. In the first, protection-oriented firms are more likely to be active since advantages to them are more concentrated compared to the diffuse benefits that are present for consumers and those favoring free trade. In the second, firms will accept satisfactory levels of profit independent of protection levels, but a move towards protection occurs when there is a downturn in the business cycle. A preliminary empirical test of the two theories found both to be equally applicable in the case of the United States and Germany in the last half of the nineteenth century and the early part of the twentieth.

* 2.71 *
Wellisz, Stanislaw, and John D. Wilson. "Lobbying and Tariff Formation: A Deadweight Loss Consideration." *Journal of International Economics* 20:3-4 (May 1986): 367-375.

Small groups are more effective in lobbying to gain tariffs than larger ones according to the authors' model. Small groups can more readily eliminate free riders that gain tariff benefits without contributing to the lobbying costs than large groups.

* 2.72 *

Young, Leslie, and Stephen P. Magee. "Endogenous Protection, Factor Returns, and Resource Allocation." *Review of Economic Studies* 53: (July 1986): 407–419.

Preferred economic outcomes often do not appear because of political influences. While free trade is beneficial if the relevant resource is readily available, it hurts areas where the relative resource availability is low. When lobbies expend resources on political activities, they may actually hurt the level of returns for their industry.

NON-TARIFF BARRIERS TO TRADE

A wide variety of non-tariff barriers (NTBs) hinder trade by obstructing imports. These barriers have been of increasing importance in recent years, and many of them are directly associated with the new protectionism. The works contained in this chapter are either general discussions or theoretical analyses of non-tariff barriers.

A particularly significant indication of the new protectionism among the countries of the world has been the increasing prevalence of non-tariff barriers to trade (NTBs). These measures take a variety of forms and have been defined as: "Measures and practices, public or private, other than a customs tariff operated in a country, or by a common agreement in two or more countries, which have, directly or indirectly, the effect of hindering the sale in that country or those countries of goods or services from other countries, and/or artificially facilitating the sale of goods or services originating in that country or those countries."[1] This broad definition indicates the multitude of forms that NTBs can take. NTBs have in many cases replaced tariffs as the primary limitation on imports into many countries; the amount of protection that they provide domestic producers can be substantial. They are increasingly used to defend industrial sectors undergoing economic difficulties and facing import competition.

Unlike tariffs, which are a readily understood measure in all countries, generally transparent, and roughly equivalent in form in different states, NTBs are more difficult to classify, given the variety of types that exist. International negotiators have had problems even agreeing on what constitute such barriers, a lack of agreement that has made efforts to limit their effects on trade even more difficult. At a very general level, NTBs can be placed in two groups of restrictive trade practices. The first includes quota systems that operate to limit imports in a variety of guises. The second, more general, type of NTB includes many governmental practices that may directly or indirectly limit imports.

Quotas

There are several different kinds of quotas. The simplest places a limit on the amount or numbers of particular items that can be imported, or, more rarely, on the total value of a certain kind of product that can be imported. Such an import quota, established by the importing country, is designed to maintain the share of domestic industries in the local market. In some cases, quotas will not directly discriminate against a particular foreign producing country but leave it up to domestic importers to choose the source from which to buy. In other cases, the quota may limit the imports from a specified country or countries to some maximum level. The quotas in question may even be auctioned off among potential importers, providing some government revenues as well as introducing an element of economic supply and demand into the import situation. Such import quotas have often been compared to tariffs in the models used by economists mentioned in Chapter 2. The models have generally indicated that these quotas work less well than tariffs in most circumstances.

In many respects such quotas, particularly if auctioned off or subject to an import fee, may be roughly equivalent to a tariff even if not an exact substitute. Unlike tariffs, they are essentially based on volume rather than cost; they may limit the ability of the domestic economy to take full advantage of foreign produced, low-cost versions of some items. Another potential disadvantage to quotas is that in some circumstances they may effectively place a limit on the responsiveness of segments of the domestic economy to changing market conditions.

Voluntary Export Restraints (VERs) and Orderly Marketing Arrangements (OMAs) are two major examples of quota types that go beyond the simple import quota. A VER is an agreement by a foreign government, foreign governments, or a group of foreign firms to voluntarily restrict their exports to a particular country. Such agreements do not officially constitute a restriction of trade under GATT rules since it is the exporter that agrees to the limitation voluntarily and not the importer that imposes the barrier. In actual fact, the voluntary nature of compliance by the affected exporter may be greatly influenced by the relative political or economic positions of the exporting country and the importing nation. VERs are also entered into by exporters, albeit often reluctantly, because even greater protectionist measures are threatened by the importing countries or are seen as likely given the level of domestic political pressures in the importing country.

OMAs are similar to VERs except that they provide for a managed increase in imports over time and are designed to ameliorate some of the negative impacts of the sudden appearance of major foreign competition on domestic producers. In theory, they are temporary measures designed to ease industrial adjustment problems in the importing countries and control the rate of growth of these imports, although once established a precedent has been set for their continuation. OMAs are also not directly prohibited by GATT, since exporters agree to the limitation voluntarily, even though an exporting country could face the same political and economic pressures to agree to an OMA as are present with VERs.

Quotas, in whatever form, clearly limit the level of imports and provide protection to domestic producers. Additionally, they will raise the costs of the protected items to domestic consumers. As is the case when higher costs result from tariffs, these additional costs could also hamper exports if the imported items are inputs into sectors that would normally be competitive in the world market if the higher costs were not present. Quotas also lack flexibility in that VERs and OMAs as international agreements must be renegotiated to keep abreast of changing economic circumstances in the world economy or of changes in the domestic economies of the protected importing states. Quantitative quotas may not even provide the protection that domestic interests desire.

If the quota is for a fixed volume of imports, as is normally the case, the exporting countries may shift to higher priced versions of the items under quota. Japanese auto exports to the United States, for example, have followed this pattern. The VER limited the number, not the quality, of the automobiles that would be imported. As a result, the vehicles imported were generally the more expensive items in the product line. The quota has had a smaller effect on the U.S. trade deficit with Japan than expected given the importation of the higher cost automobiles, and U.S. auto producers have had to face new competition in additional product lines. The U.S. consumer thus had to deal with higher costs for imported autos in addition to the higher costs for the protected domestic vehicles.[2] OMAs designed to protect the U.S. producers of footwear had led to the same result, leaving foreign producers in an even stronger competitive position.[3] Such arrangements can be useful for the exporting country since it is a convenient means for the government to encourage firms to improve the quality of the products in question.[4] Domestic producers may find that the benefits of the quotas decline even more if new foreign producers begin to export into the new import niche for the lower priced items vacated by the old exporters as they shift to the higher priced versions. The only way of dealing with these new competitors, should they appear, is through the imposition of new quotas or the negotiation of yet more VERs and OMAs.

While various government actions that constitute NTBs may not always be intended as protectionist measures, quotas in their various forms clearly have had a protectionist intent. VERs and OMAs have become more frequently used. In the 1950s and 1960s, Japan was often the exporting country that had to meet requests for the voluntary limitation of exports. In the 1970s, the newly industrializing countries of Asia faced similar requests. Since that time other developing nations have begun to face similar pressures for restraint.

The culmination of such voluntary quotas in the 1970s was the negotiation and the subsequent extension of the Multi-Fibre Arrangements (MFA), which established, through bilateral negotiations, quotas for the exports of textiles and garments from most of the developing states of the world to the industrialized countries. The MFA has allowed controlled growth in trade in textiles and in exports from the developing states, but greater growth and lower costs to the eventual consumers would have resulted from the absence of such protection.[5] This quota arrangement has often provided only limited relief. Not only have the exporters changed to exporting higher quality items within their quotas, but firms from the more advanced Asian developing countries have set up factories in other developing states that were not meeting their quotas.[6] The result has been less protection than the MFA was intended to provide.

Safeguard and Escape Clauses

In negotiating international agreements designed to further trade liberalization or to reduce protectionism, many countries have insisted on the inclusion of escape clauses or safeguard procedures. Such clauses permit the government in question to limit imports when a domestic industry faces distress from an unexpected influx of imports. Safeguards are in theory designed to permit the government or industry to undertake necessary economic adjustments, and the limitations on imports are presumed to be temporary. Although allowed under GATT rules, such clauses have often been abused.

They have become a typical inclusion in international trade agreements of all kinds. In fact, safeguard clauses are often invoked not only when domestic industries are threatened by sudden import competition but also when these industries lose sales to imports due to a variety of economic difficulties, ranging from poor management decisions, and declining domestic or world sales, to

global economic recessions such as those that took place in the last half of the 1970s.

Since the use of the escape clause or safeguard procedure is a policy decision available at the discretion of government political leaders, it is often one that is made under political pressure from the threatened domestic producers. The use of these clauses, which invariably involve a quota or a special import levy, then provides important protection for domestic firms. Minimum import prices, safeguard or escape clauses in domestic legislation, or trigger prices--where protection will occur if imports fall below a specified price--are additional examples of NTBs designed to deal with the same type of competitive pressure on domestic firms and reflect the political pressures on governments negotiating international agreements.

Subsidies, Dumping, and Countervailing Duties

Subsidies to various industries may enable them to lower prices for domestic consumption and thus to undersell foreign imports when it would not otherwise be possible to do so. While such subsidies do not directly increase the cost to the final consumer, they do increase the costs to the nation since such subsidies come from tax revenues. Subsidies to encourage the location of factories in depressed areas of a given country, a rather common practice in many developed nations, can have the same effect on imports. When such subsidized products are exported, other states may retaliate by claiming that the subsidies for the exports constitute unfair trade practices.

Countries facing what they perceive to be subsidized imports into their markets have increasingly taken advantage of the option of imposing countervailing duties. The application of countervailing duties is permissible under GATT to negate unfair advantages that are gained by foreign exporters through such mechanisms as subsidies. Unfortunately for the application of such additional duties, GATT rules are imprecise in stating what constitutes an export subsidy that can be countered. National legislation in individual countries, consequently, defines the use of countervailing duties. Such countervailing duties are applied to raise the cost of the subsidized import to reflect its true production cost and to eliminate the unfair advantages that the imports have over domestic production.

Controversies over the dumping of foreign products in a particular domestic market can also induce governments to take action to provide protection. Under GATT regulations, a country can legitimately retaliate against an exporting state that is dumping goods in its domestic market. Dumping is generally defined as selling below the actual cost of production or pricing exports below domestic costs. Domestic prices in the producing country could be higher if that market is sufficiently protected from import competition through tariffs or NTBs. If such is the case, one type of protectionist practice can become interlinked with others, and one form of protection leads to demands for protection elsewhere, either directly or indirectly. Dumping of goods, if consistently and successfully used, can even drive domestic producers out of business, permitting a later increase in the price of the imports in question.

Charges of dumping against foreign producers have often been made by domestic firms facing competition from imports. Not surprisingly, such charges have occurred more frequently when the domestic industries in question have been facing increased competition from imports regardless of whether the competition is related to dumping or not.[7] The existence of dumping is often difficult to confirm in a satisfactory fashion. One key question is whether the price of the import is based on the marginal cost of additional production or the average cost for all production. Since the marginal cost of producing one additional item from the same factory may be relatively low, the price of the import may be priced below that of the same item in the exporter's domestic market. The average cost for all production from the same factory, however, will be much higher when allocated to each additional unit.

How a government chooses to construe an apparent act of dumping can then constitute a significant NTB. A harsh interpretation has the advantage of meeting domestic political pressures, of operating within the GATT framework, and of not necessarily being seen as the application of protectionist practices since it is designed to promote fair trade. When anti-dumping actions have been taken, however, they have had the tendency to limit not only imports of the product allegedly being dumped but to decrease other imports as well.

State Trading and Purchasing

The government can also provide effective protection for its domestic industries by helping to organize production and trade. State trading practices are particularly prevalent in the centrally planned economies of Eastern Europe. The increasing trade of these countries with other nations has raised new issues and led to some charges of unfair trading practices by firms in other countries. In countries other than the centrally planned economies, which are a special case, state trading companies may be able to limit imports by their purchasing policies and to subsidize exports by their pricing policies. The prices applied to the imports, if high enough, may also be used to guarantee domestic producers a minimum share of the market.

State-owned companies or marketing boards are likely to be subject to great pressures from domestic opinion since the gains and losses from their activities are more obvious than are those of private firms. Such transactions can clearly provide the government with an opportunity to protect domestic producers. Bilateral barter agreements among states, whether by state trading firms or through government-to-government negotiations may also have the effect of limiting imports of certain goods from other sources. Governments may also organize domestic cartels to provide assured market shares for domestic firms with prices being fixed to guarantee a profit, thus maintaining the position of domestic firms and very effectively limiting import competition.

The presence of government corporations or nationalized industries can have an impact beyond state trading. Through either legislation or common practice, government purchases will be limited to domestic firms or be placed predominately with them. Lower prices for imports, with or without tariff duties, are inconsequential when as a matter of policy orders for goods are placed with the domestic firms. Domestic content requirements may also be mandatory for firms doing contracting or subcontracting work for government agencies. Where there are a significant number of public corporations or state agencies making these purchases, the barriers to imports may be very great indeed.

Government corporations, industries created by governments in the past or nationalized by them, or industries where the government owns important shares, often as a result of a previous decision to infuse new capital into firms in trouble, are becoming more common in both developed and developing countries.

Japan and many European countries have a large number of state or quasi-state corporations that use such purchasing policies to aid the market position of domestic firms. These corporations or firms may also be preferred suppliers for other government agencies or private firms with government contracts, notwithstanding their higher costs compared to imports, and thus further contribute to limitations on imports without a specific transparent barrier appearing at the border. Purchases of the kind described in many states can cumulatively diminish the total flow and level of international trade. These policies can also be used to help domestic firms establish themselves in the face of foreign competition and thus create protection for an infant industry. Government purchase policies might also guarantee domestic firms sufficient economies of scale that would not otherwise be possible, thus permitting them to more effectively compete with foreign producers.

Other Non-Tariff Barriers

Many additional NTBs result from the application of a variety of government policies. The choice of specific tariffs rather than *ad valorum* duties, the use of different or complicated tariff classifications, and country of origin regulations that are part of the tariff schedules, can all reflect government efforts to limit imports through the manipulation of the tariff structure. There may be labeling requirements that make it difficult for some or all foreign producers to export to a particular market. Requirements that products be graded or sized according to domestic standards may inhibit exporters from attempting to enter a market, particularly if such exports would account for a relatively small portion of the total production of the country or of the total exports.

Safety and health requirements for particular types of products can also restrict imports. Japan once required that Perrier water from France be boiled before entering the country as a health measure.[8] A health regulation such as this one clearly constituted a total NTB. If a country establishes health, safety, or environmental standards that are sufficiently different from those in use in most other countries, the barrier might be particularly significant since foreign producers could be much less likely to attempt to meet such special provisions. The barrier would be more important if the market were either a small one in total terms or a marginal one for a specific exporter.

Other government regulations can also be used to provide significant obstructions to imports. For example late in 1982 the French government required that all imports of Japanese video recorders be cleared at the inland customs post at Poitiers. Since that post's small staff was not augmented, the requirement effectively prevented the Japanese imports from reaching the French domestic market during the peak Christmas season.[9] Such a requirement constituted an extremely effective, although temporary, non-tariff barrier to trade. Japan in turn was effective in preventing imports of cheap American aluminum bats. It passed legislation that required the approval of Japanese baseball leagues for the use of particular brands of bats. Since such approval was not forthcoming, Japanese firms kept their domestic markets for this product.[10] Both of these examples, while somewhat trivial, demonstrate how governments can give direct or indirect protection to domestic producers at the expense of foreign producers.

A variety of other NTBs can be used to provide some protection to domestic firms. Counter-trade between countries has become a new tactic that can create obstacles to trade. In a countertrade agreement, two countries agree to increase their imports from each other with each guaranteeing to purchase goods from the other. Such agreements discriminate against other exporters and may even distort the export trade of the countries involved in the agreement. Minimum import prices may be set for some items, providing at least an element of protection. Transportation rate structures may effectively discriminate against imports, structures that are often determined by government agencies or are subject to some form of regulation. Use taxes may be applied in a fashion that discriminates against foreign imports.

Other policies may have the effect of hindering goods that would otherwise compete with domestic producers. Accelerated depreciation schedules, tax credits, guaranteed government loans with or without especially low interest rates, provisions for loss write-offs, and tax loopholes, all of which may generally be available only to domestic firms, could have the effect of obstructing imports or of providing effective subsidies for exports.

These various forms of NTBs have tended to restrict trade, of course, just as tariffs reduce imports and sometimes exports. NTBs, however, seldom serve a revenue function for the states in question. Complaints about unfair trade practices involving NTBs have proliferated, and the variety of NTBs has expanded greatly. In the early 1970s, the secretariat of GATT identified over 800 NTBs in operation with the identification based on complaints from more than one country over a particular limitation on imports.[11]

While some of the NTBs are designed explicitly as protectionist devices, others are the by-products of governmental actions intended to achieve other goals. NTBs in this category have become more common. Due to the increased complexity of national economies, government policies dealing with economic issues have had trade-distorting side effects. Policies to help depressed regions are one example of such effects. Industries in these regions are given subsidies, a guaranteed percentage of government purchases or preferences in such purchases, tax credits or tax relief, or lowered transport costs, all of which may also come to provide an effective limitation on imports.

Other government policies may constitute unintentional barriers as well. Health, safety, and environmental regulations often have initially reflected other concerns but have since come to be important NTBs in some cases. While the initial cause for the creation of a policy that constitutes a barrier may be uncertain, the result has been a limitation on trade.

NTBs raise the prices of goods for domestic consumers in the protected markets and undoubtedly constitute a net economic cost to the nation using them, although it is difficult to quantify all the costs and benefits from such actions as the application of health measures. NTBs, whether they are quotas, or government policies or regulations, once adopted in one state may diffuse to other countries, either as imitations or as retaliatory measures. One type of NTB, such as an industry subsidy, may lead to the imposition of other NTBs, such as anti-dumping regulations or countervailing duties in another state, thus further increasing the barriers to trade. Just as there are tariff wars, there can be trade conflicts that rely on NTBs as the basic weapons in national economic arsenals.

International negotiations dealing with these obstacles to trade have not been very successful in reducing their prevalence. Removal of barriers or a diminution of their effects is made more difficult by the number of forms that they can take and as a consequence of the fact that many of them are by-products of other policies, designed to deal with domestic problems or to achieve domestic political and economic goals. These policies are generally seen as being appropriate ones for governments to adopt when they are directed to appropriate goals. The resulting trade distortions and the real protectionism that results is thus going to be a continuing factor in the international economic system and a major obstacle to any efforts to liberalize international trade.

End Notes

1. Middleton, Robert. *Negotiating on Non-Tariff Distortions of Trade: The EFTA Precedents.* New York: St. Martin's Press, 1975.

2. Feenstra, Robert C. "Voluntary Export Restraint in U.S. Autos, 1980-81: Quality, Employment, and Welfare Effects." In: *The Structure and Evolution of Recent U.S. Trade Policy*, ed. Robert E. Baldwin and Anne O. Krueger. Chicago: University of Chicago Press, 1984. pp.35-59.

3. Yoffie, David B. "Adjustment in the Footwear Industry: The Consequences of Orderly Marketing Arrangements." In: *American Industry in International Competition: Government Policies and Corporate Strategies*, edited by John Zysman and Laura Tyson. Ithaca: Cornell University Press, 1983. pp. 313-349.

4. Donnenfeld, Shabtai and Wolfgang Mayer. "The Quality of Export Products and Optimal Trade Policy," *International Economic Review* 28:1 (February 1987):159-174.

5. Pearson, Charles and Nils Johnson. *The New GATT Trade Round.* Foreign Policy Institute Case Studies No. 2. Washington, D.C.: School of Advanced International Studies, Johns Hopkins University, 1986. p.20

6. Kumar, Krishna and Kee Young Kim. "The Korean Manufacturing Multinationals," *Journal of International Business Studies* 15:1 (Spring 1984):52.

7. Lloyd, Peter. *Anti-Dumping Actions and the GATT System.* Thames Essay No. 9. London: Trade Policy Research Centre, 1977.

8. Ziegler, David W. *War, Peace, and International Politics.* 4th ed. Boston: Little, Brown, 1987. p. 424

9. Kihl, Young Whan and James M. Lutz. *World Trade Issues: Regime, Structure, and Policy.* New York: Praeger, 1985. p.176

10. *Ziegler.* op. cit. p.423

11 Hindley, Brian. "Negotiations for Overcoming Non-Tariff Barriers to Trade." In: Towards an Open Economy, edited by Frank McFadzean, Sir Alex Cairncross, Sidney Golt, James Meade, W. M. Corden, Harry G. Johnson, and T. M. Rybczynski. London: Macmillan, 1972. p.127

Chapter 3: Annotated Bibliography

General Works

* 3.1 *

Agmon, Tamir. "Direct Investment and Intra-Industry Trade: Substitutes or Complements." In: *On the Economics of Intra-Industry Trade: Symposium 1978*, edited by Herbert Giersch. Tubingen: J.C.B. Mohr, 1978. ISBN 0-89563-548-8.

Individual firms have used intra-industry trade as a means around imperfect international markets. Government policies have affected these markets indirectly through import substitution and export promotion.

* 3.2 *

Balassa, Bela. "Incentive Measures: Concepts and Estimation." In: *Development Strategies in Semi-Industrial Economies*, edited by Bela Balassa. Baltimore: Johns Hopkins University Press, 1982. ISBN 0-8018-25709.

 Balassa discusses a variety of measures that can offer protection, including tariffs, quantitative protection, and tax preferences, as well as methods for estimating rates of effective protection.

* 3.3 *

Brander, James A., and Barbara J. Spencer. "Trade Warfare: Tariffs and Cartels." *Journal of International Economics* 16:3-4 (May 1984): 227-242.

 Tariffs--both specific and *ad valorum*--cartels, and subsidies are effective weapons in trade warfare. The determination of which device is most effective varies with particular circumstances.

* 3.4 *

Cao, A. D. "Non-Tariff Barriers to U.S. Manufactured Exports." *Columbia Journal of World Business* 15:2 (Summer 1980): 93-102.

 The author identifies some of the major nontariff barriers U.S. exporters face in other countries. He argues for the mutual reduction of such obstacles to trade.

* 3.5 *

Cassing, James H. "Alternatives to Protectionism." In: *Western Economies in Transition: Structural Change and Adjustment Policies in Industrial Countries*, edited by Irving Levenson and Jimmy W. Wheeler. Boulder, CO: Westview, 1980. ISBN 0-891-58589-3.

 Cassing notes the various forms that protectionism can take and provides examples of the use of non-tariff barriers for a number of developed countries. Pressure for protectionism arises because imports threaten the owners of resources in use. He suggests a variety of government adjustment programs to spread the costs and gains of such import competition and to diffuse domestic political pressures for protection.

* 3.6 *

Cornes, Richard, and Avinash Dixit. "Comparative Effects of Devaluation and Import Controls on Domestic Prices." *Economica* 49 (February 1982): 1-10.

 The relative effects of import controls and currency devaluations on prices will vary according to other factors. The benefits of adopting either policy have to be analyzed on a case-by-case basis.

* 3.7 *

Curzon, Gerard, and Victoria Curzon. *Global Assault on Non-Tariff Trade Barriers*. Thames Essay no. 3. London: Trade Policy Research Centre, 1972. ISBN 0-900-84218-0.

 The authors analyze the various existing general types of non-tariff barriers to trade. They argue that reductions in these barriers are necessary and should be brought about within the GATT framework so that the reduction is a global one.

* 3.8 *

Golt, Sidney. "The New Protectionism." In: *Western Economies in Transition: Structural Change and Adjustment Policies in Industrial Countries*, edited by Irving Leveson and Jimmy W. Wheeler. Boulder, CO: Westview, 1980. ISBN 0-891-58589-3.

 The industrialized states have increasingly relied on a variety of non-tariff barriers to limit imports, thus undercutting the liberal trade principles of GATT. Subsidies to industries have become increasingly prevalent, as have other trade limiting policies adopted as part of adjustment policies.

* 3.9 *

Hindley, Brian. "Negotiations for Overcoming Non-Tariff Barriers to Trade." In: *Towards an Open Economy*, edited by Frank McFadzean et al. London: Macmillan, 1972. ISBN 0-312-81060-1.

 While tariffs are similar across countries, non-tariff barriers are very diverse. The effects of these barriers have increased with tariff reductions. Hindley argues that while free trade may be an ideal, negotiations should center on achieving national objectives with a minimum of harm to other countries and limited government interventions in trade.

* 3.10 *

Kelly, William B. "Nontariff Barriers." In: *Studies in Trade Liberalization: Problems and Prospects for the Industrial Countries*, edited by Bela Balassa. Baltimore: Johns Hopkins Press, 1967. ISBN 0-317-19827-0.

 Kelly offers an extensive and useful overview of the non-tariff barriers in use in the 1960s and their effects on trade. He also correctly notes that the reduction of tariff barriers, ongoing during that decade, made non-tariff obstacles more important.

* 3.11 *

Lloyd, Peter J., and Rodney E. Falvey. "The Choice of Instruments for Industry Protection." In: *Issues in World Trade Policy: GATT at the Crossroads*, edited by R. H. Snape. New York: St. Martin's, 1986. ISBN 0-312-43724-2.

 Non-tariff barriers have increasingly been invoked to provide protection. The authors analyze some of the reasons for the use of these kinds of obstacles to imports, with particular reference to Australia.

* 3.12 *

Marks, Matthew J., and Harald B. Malmgren. "Negotiating Nontariff Distortions to Trade." *Law and Policy in International Business* 7:2 (1975): 327-411.

The authors discuss some of the major U.S. non-tariff barriers to trade and the problems that they present for U.S. negotiators attempting to eliminate them. The discussion elucidates their complexity and demonstrates that many of them are intimately linked with other domestic policies and practices, thus making them more difficult to remove or modify.

* 3.13 *

Middleton, Robert. *Negotiating on Non-Tariff Distortions of Trade: The EFTA Precedents.* New York: St. Martin's, 1975. ISBN 0-312-56315-9.

EFTA (European Free Trade Association) managed to reduce non-tariff barriers among its members, but its experience is not directly transferable to other circumstances. The EFTA countries attempted to find solutions to specific problems at low cost with few limitations on the national sovereignty of the member states.

* 3.14 *

Mussa, Michael. "Government Policy and the Adjustment Process." In: *Import Competition and Response*, edited by Jagdish N. Bhagwati. Chicago: University of Chicago Press, 1982. ISBN 0-226-04538-2.

In his model of adjustment processes, Mussa shows, among other points, that a quota that varies in an optimal fashion is equivalent to an optimally varying tariff in terms of meeting government objectives. He also models constant tariffs, constant quotas, production subsidies, and consumption taxes. He concludes that in an economy with private decision makers, the appropriate government policy is to remove general distortions, including taxes and transfer payments that cause the benefits received by private decision makers to diverge from the societal optimum.

* 3.15 *

Walter, Ingo. "Barriers to International Competition: The Application and Liberalization of Nontariff Distortions." In: *The United States and International Markets: Commercial Policy Options in an Age of Controls*, edited by Robert G. Hawkins and Ingo Walter. Lexington, MA: Lexington Books, 1972. ISBN 0-669-84020-3.

Non-tariff barriers have become more important as protectionist measures because tariffs are based on a complex set of multilateral agreements.

The threat of NTBs can also be effective in convincing major competitive suppliers to voluntarily decrease their exports. Overall, the NTBs seem to have a greater impact on exports from the developing countries.

* 3.16 *

Walter, Ingo. "Barriers to International Competition: The Nature of Nontariff Distortions." In: *The United States and International Markets: Commercial Policy Options in an Age of Controls*, edited by Robert G. Hawkins and Ingo Walter. Lexington, MA: Lexington Books, 1972. ISBN 0-669-84020-3.

Walter analyzes non-tariff barriers, including the levels of effective protection that are offered. He classifies non-tariff barriers in three groups--the most common, those designed to protect domestic industries; those that distort trade as a means of dealing with non-trade problems; and those designed to deal with other problems having trade-distortion effects as a by-product.

Quotas

* 3.17 *

Anderson, James E. "The Relative Inefficiency of Quotas: The Cheese Case." *American Economic Review* 75:1 (March 1985): 178-190.

Anderson analyzes the U.S. import quota on cheese as an example of a commodity group with heterogeneous components. He finds that the import quota is a relatively inefficient instrument as long as aggregated commodity groups are used.

* 3.18 *

Buffie, Edward F., and Pablo T. Spiller. "Trade Liberalization in Oligopolistic Industries: The Quota Case." *Journal of International Economics* 20:1-2 (February 1986): 65-81.

The presence of a small number of firms in an industry will affect the probability that reducing quotas will lead to price declines. In the short run prices may go down, but in the long term they may increase as firms leave the industry due to lower profits. Trade liberalization could have a perverse effect.

* 3.19 *

Casas, F. R., and E. Gelbard. "Tariffs and Quotas in the Presence of Foreign Monopoly." *International Trade Journal* 1:3 (Spring 1987): 289-303.

With a foreign monopoly present, both a tariff and a quota will have negative effects on terms of trade and costs. A tariff is better than a quota, and a quota is better than a voluntary export restraint as a means of avoiding a portion of these negative impacts.

* 3.20 *

Donnenfeld, Shabtai, and Wolfgang Mayer. "The Quality of Export Products and Optimal Trade Policy." *International Economic Review* 28:1 (February 1987): 159-174.

Voluntary export restraints can be socially useful in an exporting country. If the firms involved are few in number, the restraint can be an effective means of upgrading the quality of the exports without direct government intervention.

* 3.21 *

Falvey, Rodney E. "The Composition of Trade within Import-Restricted Product Categories." *Journal of Political Economy* 87:5 (October 1979):1105-1114.

Falvey provides a model of the process by which quantitative import restrictions can lead to the importation of higher priced items in the product line. Greater substitutions of this type occur with protectionism than would be the case with free trade.

* 3.22 *

Hamilton, Carl. "An Assessment of Voluntary Restraints on Hong Kong Exports to Europe and the USA." *Economica* 53 (August 1986): 339-350.

Voluntary restraints on exports have not been particularly effective in limiting imports into the individual EC nations from Hong Kong. The policies of the EC rather than individual national policies are the important factor. Hamilton also provides a means of estimating the costs of such quotas to importing nations.

* 3.23 *

Harris, Richard. "Why Voluntary Export Restraints Are 'Voluntary'." *Canadian Journal of Economics* 18:4 (November 1985): 799-809.

Voluntary export restraints (VERs) accepted by exporting firms in one country increase profitability for those firms due to their ability to raise prices. VERs are thus a particularly bad form of protectionism, and they raise the ultimate cost of goods to consumers.

* 3.24 *

Hindley, Brian. "Voluntary Export Restraints and Article XIX of the General Agreement on Tariffs and Trade." In: *Current Issues in Commercial Policy and Diplomacy*, edited by John Black and Brian Hindley. New York: St. Martin's, 1980. ISBN 0-312-17926-x.

Voluntary export restraints (VERs) are considered in theory to be emergency agreements implemented to deal with a surge in imports; their regulation is not covered under GATT regulations. VERs are often not efficient as a means of aiding troubled industries, and they increase pressure for

VERs in other countries that become the new recipients of the threatening exports. The developing countries have sought greater regulation of VERs under GATT, but the industrialized states have not agreed.

* 3.25 *

Hollerman, Leon. "Japan's Economic Impact on the United States." *Annals of the Academy of Political and Social Sciences* 460 (March 1982): 127-135.

The U.S. success in securing voluntary export restraints on Japanese exports could have consequences beyond higher U.S. costs. The restraints require the formation of cartels in Japan to apportion the lower level of exports. These cartels, alone or in conjunction with cartels in the EC, could operate to the extreme disadvantage of the United States in times of economic difficulties in the cartel countries or in the international economy.

* 3.26 *

Jones, Kent. "The Political Economy of Voluntary Export Restraint Agreements." *Kyklos* 37:1 (1984): 82-101.

Although voluntary export restraints shift imports away from the most efficient producers, they have advantages for all the participants to the agreement in the exporting and importing countries. Consumers in the importing countries, however, will pay higher costs. Such restraints also tend to shift exports to new markets where additional protectionist pressures may appear.

* 3.27 *

Lynch, John. *Toward an Orderly Market: An Intensive Study of Japan's Voluntary Quota in Cotton Textile Exports.* Tokyo: Sophia University, 1968. ISBN 0-8048-0652-7.

Lynch analyzes in detail the events and negotiations leading up to the voluntary export arrangement that began in 1955. Among the consequences of the quota were a shift of textile production for the U.S. market to other nations and the setting of a precedent for further quotas in other product areas.

* 3.28 *

Melvin, James R. "The Nonequivalence of Tariffs and Import Quotas." *American Economic Review* 76:4 (September 1986): 1131-1134.

Tariffs and imports quotas can never be equivalent policy measures controlling the trade between two countries when both practice protection. The use of quotas will lead to retaliation and decreases in trade, while the use of tariffs will stabilize trade.

* 3.29 *

Murray, Tracy, Wilson Schmidt, and Ingo Walter. "Alternative Forms of Protection against Market Disruption." *Kyklos* 31:4 (1978): 624-637.

Voluntary export restraints and orderly marketing arrangements are directed against specific suppliers of goods. These approaches are more restrictive of trade than general quotas if the export licenses are tradeable, as they often are.

* 3.30 *

Ono, Yoshiyasu. "Profitability of Export Restraint." *Journal of International Economics* 16:3-4 (May 1984): 335-343.

The author's model indicates that voluntary export restraints can increase profits for participating firms. Such export restraints may actually be sought by foreign producers.

* 3.31 *

Smith, Malcolm D. H. "Voluntary Export Quotas and U.S. Trade Policy--A New Nontariff Barrier." *Law and Policy in International Business* 5:1 (1973):10-55.

Smith discusses the development and implementation of VERs by the United States, with particular reference to textiles. He considers the use of VERs a significant new non-tariff barrier. Their negotiation has revealed the weakness of GATT in dealing with trade problems.

* 3.32 *

Takacs, Wendy E. "The Nonequivalence of Tariffs, Imports Quotas, and Voluntary Export Restraints." *Journal of International Economics* 8:4 (November 1978): 565-573.

Voluntary export restraints can have effects quite different from tariffs or other quotas, particularly if not all foreign producers are involved. Usually they will lead to higher import prices than tariffs or quotas. The country imposing this form of protection will suffer higher costs in many circumstances.

* 3.33 *

Turner, Louis. "Consumer Electronics: The Colour Television Case." In: *The Newly Industrializing Countries: Trade and Adjustment*, edited by Louis Turner and Neil McMullen. London: George Allen & Unwin, 1982. ISBN 0-04-382036-0.

Japan and the NICs have made serious inroads into markets in Europe and the United States with their exports of colour television sets, resulting in the imposition of quotas and orderly marketing arrangements, charges of dumping, and requests for adjustment assistance. Japanese firms have invested in Singapore and Taiwan as a way of getting around quota restrictions in the industrialized countries.

* 3.34 *

Yoffie, David B. "Adjustment in the Footwear Industry: The Consequences of Orderly Marketing Arrangements." In: *American Industry in International Competition: Government Policies and Corporate Strategies*, edited by John Zysman and Laura Tyson. Ithaca, NY: Cornell University Press, 1983. ISBN 0-8014-1577-2.

The experience of the U.S. footwear industry indicates that Orderly Marketing Arrangements do not provide effective protection. Foreign exporters shift to higher priced items leaving them in an even stronger position in the American market.

* 3.35 *

Young, Leslie, and James E. Anderson. "Risk Aversion and Optimal Trade Restrictions." *Review of Economic Studies* 49 (April 1982): 291-305.

If consumers are adverse to taking risks with price changes, trade controls can be used to reduce imports with their uncertain prices and to increase domestic prices. A quota is superior to a tariff in achieving a desired ceiling on imports.

Safeguard and Escape Clauses

* 3.36 *

Merciai, Patrizio. "Safeguard Measures in GATT." *Journal of World Trade Law* 15:1 (Jan/Feb 1981): 41-66.

The author argues that the inability of multilateral negotiations to resolve the use of safeguards under GATT has resulted in the formulation of no new rules and a severe weakening of the old ones. The issue is difficult to resolve because governments have been very sensitive about the problem, particularly at times when protectionist public opinion has been on the increase.

* 3.37 *

L'Huillier, Jacques. "Escape Clauses and the Multi-Fibre Agreement." In: *The New Economic Nationalism*, edited by Otto Hieronymi. London: Macmillan, 1980. ISBN 0-333-26173-9.

Safeguard measures such as escape clauses have been used in a discriminatory fashion in the past. L'Huillier suggests that their use be reformed so that, while they are easier to invoke, their invocation would be under strict GATT supervision.

* 3.38 *

Tumlir, Jan. "A Revised Safeguard Clause for GATT?" *Journal of World Trade Law* 7:4 (July/August 1973): 404-420.

If nations are going to reduce barriers to trade, safeguard clauses are essential to protect against sudden disruptions in domestic markets. The availability of safeguards, however, should be limited to emergency situations and then only under GATT rules.

* 3.39 *
Robertson, David. *Fail Safe Systems for Trade Liberalisation.* Thames Essay no. 12. London: Trade Policy Research Centre, 1977. ISBN 0-900-84234-2.

Robertson argues that safeguards against disruptions from imports are necessary to further overall trade liberalization. Safeguards include temporary measures to meet import disruption by limiting the level of imports and adjustment assistance to the affected sector. The use of safeguards does need to be integrated into GATT to limit abuses and to define situations in which they can be legitimately used.

* 3.40 *
Robertson, David. "Provisions for Escape Clauses and Other Safeguards." In: *Towards an Open World Economy*, edited by Frank McFadzean et al. London: Macmillan, 1972. ISBN 0-312-81060-1.

Robertson discusses various safeguards and escape clauses that allow countries to avoid the obligations of international agreements and the GATT framework. Nations regard escape clauses as essential. In the face of tariff reductions, they have increasingly used them to protect industries threatened by imports.

Subsidies, Dumping, and Countervailing Duties

* 3.41 *
Barcelo, John J. "Subsidies and Countervailing Duties--Analysis and a Proposal." *Law and Policy in International Business* 9:3 (1977): 779-853.

Barcelo provides a detailed analysis of the use of subsidies and countervailing duties and recommends that they be used only to further free trade and economic efficiency. He concludes that GATT rules will have to be changed to improve existing regulation of such subsidies and duties.

* 3.42 *
Bloch, Henry Simon. "Export Financing Emerging as a Major Policy Problem." *Columbia Journal of World Business* 11:3 (Fall 1976): 85-95.

Bloch argues that export insurance is essential for maintaining trade with the developing countries. He considers export subsidies and import restrictions to be counterproductive.

* 3.43 *
Cragg, Chris. "Shipping and Shipbuilding." In: *The International Politics of Surplus Capacity*, edited by Susan Strange and Roger Tooze. London: Allen & Unwin, 1981. ISBN 0-04-382034-4.

Protectionism in shipbuilding has usually been in the form of subsidies by governments in the developed countries and NICs. Ultimately, the shipbuilding industry and the shipping sector are hurt by protectionism, since, as Cragg notes, the real solution to their problems would be an increase in total world trade.

* 3.44 *
Dale, Richard. *Anti-Dumping Law in a Liberal Trade Order.* New York: St. Martin's, 1980. ISBN 0-312-04373-2.

Dale reviews the anti-dumping measures that have been taken in response to import dumping. He considers regulations in various countries, the GATT rules, and the special case of East-West trade as well as particular industries. He concludes that anti-dumping measures limit not only imports of the product allegedly dumped but other imports as well.

* 3.45 *
DeMeza, David. "Export Subsidies and High Productivity: Cause or Effect." *Canadian Journal of Economics* 19:2 (May 1986): 347-350.

DeMeza develops a formal model on the impact of export subsidies on productivity and discovers that countries with the lowest costs will have the higher subsidies. Higher subsidies could also occur in a country where production in an industry was concentrated in a few or only one firm.

* 3.46 *
Denton, Geoffrey, and Seamus O'Cleireacain. *Subsidy Issues in International Commerce.* Thames Essay no. 5. London: Trade Policy Research Centre, 1972. ISBN 0-900-84220-2.

Non-tariff interventions may be used to deal with import competition or as stimulants to encourage trade. Subsidies, including regional subsidies, can be used for both these purposes. Industry subsidies in one state, however, can lead to countervailing subsidies in other countries, thus introducing additional distortions into the trade system.

* 3.47 *
Diamond, Peter A. "Protection, Trade Adjustment Assistance and Income Distribution." In: *Import Competition and Response*, edited by Jagdish N. Bhagwati. Chicago: University of Chicago, 1982. ISBN 0-226-04538-2.

Diamond examines subsidies as a form of protection and as a means of adjustment assistance for workers in industries suffering from foreign competition. Much of his analysis focuses on the need to meet the costs of workers moving from declining industries to more viable ones.

* 3.48 *
Feenstra, Robert C. "Trade Policy with Several Goods and 'Market Linkages'." *Journal of International Economics* 20:3-4 (May 1986): 249-267.

Export subsidies can benefit an exporting country while quotas in the form of voluntary export restraints can help the importer. A countervailing duty may also be of benefit to an importing state.

* 3.49 *
Grossman, Gene M. "Strategic Export Promotion: A Critique." In: *Strategic Trade Policy and the New International Economics*, edited by Paul R. Krugman. Cambridge, MA: MIT Press, 1987. ISBN 0-262-11112-8.

Arguments can be made for an industrial strategy promoting exports through subsidies and other means. While such an ideal strategy can be formulated, it is doubtful that the mechanisms of governmental policy can determine and implement such a strategy.

* 3.50 *
Grubel, Herbert G. "Free Trade Zones and Their Relation to GATT." In: *Issues in World Trade Policy: GATT at the Crossroads*, edited by R. H. Snape. New York: St. Martin's, 1986. ISBN 0-312-43724-2.

Free trade zones have appeared in many countries where domestic groups favor them as a means of avoiding government policies that limit trade. Such zones, however, provide government subsidies to firms located there, possibly in violation of GATT rules on such subsidies.

* 3.51 *
Guido, Robert V., and Michael F. Morrone. "The Michelin Decision: A Possible New Direction for U.S. Countervailing Duty Law." *Law and Policy in International Business* 6:1 (1974): 237-266.

In 1973, the U.S. Department of the Treasury imposed a countervailing duty on imports of Michelin tires from Canada due to subsidies granted by local, provincial, and national governments. This decision established a new precedent for counteracting such subsidies. The precedent also provided an important new non-tariff barrier to trade.

* 3.52 *
Hoh, Motoshighe, and Kazuharu Kiyono. "Welfare Enhancing Export Subsidies." *Journal of Political Economy* 95:1 (February 1987): 115-137.

Export subsidies on otherwise marginal goods that would be traded only in small amounts can contribute to national welfare. Subsidies on non-marginal goods diminish national welfare.

* 3.53 *
Lloyd, Peter. *Anti-Dumping Actions and the GATT System*. Thames Essay no. 9. London: Trade Policy Research Centre, 1977. ISBN 0-900-48231-8.

Lloyd analyzes the GATT codes on dumping and the anti-dumping measures that individual countries take. Charges of dumping do increase in the face of import competition. Anti-dumping codes have reduced conflicts and, as a consequence, provide a guide for dealing with other non-tariff measures.

* 3.54 *
Low, Patrick. "The Definition of 'Export Subsidies' in GATT." *Journal of World Trade Law* 16:5 (September/October 1982): 375-390.

GATT does not define export subsidies in a definitive fashion; there are a number of interpretations. In some cases, export subsidies may favor trade liberalization by replacing other forms of domestic protection. In other circumstances, they may distort trade patterns.

* 3.55 *
Malmgren, Harald B. *International Order for Public Subsidies*. Thames Essay no. 11. London: Trade Policy Research Centre, 1977. ISBN 0-900-84230-x.

There are many subsidies applied to exports. An international agreement needs to be reached on their proper use, one that eliminates unfair advantage. The problems are different for different countries, and a solution to their role in domestic economies and the international economy will of necessity be a complex one.

* 3.56 *
Meuser, Robert L. "Dumping from 'Controlled Economy' Countries: The Polish Golf Cart Case." *Law and Policy in International Business* 11:2 (1979): 777-803.

U.S. anti-dumping regulations had to be modified to deal with the difficulties of establishing fair market values for goods produced in Poland. The case of Polish golf carts illustrates the difficulties of applying standard measures to goods originating in the centrally planned economies.

* 3.57 *
Phegan, Colin. "GATT Article XVI.3: Export Subsidies and 'Equitable Shares'." *Journal of World Trade Law* 16:3 (May/June 1982): 251-264.

GATT articles designed to limit export subsidies have been ineffective. It is difficult to define what constitutes a more than equitable share of world trade as specified in the GATT articles and to demonstrate that the subsidies are the cause of increased exports.

* 3.58 *
Rodrik, Dani. "Tariffs, Subsidies and Welfare with Endogenous Policy." *Journal of International Economics* 21:3-4 (November 1986): 285-299.

Subsidies have normally been considered to be superior to tariffs as instruments of national policy. Dependent upon the nature of the industrial sector or firms within it, however, tariffs on occasion may be preferable to subsidies.

* 3.59 *
Stegemann, Klaus. "Anti-Dumping Policy and the Consumer." *Journal of World Trade Law* 19:5 (September/October 1985): 466-484.

The present use of anti-dumping laws in many countries favors domestic producers and hurts consumers. Consumers would be better served if prohibitions extended only to truly predatory dumping.

* 3.60 *
Van Bael, Ivo. "Ten Years of EEC Anti-Dumping Enforcement." *Journal of World Trade Law* 13:5 (September/October 1979): 395-408.

Out of 60 cases heard by the European Court that the author considers, only five resulted in the imposition of additional duties. In other cases, however, the exporters agreed to undertake price revisions.

State Trading and Purchasing

* 3.61 *
Baban, Roy. "State Trading and GATT." *Journal of World Trade Law* 11:4 (July/August 1977): 334-353.

The author reviews various state trading practices that can take numerous forms in the centrally planned economies of Eastern Europe. These practices are hard to integrate with GATT rules. Defining trade levels that are acceptable becomes particularly difficult when there are many products involved.

* 3.62 *
Curran, Timothy J. "Politics and High Technology: The NTT Case." In: *Coping with U.S.-Japanese Economic Conflicts*, edited by I. M. Destler and Hideo Sato. Lexington, MA: Lexington Books, 1982. ISBN 0-669-05144-6.

Nippon Telephone and Telegraph (NTT), a state-owned public corporation, followed a procurement procedure that limited virtually all bidding to Japanese firms. Under U.S. pressure, the bidding procedure in some cases was opened to U.S. firms,

negating some of the protection offered to Japanese firms by this non-tariff barrier.

* 3.63 *
Ianni, Edmond M. "The International Treatment of State Trading." *Journal of World Trade Law* 16:6 (November/December 1982): 480-496.

GATT assumptions on state trading were initially based on such activities as those present in the market economies. The rules that were formulated are not readily applicable to socialist countries. The United States, as demonstrated by its trade with China, has accommodated trade with centrally planned economies better than GATT has.

* 3.64 *
Kostecki, M. M. "State Trading in Industrialized and Developing Countries." *Journal of World Trade Law* 12:3 (May/June 1978): 187-207.

The author discusses the variety of forms that state trading can take in different countries and some of the implications of such activity. State trading in some circumstances performs the same functions as tariffs, subsidies, and quotas.

* 3.65 *
Vernon, Raymond. "The International Aspects of State-Owned Enterprises." *Journal of International Business Studies* 10:3 (Winter 1979): 7-15.

State-owned companies can perform a number of protectionist functions such as bilateral trading, developing or protecting a threatened industrial sector, or increasing exports. They also face greater political pressure to use domestic inputs in production.

* 3.66 *
Warr, Peter G., and Brian R. Parmenter. "Protection through Government Procurement." In: *Issues in World Trade Policy: GATT at the Crossroads*, edited by R. H. Snape. New York: St. Martin's Press, 1986. ISBN 0-312-43724-2.

Although government procurement policies used to protect domestic industries have costs for the domestic economy, they are often lower than the costs that result from tariffs. The 1979 Agreement on Government Procurement, signed under the GATT framework by 20 countries, was designed to limit the use of this practice to favor domestic suppliers, with exceptions possible for national security reasons.

* 3.67 *
Zysman, John. "The State as Trader." *International Affairs* (London) 54:2 (April 1978): 264-281.

State trading entities have become more common, and they can be used to supply protection in threatened industries. State traders are subject to greater political pressures since the gains and losses with these firms are more immediately obvious than is the case with multiple market transactions.

Other Non-Tariff Barriers

* 3.68 *

Baylis, Arthur E. "The Documentation Dilemma in International Trade." *Columbia Journal of World Business* 11:1 (Spring 1976): 15-22.

Documentation problems for international shipments have become one of the major non-tariff barriers to trade. The presence of documentation requirements often discourages potential exporters.

* 3.69 *

Bond, Eric W. "Investment Incentives as Tariff Substitutes: A Comprehensive Measure of Protection." *Review of Economics and Statistics* 67:1 (February 1985): 91-97.

Investment incentives such as tax holidays or capital grants can be an effective non-tariff barrier. In the case of Ireland, such incentives did supply effective protection when tariffs were declining.

* 3.70 *

Davidson, Carl. "Cartel Stability and Tariff Policy." *Journal of International Economics* 17:3-4 (November 1984): 219-237.

Low tariff rates can encourage cartels if there is a domestic oligopoly. If tariff levels are high, the formation of a cartel is less likely.

* 3.71 *

Dixit, Avinash K., and Gene M. Grossman. "Trade and Protection with Multistage Production." *Review of Economic Studies* 49 (October 1982): 583-594.

The authors' model of the steps of a production process demonstrates that both tariffs and domestic content legislation can cause shifts in comparative advantage by affecting the cost of the value added. Both types of protection, however, can be counter-productive and move resources away from the protected sector.

* 3.72 *

Frankena, Mark. "The Industrial and Trade Control Regime and Product Design in India." *Economic Development and Cultural Change* 22: 2 (January 1974): 249-264.

Frankena analyzes the Indian government's policy on certain engineering goods produced in the country. Imports of these goods licensed for production are prohibited, providing total protection. Frankena concludes that the result is inefficiency, with inappropriate technological decisions being made in the choice of designs. Although Frankena does not use the term, the Indian licens-

ing procedure is a good example of an important non-tariff barrier to trade.

* 3.73 *

Grossman, Gene M. "Border Tax Adjustments: Do They Distort Trade." *Journal of International Economics* 10:1 (February 1980): 117-128.

The European countries use many indirect taxes, particularly the value added tax (VAT). Generally, the VAT can be rebated on exports and an equivalent tax imposed on competing imports. When intermediate inputs into production are taken into account, the imposition of taxes based on point of origin can distort trade and neutralize the effects of trade liberalization.

* 3.74 *

Grossman, Gene M. "The Theory of Domestic Content Protection and Content Preference." *Quarterly Journal of Economics* 96:4 (November 1981): 583-603.

Domestic content regulations provide a variable degree of protection that is difficult to predict. Such protection may not achieve the desired goals such as increasing outputs of intermediate goods or goods for export.

* 3.75 *

Jansson, Jan Owen, and Dan Shneerson. "The Effective Protection Implicit in Liner Shipping Freight Rates." *Review of Economics and Statistics* 60:4 (November 1978): 569-573.

The authors derive estimates of the protection offered by freight charges for ocean shipping. Variations in rates provide real protection for some industries. While this protection is not as great as that offered by tariffs, it is large enough to be considered in policy decisions on trade.

* 3.76 *

Kostecki, Michel. "Should One Countertrade?" *Journal of World Trade Law* 21:2 (April 1987): 7-21.

Countertrading may be efficient in some cases, but overall it is inefficient since it is bilateral. Government support of counter-trading encourages such inefficient trade, but government prohibition could place a country at a competitive disadvantage.

* 3.77 *

McVey, Thomas B. "Countertrade: Commercial Practices, Legal Issues and Policy Dilemmas." *Law and Policy in International Business* 16:1 (1984): 1-69.

McVey considers the various aspects of countertrade, a practice where a country agrees to balance its trade with a partner. Countertrade is often considered to interfere with the free flow of trade, and control of its use requires a co-ordinated, consistent response from the developed countries.

* 3.78 *

Organisation for Economic Co-Operation and Development. *Export Cartels: Report of the Committee of Experts on Restrictive Business Practices.* Paris: OECD, 1974.

Export cartels appear to have strengthened the existing barriers to international trade as well as creating some new obstacles. International cartels, as opposed to national ones, in particular have this effect.

* 3.79 *

Patrick, Hugh, and Hideo Sato. "The Political Economy of United States-Japan Trade in Steel." In: *Policy and Trade Issues of the Japanese Economy: American and Japanese Perspectives*, edited by Kozo Yamamura. Seattle: University of Washington Press, 1982. ISBN 0-295-95900-2.

For many years, U.S. steel producers were content with the large domestic market that foreign producers were allowed to penetrate. U.S. steel producers then pressed for protection, culminating in the trigger price mechanism in late 1977, the development of which the authors discuss in detail. The trigger price mechanism is superior to quotas and anti-dumping regulations, both of which invite retaliation.

* 3.80 *

Rajski, Jerzy. "Some Legal Aspects of International Compensation Trade." *International and Comparative Law Quarterly* 35:1 (January 1986): 128-137.

Compensatory trade agreements, wherein countries agree to buy goods from each other through barter deals or other arrangements, have become more prevalent. International institutions need to generate some common standards to judge and clarify these arrangements so as to protect the contracting parties.

* 3.81 *

Roessler, Frieder. "Countertrade and the GATT Legal System." *Journal of World Trade Law* 19:6 (November/December 1985): 604-614.

The practice of countertrade is increasing, notwithstanding the fact that multilateral trade without these restrictions contributed to the un-precedented growth of world trade. Countertrade may violate GATT principles in some cases but not in others.

* 3.82 *

Ruyak, Robert F. "United States Country of Origin Marking Requirements: The Application of a Nontariff Trade Barrier." *Law and Policy in International Business* 6:2 (1974): 485-531.

The U.S. requirement that the country of origin be identified on each imported item, established in 1890, constitutes an important barrier to imports in many cases. The complexity of this requirement, and the costs involved in meeting it, clearly limit trade and provide protection for domestic producers.

* 3.83 *

Walsh, James A. "Countertrade: Not Just for East-West Anymore." *Journal of World Trade Law* 17:1 (January/February 1983): 3-9.

Walsh provides numerous examples of agreements providing for countertrade between developed and developing countries. The increasing use of this mechanism requires that it be brought within the GATT structure and be subject to GATT principles.

* 3.84 *

Walsh, James A. "The Effect on Third Countries of Mandated Countertrade." *Journal of World Trade Law* 19:6 (November/December 1985): 592-603.

Countertrade agreements between two countries can limit the trade of non-participants. Non-participating countries face difficulties because the involved governments put restrictions on both exports and imports to achieve their goals.

* 3.85 *

Woolcock, Stephen. "Iron and Steel." In: *The International Politics of Surplus Capacity*, edited by Susan Strange and Roger Tooze. London: Allen & Unwin, 1981. ISBN 0-04-382034-4.

Surplus capacity in the steel industry in West Europe and the United States has led to the imposition of a variety of non-tariff barriers. These have included voluntary export restraints, trigger prices, and base import prices.

INTERNATIONAL REGIMES, HEGEMONY, AND TRADE LIBERALIZATION

The international trading system's overall level of openness may be a consequence of the distribution of political power among the major countries. A key question has been whether the presence or absence of a dominant state has had an influence on the general level of protectionism in place. In the past the presence of such a major state has often been associated with greater levels of free trade. Current studies suggest the possibility that political relationships may have an effect upon economic relationships.

It has been postulated that if there is a leading military and economic state present in the international system, it can play a major role in structuring international economic exchange. Such a state is also in a position to play an instrumental role in establishing a trade regime, with the regime consisting of explicit or implicit rules, norms, and principles.[1] These regimes may persist without the presence of a leading state or hegemon if many countries find it advantageous to adhere to the established patterns, but a hegemon may find it easier to create a regime or bring about change in an existing regime. Alternately, the lack of a hegemon may reduce adherence to the rules and norms of the regime since there is no one state to enforce them, persuade other states to cooperate, or offer other tangible benefits and resources for adherence.[2] For example, at the end of World War II, the United States was one of the two leading political and military powers in the world and the leading economic actor.

United States Hegemony

The United States had a dominant role in the international organizations that dealt with economic issues. Japan and the countries of Western Europe were just beginning their efforts at reconstruction, and they were not yet in a position to mount an effective challenge to the position of the United States. The Soviet Union under Stalin and his successors opted to keep the USSR and the associated centrally planned economies of Eastern Europe as uninvolved in economic interaction with the West as possible. Western economic penetration of their economies was seen as a threat to the autonomy, both economic and political, of these states. As a consequence, the United States was in a key position to influence the international trade regime and to form international organizations such as GATT and to pursue its policy of general free trade advocacy for the non-Communist countries of the world.

The hegemonic position of the United States after World War II was one example of situations that led to the formulation of the view that a position of hegemony by one country permitted the leading state to structure the international economic regime in conformity to its own particular idea of a desirable regime. In order for hegemony to be present, the dominant country should be able to provide both economic and political leadership. A militarily strong state that is not in a strong economic position may be able to extract resources from other members of the system, but it will have difficulty in structuring the international economic relations among the other countries in the system. It will also lack the economic resources that can be used to persuade other countries to conform to the desired regime. A dominant economic power that is lacking the appropriate military strength will find it difficult to assume the position of a hegemon since it will lack the power to defend its position militarily should such challenges arise, to exert coercive pressure on other members of the system, or to defend other members of the system from coercive pressure from other states.

Hegemony and Free Trade

If a political and economic hegemon does exist, an emphasis on free trade has often been considered to be one of the consequences. A position of economic leadership usually implies that productive facilities located in the hegemon are more efficient than those in other states and that the hegemon will have important comparative advantages in key industrial sectors. The hegemon will thus be in a position to increase its wealth in a general system of free trade. Economic, diplomatic, and military pressure can be exerted to encourage other states in the system to adopt a free trade orientation. Followers can be rewarded in a variety of ways as well. While totally free trade may not be the result, the level of protectionism could be limited. If no hegemon exists, then the creation of trade barriers could begin, and trade wars could also become possible. The different states in the international system will maneuver for positions of national advantage and economic nationalism and competition can take place.

Krasner[3] was among the first to argue that a liberal international trading regime was likely to be present when there was a hegemonic state in the international system. He found in his study that from 1820 to 1879 there was increasing openness in the international system, corresponding to the rise of Great Britain to a position of hegemony. Similarly, from 1945 to 1960 there was again a period of openness corresponding to the period of U.S. hegemony. In periods when no state occupies a position of both political and economic hegemony, the international trading system can become less open. Beginning in the late nineteenth century, Great Britain was challenged militarily and economically by Germany. The United States was also rising to a position of economic competitiveness with Great Britain to some extent. The level of protectionism present in the international system increased in this period. In the years between the two world wars, there was no dominant global military power or economic power, and this period was one of great trade conflicts and tariff wars.

After 1960, the United States still remained the major western military power, but its position of economic leadership had begun to wane. The creation of the European Common Market accelerated the economic challenge from the Federal Republic of Germany, and somewhat later Japan also began to challenge the United States in the economic arena. Although neither state was a military equal of the United States, economic competition became increasingly clear through the years. Thus, the rise of the new protectionism in the 1970s may reflect, at least in part, the decline of the United States as a hegemon and the failure of a successor to appear.

New Perspectives on Hegemony

Additional research has refined or challenged the idea that there is a connection between hegemony and the openness of the international trade regime. The decline of the United States as a hegemonic state may in fact have facilitated the rise of protectionism by removing obstacles to the implementation of protectionist practices in other states. Such a decline in turn may give greater opportunities to protectionist sentiment within the former hegemon from domestic groups suffering as a result of this declining economic position. The loss of hegemony and consequent inability to prevent the adoption of protectionist practices elsewhere may mean that the government is less likely to be able to control such domestic pressures.

The hegemony concept has been applied to other time periods or to different parts of the world, and in some cases the hypothesized connection between hegemony and freer trade has not been found. Other studies have suggested different years in which there was a correspondence between hegemony and freer trade or have concentrated on the appearance of non-hegemonic strong states that have disrupted the openness of the system or supported it, depending upon individual national needs.[4]

To the extent that the presence or absence of a hegemon is relevant to the level of protectionism present in the international system, the resurgence of protectionism and the decline of the commitment to free trade in the 1970s and 1980s does reflect the wider distribution of economic power in the international system. The presence of a number of important state actors in the economic sphere that need to agree on the structure of the regime has led to a lack of leadership. While a multilateral consensus on the form of the international trading regime and structure is not impossible to achieve, it is surely more difficult to create or modify a regime with multiple actors.[5] This difficulty can be seen in part in the next chapter, which deals with other aspects of the international economic system, including international negotiations and the relevance of GATT as an international organization designed to maintain or further trade liberalization.

End Notes

1. Krasner, Stephen D. "Structural Causes and Regime Consequences: Regimes as Intervening Variables," *International Organization* 36:2 (Spring 1982):186.

2. Keohane, Robert O. "The Theory of Hegemonic Stability and Changes in International Economic Regimes, 1967-1977." In: *Change in the International System*, edited by Ole R. Holsti, Randolph M. Siverson, and Alexander L. George. Boulder, CO: Westview Press, 1980, p.136

3. Krasner, Stephen D. "State Power and the Structure of International Trade." *World Politics* 28:3 (April 1976):317-347.

4. Lake, David A. "International Economic Structure and American Foreign Economic Policy, 1887-1934," *World Politics* 35:4 (July 1983):517-543.

5. Lake, David A. "Beneath the Commerce of Nations: A Theory of International Economic Structures," *International Studies Quarterly* 28, 2 (June 1984): 143-170.

Chapter 4: Annotated Bibliography

* 4.1 *
Aggarwal, Vinod K. *Liberal Protectionism: The International Politics of Organized Textile Trade*. Berkeley: University of California Press, 1985. ISBN 0-520-05396-6.

Aggarwal discusses the rise of restrictive trade practices for textiles in the context of changes in international economic regimes and the level of hegemony existing from 1950 to 1982. Much of the existing protectionism resulting from the weakened international regime for trade has been supported by those favoring free trade as a means of avoiding even more barriers to trade.

* 4.2 *
Bergsten, C. Fred, Robert O. Keohane, and Joseph S. Nye. "International Economics and International Politics: A Framework for Analysis." In: *World Politics and International Economics*, edited by C. Fred Bergsten and Lawrence B. Krause. Washington, DC: Brookings Institution, 1975. ISBN 0-317-20637-0.

The hegemonic period of U.S. leadership passed in part because the United States permitted a resurgence of other economic leaders such as Japan and West Europe, as well as the appearance of new international economic issues. More recent domestic pressures resulting from economic interdependence have led to the rise of economic nationalism and protectionism.

* 4.3 *
Conybeare, John A. C. "Public Goods, Prisoners' Dilemmas and the International Political Economy." *International Studies Quarterly* 28:1 (March 1984): 5-22.

Hegemons in the international system may not be proponents of free trade. Their position of dominance may permit them to gain economically from smaller powers through other policies.

* 4.4 *
Conybeare, John A. C. "Tariff Protection in Developed and Developing Countries: A Cross-Sectional and Longitudinal Analysis." *International Organization* 37:3 (Summer 1983): 441-463.

Conybeare analyzes tariff levels for 35 countries during the 1960s and 1970s and in 1902 for 18 of them in an effort to determine factors affecting those levels. There was little support for a connection between high state power and lower tariffs (hegemony theory)--an indication that rational domestic economic policy action did explain tariffs, little evidence of intra-governmental politics having an impact, and ambiguous evidence on the role of interest groups. As the author notes, the findings must be viewed cautiously given the nature of the data drawn from a variety of sources.

* 4.5 *

Drysdale, Peter. "The Pacific Basin and Its Economic Vitality." *Proceedings of the Academy of Political Science* 36:1 (1986): 11-22.

One of the key issues facing countries in the Pacific Basin has been the rise of protectionism. In the past, countries in the area relied on the United States to sustain the trade regime. The countries in the region, particularly Japan, need to make greater efforts to revitalize GATT.

* 4.6 *

Grassman, Sven. "Long-Term Trends in Openness of National Economies." *Oxford Economic Papers* n.s.32:1 (March 1980): 123-133.

An analysis of the openness of the economies of the United Kingdom, Italy, Sweden, Norway, and Denmark found no consistent patterns from 1875 to 1975. The openness varied, demonstrating no support for the idea that a hegemonic state had a liberalizing effect on trade.

* 4.7 *

Keohane, Robert O. *After Hegemony: Cooperation and Discord in the World Political Economy.* Princeton: Princeton University Press, 1984. ISBN 0-691-07676-6.

Keohane provides an overview of the hegemonic approach to the question of stability in the international system. He specifically discusses protectionism in various parts of the volume, and offers a wider context in which to view the effect of the presence or absence of a hegemon.

* 4.8 *

Keohane, Robert O. "The International Political Economy of the 1980s." In: *Tariffs, Quotas, & Trade: The Politics of Protectionism*, edited by the Institute for Contemporary Studies. San Francisco: Institute for Contemporary Studies, 1979. ISBN 0-917-616-34-0.

The lack of a leading international actor has led to a decline of the rules and norms of behavior for interactions among various state actors and hence to economic conflict among industrialized states. The possible losers from these changes include groups with weak political resources within the industrialized states and the weaker developing countries that will face more restrictions on some of their exports to the developed states.

* 4.9 *

Keohane, Robert O. "The Theory of Hegemonic Stability and Changes in International Economic Regimes, 1967-1977." In: *Change in the International System*, edited by Ole R. Holsti, Randolph M. Siverson, and Alexander L. George. Boulder, CO: Westview, 1980. ISBN 0-89158-895-7.

An analysis of the decade from 1967 to 1977 finds that changes in the system of international trade, including the proliferation of non-tariff barriers and the further undermining of the principle of non-discrimination, were related in part to the declining role of the United States as the leading economic actor. Keohane concludes that the theory of hegemonic stability is useful as a partial explanation of changes, perhaps least so in the trade area compared to other economic issues in this decade.

* 4.10 *

Krasner, Stephen D. "American Policy and Global Economic Stability." In: *America in a Changing World Political Economy*, edited by William P. Avery and David P. Rapkin. New York: Longman, 1982. ISBN 0-582-28269-1.

The U.S. hegemonic position after World War II permitted the pursuance of international political objectives rather than specific economic interests, including those resulting from pressure from domestic groups. One result was tolerance, even support, of protectionism in other countries while the U.S. market was relatively open. One consequence of the decline of U.S. hegemony has been greater protectionism in the world economy and in the U.S. market.

* 4.11 *

Krasner, Stephen D. "State Power and the Structure of International Trade." *World Politics* 28:3 (April 1976): 317-347.

In an important early article on the interrelationship between state power and the international economy, Krasner argues that a more open international trading system i.e., one with less protectionism is likely to appear when there is a hegemonic, or dominating, state actor in the international system. When there is no hegemon, restrictions on international trade appear and regional trading blocks are formed. An analysis from 1820 to the 1970s found support for this view, although there was a time lag on occasion in changes in the international trading system after changes occurred regarding the presence or absence of a hegemon.

* 4.12 *
Krasner, Stephen D. "United States Commercial and Monetary Policy: Unravelling the Paradox of External Strength and Internal Weakness." *International Organization* 31:4 (Autumn 1977): 635-671.

Trade policy in the United States was more affected by domestic pressure groups after World War II than was the more insulated monetary policy. The decline of U.S. power in the 1960s led to growing pressures for protection, resulting in a less coherent economic policy and instability in the international economy.

* 4.13 *
Lake, David A. "Beneath the Commerce of Nations: A Theory of International Economic Structures." *International Studies Quarterly* 28: 2 (June 1984): 143-170.

Hegemony by one state and free trade do not necessarily correspond. Other factors in the international economic system play important roles. Trade liberalization can occur under the multilateral sponsorship of a number of states.

* 4.14 *
Lake, David A. "International Economic Structure and American Foreign Economic Policy, 1887-1934." *World Politics* 35:4 (July 1983): 517-543.

Lake analyzes the role of American economic policy in the context of the hegemonic model of the international political economy. In general, the United States played the role of a free trade supporter to the United Kingdom during that country's period of hegemonic leadership and then began to move towards hegemonic leadership itself. Other countries were "spoilers" during various periods in their reliance on protectionist practices.

* 4.15 *
Lawson, Fred H. "Hegemony and the Structure of International Trade Reassessed: A View from Arabia." *International Organization* 37:2 (Spring 1983): 317-337.

Lawson disputes the relationship between an established hegemon and free trade in the international economy based on the commercial policies of Muscat, Aden, and Mocha on the littoral of the Arabian Peninsula in the nineteenth century. While his findings do not support general hegemony theory, he does suggest that small markets in the world periphery may be exceptions to the general patterns found in the wider international trading system.

* 4.16 *
McKeown, Timothy J. "The Limitations of 'Structural' Theories of Commercial Policy." *International Organization* 40:1 (Winter 1986): 43-64.

McKeown argues that structural theories of the international system are insufficient to explain the level of openness in the international economic system. He presents a number of theories and approaches related to domestic political processes that can potentially be included in an analysis to help understand the commercial policies of nations.

* 4.17 *
Milward, Alan. "Tariffs as Constitutions." In: *The International Politics of Surplus Capacity*, edited by Susan Strange and Roger Tooze. London: Allen & Unwin, 1981. ISBN 0-04-382034-4.

Tariff structures have responded more to internal political circumstances than to international economic situations. The acquisition of domestic political power by certain economic pressure groups first led to trade liberalization in the 1860s, while the later inclusion of additional groups then led to restrictions on trade in the late nineteenth and early twentieth centuries.

* 4.18 *
Price, Victoria Curzon. "Recessions and the World Economic Order." In: *The International Policies of Surplus Capacity*, edited by Susan Strange and Roger Tooze. London: Allen & Unwin, 1981. ISBN 0-04-382034-4.

The state of the global economy influences the likelihood of free trade rather than the reverse. Institutional supports for freer trade are built up in time of global expansion and suffer breakdowns in periods of recession.

* 4.19 *
Ruggie, John Gerard. "Another Round, Another Requiem? Prospects for the Global Negotiations." In: *Power, Passions, and Purpose: Prospects for North-South Negotiations*, edited by Jagdish N. Bhagwati and John Gerard Ruggie. Cambridge, MA: MIT Press, 1984. ISBN 0-262-02201-x.

The openness of the trade regime is not a consequence of the presence or absence of a hegemon. The regime reflects the projection of domestic patterns within states. When there are differences among domestic patterns for major trade as in the 1930s or the present time, the trade regime will reflect this lack of consensus. The present disorganization of the trade regime will make it difficult for the developing states to attain the changes that they desire.

* 4.20 *
Schmid, Gregory. "Interdependence Has Its Limits." *Foreign Policy* 21 (Winter 1975-1976): 188-197.

Trade liberalization after World War II proceeded so quickly because of the dominant U.S. economic position, a special condition that has not lasted.

The new mercantilism reflects the domestic economic concerns of the developed states, and the era of free trade under U.S. leadership was a relatively unusual period in history.

* 4.21 *
Stein, Arthur A. "The Hegemon's Dilemma: Great Britain, the United States, and the International Economic Order." *International Organization* 38: 2 (Spring 1984): 355-386.

Stein argues that the hegemonic view of an international free trade system is not totally correct for a variety of reasons. Hegemons need followers to open up the economic system; they cannot do it alone. In addition, hegemony leads to freer trade, not free trade; such trade involves only sections of the world economy, not all of it; and the decline of the hegemon does not automatically mean the end of an open international economic system.

* 4.22 *
Wallerstein, Immanuel. "Friends as Foes." *Foreign Policy* 40 (Fall 1980): 119-131.

The decline of U.S. hegemony is just one example of cyclical rises and declines of hegemons in the capitalist world economy. West European and Japanese industries have been gaining at the of U.S. manufacturers, even in the U.S. domestic market. Other countries have gained bargaining power vis-a-vis the United States as a result of these changes in economic strength.

* 4.23 *
Whitman, Marina V. N. "Leadership without Hegemony." *Foreign Policy* 20 (Fall 1975): 138-160.

The decline of U.S. hegemony has contributed to much of the uncertainty in the international economic system. The United States needs to develop mechanisms for leading without hegemony, while Europe and Japan will have to assume leadership responsibilities if they undermine U.S. leadership capabilities.

* 4.24 *
Yarbrough, Beth V., and Robert M. Yarbrough. "Cooperation in the Liberalization of International Trade: After Hegemony, What?" *International Organization* 41:1 (Winter 1987): 1-26.

Trade liberalization need not be multilateral, and the absence of multilateralism does not leave protectionism as the only alternative. The presence of a hegemon facilitates multilateralism, but in the absence of a hegemon, agreements among two or a few states are more likely to be successful.

INTERNATIONAL ORGANIZATIONS, DISPUTES, and NEGOTIATIONS

The General Agreement on Tariffs and Trade (GATT) has been the most important international organization concerned with trade issues. Its framework of rules and principles has been very important in structuring much of the discussions dealing with trade and protectionism. Multilateral negotiations under GATT's auspices were very important in reducing barriers to trade after World War II, and the organization remains as a focus of many efforts to liberalize trade or limit the effects of protection. There have been some suggestions that the shortcomings and weaknesses of GATT have contributed to the rise of the new protectionism.

While the presence or absence of a hegemon, as well as the characteristics of that hegemon, can have an effect on the overall level of protectionism in the international economy, other aspects of the international system are also relevant. Since the General Agreement on Tariffs and Trade has served as the major international trade organization, its rules and regulations have provided a framework for discussions of trade issues since 1947. In addition, most of the multilateral negotiations on trade liberalization that have been undertaken have occurred under GATT auspices. Even other bilateral negotiations have been conducted within the overall GATT framework in many cases. The GATT rules and regulations have served as points of reference and have provided the agenda for these other discussions.

The GATT Framework

GATT was not originally intended as the international organization that would deal with trade issues. It was signed in 1947 as an interim agreement to be replaced by the International Trade Organization (ITO) that was then being negotiated. The proposed ITO was stillborn, however, due to political opposition in the U.S. Congress, an ironic failure since the United States was one of the strongest supporters of the idea of trade liberalization and general free trade that ITO was designed to further. The ITO itself was a complex compromise among the countries involved in the negotiations surrounding its creation. Congressional opposition comprised those who believed that the organization went too far towards free trade and those who thought it was inadequate. The failure of the United States to join the ITO meant that it would not be put into place since the leading international economic actor was not a member.[1]

GATT then became the replacement for ITO and assumed an organizational structure and purpose not initially intended for a "general agreement." The use of GATT as an international trade organization, even if unintentional initially, did reflect the continuing U.S. concern with trade liberalization after World War II. GATT, like ITO, was an organization designed to encourage free trade. The U.S. free trade philosophy was reflected in GATT, and GATT was in part an effort to avoid the trade conflicts and tariff wars that led to the breakdown of the international economy in the 1930s, that generated economic conflicts and economic nationalism, and that were a contributing factor in the outbreak of war. In some respects the appearance of GATT as an organization to promote free trade reflected the position of U.S. hegemony after World War II.

The rules set forth in GATT are in theory binding on all nations that have signed the agreement. While GATT is not universal in the sense that all countries adhere to it, the most important trading states in the world are signatories. The GATT principles call for the liberalization of trade among member countries and require that each member treat the others equally. Japan was the last major trader to adhere to the agreement in 1955. Equal treatment was not initially accorded to Japan, however, because Japanese products were already beginning to compete in European markets.

Many European countries, fearful of this competition, did not grant Japan all the GATT privileges. They retained a variety of restrictions on Japanese trade, as permitted by a GATT escape clause that allows established members to withhold from new members some of the existing advantages of GATT.[2] Even this partial acceptance of Japan was due to the pressure the United States exerted during the time when it was making major efforts to integrate Japan into the liberal trading system that was to incorporate its free trade orientation. Although most of the nations that initially withheld full GATT privileges from Japan eventually did accord them, the initial refusal did indicate that protectionist impulses were present in Europe even at this time. More recently, the European centrally planned economies have begun to join GATT. Poland, Hungary, and Rumania are members, and the Soviet Union has recently indicated its interest in joining.

GATT does provide a framework in which international trade can occur. Various articles in the agreement set forth the principles for the conduct of trade. Among these are reciprocity and non-discrimination. The most favored nation concept is an integral part of these ideas that are supportive of free trade. Any concession made by one state must be accorded to all the other countries that have been granted the most favored nation status by the country making the concessions. This principle automatically extends trade liberalization efforts since any agreements between countries in bilateral negotiations will have broader applicability, generally, to all the other members of GATT. GATT also provides clauses for exceptions to the general practice of free trade.

Customs unions and free trade areas are specifically noted as acceptable exceptions to the ideas of reciprocity and non-discrimination. Countries are also permitted to establish new trade barriers or to raise tariffs in times of economic distress. Balance of payments difficulties are considered an acceptable justification for such measures, but problems in the general economy and in specific sectors have also been used. Such exceptions are presumably temporary while the necessary domestic re-adjustments are being made. GATT rules also specify that countries can impose countervailing duties and other sanctions when faced with unfair trade practices by other states. GATT also provides a set of guidelines in which trade conflicts and disputes can be settled. In addition, GATT rules prohibit trade agreements outside of customs unions or free trade areas where reverse preferences are granted among the signatories in violation of the most favored nation principle, although such agreements have indeed occurred (see Chapter 10). Existing preferences among states at the time GATT was signed were not affected, although it was expected that these arrangements would decline as trade liberalization proceeded.

GATT and the Developing Countries

The United Nations, the major global international organization, and its various agencies have been much less involved in the issue of protectionism in the international trading system. Initially, GATT served the interests of its member states, while the United Nations included non-GATT states, such as the Soviet Union and East European countries. In addition, by the 1960s, the UN General Assembly and its specialized agencies increasingly reflected the presence of a large number of developing states that had interests different from those of the major, industrialized trading countries.

The dissatisfaction of the developing countries with GATT and the international trade regime in general led to the creation of the United Nations Conference on Trade and Development (UNCTAD), designed to reflect their interests. The various UNCTAD meetings have concentrated principally on issues involving the restructuring of international economic relations in order to aid economic development and growth of the developing states. UNCTAD, as a consequence, has not been primarily concerned with issues of protectionism as such. One exception has been the concept of a Generalized System of Preferences (GSP). UNCTAD has been the forum in which calls for the adoption of GSPs by the developed states has been relatively successful. The GSP schemes adopted by the developed states accord certain exports from the developing countries, usually manufactured products, a margin or preference in their tariff structures. The tariff on goods from the developing countries is lower than that for products from other industrialized states to provide an additional incentive for efforts at industrialization in the developing countries. Chapter 8 also discusses GSP schemes in relation to the developing states.

Multilateral Negotiations

GATT, rather than the United Nations, has provided the framework for a series of multilateral negotiations designed to reduce tariffs. Seven sets of negotiations have occurred since 1947, including the Dillon Round in the early 1960s, the Kennedy Round later in the 1960s, and the Tokyo Round in the 1970s. There has been recent interest (1987) in starting a new round of such negotiations, and one is likely in the immediate future. Each of the sets of negotiations reduced tariffs among the principal trading nations. Each recent round has taken a number of years to reach agreement on the reductions. It was essential that the meetings be multilateral so that all the major trading states would be required to make concessions on tariffs. The need for multilateralism in the negotiations is a reflection of the fact that a state not involved in tariff reductions would gain from the resulting trade liberalization from these agreements if it had most favored nation status with any of the negotiators. The absent state would not have to make any concessions in return.[3]

The emphasis in GATT on the most favored nation principle not only permits some states to gain unilaterally from tariff reductions, but it also makes it difficult for a state to institute sanctions or refuse to lower barriers in retaliation for protectionist practices in other nations.[4] The multilateral approach, however, is one means of avoiding free riders i.e., states that gain without cost to themselves. One result of the need for multilateralism is often that it is more difficult to reduce those initially higher national tariffs in a manner to make them conform to the average levels in other states that originally had lower tariff structures. All participants in the negotiations tend to concede reductions more or less equally. Trade is liberalized, but the more protectionist states at the beginning of the negotiations are often

likely to remain with higher average barriers at the finish.

The United States, Japan, and the European Community, with its common external tariff, have been the most important participants in these negotiations, although other states have been important contributors. The developed countries have had some difficulties in taking consistent stands in the recent rounds of the negotiations due to domestic political pressures. In some cases, a country will favor trade liberalization since its domestic industries are competitive in world markets. In other cases, the same country will oppose removing obstacles in order to protect industries that would be hurt by import competition. Even with the difficulties, these negotiations have been effective in reducing the levels of tariffs in the world, although the reductions have often excluded those products that are of particular importance to the developing states. As already noted in earlier chapters, these reduced tariff levels have been one of the reasons for the increasing importance and utilization of NTBs.

The various rounds have aided in the liberalization of trade, but future negotiations are likely to have limited results. Remaining tariffs are often those that the levying nations have considered to be crucial; thus, they are not likely to negotiate them away. There have been increasing calls for negotiations on NTBs, but little progress has been made in this aspect of protectionism. In the Tokyo Round of negotiations, an agreement on standards of conduct for the use of subsidies, government procurement practices, and countervailing duties was reached. Not all GATT members have signed this agreement, and there has been relatively little indication to date that existing NTBs have been reduced as a result. The European countries have also been reluctant to enter a new round of multilateral reductions given the increasing import competition that European industries have faced from Japan and the NICs, competition which gave much of the impetus to demands for new protection. Many of the more advanced developing countries also oppose further tariff cuts since they would erode the GSP margins that have benefited them in particular.[5] In general, however, it has been thought that the NICs and other developing states would normally gain more from greater trade liberalization than from the existing GSP benefits.

Bilateralism and the Weakening of GATT

The multilateral approach to trade liberalization has weakened with the appearance of the new protectionism. The inability of multilateral meetings to reach agreement on some of the trade problems that have arisen has led to the increasing use of bilateral negotiations to deal with many topics.

The bilateral approaches, often between the United States and Japan, the EC and the United States, or the EC and Japan, have dealt with specific difficulties between pairs of traders rather than with broader issues or general trade liberalization. The bilateral negotiations have often resulted in agreements to establish VERs, OMAs, or other types of protection against imports. Even the MFA agreements on textiles simply set up a broad framework under which trade restrictions would be negotiated in bilateral settings between a developed nation and a developing country. Although bilateralism was also used in earlier periods, the increasing use of this technique is a reflection of a decline in the GATT trade regime.

It has been suggested that these bilateral approaches are not totally counterproductive in facilitating trade since they have prevented an even further deterioration in the freedom of trade. Bilateral arrangements, however, could effectively limit future efforts at trade liberalization since a proliferation of such agreements could be difficult to undo in some general negotiation designed to remove protectionist barriers. Another sign of the weakening of GATT has been the economic summit meetings of the leaders of the United States, Canada, Japan, France, the United Kingdom, Germany, and Italy. These annual meetings that began in 1975 have dealt with many of the problems present in the international trade regime and with protectionism. While the meetings have had a relatively limited influence, their appearance is a further reflection of the inability of GATT to deal with many of the recent trade problems and disputes.

Decline of GATT and Reform Proposals

The increasing utilization of bilateral negotiations is just one indication of the relative decline of the role of GATT, and its principle of free trade, in the structuring of the trade regime. Adherence to GATT's rules and regulations has also declined in other areas. The use of VERs, OMAs, dumping charges, countervailing duties, and other NTBs violate the spirit if not the letter of GATT and demonstrate the willingness of countries to bypass the organization. The inability of multilateral negotiations to address effectively the problems of NTBs also attests to decreased support for GATT and its principles. The decrease in adherence to GATT rules may be one symptom of the loss of U.S. hegemony in the international system.[6] This decline has in turn contributed to the increase in protectionism.

There have been calls for strengthening the ability of GATT to judge or settle trade disputes as a means of reviving the organization and the

commitment to free trade.[7] The GATT procedures in the early years of the organization were effective in dealing with many claims of unfair trading practices, perhaps because the United States more clearly backed these procedures. More recently GATT's loss of effectiveness in this area has led to calls for greater enforcement capabilities. One problem with the existing rules is that while a state can impose sanctions under certain circumstances, a small trading nation may not be able to bear the economic consequences of applying countervailing duties if engaged in a dispute with a larger state.

In effect, the scales are often tipped in favor of the larger country. One suggested advantage of a greater reliance on bilateral arrangements, beyond their ability to prevent the further deterioration of free trade, is that such agreements provide one means for regulating trade relations and even specify the type of sanctions that can be used to enforce fair trade in the absence of stronger international rules.[8] The call for a greater mechanism for settling disputes in GATT reflects these difficulties and the declining importance of the organization in the face of increasing protectionism. In many respects the focus on trade issues has partially shifted from GATT, and other international organizations, to individual states, whose varying roles will be considered in the next three chapters.

End Notes

1. Spero, Joan Edelman. *The Politics of International Economic Relations.* 3rd ed. New York: St. Martin's, 1985. pp.94-96

2. Hollerman, Leon. "Foreign Trade in Japan's Economic Transition." in: *The Japanese Economy in International Perspective*, edited by Isaiah Frank. Baltimore: Johns Hopkins University Press, 1975. pp.186-187.

3. McCulloch, Rachel "U.S. Relations with Developing Countries: Conflict and Opportunity," *Annals of the Academy of Political and Social Sciences* 460 (March 1982):125

4. Corbet, Hugh. "Position of MFN Principle in Future Trade Negotiations," In: *Towards an Open Economy*, ed. Frank McFadzean, Sir Alec Cairncross, Sidney Golt, James Meade, W. M. Corden, Harry G. Johnson, and T. M. Rybczynski. London: Macmillan, 1972. pp. 157-167.

5. Ahmad, Jaleel. "Tokyo Rounds of Trade Negotiations and the Generalized System of Preferences." *Economic Journal* 88:350 (June 1978):285-295.

6. Lipson, Charles. "The Transformation of Trade: The Source and Effects of Regime Change." *International Organization* 36:2 (Spring 1982):45.

7. Baldwin, Robert E. and T. Scott Thompson. "Responding to Trade-Distorting Policies of Other

Countries." *American Economic Review* 74:2 (May 1984):271-276.

8. Yarbrough, Beth V. and Robert M. Yarbrough. "Reciprocity, Bilateralism, and Economic 'Hostages': Self-Enforcing Agreements in International Trade," *International Studies Quarterly* 30:1 (March 1986):7-22.

Chapter 5: Annotated Bibliography

General Works

* 5.1 *
Baldwin, Robert E., and David A. Kay. "International Trade and International Relations." In: *World Politics and International Economics*, edited by C. Fred Bergsten and Lawrence B. Krause. Washington, DC: Brookings Institution, 1975. ISBN 0-317-20637-0.

The authors discuss prospects for trade within existing international agreements, liberalization of all trade, increasing regionalism, and a less emphasis on liberalization, both globally and regionally. They expect increased protectionist actions by many countries, but they also think there are economic and political reasons for liberalizing trade that will lead to a mixed pattern.

* 5.2 *
Bare, C. Gorden. "Trade Policy and Atlantic Partnership: Prospects for New Negotiations." *Orbis* 17:4 (Winter 1974): 1280-1305.

World trade conducted according to the most favored nation principle declined between 1955 and 1970, largely due to the effects of the formation of the EC. International negotiations on tariffs, non-tariff barriers, preference schemes, and agricultural trade are hampered by the complexity of the issues and the differing views and interests of the developed countries.

* 5.3 *
Curzon, Gerard, and Victoria Curzon. "The Multi-Tier System." In: *The New Economic Nationalism*, edited by Otto Hieronymi. London: Macmillan, 1980. ISBN 0-333-26173-9.

Multilateral tariff reductions have been very successful in liberalizing trade. There is a need, however, to deal with non-tariff barriers. At least some of the developing countries need to be fully integrated into a liberal world trading system.

* 5.4 *
Lipson, Charles. "The Transformation of Trade: The Sources and Effects of Regime Change." *International Organization* 36:2 (Spring 1982): 417-455.

Lipson provides an overview of changes in the international trade regime. He describes negotiations that have taken place, types of protectionism that exist, and how the rules and norms of the system have affected negotiations and their results. The decline of the United States as the leading economic power in the system has played at least some role in the weakening of the norms of behavior and the increase in protectionism.

* 5.5 *
Michaely, Michael. "Trade in a Changed World Economy." *World Development* 11:5 (May 1983): 397-403.

The downturn in the business cycle in 1973 did not lead to a relative reduction in world trade or a decline in the importance of trade in manufactures. The presence of free trade structures, including GATT, have lessened the effect of the business cycle on trade.

* 5.6 *
Zacher, Mark W. "Trade Gaps, Analytical Gaps: Regime Analysis and International Commodity Trade Regulation." *International Organization* 41:2 (Spring 1987): 173-202.

Neither the presence of hegemons or of international institutions explains the openness of a trade regime. The patterns of power and interests of various states and other actors determines whether trade is open or restricted. International institutions reflect these underlying factors, although they are not without an independent effect.

The GATT Framework

* 5.7 *
Baldwin, Robert E., and T. Scott Thompson. "Responding to Trade-Distorting Policies of Other Countries." *American Economic Review* 74:2 (May 1984): 271-276.

The authors argue that the GATT system has to be strengthened to deal with the effects of protectionism. The GATT framework needs to provide redress for countries hurt by various government actions, particularly the use of non-tariff barriers.

* 5.8 *

Conybeare, John. "Trade Wars: A Comparative Study of Anglo-Hanse, Franco-Italian, and Hawley-Smoot Conflicts." *World Politics* 38:1 (October 1985): 147-172.

Conybeare makes an innovative use of game theoretic approaches to economic disputes among nations, focusing on three trade wars that utilized tariff devices and other forms of protectionism. One conclusion from the analysis is that the GATT framework has been helpful in easing the problems of reciprocity inherent in some games that are useful analogies for these trade wars by increasing the advantages of cooperation as well as the costs of conflict. GATT, however, is relatively ineffective in dealing with issues related to non-tariff barriers.

* 5.9 *

Corbet, Hugh. "Position of MFN Principle in Future Trade Negotiations." In: *Towards an Open Economy*, edited by Frank McFadzean et al. London: Macmillan, 1972. ISBN 0-312-17926.

Corbet argues that the most favored nation (MFN) principle should be modified since some nations can gain without making reciprocal concessions. Under the MFN principle, nations have also had difficulty in withdrawing concessions from trading partners as a retaliatory measure for protection under the existing GATT rules.

* 5.10 *

Curzon, Gerard, and Victoria Curzon. "The Management of Trade Relations in the GATT." In: *International Economic Relations of the Western World, 1959-1971: Vol.1, Politics and Trade*, edited by Andrew Shonfield with Hermia Oliver. London: Oxford University Press, 1976. ISBN 0-19-218314-1.

The authors provide a comprehensive review of the manner in which the GATT system has functioned to reduce protectionism. They note that U.S. trade partners have benefited from trade liberalization, negating the idea that the United States imposed liberal trade for its own purposes. The United States may even have lost from trade liberalization.

* 5.11 *

Finlayson, Jock A., and Mark W. Zacher. "The GATT and the Regulation of Trade Barriers: Regime Dynamics and Functions." *International Organization* 35:4 (Autumn 1981): 561-602.

The authors discuss the substantive norms of GATT such as non-discrimination, liberalization, reciprocity, safeguards, and growth of developing states. Procedural norms and mechanisms include multilateralism and greater influence accorded to the actors with the greatest stake. The article concludes with an overview of the major functions of GATT.

* 5.12 *

Gardner, Richard N. *Sterling-Dollar Diplomacy in Current Perspective: The Origins and the Prospects of Our International Order*. New York: Columbia University Press, 1980. ISBN 0-231-04944-7.

Gardner discusses the creation of international institutions, including GATT, that dealt with monetary and trade policies at the end of World War II. The activities of the United States and Great Britain were key to establishing postwar policies, and in both countries domestic political activities were important factors.

* 5.13 *

Holzman, Franklyn D., and Robert Legvold. "The Economics and Politics of East-West Relations." In: *World Politics and International Economics*, edited by C. Fred Bergsten and Lawrence B. Krause. Washington, DC: Brookings Institution, 1975. ISBN 0-317-20637-0.

Trade liberalization between East and West would benefit the Eastern states, although the Soviet Union is concerned about the political implications of permitting increased trade. Poland, Rumania, and Hungary became full members of GATT, but only small increases in trade are likely to result. The pricing policies of the centrally planned economies have led to dumping charges in the West, which has usually resulted in the Eastern states withdrawing their exports from the market.

* 5.14 *

Hudec, Robert E. "The GATT Legal System: A Diplomat's Jurisprudence." *Journal of World Trade Law* 4:5 (September/October 1970): 615-665.

Hudec provides a lengthy discussion of the GATT legal system, complete with case examples. He emphasizes that the GATT rules reflect diplomatic agreements and compromises rather than efforts to create a functioning legal code.

* 5.15 *

Hufbauer, Gary C. "Should Unconditional MFN Be Revived, Retired, or Recast?" In: *Issues in World Trade Policy: GATT at the Crossroads*, edited by R. H. Snape. New York: St. Martin's, 1986. ISBN 0-312-43724-2.

The idea of unconditional most favored nation treatment was included in GATT at U.S. insistence rather than conditional most favored nation treatment where third states only gain if they reciprocate on trade concessions. Hufbauer argues that the unconditional principle has hindered trade liberalization as nations are less likely to make concessions.

* 5.16 *
Jackson, John H. "The Birth of the GATT-MTN System: A Constitutional Appraisal." *Law and Policy in International Business* 12:1 (1980): 21-58.

While GATT in general and multilateral tariff reductions have had important results for liberalizing trade, they have failed to address the need for long-term and institutional mechanisms for dealing with disputes in the international economic system. There is a possibility of developing rules and procedures that can be applied in trade disputes, and this need is the challenge of the future.

* 5.17 *
Kostecki, M. M. *East-West Trade and the GATT System.* New York: St. Martin's, 1978. ISBN 0-312-22500-8.

Kostecki analyzes the effect of GATT rules on trade between Western countries and centrally planned economies, particularly Hungary, Rumania, and Poland as these state traders have joined GATT. The GATT framework has not been particularly effective as many countries have retained restrictions on exports from these countries.

* 5.18 *
Patterson, Eliza R. "Improving GATT Rules for Nonmarket Economies." *Journal of World Trade Law* 20:2 (March/April 1986): 185-205.

Patterson analyzes the effects of GATT membership on non-market or centrally planned economies. She argues that GATT membership will be useful for these states and the existing members, but membership should be assumed on a step-by-step basis given the nature of the centrally planned economies.

* 5.19 *
Snape, R. H. "Introduction." In: *Issues in World Trade Policy: GATT at the Crossroads*, edited by R. H. Snape. New York: St. Martin's, 1986. ISBN 0-312-43724-2.

GATT has been successful in facilitating tariff reductions, but its other provisions have not been used effectively to liberalize trade. GATT has not prevented preferential trade agreements. Efforts to regulate the use of trade obstacles such as subsidies and quotas have created complicated procedures that have not worked.

* 5.20 *
Vernon, Raymond. "International Trade Policy in the 1980s: Prospects and Problems." *International Studies Quarterly* 26:4 (December 1982): 483-510.

The United States has supported free trade in principle but deviated from that principle in specific cases. GATT does reflect the U.S. general position, but it has been greatly weakened, and there is little prospect of recovery. Initiatives for liberalizing trade that are less than global in geographic scope may be one means of maintaining open markets.

GATT and the Developing Countries

* 5.21 *
Ahmad, Jaleel. "Prospects of Trade Liberalization Between the Developed and Developing Countries." *World Development* 13:9 (September 1985): 1077-1086.

The author considers a number of approaches to liberalizing trade between the developed and developing countries and reducing protection. The developed states must adopt appropriate domestic adjustment policies for whichever path they follow. He notes also that since domestic pressures lead to protection, trade liberalization is a political process.

* 5.22 *
Erb, Guy F. "The Developing Countries in the Tokyo Round." In: *The U.S. and the Developing World: Agenda for Action, 1974*, edited by James W. Howe. New York: Praeger, 1974. ISBN 0-275-05260-5.

Developing countries face obstacles in exporting to the developed nations due to higher tariffs and non-tariff barriers. Tariff preferences for developing country exports are a partial help, but other changes should be sought through international negotiations. Cooperation among developing countries in GATT negotiations has changed the nature of international interactions to the extent that agreements among Europe, Japan, and the United States no longer can settle issues or disputes.

* 5.23 *
Golt, S. "World Trade and the Developing Countries." In: *The New Mercantilism: Some Problems in International Trade, Money, and Investment*, edited by Harry G. Johnson. New York: St. Martin's, 1974. ISBN 0-312-56840-1.

GATT has not functioned as well for the developing countries as for the industrialized ones. The developing states have turned to UNCTAD as a result, in effect preventing changes in GATT that might have benefited them. The developing countries as a group, however, are so diverse that changes in international trading practices invariably favor some and may hinder others, thus making a unified front difficult.

* 5.24 *
Gosovic, Branislav. *UNCTAD, Conflict and Compromise: The Third World's Quest for an Equitable World Economic Order through the United Nations.* Leiden: A. W. Sijthoff, 1972. ISBN 90-286-0091-4.

Gosovic discusses the factors and events leading to the formation of UNCTAD and provides a description of many of its early activities. Issues included are trade liberalization for primary products, multilateral negotiations and the role of developing countries, special preferences for the developing countries, the role of GATT, and the interactions between GATT and UNCTAD.

* 5.25 *

Green, Reginald Herbold. "Access for Exports, the New Protectionism and GATT: Notes Towards Negotiable Proposals." In: *Commodities, Finance and Trade: Issues in North-South Negotiations*, edited by Arjun Sengupta. Contributions in Economics and Economic History, no. 30. Westport, CT: Greenwood Press, 1980. ISBN 0-313-21469-7.

Since 1974 the movement toward free trade has stopped and protectionism has increased, frequently to the disadvantage of developing economies. Since the new protectionism exists, even if it is undesirable, GATT should be strengthened to deal with the resulting difficulties. Orderly marketing arrangements, as well as changes in them, should be negotiated in the GATT framework, thus limiting some of their negative effects.

* 5.26 *

Ibrahim, Tigani. "Developing Countries and the Tokyo Round." *Journal of World Trade Law* 12: 1 (January/February 1978): 1-26.

The Tokyo Round is unlikely to lead to any major benefits for the developing states. GSPs have too many exceptions to be of much aid. Ultimately, GATT institutions need to be changed to prevent the dominance of the major trading countries and to provide more input for the developing states.

* 5.27 *

Krasner, Stephen D. "Transforming International Regimes: What the Third World Wants and Why." *International Studies Quarterly* 25:1 (March 1981): 119-148.

The developing countries have sought to change the structure of international norms and practices in their favor. They have supported the idea of special preferences for the developing countries and have had them accepted in many international forums.

* 5.28 *

McCulloch, Rachel. "U.S. Relations with Developing Countries: Conflict and Opportunity." *Annals of the Academy of Political and Social Sciences* 460 (March 1982): 118-126.

Trade from developing countries has faced new protectionist obstacles limiting the expansion of markets for their products. The developing countries have been relatively inactive in GATT negotiations since they have gained from their most favored nation status without making concessions in return. Bilateral talks between the United States and the developing nations may accomplish more in terms of creating new markets than multilateral GATT negotiations.

* 5.29 *

Weintraub, Sidney. "The Role of the United Nations in Economic Negotiations." *Proceedings of the Academy of Political Science* 32:4 (1977): 93-105.

This issue of the *Proceedings* bears a separate title: *The Changing United Nations Options for the United States*, edited by David A. Kay. The United States has preferred to avoid involving the United Nations in negotiations on economic issues. GATT has been useful in the efforts of the developed states to liberalize trade among themselves, while the United Nations and UNCTAD have been used by the developing countries to press their demands. UNCTAD's effective efforts in gaining special preferences for exports from the developing states are a case in point.

* 5.30 *

Yoder, Amos. "UNCTAD III--Insights into Development Policies." *Orbis* 17:2 (Summer 1973): 527-544.

The most common theme of developing countries' presentations at the 1972 UNCTAD meeting involved trade policy and the need for developed states to reduce import barriers and to provide preferences. The developed countries approved the idea of preferences but did not consider import barriers as important a topic.

Multilateral Negotiations

* 5.31 *

Ahmad, Jaleel. "Tokyo Rounds of Trade Negotiations and the Generalized System of Preferences." *Economic Journal* 88 (June 1978): 285-295.

The author demonstrates that tariff reductions considered at the Tokyo Round of tariff negotiations would effectively reduce the benefit of preferences given to the developing countries since their margin of preference would be eroded. He argues that tariffs on some products under consideration should not be reduced.

* 5.32 *

Aho, C. Michael, and Jonathan David Aronson. *Trade Talks: America Better Listen*. New York: Council on Foreign Relations, 1985. ISBN 0-87609-009-9.

Upcoming trade negotiations, which are very important for the United States, should be concerned with promoting growth and discipline in trade rather than focusing on the free trade-protectionism debate. Any agreements negotiated should take into account the important interests of the major participants.

* 5.33 *
Baldwin, Robert E. *Beyond the Tokyo Round Negotiations*. Thames Essay no. 22. London: Trade Policy Research Centre, 1979. ISBN 0-900-84247-4.

The Tokyo Round not only failed to make major tariff cuts, it also failed to deal with other protectionist issues. A number of areas are identified as being subjects for further negotiations, including non-tariff barriers, state trading activities, and trade in services.

* 5.34 *
Baldwin, Robert E. *The Multilateral Trade Negotiations: Toward Greater Liberalization?* Washington, DC: American Enterprise Institute, 1979. ISBN 0-8447-1082-2.

Baldwin analyzes the results of the Tokyo Round of trade negotiations, particularly in the area of non-tariff barriers. He notes that many protectionist concessions were made to the U.S. Congress in the course of these negotiations.

* 5.35 *
Behrman, Jack N. "International Sectoral Integration: An Alternative Approach to Freer Trade." *Journal of World Trade Law* 6:3 (May/June 1972): 269-283.

Although free trade is an ideal, it is unlikely to be established any time in the near future. A more useful approach would be to liberalize trade on a sectoral basis. Multilateral negotiations should focus on one industrial sector at a time.

* 5.36 *
Blackhurst, Richard. "Estimating the Impact of Tariff Manipulation: The Excess Demand and Supply Approach." *Oxford Economic Papers* n.s. 25:1 (March 1973): 80-87.

Blackhurst develops a model that estimates the effect of tariff changes on imports, taking into account the presence of excess demand or supply. He notes that this model will provide useful, though not perfect, estimates for persons engaged in tariff negotiations.

* 5.37 *
Brown, Fred, and John Whalley. "General Equilibrium Evaluations of Tariff-Cutting Proposals in the Tokyo Round and Comparisons with More Extensive Liberalization of World Trade." *Economic Journal* 90 (December 1980): 838-866.

The authors construct a model to determine the effect of various tariff reductions, suggested at the 1979 Tokyo Round of negotiations, on the United States, the EEC, Japan, and the rest of the world. Their analyses indicate that the rest of the world has negative welfare gains while the other three have positive ones, most particularly the EEC. The world total is positive. The rest of the world does gain if all tariffs and non-tariff barriers on trade in agricultural and primary commodities, items not generally considered in the negotiations, are removed.

* 5.38 *
Chan, Kenneth S. "The International Negotiation Game: Some Evidence from the Tokyo Round." *Review of Economics and Statistics* 67:3 (August 1985): 456-464.

The author uses various cooperative games from game theory to analyze the Tokyo negotiations. The eventual choice of the Swiss proposal in these meetings was at least partially related to the fact that potential disruptions affected all major actors equally.

* 5.39 *
Cline, William R., Noburu Kawanabe, T.O.M. Kronsjo, and Thomas Williams. *Trade Negotiations in the Tokyo Round: A Quantitative Assessment*. Washington, DC: Brookings Institution, 1978. ISBN 0-8157-1472-6.

The authors consider the effects of various tariffs and non-tariff barriers in the developed countries. Their estimates indicate that the negotiations were leading to insufficient trade liberalization. Negotiations have been hampered by protectionist pressures in the developed states.

* 5.40 *
Corbet, Hugh, and Harry G. Johnson. "Optimal Negotiating Techniques on Industrial Tariffs." In: *Towards an Open World Economy*, edited by Frank McFadzean, Sir Alec Cairncross, Sidney Golt, James Meade, W. M. Corden, Harry G. Johnson, and T. M. Rybczynski. London: Macmillan, 1972. ISBN 0-312-81060-1.

Even with reductions, tariffs remain important because of the effective rate of protection offered. Non-tariff barriers also have become more important, particularly for trade in agricultural products. The authors suggest that if the industrial countries were to agree to trade liberalization, the developing countries would forgo uneconomic import substitution.

* 5.41 *
Deardorff, Alan V., and Robert M. Stern. "The Structure of Tariff Protection: Effects of Foreign Tariffs

and Existing NTBs." *Review of Economics and Statistics* 67:4 (November 1985): 539-548.

Tariff reductions in other countries as part of multilateral negotiations are very important for the larger industrialized countries. Reduction of non-tariff barriers is less important for trade among the developed states.

* 5.42 *
Deardorff, Alan V., Robert M. Stern, and Christopher F. Baum. "A Multi-Country Simulation of the Employment and Exchange-Rate Effects of Post-Kennedy Round Tariff Reductions." In: *Trade and Employment in Asia and the Pacific*, edited by Narongchai Akrasanee, Seiji Naya, and Vinyu Vichit-Vadakan. Honolulu: University Press of Hawaii, 1977. ISBN 0-8248-0573-9.

The results of a detailed modeling of the effects of multilateral tariff reductions suggest that the United States can pursue tariff reductions actively since effects on employment and exchange rates will be small. Particular industries will be more adversely impacted and require adjustment assistance. The reductions will not help developing countries very much since exempted industrial sectors such as textiles will not face tariff reductions, and non-tariff barriers will limit exports that the developing countries are most capable of producing.

* 5.43 *
Denis, Jean-Emile, and Rene Poirier. "The North American Chemical Industry in the Tokyo Round: Participation of Canadian and American Firms in the GATT Negotiation Process." *Journal of World Trade Law* 19:4 (July/August 1985): 315-342.

The positions and goals of the U.S. chemical industry were better supported by negotiators in the Tokyo Round than were those of their Canadian counterparts. The U.S. firms were better able to present their interests to the negotiators by lobbying Congressional committees, the special trade representative, and the International Trade Commission.

* 5.44 *
Evans, John W. *The Kennedy Round in American Trade Policy: The Twilight of GATT?* Cambridge: Harvard University Press, 1971. ISBN 0-674-50275-2.

Evans deals with a variety of specific problems and issues covered in the Kennedy Round of multilateral trade negotiations. He concludes that the tariff reductions that occurred were the end of a process, not a beginning. Attitudes in the United States, including those in Congress, were becoming more protectionist. In addition, the GATT framework was being weakened by the appearance of preferences in some areas for exports from developing countries, various non-tariff barriers, and the appearance of common markets, free trade areas, and other forms of trading blocs in the world.

* 5.45 *
Hatta, Tatsuo, and Takashi Fukushima. "The Welfare Effect of Tariff Rate Reductions in a Many Country World." *Journal of International Economics* 9:4 (November 1979): 503-511.

The authors' model demonstrates that all countries gain when tariffs are the only protective device and when either the highest tariff country unilaterally reduces its tariff to the level of the second highest state or when all countries reduce tariffs proportionally. The second finding is supportive of the general results of the Kennedy and Tokyo Rounds of negotiations with their proportional tariff reductions.

* 5.46 *
Hufbauer, Gary Clyde, and Jeffrey J. Schott. *Trading for Growth: The Next Round of Trade Negotiations.* Policy Analyses in International Economics 11. Washington, DC: Institute for International Economics, September 1985. ISBN 0-88132-033-1.

The world trading system faces many problems. Multilateral negotiations present opportunities to liberalize trade that will increase the prospects for greater growth. The authors argue that these negotiations are needed and suggest strategies that will increase their likelihood of success.

* 5.47 *
Keohane, Robert O., and Joseph S. Nye, Jr. "Two Cheers for Multilateralism." *Foreign Policy* 60 (Fall 1985): 148-167.

The authors argue that regimes, including the trade regime, are essential for international interactions. The trade regime has limited protectionism, provided mechanisms for multilateral negotiations, and led to greater continuity in policies in states where the democratic leadership has changed.

* 5.48 *
Krasner, Stephen D., "The Tokyo Round: Particularistic Interests and Prospects for Stability in the Global Trading System." *International Studies Quarterly* 23:4 (December 1979): 491-531.

The U.S. approach to the Tokyo Round for reductions of tariffs and other barriers to trade varied according to the situation of U.S. industries in the global economy. For all the developed countries, there were similar cross pressures leading to a more open trading system in some cases but not in others.

* 5.49 *

Mayer, Wolfgang. "Theoretical Considerations on Negotiated Tariff Adjustments." *Oxford Economic Papers* n.s. 33:1 (March 1981): 135-153.

Mayer develops a model for studying tariff negotiations. He ascertains that free trade is an unlikely outcome, although more optimal tariff patterns could result. Interest groups are introduced into the model in a highly simplified form, and the results indicate that they hinder the development of free trade.

* 5.50 *

Middleton, R. W. "The GATT Standards Code." *Journal of World Trade Law* 14:3 (May/June 1980): 201-219.

Middleton describes the GATT agreement that was designed to reduce non-tariff barriers to trade. He believes the code will reduce such barriers and support the principle of non-discrimination. The mechanism established for dispute settlement will also be important.

* 5.51 *

Pearson, Charles, and Nils Johnson. *The New GATT Trade Round*. Foreign Policy Institute Case Studies no. 2. Washington, DC: Foreign Policy Institute, School of Advanced International Studies, Johns Hopkins University, 1986.

The authors discuss the views of the major participants involved in the negotiations leading to a new round for the multilateral reduction of trade barriers as well as the key underlying issues. The authors also note that the weakening of GATT and increasing protectionism were factors that led to the beginning of new multilateral negotiations.

* 5.52 *

Pomeranz, Morton. "Toward a New International Order on Government Procurement." *Law and Policy in International Business* 11:4 (1979): 1263-1300.

The author discusses the background to government purchasing policies. He also analyzes the various provisions for the new agreement on such policies established under GATT auspices. The Code on Government Procurement has a number of weaknesses, but Pomeranz believes it could expand its scope over time.

* 5.53 *

Rivers, Richard R., and John D. Greenwald. "The Negotiation of a Code on Subsidies and Countervailing Measures: Bridging Fundamental Policy Differences." *Law and Policy in International Business* 11:4 (1979): 1447-1495.

The negotiation of a code on subsidies and countervailing duties at the Tokyo Round reflected compromises among key countries. Different nations had different definitions and varying views, resulting in an agreement with some weaknesses but many strengths as well.

* 5.54 *

Russell, Robert William. "Political Distortions in Trade Negotiations among Industrialized Countries." In: *Prospects for Eliminating Non-Tariff Distortions*, edited by Anthony E. Scaperlanda. Leiden: A. W. Sitjhoff, 1973. ISBN 90-286-0063-9.

Russell argues that the outlook for reduction of non-tariff barriers in the then approaching Tokyo Round of negotiations was not bright. Domestic pressures were such that the necessary negotiating freedom would not be granted by the U.S. Congress or the member states of the EC.

* 5.55 *

Seyoum, Belayneh. "Export Subsidies under the MTN." *Journal of World Trade Law* 18:6 (November/December 1984): 512-541.

The author surveys the agreement reached on export subsidies at the Tokyo Round of tariff negotiations. The agreement provides some regularity for dealing with the use of these measures. He argues that some exceptions should be made for the developing countries.

* 5.56 *

Stern, Robert M. "Evaluating Alternative Formulae for Reducing Industrial Tariffs." *Journal of World Trade Law* 10:1 (January/February 1976): 50-64.

Stern discusses various issues that are important for negotiations on multilateral tariff reductions. Among other points, he notes that special attention should be given to items that the developing countries have the opportunity to produce for export and that measurements and evaluations of the consequences of reductions should directly take into account the domestic effects of the cuts.

* 5.57 *

Whitman, Marina V. N. "A Year of Travail: The United States and the International Economy." *Foreign Affairs* 57:3 (1978): 527-554.

The year 1978 witnessed the increasing use of non-tariff barriers such as export subsidies and countervailing duties. GATT negotiations in Tokyo dealt with some of these issues for the first time as well as restrictions involving agricultural trade.

* 5.58 *

Winham, Gilbert R. "The Mediation of Multilateral Negotiations." *Journal of World Trade Law* 13:3 (May/June 1979): 193-208.

The author discusses various aspects of negotiating in multilateral settings based on the activities in the Kennedy Round of tariff reductions. He suggests that the GATT secretariat is important not only as a mediator but also as a negotiator.

Bilateralism and the Weakening of GATT

* 5.59 *

Barden, Benjamin. "The Cotton Textile Agreement, 1962-1972." *Journal of World Trade Law* 7:1 (January/February 1973): 8-35.

Barden describes the cotton textile arrangement that was in effect for 11 years. While the agreement limited exports from some countries, it is likely that without the international agreement individual developed countries would have placed more severe limitations on imports to their domestic markets.

* 5.60 *

Bergsten, C. Fred. "What To Do About the U.S.-Japan Economic Conflict." *Foreign Affairs* 60:5 (Summer 1982): 1059-1075.

Japan's competitiveness in the world and the increasing penetration of the U.S. market by Japanese imports have led to conflicts and protectionist action. Bergsten argues that many of the difficulties and areas of conflict could be dealt with through reform of currency exchange and related issues that would strengthen the yen relative to the dollar.

* 5.61 *

Bergsten, C. Fred, and William R. Cline. *The United States-Japan Economic Problem*. Policy Analyses in International Economics 13. Washington, DC: Institute for International Economics, 1985. ISBN 0-262-52108-3.

The trade problems between the United States and Japan are a result of many factors, including currency exchange rates, Japanese protection, inadequate GATT mechanisms for dealing with disputes, structural differences in the two societies, and macroeconomic policies related to savings levels and budget deficits. Changes in trade policies will only solve some of the problems since some of the causes of the current trade imbalances are a result of these other factors.

* 5.62 *

Bilzi, Carol. "Recent United States Trade Arrangements: Implications for the Most-Favored-Nation Principle and United States Trade Policy." *Law and Policy in International Business* 17:1 (1985): 209-236.

While bilateral negotiations and agreements have a role to play in trade policy, they should be used only to a limited extent. Multilateral negotiations will promote free trade and strengthen

GATT. Bilateralism will further encourage regional trading blocs.

* 5.63 *

Bressand, Albert. "Mastering the 'Worldeconomy'." *Foreign Affairs* 61:4 (Spring 1983): 745-772.

Protectionist measures in Europe against Japanese imports have been designed in part to preserve European involvement in key industrial sectors such as electronics. The European experience is an indication of future problems that the United States may face. The redistribution of economic power and increased international industrial competition will make trade relations more subject to conflict, and potentially more bound to protection.

* 5.64 *

Das, Bhagirath L. "The GATT Multi-Fibre Arrangement." *Journal of World Trade Law* 17:2 (March/April 1983): 95-105.

The third agreement on textiles is less restrictive than the second but more restrictive than the first. Multilateral observation of the trade is easier under the most recent agreement, and there is the possibility that textiles may eventually be re-integrated into the GATT general rules on trade.

* 5.65 *

Destler, I.M., Haruhiro Fukui, and Hideo Sato. *The Textile Wrangle: Conflict in Japanese-American Relations, 1969-1971*. Ithaca, NY: Cornell University Press, 1979. ISBN 0-8014-1120-3.

The negotiations leading up to the voluntary restraint on Japanese exports of textiles in 1971 indicate the severity of the problems involved in international negotiations on protectionist issues. The analysis also indicates the importance of domestic political pressures, bureaucratic interests, and of different political structures on such negotiations.

* 5.66 *

Destler, I. M., and Hideo Sato. "Coping with Economic Conflicts." In: *Coping with U.S.-Japanese Economic Conflicts*, edited by I. M. Destler and Hideo Sato. Lexington, MA: Lexington Books, 1982. ISBN 0-669-05144-6.

Trade issues and protectionism have caused conflicts between Japan and the United States. The Japanese government and industrial sectors have been relatively willing to restrain exports when U.S. industries have suffered. U.S. efforts to open the Japanese market to American goods have been more difficult, given internal opposition to concessions by the Japanese government.

* 5.67 *

Drovin, Marie-Josee, and Harald B. Malmgren. "Canada, the United States, and the World Economy." *Foreign Affairs* 60:2 (Winter 1981/1982): 393-413.

Canada's efforts to distance itself politically and economically from U.S. influences have included export subsidies and import substitution measures. The U.S. government has sought to have many of the existing restrictions to trade and investment removed.

* 5.68 *

Hager, Wolfgang. "Political Implications of US-EC Economic Conflicts (II): Atlantic Trade--Problems and Prospects." *Government and Opposition* 22:1 (Winter 1987): 49-63.

Managed trade has been the norm for trade between North America and Pacific countries and between the United States and Canada. Although U.S.-European trade has not yet followed this pattern, the presence of significant differences in approaches to trade between the two sides and the general rise of neo-mercantilism suggest that future adherence to free trade is unlikely.

* 5.69 *

Hanabusa, Masamichi. *Trade Problems Between Japan and Western Europe.* New York: Praeger, for the Royal Institute of International Affairs, 1979. ISBN 0-03-053361.

Japan's increasing role in international trade between 1958 and 1978 and the penetration of European markets by Japanese products has led to strains between Japan and Western Europe. Among these strains are the European practice of giving preferences to third countries, protectionist practices in Europe, and the European perception that Japan's domestic markets are highly protected.

* 5.70 *

Odell, John S. "The Outcomes of International Trade Conflicts: The U.S. and South Korea, 1960-1981." *International Studies Quarterly* 29:3 (September 1985): 263-286.

An analysis of 13 trade conflicts between the United States and South Korea indicates that U.S. protectionism was unrelated to the level of import penetration or the domestic political power of U.S. industries. While the decline of the U.S. position of hegemony encouraged protectionism, the general free trade policy of the government limited the restrictions imposed.

* 5.71 *

Pinder, John. "Integration Groups and Trade Negotiations." *Government and Opposition* 14:1 (Winter 1979): 149-171.

Trade negotiations between the EC and Comecon countries have not proceeded very rapidly, in part due to protectionist practices in the EC that have hurt the exports of some Eastern European countries. Negotiations have been hampered by the refusal of the USSR and the other Comecon members to recognize the EC as the bargaining instrument for its members.

* 5.72 *

Putnam, Robert D., and Nicholas Bayne. *Hanging Together: The Seven-Power Summits.* Cambridge: Harvard University Press, 1984. ISBN 0-674-37225-5.

The seven largest industrialized democracies --the United States, Canada, Japan, the United Kingdom, Germany, France, and Italy--have met annually in economic summits since 1975. Trade issues, including the rise of protectionism, have been important items on the agendas, although promises to reduce trade barriers have often not been fulfilled. The lack of any hegemonic state has been one factor that has led to a need for such collective leadership.

* 5.73 *

Rugman, Alan M. "U.S. Protectionism and Canadian Trade Policy." *Journal of World Trade Law* 20:4 (July/August 1986): 363-380.

Canada has declared its intention to seek a bilateral agreement with the United States to counter creeping protectionism in its neighbor. American protectionism has resulted from increasing Congressional involvement in trade policy. Both Canada and the United States would gain from such an agreement, and a successful bilateral arrangement could provide a blueprint for future GATT negotiations.

* 5.74 *

Sato, Hideo, and Michael W. Hodein. "The U.S.-Japanese Steel Issue of 1977." In: *Coping with U.S.-Japanese Economic Conflicts*, edited by I. M. Destler and Hideo Sato. Lexington, MA: Lexington Books, 1982. ISBN 0-6690-05144-6.

U.S. steel manufacturers complained of unfair trade practices and gained support in Congress for protection. The Carter administration could not ignore the pressure since it needed Congressional approval for multilateral trade negotiations. Japanese producers even favored an orderly marketing agreement, partially so that they could keep their share of the important U.S. market.

* 5.75 *

Silk, Leonard. "The United States and the World Economy." *Foreign Affairs* 65:3 (1987): 458-476.

Multilateralism is necessary to deal with the problems in the world economy, although many developed states, including the United States, are increasingly using bilateralism in trade negotiations. A re-occurrence of the trade wars of the 1920s and 1930s must be avoided.

* 5.76 *
Solomon, Anthony M. "Toward Realistic Cooperation." In: *Economic Summitry*, edited by George de Menil and Anthony M. Solomon. New York: Council on Foreign Relations, 1983. LC 83-071273.

Solomon argues that the 1983 economic summit involving the seven largest Western developed states will need to deal with issues involving a recovering global economy. He suggests creating a monitoring group to deal with protectionist practices to supplement GATT, but not to replace it.

* 5.77 *
Stoga, Alan J. "If America Won't Lead." *Foreign Policy* 64 (Fall 1986): 79-97.

The U.S. commitment to a leadership role in the international economy has faltered. There are increased demands for protection by many sectors and increasing reliance on bilateral arrangements, even though bilateralism is only preferable to the chaos that would occur with no agreements. The United States has become too integrated into the global economy to ignore the need for its leadership.

* 5.78 *
Trezise, Philip H. "US-Japan Trade: The Bilateral Connection." In: *The Politics of Trade: U.S. and Japanese Policymaking for the GATT Negotiations*, edited by Michael Blaker. Occasional Papers of the East Asian Institute. New York: Columbia University, 1978. ISBN 0-317-17100-3.

Trade disagreements, including disputes over protectionist practices, between the United States and Japan have generally been dealt with bilaterally rather than through GATT mechanisms. Each nation has in effect complained about practices of the other that both use. Common, international definitions of violations of the GATT framework, while useful, are unlikely, given the varied interests of major traders. Bilateral dealings will continue to be necessary.

* 5.79 *
Tsoukalis, Loukas, and Antonio da Silva Ferreira. "The Response of the European Community." In: *The International Politics of Surplus Capacity*, edited by Susan Strange and Roger Tooze. London: Allen and Unwin, 1981. ISBN 0-04-382034-4.

The European Community, as opposed to individual national governments, has been forced to sanction protectionism by those governments and their unilateral actions. It has negotiated voluntary export restraints and bilateral agreements, used anti-dumping measures, and helped to set up a steel cartel.

* 5.80 *
Wellenstein, Edmund. "Political Implications of US-EC Economic Conflicts (I): Euro-American Turbulence--The Trade Issue." *Government and Opposition* 21:4 (Autumn 1986): 387-395.

Wellenstein reviews the trade problems between the United States and the EC, noting that GATT has become increasingly ineffective and that the pressures for protectionism are increasing on both sides of the Atlantic. While GATT affords many advantages, its inability to supervise trade effectively is a major shortcoming.

* 5.81 *
Woolcock, Stephen. "US-European Trade Relations." *International Affairs (London)* 58:4 (Autumn 1982): 610-624.

Woolcock summarizes various conflicts over trade between the United States and West Europe, including issues in which protectionism is prominent. These disputes have weakened confidence in multilateral negotiations as a means of liberalizing trade.

* 5.82 *
Yarbrough, Beth V., and Robert M. Yarbrough. "Reciprocity, Bilateralism, and Economic 'Hostages': Self-Enforcing Agreements in International Trade." *International Studies Quarterly* 30:1 (March 1986): 7-22.

Various bilateral agreements and uses of protectionist measures, through regulatory applications, have been one means of dealing with domestic pressures for protection. These measures, however, also afford a means of enforcing fair trade among major trading countries in the absence of an effective international agency to guarantee fair trade.

Decline of GATT and Reform Proposals

* 5.83 *
Aggarwal, Vinod K. "The Unraveling of the Multi-Fiber Arrangement, 1981: An Examination of International Regime Change." *International Organization* 37:4 (Autumn 1983): 617-645.

A multilateral effort was made to reach an agreement over international textile trade to facilitate protectionist measures in the developed states while avoiding the possibility that either the EC or the United States would become more protectionist than the other. The international agreement was designed to control trade rather than free it. Domestic pressures in the developed states have led to efforts that increase protection. It is possible that this sentiment could overwhelm the idea of organized trade with only some protection.

* 5.84 *
Bergsten, C. Fred. "Reforming the GATT: The Use of Trade Measures for Balance-of-Payments Purposes." *Journal of International Economics* 7:1 (February 1977): 1-18.

Bergsten argues that using quotas and tariff surcharges as allowed by GATT is one of the agreement's greatest weaknesses. Ideally, such actions should no longer be allowed; if they are, major alterations are necessary in terms of when and how they can be used.

* 5.85 *
Bratschi, Peter. "GATT: Targets for Reform." *Journal of World Trade Law* 7:4 (July/August 1973): 383-403.

Bratschi reviews some of the shortcomings of GATT. He argues that a number of reforms are necessary to strengthen the organization and to facilitate its goals.

* 5.86 *
Camps, Miriam, and William Diebold, Jr. *The New Multilateralism: Can the World Trading System Be Saved?* New York: Council on Foreign Relations, 1986. LC 83-71627.

Multilateral relations among states have changed in recent years. The GATT system could be modified to deal with the new situation. GATT should also be more closely integrated with other international organizations that deal with trade matters.

* 5.87 *
Curzon, Gerard, and Victoria Curzon. "GATT and NTD's." In: *Prospects for Eliminating Non-Tariff Distortions*, edited by Anthony E. Scaperlanda. Leiden: A. W. Sijthoff, 1973. ISBN 90-286-0063-9.

GATT has proven to be ineffective in terms of dealing with protectionism. Efforts to reduce non-tariff barriers in the Kennedy Round largely failed, and GATT's general inability to enforce existing rules make it unlikely that the organization will be able to cope with trade distortions arising from non-tariff barriers.

* 5.88 *
Curzon, Gerard, Juergen B. Donges, Jean Waelbroeck, Jose de la Torre, Alasdair I. MacBean, and Martin Wolf. *MFA Forever? Future of the Arrangement for Trade in Textiles.* International Issues no. 5. London: Trade Policy Research Centre, 1981.

The authors analyze the various agreements for protection in textiles, particularly in the EC, and they argue in turn that trade liberalization is a better approach than continuation of the Multi-Fibre Arrangements. The protectionism implicit in the MFA is particularly harmful to the developing countries that could competitively export textiles.

* 5.89 *
Czinkota, Michael R., and Anne Talbot. "GATT Regulation of Countertrade: Issues and Prospects." *International Trade Journal* 1:2 (Winter 1983): 155-174.

Countertrade, an extension of barter agreements requiring purchases in exchange for market access, is a means of husbanding scarce foreign exchange. While countertrade is in effect opposed to basic GATT principles, it has proven to be an appropriate response to recent trade dislocations.

* 5.90 *
Diaz-Alejandro, Carlos F., and Gerald K. Helleiner. *Handmaiden in Distress: World Trade in the 1980s.* Development Paper 34. Washington, DC: Overseas Development Council. 1982. LC 82-19067.

The GATT system needs to be revitalized, and its credibility restored. The need for a liberal trade regime is as important as ever. Among the changes needed are an end to the abuse of the safeguard clause, the end of conditional applications of GATT principles, and fairer treatment for the exports of the developing countries.

* 5.91 *
Farran, Andrew. "The Interplay of Law and Economics in International Trade Regulation." In: *Issues in World Trade Policy: GATT at the Crossroads*, edited by R.H. Snape. New York: St. Martin's, 1986. ISBN 0-312-43724-2.

Farran argues that GATT rules should be strengthened and that countries should negotiate to establish what would essentially be a legal framework to deal with trade disputes. Symmetry needs to be restored to the trade regime so that all states can protect their opportunities to trade.

* 5.92 *
Farrands, Chris. "Textile Diplomacy: The Making and Implementation of European Textile Policy, 1974-78." *Journal of Common Market Studies* 18:1 (September 1979): 22-39.

Even though the different positions of the nine members of the EC made re-negotiation of the Multi-Fibre Agreement on textiles difficult and many of the NICs desired a greatly revised agreement, the NICs accepted a less than ideal document. If the MFA had been allowed to lapse, individual European countries would have been able to impose greater protection against textile exports from individual developing countries or countries that did not sign the new MFA.

* 5.93 *
Graham, Thomas R. "Global Trade: War & Peace."
Foreign Policy 50 (Spring 1983): 124-137.

The series of *ad hoc* restrictions on trade in the 1980s will limit economic recovery and could contribute to the appearance of worldwide depression. The GATT system has deteriorated and is no longer capable of dealing with trade conflicts. The United States needs to develop mechanisms to distinguish between industry problems due to unfair trade practices by other countries and those problems due to natural decline.

* 5.94 *
Graham, Thomas R. "Revolution in Trade Politics."
Foreign Policy 36 (Fall 1979): 49-63.

Protectionism has increased due to government actions, some directly limiting imports and others doing so indirectly as a result of domestic policies. Imposition of obstacles to imports in one state tends to lead to such actions elsewhere. The Tokyo Round of tariff reductions failed to deal with the key hindrances to international trade.

* 5.95 *
Grey, Rodney de C. "The Decay of the Trade Relations System." In: *Issues in World Trade Policy: GATT at the Crossroads*, edited by R.H. Snape. New York: St. Martin's, 1986. ISBN 0-312-43724-2.

GATT has not been effective for protecting the interests of smaller countries or even the larger ones as managed trade has increased. GATT regulations providing for the possibility of countries seeking compensation for trade injuries are ineffective and little used.

* 5.96 *
Hudec, Robert E. *Adjudication of International Trade Disputes*. Thames Essay no. 16. London: Trade Policy Research Centre, 1978. ISBN 0-900-84239-3.

GATT procedures for dispute settlement and formalizing sanctions to counter protectionism are not particularly effective beyond the normative pressure exerted. The right to impose countersanctions is not effective for small states in disputes with large states since the large state is better able to bear equal costs. Hudec suggests greater use of national laws to reinforce GATT procedures.

* 5.97 *
Hufbauer, G. C., J. Shelton Erb, and H. P. Starr. "The GATT Codes and the Unconditional Most-Favored-Nation Principle." *Law and Policy in International Business* 12:1 (1980): 59-93.

The most favored nation principle has been a cornerstone of the GATT system, but it has been violated by countries making special concessions

in order to liberalize general trade. Rules permitting limited, conditional treatment in bilateral agreements are suggested as the best approach to reconcile chances of continued liberalization and the GATT rules.

* 5.98 *
Jackson, John H. "The Crumbling Institutions of the Liberal Trade System." *Journal of World Trade Law* 12:2 (March/April 1978): 93-106.

Countries have undermined the GATT system by allowing its rules to be infringed. These infringements have exacerbated world economic problems. Jackson argues that support for GATT is essential for the future of the trading system.

* 5.99 *
Jackson, John H. "Governmental Disputes in International Trade Relations: A Proposal in the Context of GATT." *Journal of World Trade Law* 13:1 (January/February 1979): 1-21.

Jackson argues that methods for settling disputes in GATT should be strengthened. He even provides a draft of an agreement for such dispute settlement.

* 5.100 *
Kramer, Hans R. "Changing Principles Governing International Trade." *Journal of World Trade Law* 8:3 (May/June 1974): 227-237.

General norms for international trade are decreasing in effectiveness. Reciprocity and most favored nation treatment are declining as special preferences have increased. Voluntary limits on exports have further eroded the idea of free trade.

* 5.101 *
Krause, Lawrence B. "The Developing Countries and American Interests." *Proceedings of the Academy of Political Science* 36:1 (1986): 150-160.

U.S. efforts to promote free trade through multilateral GATT negotiations are likely to fail given the reluctance of the EC and some developing countries to participate. Such GATT negotiations would deflect protectionist pressures in the United States, however, offering encouragement to such participation. The developing countries in the Pacific Basin are ambivalent on new GATT negotiations since they would probably gain by trade liberalization in general, but would lose their margin of preferences under GSP schemes.

* 5.102 *
Krauss, Melvyn B. "Border-Tax Adjustments: A Potential Trans-Atlantic Trade Dispute." *Journal of World Trade Law* 10:2 (March/April 1976): 145-156.

Border tax adjustments could become a source of friction between the United States and Europe. U.S. firms have sought the imposition of countervailing duties. Reform of GATT principles to deal with this issue would be the best solution to the problem.

* 5.103 *
Meltzer, Ronald I. "Contemporary Security Dimensions of International Trade Relations." In: *Economic Issues and National Security*, edited by Klaus Knorr and Frank N. Traeger. Lawrence: Regents Press of Kansas, 1977. ISBN 0-7006-167-8.

Multilateral trade negotiations have involved security concerns of the participating nations. Questions of export controls and access to supplies have been one major concern, while concern for safeguards against sudden import increases and the opportunity for adjustments in the face of competition have been another. The inadequacy of GATT mechanisms in recent years has led to greater emphasis over short-term national objectives at the expense of broader international problems such as trade liberalization.

* 5.104 *
Renner, John C. "Trade Barriers, Negotiations, and Rules." *Columbia Journal of World Business* 8:2 (Summer 1973): 51-58.

Renner discusses a number of existing barriers to trade, including tariffs and non-tariff barriers. He suggests methods for improving rules on trade, such as GATT regulations, safeguards, and methods of dispute settlement.

THE RISE OF PROTECTIONISM IN THE UNITED STATES

The United States has played a central role in facilitating or hindering free trade. It has held a key position in the international economy because of the size of its domestic market and its leadership in GATT after World War II. The sharp rise of protectionist sentiment in the United States has become a matter of grave concern to advocates of free trade.

The United States is a particularly important country in the international economic system for a number of reasons; as a consequence, a great deal has been written about attitudes in the United States towards free trade and protectionism. Although the total effects of the role of a hegemon in the trade regime have been debated, the United States was in a key position to influence the structuring of trading relationships after World War II. The United States has continued to be a key actor in GATT, and is one of the nations whose cooperation has been essential in the multilateral negotiations directed toward greater trade liberalization.

The United States is the single largest national market in the world, although it has been surpassed in economic size by the common market that was created by the formation and later enlargement of the EC. Thus, the actions of the United States on trade issues, and its willingness to support free trade or to resort to protectionism, have great influence on the global trade regime and on the actions of other countries. The fear of growing pressure for protection in the United States has already had major repercussions in other countries. Should the United States wholeheartedly embrace protectionism as a general policy, the liberal trade regime created after World War II would undoubtedly collapse.

U.S. Advocacy of Free Trade

At the end of World War II, the United States became the leading advocate of free trade, an advocacy that was apparent in the support given to GATT and to the various rounds of multilateral negotiations on tariff reductions in subsequent years. Initial reasons for supporting free trade included the idea that it would speed the economic recovery of the European nations, that the resulting economic interdependence would limit future hostilities in Europe, and that free trade would also facilitate the creation of a political and diplomatic grouping of democratic states under U.S. leadership. The United States even accepted the continuation of preferences within the European colonial empires after World War II as a necessary, and ideally temporary, exception to free trade principles that would facilitate European reconstruction and economic recovery. U.S. aid for such recovery, however, was often implicitly, and sometimes explicitly, tied to the idea of trade liberalization. The United States later even encouraged the formation of customs unions among the European states on the assumption that such unions, in breaking down trade barriers among the members, would also lead to general trade liberalization. The United States also encouraged Japanese adherence to trade liberalization for much the same reasons and was a vigorous supporter of Japanese membership in GATT.

The U.S. advocacy of free trade as a principle was not limited to perceptions of a trade regime as an aid to economic reconstruction in the aftermath of war. Freer trade also was seen as aiding the United States, which had the productive capacity to supply exports to many parts of the world. The removal of trade barriers that existed in the 1930s would favor U.S. industries in many cases by opening new markets. The availability of such overseas markets also would facilitate the transition of the U.S. economy from a war to a peace basis. Likewise the economic recovery of Europe and Japan was sought since it would further fuel the national economy. U.S. access to raw materials in the world would also increase with trade liberalization, particularly when some of the European colonies were opened to U.S. purchases and investments. Trade liberalization was seen then, and continues to be seen, as one means of increasing the efficiency of the U.S. economy and providing competition for product areas dominated by a few U.S. firms, with resulting benefits to consumers.[1] Thus, to some extent at least, the United States advocated trade liberalization through the years because that policy was thought to be in the best interests of many sectors of the economy.

Although its positive response to trade liberalization was in part self-serving, the United States remained generally consistent into the 1970s in supporting free trade. Even later it continued to make efforts towards trade liberalization, but perhaps not as strongly as before. At times, sacrifices were made to uphold the ideal of free trade even when domestic industries or interest groups were complaining about the costs that resulted from import competition or when damage occurred because other countries did not make the desired reciprocal concessions. In any international regime, it may be necessary for its supporters to make sacrifices for its long-term maintenance, and the United States has often been the nation that did so in the case of the free trade regime.

It has been argued that this commitment to free trade became so imbedded in U.S. economic policy that it has been continued past the point of valid applicability. There has been increasing political discontent within the United States with this support of free trade, a discontent fueled by economic considerations. The position of the United States in the world economy has changed since the end of World War II, and unthinking adherence to an ideal of free trade is no longer seen as being automatically in the best interests of the United States by many groups. It has been argued that the United States should instead pursue economic policies that are in its national interest, whether those policies rely either on free trade or on neo-mercantilist ideas.

The Executive Branch

The system of checks and balances in the U.S. government has meant that a unified trade policy is not always possible. Different branches can take different and conflicting positions on trade issues. It has often been thought that in the formation of trade policy the executive branch has generally favored freer trade while Congress has been more inclined to support protectionist measures. U.S. presidents since World War II have in fact been generally supportive of trade liberalization, and many efforts directed toward maintaining free trade or liberalizing trade have originated in the executive branch of the government. At times, individual presidents have made exceptions in particular cases where the industry has been considered to be a critical one, when the level of potential job losses would have been unacceptable, or when the imports have originated from a nation that was perceived to be using unfair trade practices.

At other times protectionist policies have been grudgingly supported by presidents in order to prevent even greater barriers to trade being erected by Congressional action. The presidency is seen as the focus of the freer trade point of view in part because the president is the elected official who must consider the overall costs and benefits of protection to the U.S. economy as a whole rather than the costs or benefits to specific industries, geographical areas, or interest groups. The president must also be aware of the possible effects of retaliation by foreign nations on the U.S. export position and be concerned with the role that trade policy may play in the context of broader foreign policy issues and the potential effects of protection on overall relations with specific countries. Trade policy cannot be made in isolation from other aspects of foreign policy. In effect, the president, as the only nationally elected public official, is often more interested in broad national issues rather than in local ones.

Other portions of the executive branch of the government have also played an important role in trade policy. These other agencies have also generally been supportive of more liberal trade policies. The International Trade Commission, a relatively new agency that evolved out of the old Tariff Commission, is central for some trade issues. It is the agency that considers charges of unfair trading practices leveled against other countries and that can grant relief to industries suffering from import competition. Such relief can be provided by limiting imports on the basis of escape clauses and safeguard provisions in existing legislation and international agreements, when serious damage to domestic industries can be demonstrated. In many of the cases the commission has heard, its actions have not favored the domestic interests seeking protection. Its rulings have often been supportive of free trade, and it has only been willing to grant relief to industries when clear justification is present. Various special trade negotiators appointed by presidents to deal with GATT negotiations or bilateral problems in trade with particular countries have also usually been part of the executive branch consensus favoring trade liberalization.

Congress

Congress has been the branch of government considered to be most responsive to increasing domestic demands for limits on imports. Local interests are better represented in Congress than in the presidency, and pressure can be brought to bear on individual members of Congress to save jobs or threatened industrial plants that are important in their districts or states. Members of Congress in fact are more likely to respond to constituency interests in this area without regard to party affiliation, being aware that failure to respond may carry a heavy price when they seek re-election. Industries facing import competition and declines in sales and workers facing unemployment or wage cuts are groups that clearly can see the benefits of protection. The costs of protection to consumers are diffused throughout the population in general and are less apparent as a result. Workers whose jobs have been saved are seen as more likely to vote to re-elect a supportive member while the average consumer is not likely to make his or her voting decision on the basis of legislative votes for or against protection. The concentration of benefits from protection and the diffuse nature of costs facilitates interest group activity directed towards creating trade barriers and makes active support for free trade more difficult to mobilize.

Pressure from one particular industry is effective only infrequently, but the U.S. automotive industry is an obvious example of the effect that an important industry in the economy, with plants and facilities located in many districts and states, can have. In other cases, the more logical way for industries to gain favorable Congressional action is by vote trading on legislation that will provide protection for a number of industries, such as occurred with the Smoot-Hawley Tariff Act that was passed in 1930. Such a legislative coalition might then be able to muster sufficient votes to raise barriers to trade in a number of product areas. Presidential concessions to Congress on protection in some product areas have been one means of preventing such a coalition from forming, a coalition that would raise greater barriers to trade than those contained in the concessions.

Even though Congress has often been assumed to respond to domestic pressures for protection, the evidence for such a preference has not been overwhelming. If Congressional opinion forces concessions from presidents, the effect is less obvious than if a new tariff law were passed. Congress will still have succeeded, however, in increasing the level of protection available. Even though such Congressional success may be indirect, it is still important. Analyses of the industrial characteristics of districts, the level of unemployment, the degree of unionization, and other factors that might influence Congress, have not consistently found evidence to support the idea that domestic pressures are effective in leading to the introduction of and support for legislation directed towards limiting imports. One exception to the previous mixed findings has been the evidence that, of all industries facing import competition, geographically concentrated industries that can readily mount lobbying campaigns on their representatives and senators, have been most successful in achieving some limitations on imports.[2]

One possible reason for the lack of direct links between Congressional voting patterns and constituency characteristics in some cases might be that some researchers have misread the protectionist sentiment supposedly present in Congress. Legislative expressions of the need for protection have often constituted signals to foreign countries. These signals are intended to bring about changes in the trade practices of the foreign countries by raising the specter of legislation that would limit their imports as a consequence of their trade barriers or unfair trading practices. This political rhetoric is not directly intended to create domestic barriers to trade; thus, it is not surprising that these efforts often fail to do so.[3]

The effort may be quite successful, however, in changing practices abroad. Congressional interest in trade policy has focused both on the need to open up foreign markets and the need to provide protection. Even with the possibility that Congress is in reality less protectionist than often portrayed, there have been indications that previous Congressional practices, which worked to defuse domestic political pressures for protection, have been less successful recently and that real protectionist sentiment is increasing in the body in response to public opinion and the trade problems that the United States has been facing.

The Rise in Protectionist Sentiment

In the 1970s, increasing domestic pressure for protection appeared in the United States, although the demand for protection from import competition had never been totally absent in earlier years. To some extent the increasing domestic discontent with free trade reflected the success of the post-war efforts of the United States in aiding Europe and Japan to rebuild. The initial U.S. edge in the world marketplace had to decline as the ability of other countries to produce increased. The appearance of the NICs as new competitors in certain products was also a logical consequence of shifts in comparative advantage among nations. Changes in the nature of the international economy, some permanent and some transitory, led to an increase in protectionist sentiment within the United States. One such change was that the United States had become more involved in the global economy as a consequence of its free trade orientation. As a result, it was more vulnerable to international economic events than it had been in the past.[4]

The rise in import competition, of course, has been the main factor underlying this increase in protectionist feelings, but the change occurred when it did for other reasons as well. Import competition for declining industries was more critical since the U.S. government was not able to come up with effective adjustment policies to deal with the problems. Job re-training programs and government assistance for displaced workers have been utilized to some extent, but these programs have been isolated attempts to deal with the problems and not part of any major co-ordinated policy approach.

Greater support for continuation of free trade might have been present if legislation had provided for the phased elimination of obsolete plants as a means of dealing with declines in market shares. Such legislation could also have provided for worker relocation or subsidies as plants phased down, as opposed to subsidies for continued production. When protection is applied as a remedy, however, the more efficient sectors, plants, or companies may actually gain sales while the troubled portions of the industry decline still more. Incentives to companies to re-invest profits, install new technology, or upgrade productivity have not been noticeably successful. Tax breaks for firms in these industrial sectors have led many of them to deal with profit difficulties by diversifying manufacturing operations through the acquisition of companies in unrelated production or service areas rather than by upgrading old plants or introducing new technologies. This lack of an industrial adjustment alternative to protection has been one of the other factors that has led to increased domestic demands for the use of trade barriers as a means of saving jobs and industries.

Protectionism and Global Recession

The global recession in the latter part of the 1970s and into the 1980s aggravated domestic discontent with competition from imports. The recession meant that there was a lack of expanding markets for industries in the developed as well as the developing states, and competition for the existing markets became greater. It became more difficult for firms to shift resources into expanding product lines since such new opportunities for sales were disappearing. Industries or firms that derived little benefit from trade liberalization because they produced primarily for the domestic market were even more likely to favor protection under these circumstances. Workers in threatened industries faced problems as well. In this period they were less able to find new manufacturing jobs if the old ones were lost. The lack of new employment opportunities again increased the pressure for protecting the domestic markets that were still available. It is symptomatic of the effects of the general recession that allegations of dumping and requests for countervailing duties increased rather noticeably during this period. The decrease in market opportunities clearly led businesses to challenge previous practices that had not been a major concern in times of economic expansion. It is also quite possible that other nations were reacting to the same depressed world economic situation by a greater use of such practices as export subsidies and dumping as part of an effort to find outlets for a sudden excess capacity in a number of their industries.

Organized Labor and Protectionism

Organized labor has also reacted in a more protectionist fashion in the face of the recent economic difficulties. Labor had traditionally been in favor of free trade, presumably due to the jobs that became available in export industries at the end of World War II when the United States did have a major productivity advantage. Unemployment in basic industries, many of which are heavily unionized, has also led to a change of orientation. Re-negotiation of contracts with lower wages or loss of benefits in some cases also undoubtedly played a role in the changing attitudes. The recent emphasis by many labor spokespersons has been on "fair trade" rather than free trade. It is argued that other countries have used export subsidies, state trading, dumping, and other practices to penetrate the U.S. domestic market. Extremely low wages paid in some foreign countries, particularly developing ones, have also come under criticism for in effect constituting an unfair trading practice. As a consequence, labor has argued that some form of U.S. protection is necessary to counteract the effects of the unfair trading practices of these foreign states. A frequent associated demand is that U.S. multinational corporations should be prevented from relocating production facilities abroad to take advantage of excessively cheap labor. If protection were instituted at the U.S. borders, it would limit the advantages that would accrue from moving plants offshore if the production were destined for the domestic market.

Tariff Levels

The level of U.S. tariffs is relatively low compared to those of many other industrialized states. Tariffs have actually been relatively low during many periods of U.S. history, although the Smoot-Hawley tariff levels that existed before World War II were very high and contributed to the restriction of trade during that period. After World War II tariffs have been consistently reduced to the present low levels, in large measure as a result of the various multilateral GATT rounds of negotiations. In some product areas, however, tariffs have been prohibitive at times. The effect of the tariffs overall has been to raise prices to consumers and to increase the profit levels in the industries that have benefited. The tariff schedule in the early 1970s also provided incentives for firms to concentrate on production for the domestic market rather than for foreign markets.[5] The U.S. tariff structure, like that of many other industrialized countries, also tends to raise greater obstacles to some exports from the developing countries. Special preferences for some exports

from the developing states have been established, but the U.S. GSP is relatively complicated, limiting the extent of its benefits.[6] The tariff schedule also contains a number of other technical considerations that have presented at least some obstacles to imports.

Non-Tariff Barriers

Non-tariff barriers have become a more important form of protectionism in the United States as they have in other countries. Quotas have been used in a variety of forms to provide protection to domestic industries, particularly voluntary export restraints. The quotas have been applied in an *ad hoc* fashion in response to political pressures rather than as part of a consistent national industrial policy. Textiles, apparel, footwear, and automobiles have been some of the product areas in which quotas have commonly been utilized. Japan, as well as many of the NICs, has been among the states most often requested to restrain their exports or to provide for orderly marketing processes. The quotas have raised costs to consumers, and have often been less effective than corresponding tariffs would have been, although the tariff option has been limited due to the international agreements reached in GATT negotiations. The quotas have had mixed results in providing protection. The U.S. textile industry may actually have gained from the quotas that were imposed since they gave the industry time to restructure itself. The restructuring was possible because the quotas provided a guaranteed market for purposes of planning and making the necessary investments.[7] Quotas in other areas have often been less effective. Industries have not restructured and no appreciable number of jobs have been saved. Limitations on the imports of Japanese automobiles have been a case in point. The result has been higher costs for the consumers, and higher profits for both domestic and Japanese producers. The Japanese firms have gained by moving into more sophisticated model lines. The sub-compact market, which was formerly dominated by the Japanese, has more recently seen the introduction of imports from Korea and Yugoslavia fill the gap created by the Japanese shift to larger models, thus negating one of the goals of the quota.

Other NTBs are also important barriers to imports. Anti-dumping charges have been leveled and requests for countervailing duties put forward, sometimes successfully. Although the International Trade Commission has not been overly protectionist in its rulings, the existence of this agency, however, can be used to pressure foreign firms or governments to limit their exports to the United States. The possibility of facing administrative proceedings, or even court trials, can discourage potential importers from making purchases from foreign firms.[8] The trigger price mechanism used for steel imports has provided some relief for the domestic industry. When foreign imports fall below a specified price level, the foreign producers can be required to demonstrate that the price reflects the true production costs. European and Japanese steel producers reluctantly accepted this limitation in order to avoid the possibility of even more severe protectionist measures being imposed. One result of this measure has been the appearance of new imports of steel originating from the NICs to replace some of the markets lost by the European and Japanese producers.[9] There are also a variety of export subsidies that afford protection to domestic firms by keeping them competitive and by contributing to their overall sales levels. There are other administrative practices that can provide some protection such as government purchasing decisions and preferences--particularly in defense industries--health and safety standards, grading requirements, and the like. Some of the American states have passed legislation favoring domestic producers for state or local contracts.

End Notes

1. Shepherd, William G. "Causes of Increased Competition in the U.S. Economy, 1939-1980." *Review of Economics and Statistics* 64:4 (November 1982): p.622

2. Godek, Paul E. "Industry Structure and Redistribution through Trade Restrictions." *Journal of Law and Economics* 28:3 (October 1985): pp.687-703

3. Pastor, Robert. "The Cry-and-Sigh Syndrome: Congress and Trade Policy." In: *Making Economic Policy in Congress*, edited by Allen Schick. Washington, D.C.: American Enterprise Institute, 1983. p.184.

4. Faux, Jeff. "The Democrats and the Post-Reagan Economy." *World Policy* 3:2 (Spring 1986): p.186.

5. Witthans, Fred. "Estimates of Effective Rates of Protection for United States Industries in 1967." *Review of Economics and Statistics* 55:3 (August 1973): pp.362-364.

6. Erb, Gary F. "U.S. Trade Policies Toward Developing Areas." *Columbia Journal of World Business* 8:2 (Summer 1973): pp.59-67.

7. Pelzman, Joseph. "The Textile Industry," *Annals of the Academy of Political and Social Sciences* 460 (March 1982): pp.92-100.

8. Soltysinski, Stanislaw. "The U.S. Antidumping Laws and State-Controlled Economies." *Journal of World Trade Law* 15:3 (May/June 1981): p.265.

9. Canto, Victor A., Arthur B. Laffo, and Richard B. Eastin. "Failure of Protectionism: A Study of the Steel Industry." *Columbia Journal of World Business* 17:4 (Winter 1982): pp.43-57.

Chapter 6: Annotated Bibliography

General Works

* 6.1 *
Anderson, James E. "Effective Protection in the U.S.: A Historical Comparison." *Journal of International Economics* 2:1 (February 1972): 57-76.

An analysis of U.S. effective protection rates between 1939 and 1958 indicates that on average they were considerably higher than nominal rates. Efforts to protect labor intensive industries were apparent from 1939 to 1947, after which time a partial reversal of these efforts occurred.

* 6.2 *
Baldwin, Robert E. *The Political Economy of U.S. Import Policy.* Cambridge: MIT Press, 1985. ISBN 0-262-02232.

Baldwin analyzes the relationships between political and economic factors in the United States and the resultant trade policies. He also considers the roles of the presidency, Congress, and the International Trade Commission in recent trade issues, including efforts to create protectionist measures and efforts at tariff reductions in multilateral negotiations.

* 6.3 *
Bergsten, C. Fred. "The United States and the World Economy." *Annals of the American Academy of Political and Social Sciences* 460 (March 1982): 11-20.

The United States has faced new constraints in the formulation of policies related to trade. The increased importance of trade for the U.S. economy favors a continued free trade approach. Slower economic growth and rising unemployment have generated new domestic pressures for protection.

* 6.4 *
Destler, I. M. *American Trade Politics: System Under Stress*. New York: Institute for International Economics, 1986. ISBN 0-88132-058-7.

Destler discusses changes in U.S. trade policy since World War II and the increasing pressure to limit imports. He argues that there is stronger pressure for protection and that the political system is less able to deal with it. Appendix B contains a very useful listing of escape clause cases (1975-1985), countervailing duty investigations (1979-1985), and anti-dumping cases (1979-1985) brought by domestic firms as well as the outcomes of the hearings.

* 6.5 *
Diebold, William, Jr. "Past and Future Industrial Policy in the United States." In: *National Industrial Strategies and the World Economy*, edited by John Pinder. Totowa, NJ: Allanheld, Osmun, 1982. ISBN 0-86598-040-3.

Economic nationalism was strengthened in the United States by problems in the international economy in the 1970s. Barriers to imports previously existed, either in specific areas or due to national security considerations, but protectionism increased as a result of these problems, in response to which there have been some preliminary moves in the direction of establishing an industrial policy.

* 6.6 *
Gordon, Bernard K. "Truth in Trading." *Foreign Policy* 61 (Winter 1985-1986): 94-108.

Gordon argues that protectionist sentiment in the United States has increased in part because the focus has been on the level of imports rather than on the fact that the United States is the leading exporter of manufactured products. U.S. sales of services can cover the trade deficit that exists. Gordon argues that an open trading system remains preferable to protectionism.

* 6.7 *
Hayes, Robert H., and James H. Smalhout. "Defending Endangered Industries." *Columbia Journal of World Business* 13:1 (Spring 1978): 5-13.

The authors argue for a middle course between free trade and protectionism for dealing with the problems of U.S. industries such as steel, textiles, and merchant shipping that face import competition.

* 6.8 *
Kindleberger, Charles P. "U.S. Foreign Economic Policy, 1776-1976." *Foreign Affairs* 55:2 (January 1977): 395-417.

Kindleberger provides a useful brief overview of the history of U.S. economic policy, including the role of protectionism. He notes that protectionism had become an important issue in the 1970s.

* 6.9 *
Monroe, Wilbur F. *International Trade Policy in Transition*. Lexington, MA: Lexington Books, 1975. ISBN 0-669-98152-4.

The U.S. economy has increasingly become internationalized with foreign economic events impinging on domestic aspects of the U.S. economy and domestic events having international implications. Monroe discusses a wide variety of issues important in international trade in the early 1970s, including all the major protectionist ones.

* 6.10 *
Seevers, G. L., and W. R. Keeton. "Interrelationships between the Levels of U.S. Exports and Imports." In: *U.S. Trade Policy and Agricultural Exports*, edited by the Iowa State University Center for Agricultural and Rural Development. Ames: Iowa State University Press, 1973. ISBN 0-8138-1655-6.

Protection against the most likely imports of manufactures would lead to an initial decline in U.S. exports, but it would be smaller than the gains from the protection. This estimate does not take into account the possible retaliation abroad that would raise the costs of protection.

* 6.11 *
Wolff, Alan Wm. "International Competitiveness of American Industry: The Role of U.S. Trade Policy." In: *U.S. Competitiveness in the World Economy*, edited by Bruce R. Scott and George C. Lodge. Boston: Harvard Business School Press, 1985. ISBN 0-87584-173-2.

The U.S. trade policy has generally been one of free trade. More effective global competitiveness on the part of U.S. industries requires a co-ordinated government policy to aid these industries as well as cooperation between the executive and legislative branches. The strategy should be to recreate competitive industries rather than to keep a declining industry active for a longer period of time.

U.S. Advocacy of Free Trade

* 6.12 *
Ahearn, Raymond J., and Alfred Reifman. "The Future of U.S. Trade Policy." In: *Canada-United States Free Trade*, edited by John Whalley with Roderick Hill. Toronto: University of Toronto Press, 1985. ISBN 0820-7253-4.

An analysis of U.S. trade policy indicates that while protectionism has increased there is still support for liberal trade. Slower economic growth and unemployment have contributed to protectionist pressures. Many protectionist statements coming from the United States are signals to other countries to remove or lower their barriers to imports.

* 6.13 *
Baldwin, Robert E. "Trade and Employment Effects in the United States of Multilateral Tariff Reductions." *American Economic Review* 66:2 (May 1976): 142-148.

Baldwin analyzes the probable effect of further tariff reductions on the United States. He finds that negotiated reductions would not cause significant negative effects on either trade or employment.

* 6.14 *
Baldwin, Robert E., John H. Mutti, and J. David Richardson. "Crucial Issues for Current International Trade Policy." In: *The New International Economic Order: A U.S. Response*, edited by David B. H. Denoon. New York: New York University Press, 1979. ISBN 0-8147-1769-1.

Analysis indicates that the benefits of multilateral trade liberalization are great enough to offset the costs to the United States. Domestic adjustment policies will be necessary, but such liberalization will further industrialization in developing countries and reduce international inequality.

* 6.15 *
Baldwin, Robert E., John H. Mutti, and J. David Richardson. "Welfare Effects on the United States of a Significant Multilateral Tariff Reduction." *Journal of International Economics* 10:3 (August 1980): 405-423.

A fifty percent multilateral reduction in tariffs would lead to U.S. gains that would outweigh adjustment costs by twenty to one. The authors analyze the effects of reduction on a variety of industries, some of which would face significant problems and major costs and losses.

* 6.16 *
Bale, Malcolm D. "Estimates of Trade Displacement Costs for U.S. Workers." *Journal of International Economics* 6:3 (August 1976): 245-250.

If tariffs are removed, U.S. consumers will gain more than workers will lose. Only if workers displaced by imports remain unemployed for a lengthy period will the costs to society be greater than the benefits.

* 6.17 *
Bergsten, C. Fred. "Crisis in U.S. Trade Policy." *Foreign Affairs* 49:4 (July 1971): 619-635.

Free trade was supported in the United States after World War II primarily because there was domestic acceptance of its positive effects on post-war reconstruction elsewhere in the world and secondarily because it was economically beneficial. Support for these views has declined, particularly by organized labor, which has become protectionist. The formation of the European Common Market and some of its effects also helped to foster protectionism in the United States.

* 6.18 *
Blough, Roy. "U.S. Trade Policy: Past Successes, Future Problems." *Columbia Journal of World Business* 8:2 (Summer 1973): 7-19.

Views of an increasingly integrated world economy were misplaced as trade restrictions increasingly appeared. The position of the United States in the world economy has deteriorated, and there have been domestic adjustment problems. Multinational corporations have presented problems for trade policy as well.

* 6.19 *
Cline, William R. "U.S. Trade and Industrial Policy: The Experience of Textiles, Steel, and Automobiles." In: *Strategic Trade Policy and the New International Economics*, edited by Paul R. Krugman. Cambridge, MA: MIT Press, 1987. ISBN 0-262-11112-8.

Industries receiving protection should demonstrate either a reduction in production as part of a planned phasing out of activity or revitalization since such protection is costly for the country. Free trade is basically a sound policy, and U.S. policy should not shift costs from one industry to another through protection. The formulation of industrial policy and trade policy also needs to consider other issues such as exchange rates and productivity.

* 6.20 *
Cohen, Benjamin J. "U.S. Foreign Economic Policy." *Orbis* 15:1 (Spring 1971): 232-246.

U.S. efforts at trade liberalization after World War II were designed to aid in European and Japanese economic recovery. Further tariff reductions became unnecessary for this goal in the 1960s, and Cohen argues that the U.S. economy would gain little from further liberalization. He correctly anticipated a more restrictive U.S. trade policy.

* 6.21 *
Cohen, Stephen D. *The Making of United States International Economic Policy: Principles, Problems, and Proposals for Reform.* New York: Praeger, 1977. ISBN 0-03-021926-4.

Cohen analyzes the international economic policy structure of the U.S. government in the context of the economic difficulties of the 1970s. He discusses a variety of protectionist issues and domestic pressures as part of his argument for creating a more coherent arrangement for decision making in economic policy in the United States.

* 6.22 *
Curtis, Thomas B., and John Robert Vastine, Jr. *The Kennedy Round and the Future of American Trade.* New York: Praeger, 1971. LC 71-139875.

The authors analyze, primarily from a U.S. perspective, the trade negotiations of the late 1960s, the Kennedy Round, that were designed to lower tariffs and facilitate the freer flow of international trade. They note the various issues raised and the successes and failures of the negotiations. They also note perceptively that the 1960s favored the reduction of barriers but that in the 1970s greater pressure for a protectionist attitude in the United States was quite possible.

* 6.23 *
Diebold, William. "U.S.-Canada Free Trade: An American View." In: *Canada-United States Free Trade*, edited by John Whalley with Roderick Hill. Toronto: University of Toronto Press, 1985. ISBN 0820-7253-4.

The United States had not developed a policy on free trade with Canada in 1985. The decline of international free trade could lead to greater interest in both countries. Both countries could gain by freer trade on a multilateral or bilateral basis.

* 6.24 *
Diebold, William. "U.S. Trade Policy: The New Political Dimensions." *Foreign Affairs* 52:3 (April 1974): 472-496.

Diebold notes a number of difficulties that hamper the development of trade liberalization. The rise of non-tariff barriers, competition from Europe and Japan, and the increased involvement of the U.S. Congress, with its greater responsiveness to domestic protectionist pressures in trade policy, are among the factors limiting trade liberalization.

* 6.25 *
Esposito, Louis, and Frances Ferguson Esposito. "Foreign Competition and Domestic Industry Profitability." *Review of Economics and Statistics* 53:4 (November 1971): 343-353.

The authors' analysis of the effects of protection on the profitability of U.S. firms found that trade liberalization would increase competition and lower profits. They also noted the importance of non-tariff barriers in enhancing the level of profits.

* 6.26 *
Fox, Lawrence A., and Stephen Cooney. "Protectionism Returns." *Foreign Policy* 53 (Winter 1983-84): 74-90.

The authors argue that the United States should manipulate exchange rates to enhance the competitiveness of U.S. industries in the face of import competition, both domestically and abroad. Such a policy would avoid demands for protectionism by U.S. industries.

* 6.27 *
Goldstein, Judith L., and Stephen D. Krasner. "Unfair Trade Practices: The Case for a Differential Response." *American Economic Review* 74:2 (May 1984): 282-287.

Given the weakness of the GATT system for dealing with unfair trade practices, the authors suggest that the United States adopt unilateral retaliation rather than attempting multilateral negotiations. Such action must be taken to force other states to support free trade. It is particularly needed to oppose non-tariff barriers.

* 6.28 *
Hathaway, Dale E. "Trade Restrictions and U.S. Consumers." In: *U.S. Trade Policy and Agricultural Exports*, edited by the Iowa State Center for Agricultural and Rural Development. Ames: Iowa State University Press, 1973. ISBN 0-8138-1655-6.

Liberal trade would permit U.S. consumers to gain from the competition confronting domestic producers. It would also help preserve the jobs of workers in export industries. Protection would decrease domestic competition and perhaps lead to price increases larger than the benefits of the protection.

* 6.29 *
Hays, Larry D., and Thomas D. Willett. "Two Economists' View of the Case for Trade Liberalization." *Columbia Journal of World Business* 8:2 (Summer 1973): 20-25.

The authors present arguments in favor of liberalizing trade through multilateral negotiations. The United States will gain enough benefits from freer trade to more than offset the costs.

* 6.30 *
Hughes, Thomas L. "The Twilight of Internationalism." *Foreign Policy* 61 (Winter 1985-1986): 25-48.

Commitment in the United States to international cooperation and to solving international problems has declined. One symptom of this general condition has been declining support for free trade

* 6.31 *

Krasner, Stephen D. "Trade Conflicts and the Common Defense: The United States and Japan." *Political Studies Quarterly* 101:5 (1986): 787-806.

U.S. support of free trade after World War II was primarily designed to encourage democracy through liberalization in the international economy. At times the United States gained short-term benefits from freer trade, but often there were costs that had to be borne in the support of a free trade policy designed to help create democratic regimes elsewhere.

* 6.32 *

Mingst, Karen. "Process and Policy in U.S. Commodities: The Impact of the Liberal Economic Paradigm." In: *America in a Changing World Political Economy*, edited by William P. Avery and David P. Rapkin. New York: Longman, 1982. ISBN 0-582-28270-5.

The concept of free trade has pervaded U.S. trade policy in commodities. An underlying support for free trade and unco-ordinated patterns of decision making have affected U.S. trade policies. These policies have been reactive rather than anticipatory and one decision has often interfered with other decisions and limited their effects.

* 6.33 *

Pugel, Thomas A. *International Market Linkages and U.S. Manufacturing: Prices, Profits, and Patterns.* Cambridge, MA: Ballinger, 1978. ISBN 0-8841-490-7.

Import competition improves the performance of less competitive U.S. domestic firms by increasing their efficiency. Protection in the form of tariffs and non-tariff barriers results in higher prices and leads to inefficiency. Monopolies and oligopolies are likely to increase prices by amounts greater than the additional costs that result from such protection.

* 6.34 *

Shepherd, William G. "Causes of Increased Competition in the U.S. Economy, 1939-1980." *Review of Economics and Statistics* 64:4 (November 1982): 613-623.

Shepherd finds that large portions of the U.S. economy are in positions of oligopoly. He notes that free trade is important because imports constitute a significant source of competition in these cases.

* 6.35 *

Spich, Robert E. "Free Trade as Ideology, Fair Trade as Goal: Problems of an Ideological Approach in U.S. Trade Policy." *International Trade Journal* 1:2 (Winter 1986): 128-154.

Ideological commitment to free trade in the United States in the face of protectionism abroad and decreasing practice at home has resulted in some poor choices in trade policy. A more pragmatic approach to present problems, with an emphasis on fair trade practices, is suggested as a better policy approach.

* 6.36 *

Yeager, Leland B., and David G. Tuerck. *Foreign Trade and U.S. Policy: The Case for Free International Trade.* New York: Praeger, 1976. ISBN 0-674-44550-3.

Yeager and Tuerck present an argument for working towards free trade and reducing protectionism. In the process of presenting their case, they discuss most protectionist practices, emphasizing the costs involved. They also argue that the United States as a traditional supporter of free trade has been timid in working for its implementation.

The Executive Branch

* 6.37 *

Adams, Walter, and Joel B. Dirlam. "The Trade Laws and Their Enforcement by the International Trade Commission." In: *Recent Issues and Initiatives in U.S. Trade Policy*, edited by Robert E. Baldwin. Washington, D.C.: National Bureau of Economic Research, 1984.

The authors analyze the activities of the International Trade Commission, particularly in relation to escape clause cases and anti-dumping and countervailing duty proceedings. The protection offered by these measures may encourage firms to use the increased profits in other product lines or for investment in facilities abroad rather than the intended domestic restructuring to increase competitiveness and employment.

* 6.38 *

Amacher, Ryan C., Robert D. Tollison, and Thomas D. Willett. "The Divergence between Theory and Practice." In: *Tariffs, Quotas & Trade: The Politics of Protectionism*, edited by the Institute for Contemporary Studies. San Francisco: The Institute, 1979. ISBN 0-917616-34-0.

The authors conclude that political factors rather than changing economic circumstances are largely responsible for the rise of demands for protectionism in democracies, demands that have modified the underlying basis of the theory of free trade. In the United States, an additional significant factor has been the lessened ability of the executive branch, usually anti-protectionist, to control Congress, usually more protectionist, on economic and trade issues.

* 6.39 *
Baldwin, Robert E. "Trade Policies under the Reagan Administration." In: *Recent Issues and Initiatives in U.S. Trade Policy*, edited by Robert E. Baldwin. Washington, DC: National Bureau of Economic Research, 1984.

The Reagan administration has stressed free trade and has allowed economic activity to shift to countries with a comparative advantage. Even so, it has responded similarly to previous administrations in granting import relief and has placed emphasis on fair trade policies, including countervailing action against practices in other countries. The administration has also been limited by the need to act in concert with Congress, which is more responsive to those economic interests that have asked for protection.

* 6.40 *
Destler, I. M. "United States Trade Policymaking during the Tokyo Round." In: *The Politics of Trade: US and Japanese Policymaking for the GATT Negotiations*, edited by Michael Blaker. Occasional Papers of the East Asian Institute. New York: Columbia University, 1978. ISBN 0-317-17100-3.

The United States supported the organization of the multilateral negotiations that became the Tokyo Round in part because participation in such a meeting would deflect protectionist pressure at home. Such pressure would be deflected by the argument that protectionist measures would undercut the U.S. negotiating stance. The Trade Act of 1974 authorizing the negotiations was successfully maneuvered through Congress in part because the executive branch was united in supporting the negotiations.

* 6.41 *
Dobson, John M. *Two Centuries of Tariffs: The Background and Emergence of the U.S. International Trade Commission*. Washington, DC: U.S. Government Printing Office, 1976. LC 77-604260.

Dobson provides a history of U.S. tariff acts and later efforts at trade expansion. He also considers many of the arguments for protectionism and free trade in the United States through time. He details the background for the development of the International Trade Commission, now a key agency involved in the protectionist debates in the United States.

* 6.42 *
Garten, Jeffrey E. "Gunboat Economics." *Foreign Affairs* 63:3 (1985): 538-559.

In a generally negative discussion of the failed economic policies of the Reagan administration, Garten argues that the administration performed badly in the application of protectionist practices. GATT rules were violated, and the policies undertaken were unsuccessful in dealing with the problems, and were even counter-productive.

* 6.43 *
Grzybowski, Kasimierz, Victor Rud, and George Stepanyenko. "Towards Integrated Management of International Trade--The U.S. Trade Act of 1974." *International and Comparative Law Quarterly* 26:2 (April 1977): 283-323.

The authors consider the U.S. Trade Act of 1974 to provide a means for revitalizing GATT's ability to handle disputes and liberalize trade. They analyze the role of various parts of the U.S. government under the act, particularly agencies in the executive branch.

* 6.44 *
Hormats, Robert D. "The World Economy under Stress." *Foreign Affairs* 64:3 (1986): 455-478.

The reduction of tariffs in the 1960s and 1970s heightened the effect of non-tariff barriers that often hurt U.S. exports and stimulated the demand for protectionism in the United States. The Reagan administration, despite its commitment to free trade, took some protectionist action to pre-empt tougher legislation from Congress. Efforts for a new round of multilateral negotiations reflect the concern of many countries over problems in the trading system, but they also reflect a lack of consensus on what changes are necessary.

* 6.45 *
Jameson, Paul W. "Recent International Trade Commission Practice Regarding the Material Injury Standard: A Critique." *Law and Policy in International Business* 18:3 (1986): 517-577.

Jameson argues that the International Trade Commission has not been granting relief to domestic industries as often as it should. He believes that this trend needs to be reversed. The ITC should support the intent of Congress, not attempt to undermine that intent because it considers that Congress was wrong.

* 6.46 *
Jonish, James E. "Recent Developments in U.S. Antidumping Policy." *Journal of World Trade Law* 7:3 (May/June 1973): 316-327.

U.S. anti-dumping decisions were generally based on reasonable indicators for determining if action was necessary. In the early 1970s, however, criteria were changed somewhat to permit a greater likelihood of damage to domestic industry as concern over unfair trading practices abroad increased in the executive branch.

* 6.47 *

Kahler, Miles. "America's Foreign Economic Policy: Is the Old-Time Religion Good Enough." *International Affairs (London)* 56:3 (Summer 1980): 459-473.

Protectionist pressure in the United States has risen in part as the U.S. position in the world economy has changed. The American presidency is often too weak to resist concerted protectionist pressure entirely. U.S. trade policy has concentrated on openness in the world trading system but ignored the need for internal adjustment.

* 6.48 *

Lande, Steve, and Craig VanGrasstek. "Trade with the Developing Countries: The Reagan Record and Prospects." In: *U.S. Foreign Policy and the Third World: Agenda 1985-86*, edited by John W. Sewell, Richard E. Feinberg, and Valeriana Kallab. U.S.-Third World Policy Perspectives no. 3. New Brunswick, NJ: Transaction Books, 1985. ISBN 0-88738-042-5.

The record of the Reagan administration has been mixed from the point of view of the developing countries. Under domestic political pressures, protection against imports from the developing countries has been imposed in some cases, but such protection has been more limited than it could have been. The executive branch has also supported the continuation of the U.S. preferences for developing countries.

* 6.49 *

Madden, M. Stuart. "The Threat of National Injury Standard in Countervailing Duty Enforcement." *Law and Policy in International Business* 16:2 (1984): 373-416.

The International Trade Commission has provided, through its rulings, a consistent standard in the definition of an injury requiring the imposition of countervailing duties. The resulting pattern has contributed to a fair approach to complaints, avoided the capricious imposition of duties, and supported general GATT principles.

* 6.50 *

Malmgren, Harald B. "Managing Economic Policy." *Foreign Policy* 6 (Spring 1972): 42-63.

Foreign policy decisions dealing with trade issues involve many different agencies in the executive branch. Malmgren argues for a co-ordination of effort and consolidation of authority, particularly since the executive branch often faces protectionist pressures from members of Congress who respond to pressures in their districts.

* 6.51 *

Mangan, John J. "Trade Agreements Act of 1979: A Steel Industry Perspective." *Law and Policy in International Business* 18:1 (1986): 241-277.

The steel industry sought to use the Trade Agreements Act of 1979 to limit the discretion of the executive branch in imposing, or not imposing, countervailing duties against imports. The industry believed that the duties were seldom imposed, contrary to Congressional intent. Some limitations on the discretionary authority of the executive branch in this area did result from the 1979 law.

* 6.52 *

Pincus, J. J. "Why Have US Tariffs Fallen Since 1930?" In: *Issues in World Trade Policy: GATT at the Crossroads*, edited by R.H. Snape. New York: St. Martin's, 1986. ISBN 0-312-43724-2.

The decline of U.S. tariff levels from the high of 1934 was due in part to changes in the framework in which trade policy was made. Today domestic interests facing import competition have procedures to seek adjustments through the bureaucracy on a case-by-case basis. The old practice of vote trading in Congress to create protectionist barriers has been eliminated by this process.

* 6.53 *

Takacs, Wendy E. "Pressures for Protectionism: An Empirical Analyses." *Economic Inquiry* 19:4 (October 1981): 687-693.

Takacs found that cycles in economic activity in the United States between 1949 and 1979 did have an effect on pressure for protectionism as measured by the successful use of escape clause appeals to the International Trade Commission in the United States. She also found that successful appeals had a demonstration effect in the following years for other groups seeking protection.

* 6.54 *

Winham, Gilbert R. "Robert Strauss, the MTN and the Control of Faction." *Journal of World Trade Law* 14:5 (September/October 1980): 377-397.

Winham discusses the diplomatic ability of Robert Strauss, President Carter's Special Trade Representative, to achieve results. Strauss concentrated on domestic interest groups' goals in his efforts and sought support in Congress for trade liberalization as he proceeded.

Congress

* 6.55 *

Ahearn, Raymond J., and Alfred Reifman. "Trade Policymaking in the Congress." In: *Recent Issues and Initiatives in U.S. Trade Policy*, edited by Robert

E. Baldwin. Washington, DC: National Bureau of Economic Research, 1984.

The authors provide a useful summary of the Congressional role in dealing with trade policy, including the effects of Congressional organization and committee structure, attitudes towards trade issues, and the effects of the diffusion of legislative power. In response to domestic pressures, Congressional emphasis has shifted from free trade to other issues, including protection and the opening up of foreign markets.

* 6.56 *

Baldwin, Robert E. "The Changing Nature of U.S. Trade Policy Since World War II." In: *The Structure and Evolution of Recent U.S. Trade Policy*, edited by Robert E. Baldwin and Anne O. Krueger. Chicago: University of Chicago Press, 1984. ISBN 0-226-03604-9.

Although the United States led efforts at trade liberalization after World War II, support for protectionism has increased. Congress has been more inclined to meet protectionist demands, and members of Congress of both political parties react to such demands more on the basis of constituency interests than party platforms. The presidency has continued to have a free trade outlook.

* 6.57 *

Baldwin, Robert E. "Protectionist Pressures in the United States." In: *Challenges to a Liberal International Economic Order: A Conference Sponsored by the American Enterprise Institute for Public Policy Research*, edited by Ryan C. Amacher, Gottfried Haberler, and Thomas D. Willett. Washington, DC: American Enterprise Institute for Public Policy Research, 1979. ISBN 0-8447-2151-4.

Protectionist pressures on members of Congress are particularly strong in districts and states negatively affected by competition from imports. Presidents have often been forced to concede to some protectionist demands to achieve Congressional authorization for multilateral negotiations or to prevent more severe protectionist legislation. Baldwin also compiles the costs and benefits of possible multilateral tariff reductions, which would have a relatively small negative net employment effect and much larger consumer benefits.

* 6.58 *

Bauer, Raymond A., Ithiel de Sola Pool, and Lewis Anthony Dexter. *American Business and Public Policy: The Politics of Foreign Trade*. New York: Atherton Press, 1964. ISBN 0-202-24128-9.

The authors undertook an analysis of attitudes towards trade liberalization in the later 1950s and early 1960s based on numerous interviews with business leaders, members of Congress,

journalists, lobbyists, and others. They focus on attitudes, sources of information, the actions of pressure groups, and activities in Congress.

* 6.59 *

Congressional Quarterly Weekly Report. Vol. 1- Washington, DC: Congressional Quarterly, 1946-.

This is a long-standing reference publication that reviews the votes and activities in the U.S. Congress. While covering all types of legislation, it will include a summary of the legislation under consideration and the recorded votes of individual members of Congress on protectionist legislation whenever a roll call vote is taken.

* 6.60 *

Coughlin, Cletus C. "Domestic Content Legislation: House Voting and the Economic Theory of Regulation." *Economic Inquiry* 23:3 (July 1985): 437-448.

Coughlin analyzed favorable votes on the 1982 domestic content legislation in the House of Representatives and various characteristics of the districts of the Representatives. Pro-protectionist votes were found to be associated with the importance of the auto and steel industries, increased levels of unemployment, the shares of labor in interest group campaign contributions, and affiliation with the Democratic party.

* 6.61 *

Czintoka, Michael R. "U.S. Trade Policy and Congress." *Columbia Journal of World Business* 20:4 (1986): 71-77.

Although Congress has been active in proposing protectionist legislation, some of the activity has been a political response to constituent pressures. On many key votes, however, Congress has often defeated protectionist legislation. While there is still bipartisan support for free trade, the support among Democrats has waned.

* 6.62 *

Destler, I. M. "Protecting Congress or Protecting Trade?" *Foreign Policy* 62 (Spring 1986): 96-107.

Protectionist sentiment expressed in Congress in the 1960s and 1970s was not converted to action but was used to shield Congress from domestic political pressures. Recently, high trade deficits have made it more difficult for Congress to avoid demands for protection by using the old political stratagems. Lack of attention by the Reagan administration has also made it more difficult to ignore such pressures.

* 6.63 *

Destler, I. M. "Trade Consensus, SALT Stalemate: Congress and Foreign Policy in the 1970s." In: *The New Congress*, edited by Thomas E. Mann and Norman J. Ornstein. Washington, DC: American Enterprise Institute, 1981. ISBN 0-8447-3415-2.

In comparing the legislative failure of the SALT II agreement and the successful passage of approval for multilateral trade negotiations in the context of legislative-executive relations, Destler notes that members of Congress and interest groups are actually very pragmatic about trade issues. Robert Strauss, the chief trade negotiator, was a clear policy leader for the Carter administration in this policy area, a factor that facilitated Congressional agreement. The administration's approach also facilitated a bipartisan consensus in Congress.

* 6.64 *

Dymock, Paul, and Donna Vogt. "Protectionist Pressures in the U.S. Congress." *Journal of World Trade Law* 17:6 (November/December 1983): 496-512.

The executive branch has favored free trade while Congress has been more protectionist. Congressional interest in the trade policies of other countries and protectionism therein, however, could provide the impetus for reviving GATT.

* 6.65 *

Pastor, Robert A. *Congress and the Politics of U.S. Foreign Economic Policy, 1929-1976.* Berkeley: University of California Press, 1980. ISBN 0-520-04645-5.

Pastor discusses various aspects of U.S. foreign economic policy since the onset of the Great Depression. Part II of the volume considers trade policy and periods of free trade and protectionism. This portion of the book also discusses the roles of the presidency, Congress, and interest groups in the making of trade policy in some detail.

* 6.66 *

Pastor, Robert. "The Cry-and-Sigh Syndrome: Congress and Trade Policy." In: *Making Economic Policy in Congress*, edited by Allen Schick. Washington, DC: American Enterprise Institute, 1983. ISBN 0-8447-3534-5.

Although Congress has often been portrayed as protectionist, it actually has generally favored free trade. Talk of protectionism in Congress has often been designed to bring about reciprocity in open trade relations with other states. Talk of protection has been a signal to foreign countries that has at times been misjudged by analysts.

* 6.67 *

Pincus, Jonathan J. *Pressure Groups and Politics in Antebellum Tariffs.* New York: Columbia University Press, 1977. ISBN 0-2310-3963-8.

Pincus analyzes the early tariff history of the United States in the context of broader tariff theory. He argues that while sectional differences were important in the formation of the tariff, there were also local factors in various states that played a role in the pressures put on Congress.

* 6.68 *

Real, P. Lavergne. *The Political Economy of U.S. Tariffs: An Empirical Analysis.* Toronto: Academic Press, 1983. ISBN 0-12-438740-3.

Real's analysis of the role of interest groups in U.S. tariff and non-tariff barrier policies suggests that their role is generally small. Only total employment in an industry and the size of the most important producing states were related to levels of protection, indicating that the ability to form a large voting bloc might be important in gaining protection.

* 6.69 *

Schattschneider, E. E. *Politics, Pressures, and the Tariff: A Study of Free Private Enterprise in Pressure Politics as Shown in the 1929-1930 Revision of the Tariff.* Hamden, CT: Archon Books, 1935. LC 35-29634.

Schattschneider's work is a classic study of the role of economic interest groups in the formulation and passage of the Smoot-Hawley Tariff Act that greatly increased U.S. tariffs and contributed to the breakdown of the international trading system. The volume discusses the tactics of the pressure groups, factors favoring successful pleading, and geographical versus functional interest groups. Schattschneider notes that pressure for protection was more effective than probably equal opposition because producers were active in presenting their case while consumers were passive.

* 6.70 *

Shuman, Shannon Stock, and Charles Owen Verrill, Jr. "Recent Developments in Countervailing Duty Law and Policy." In: *Recent Issues and Initiatives in U.S. Trade Policy*, edited by Robert E. Baldwin. Washington, DC: National Bureau of Economic Research, 1984.

Pressure from business and labor prompted Congress to pass legislation in the 1970s that imposed countervailing duties on products receiving export subsidies from foreign governments. The legislation has limited administrative discretion in the imposition of the duties and required complex procedures of litigation. One possible disadvantage of these procedures is that the cost has placed the process beyond the reach of all but the largest firms or industry associations.

* 6.71 *

Winham, Gilbert R., and Ikuo Kabashima. "The Politics of U.S.-Japanese Auto Trade." In: *Coping with U.S.-Japanese Economic Conflict*, edited by I. M. Destler and Hideo Sato. Lexington, MA: Lexington Books, 1982. ISBN 0-669-05144-6.

By the 1980s, trade in automobiles became an issue between Japan and the United States due to Japanese imports and domestic pressure for protection. Congressional efforts to pass protectionist legislation were dropped when the Japanese agreed voluntarily to limit exports.

The Rise in Protectionist Sentiment

* 6.72 *

Ahearn, Raymond J. "Political Determinants of U.S. Trade Policy." *Orbis* 26:2 (Summer 1982): 413-429.

Decreasing U.S. support for free trade in the 1970s resulted from domestic pressure groups contesting with free trade supporters. While free trade is still the norm, concessions have been made to some of the groups seeking protection.

* 6.73 *

Aho, C. Michael, and Thomas O. Bayard. "Costs and Benefits of Trade Adjustment Assistance." In: *The Structure and Evolution of Recent U.S. Trade Policy*, edited by Robert E. Baldwin and Anne O. Krueger. Chicago: University of Chicago Press, 1984. ISBN 0-226-03604-9.

In their consideration of U.S. adjustment assistance to industries adversely affected by imports, the authors note that one of the benefits is the weakening of protectionism. Although exact costs and benefits cannot be quantified, this political result is an important subjective benefit that needs to be taken into account.

* 6.74 *

Bale, Malcolm. "United States Concessions in the Kennedy Round and Short-Run Labour Adjustment Costs." *Journal of International Economics* 7:2 (May 1977): 145-148.

While U.S. tariffs were cut during the Kennedy Round, industries with high labor adjustment costs faced lower reductions in tariff schedules. Thus, it would appear that the interests of labor were being represented by the U.S. negotiators.

* 6.75 *

Bergsten, C. Fred. "The New Economics and U.S. Foreign Policy." *Foreign Affairs* 50:2 (January 1972): 199-222.

Bergsten argues that the Nixon administration by its actions in trade and monetary policy promoted protectionism and isolation. He argues that the types of policies undertaken in response to economic problems and domestic pressures will be counter-productive, especially given the extent of these politics.

* 6.76 *

Bluestone, Barry, and Seamus O'Cleireacain. "Industrial Priorities in the Trade Jungle." *World Policy Journal* 1:2 (Winter 1984): 377-395.

The authors review U.S. industrial policy and the rise of protectionist pressures. They detail the many kinds of protectionist measures used. They argue that protectionism is not a substitute for effective fiscal and monetary policies that provide for employment and economic growth nor is it an alternative to viable adjustment policies in industries hurt by foreign competition.

* 6.77 *

Brandis, R. Buford. "The National Need for an Integrated Trade Policy: The Textile Example." In: *U.S. Trade Policy and Agricultural Exports*, edited by the Iowa State University Center for Agricultural and Rural Development. Ames: Iowa State University Press, 1973. ISBN 0-8138-16556.

Brandis argues for protection against imports of textiles since the textile industry is important for the national economy and employs significant numbers of workers. He argues that import quotas would be acceptable under GATT rules and are further justified by the fact that European countries and Japan rely on such protection.

* 6.78 *

Browne, Robert S. "Changing International Specialization and U.S. Imports of Manufactures." In: *The Challenge of the New International Economic Order*, edited by Edwin P. Reubens. Boulder, CO: Westview, 1981. ISBN 0-89158-762-4.

Protectionism in the United States results in part from the loss of jobs to imports, particularly in some low skill industries. Adjustment assistance is one response to competition from the developing countries. Since protectionism is not likely to disappear, however, Browne suggests that the developing states become more self-reliant rather than continue to rely on markets in the developed countries.

* 6.79 *

Chaikin, Sol C. "Trade Investment and Deindustrialization: Myth and Reality." *Foreign Affairs* 60:4 (Spring 1982): 836-851.

Chaikin details many of the problems that threatened industrial sectors face and the events leading to the difficulties. He concludes by arguing that the U.S. government should encourage fair trade, including global quotas in some sectors. He argues that fair trade is better than autarkic protectionism, the alternative that will result from domestic pressures if no action is taken.

* 6.80 *
Cheh, John H. "United States Concessions in the Kennedy Round and Short-Run Labor Adjustment Costs." *Journal of International Economics* 4:4 (November 1974): 323-340.

Cheh argues that in the Kennedy Round declining industries and industries with a high proportion of unskilled or older workers in the United States retained higher levels of protection. Factors other than general national welfare were obviously important in these negotiations.

* 6.81 *
Deardorff, Alan, and Robert M. Stern. "American Labor's Stake in International Trade." In: *Tariffs, Quotas & Trade: The Politics of Protectionism*, edited by the Institute for Contemporary Studies. San Francisco: The Institute, 1979. ISBN 0-917616-34-0.

American organized labor was generally free trade oriented in the past, but by 1970, it had come to favor protectionism, particularly in the form of import quotas. The authors point out that workers are potentially affected by trade policy as consumers and suppliers, as well as by industry of employment, and by area of residence. The four considerations do not necessarily coincide with being pro-free trade or protectionist. They conclude with an argument for tariffs rather than other types of protectionist measures since tariffs are more predictable over time for participants in the marketplace.

* 6.82 *
Enger, Thomas P. "Foreign Trade Policy of American Labour." *Journal of World Trade Law* 7:4 (July/August 1973): 449-460.

American labor became more protectionist after 1970 for a variety of reasons, including the increased role of multinational corporations in the international economy and shifts of U.S. employment to the service sector. Enger finds little evidence to support the fears of organized labor about import competition in the United States.

* 6.83 *
Faux, Jeff. "The Democrats and the Post-Reagan Economy." *World Policy* 3:2 (Spring 1986): 183-218.

The United States needs new approaches to solve both its domestic and international economic problems. U.S. economic leadership favoring free trade has left the U.S. economy vulnerable to external forces, requiring greater government attention to and efforts directed at these forces. Greater efforts at managing trade such as the

Multi-Fibre Arrangements would be useful in other areas.

* 6.84 *
Finger, J. Michael. "Ideas Count, Words Inform." In: *Issues in World Trade Policy: GATT at the Crossroads*, edited by R. H. Snape. New York: St. Martin's, 1986. ISBN 0-312-43724-2.

The GATT system established two mechanisms--an international negotiation system to remove trade barriers but not impose them and a domestic process whereby barriers can be imposed but not removed. Protection in the United States increasingly has come through administrative processes subject to domestic political pressures. Escape clauses in U.S. law that have been increasingly used to provide protection to local interests are an excellent case in point of such administered protection.

* 6.85 *
Fraser, Douglas A. "Domestic Content of U.S. Automobile Imports: A UAW Proposal." *Columbia Journal of World Business* 16:4 (Winter 1981): 57-61.

Fraser argues that the United States is the only major nation without policies designed to maintain employment in the auto industry. He favors domestic content legislation to pressure the Japanese to invest in U.S. plants rather than import quotas as the best policy.

* 6.86 *
Gadbow, R. Michael. "Reciprocity and Its Implications for U.S. Trade Policy." *Law and Policy in International Business* 14:3 (1982): 691-746.

Gadbow argues that the U.S. market should only be as open to imports from a foreign country as that country's domestic market is open to U.S. products. Such reciprocal requirements would be an essential means of maintaining freer trade since it would provide a mechanism to support and encourage nations to reduce trade obstacles.

* 6.87 *
Goldfinger, Nat. "The Case for Hartke-Burke." *Columbia Journal of World Business* 8:1 (Spring 1973): 22-26.

Legislation is needed to limit imports that threaten U.S. employment and the country's industrial base. It is also necessary to limit outflows of capital and technology. These limitations are necessary as a consequence of the presence of managed economies abroad and the growth of multinational corporations
.

* 6.88 *
Goodson, Roy. "American Labor's Continuing Involvement in World Affairs." *Orbis* 19:1 (Spring 1975): 93-116.

In the economic arena American labor is less supportive of free trade in part due to protectionist practices abroad. Labor has also wanted reductions in the incentives for U.S. corporations to produce abroad, greater regulation of multinational corporations, and limitations on the export of technology.

* 6.89 *

Haglund, David G. "Protectionism and National Security: The Case of Uranium Exports to the United States." *Canadian Public Policy* 12:3 (September 1986): 459-472.

The U.S. uranium industry has pressed for protection from lower cost Canadian producers. Some Canadian regulations on processing the ore could be considered an unfair trade practice under GATT regulations.

* 6.90 *

Krueger, Anne O. "Impacts of Foreign Trade on Employment in United States Industry." In: *Current Issues in Commercial Policy and Diplomacy*, edited by John Black and Brian Hindley. New York: St. Martin's, 1980. ISBN 0-312-17926.

Protectionism is justified on the basis that foreign competition has hurt domestic industries and led to job losses. In the case of the United States, there is no indication that foreign imports have led to either of these results. American labor has favored protectionism, perhaps in part to compensate less skilled union members who have been handicapped by other aspects of union policies.

* 6.91 *

Malmgren, Harald B. "The United States." In: *Economic Foreign Policies of Industrial States*, edited by Wilfrid L. Kohl. Lexington, MA: Lexington Books, 1977. ISBN 0-669-00958.

U.S. economic policy has shifted inward or outward in response to domestic political considerations and changing domestic political coalitions. The movement toward protectionism in Congress in the 1970s is one recent example of such a shift.

* 6.92 *

Meltzer, Ronald I. "Colour-TV Sets and U.S.-Japanese Relations: Problems of Trade Adjustment Policymaking." *Orbis* 23:2 (Summer 1979): 421-446.

Meltzer analyzes U.S. imports of Japanese color TVs as an example of protectionist trends. He finds that the U.S. government was not well prepared to handle domestic pressures and international structures were not totally adequate. Governments have often sought some middle ground between protection for domestic groups and general commitments to liberalized trade.

* 6.93 *

Millstein, James E. "Decline in an Expanding Industry: Japanese Competition in Color Television." In: *American Industry in International Competition: Government Policies and Corporate Strategies*, edited by John Zysman and Laura Tyson. Ithaca, NY: Cornell University Press, 1983. ISBN 0-8014-1577-2.

U.S. firms have lost domestic and world markets for their color televisions. It is principally labor that has sought protection while the companies have sought to compete by locating production facilities offshore to take advantage of low wages. Orderly marketing arrangements have not been successful due to Japanese investments in the United States and shifts in offshore production to states are not affected by the agreements.

* 6.94 *

Mueller, Hans G. "The Steel Industry." *Annals of the American Academy of Political and Social Sciences* 460 (March 1982): 73-82.

The U.S. steel industry was unable to compete effectively in an internationally competitive environment when threatened by imports. Management was not prepared for innovative strategies and labor was unwilling to compromise on work rules. The two segments combined to seek protection, but this approach will fail as a long-term solution to the problems of the industry.

* 6.95 *

Nivola, Pietro S. "The New Protectionism: U.S. Trade Policy in Historical Perspective." *Political Studies Quarterly* 101:4 (1986): 577-600.

Nivola compares the recent protectionism sentiment in the United States with earlier pressures for protection. Interest groups are more involved today, and coalitions seeking protection have been formed across industrial sectors as in the past, but sectional and party differences have been reduced. The shift of decision making to the executive branch on trade policy has increasingly been contested by Congress.

* 6.96 *

Pugel, Thomas, and Ingo Walter. "U.S. Corporate Interests and the Political Economy of Trade Policy." *Review of Economics and Statistics* 67:3 (August 1985): 465-473.

The statistical analysis of survey results for U.S. corporate executives indicates that corporate policy on trade issues, including protection, was related to the intensity of and change in import competition, likely benefits from trade liberalization, and the level of product diversification that lessens sensitivity to competition in one product area.

* 6.97 *
Reich, Robert B. "Making Industrial Policy." *Foreign Affairs* 60:4 (Spring 1982): 852-881.

One factor leading to increased protectionism in industrialized countries in the 1970s was slower economic growth which made adjustment to import penetration more difficult. Protection in one sector in the United States has had multiplier effects in other sectors, and such protection has usually been ineffective in bringing about economic revitalization. The alternative to protection in periods of slow growth is managed adjustment.

* 6.98 *
Richardson, J. David. "Trade Adjustment Assistance under the United States Trade Act of 1974: An Analytical Examination and Worker Survey." In: *Import Competition and Response: A Conference Report of the National Bureau of Economic Research*, edited by Jagdish N. Bhagwati. Chicago: University of Chicago Press, 1982. ISBN 0-226-04538-2.

Richardson discusses the history and background of trade adjustment assistance, an alternative mechanism to protectionism for dealing with problems arising from import competition. An analysis of workers receiving such assistance reveals that they are older, less educated, more unionized, and have a more stable employment history than other unemployed workers, and that they had higher average incomes as well. Surprisingly, members of the apparel and footwear industries, as well as the auto industry, fared better than persons in other industries in their later employment history.

* 6.99 *
Root, Franklin, and Bernard Mennis. "How U.S. Multinational Corporations, Unions, and Government View Each Other and the Direction of U.S. Policies." *Journal of International Business Studies* 7:1 (Spring 1976): 17-30.

Officials in unions, the government, and multinational corporations are in agreement in perceiving that Japan and the EC have restrictive trade policies. They have greatly different views, however, on the effects of U.S. trade policies, suggesting that cooperation in creating a unified policy approach is unlikely.

* 6.100 *
Vamberg, Robert G. "The American Steel Industry." *Journal of World Trade Law* 5:1 (January/February 1971): 5-28.

Import competition has resulted from inept U.S. management in domestic firms. Voluntary export restraints agreed to by Japan and the EC are expected to cost purchasers of U.S. steel an extra $4 billion over the next six years.

* 6.101 *
Walters, Robert S. "The U.S. Steel Industry: National Policies and International Trade." In: *The Emerging International Economic Order: Dynamic Processes, Constraints and Opportunities*, edited by Harold K. Jacobson and Dusan Sidjanski. Beverly Hills, CA: Sage, 1982. ISBN 0-8039-1833-x.

The U.S. steel industry sought protection on the grounds that import competition resulted from unfair trading practices by foreign firms. It opposed government adjustment programs for the industry because it feared government control. While the government has continued to support liberal trade, pressures for protection are increasing in the U.S. economy.

* 6.102 *
Zysman, John, and Stephen S. Cohen. "Double or Nothing: Open Trade and Competitive Industry." *Foreign Affairs* 61:5 (Summer 1983): 1113-1139.

The authors detail activities and events that have weakened the system of free trade and that have led to protectionism in the United States. They argue that U.S. policy should be designed to revitalize American industry and to seek to free trade from restrictions that exist elsewhere in the world.

Tariff Levels

* 6.103 *
Baldwin, Robert E. "U.S. Political Pressures Against Adjustment to Greater Imports." In: *Trade and Growth of the Advanced Developing Countries in the Pacific Basin: Papers and Proceedings of the Eleventh Pacific Trade and Development Conference*, edited by Wontack Hong and Lawrence B. Krause. Seoul: Korea Development Institute, 1981. ISBN 0-82-480791.

U.S. tariff levels are high in labor intensive industries with low wages, while non-tariff barriers are common in industries with few firms and high levels of import penetration. The ability of industries to resist reductions in protection agreed to in the Tokyo negotiations was related to sluggish growth in employment, poor profits, rising import competition, and the existence of previous protectionist measures.

* 6.104 *
Burgess, David F. "Tariffs and Income Distribution: Some Empirical Evidence for the United States." *Journal of Political Economy* 84:1 (February 1976): 17-45.

Burgess makes an attempt to test which groups gain from income redistributions concomitant with tariffs in the United States under a variety of circumstances. His findings are inconclusive, indicating that a number of additional factors could affect such redistributions.

* 6.105 *

Cassing, James, Timothy J. McKeown, and Jack Ochs. "The Political Economy of the Tariff Cycle." *American Political Science Review* 80:3 (September 1986): 843-862.

The authors analyze regional differences in U.S. industries to develop a theory of tariff cycles. Old industrial regions press for protection in poor economic times, whereas new industrial regions gain more from protection in times of expansion. The presence of tariffs is related to the relative size of old regions and new ones in the industry, as well as the general state of the economy.

* 6.106 *

Erb, Gary F. "U.S. Trade Policies Toward Developing Areas." *Columbia Journal of World Business* 8:2 (Summer 1973): 59-67.

U.S. consumers would gain by increased imports from developing countries, although costs could be localized, requiring adjustment assistance. The U.S. GSP scheme has significant features that effectively limit the expansion of developing country exports. Erb argues that simplification and improvement of the preference schedule is necessary.

* 6.107 *

Fieleke, Norman S. "The Incidence of the U.S. Tariff Structure on Consumption." *Public Policy* 19:4 (Fall 1971): 639-652.

Tariff duties are not proportional in their cost to segments of the U.S. population. They are, in fact, somewhat regressive in that a larger percentage of the income of the poor goes to paying them.

* 6.108 *

Fieleke, Norman S. "The Tariff Structure for Manufacturing Industries." *Columbia Journal of World Business* 11:4 (Winter 1976): 98-104.

An analysis of U.S. tariff rates in 1965 and 1972 found them unrelated to the level of import competition, the importance of the product to national defense, the level of or lack of industry growth, or the level of employment. The wage rate was only marginally important for the tariff rate.

* 6.109 *

Finger, J. M. "Trade and Domestic Effects of the Offshore Assembly Provision in the U.S. Tariff." *American Economic Review* 66:4 (September 1976): 598-611.

U.S. tariffs are lower on imports that contain components produced in the United States but then used as part of a final product assembled abroad. The effect of this barrier to other imports is to permit developing countries to use their comparative advantage in labor intensive assembly operations. There is a U.S. gain since the absence of the provision would probably lead to the replacement of U.S. components by German or Japanese ones.

* 6.110 *

Finger, J. M., and Dean A. DeRosa. "Trade Overlap, Comparative Advantage and Protection." In: *On the Economics of Intra-Industry Trade: Symposium 1978*, edited by Herbert Giersch. Tubingen: J.C.B. Mohr, 1978. ISBN 0-89563-548-8.

U.S. tariffs have generally protected labor intensive industries but have provided little protection for skilled labor intensive production. The Kennedy Round of tariff reductions bore no discernible relationship to U.S. industry characteristics or U.S. trade patterns as reductions were generally across the board.

* 6.111 *

Hartigan, James C., and Edward Tower. "Trade Policy and the American Income Distribution." *Review of Economics and Statistics* 64:2 (May 1982): 261-270.

When highly disaggregated economic sectors were used, it was discovered that tariffs and quotas had a much greater effect on U.S. income distribution than previously assumed. The groups that gained or lost depended upon the direction of changes in protection and whether the analysis emphasized the short-term or long-term consequences.

* 6.112 *

James, John A. "The Optimum Tariff in the Antebellum United States." *American Economic Review* 71:4 (September 1981): 726-734.

James calculates what the optimum U.S. tariff should have been in the early years of the country and compares it to the actual tariff. In expanding domestic manufacturing, trade balances, and factors of production utilized, the U.S. tariff structure was consistently below optimum levels.

* 6.113 *

Kilpatrick, John A., and Robert E. Miller. "Determinants of the Commodity Composition of U.S. Trade: A Discriminant Analysis Approach." *Journal of International Business Studies* 9:1 (Spring/Summer 1978): 25-32.

Tariffs did have an effect on some components of U.S. trade. In some cases trade was present despite high tariffs, but in other cases there was some evidence that tariffs led to a reversal of the direction of trade in product areas.

* 6.114 *
Pease, Don J., and J. William Goold. "The New GSP: Fair Trade with the Third World." *World Policy Journal* 2:2 (Spring 1985): 351-366.

The authors argue that the U.S. GSP scheme is a benefit to the United States, notwithstanding domestic pressures to end it. By fueling industrial development in the developing countries, new markets will be opened for U.S. exports.

* 6.115 *
Pincus, J. J. "Pressure Groups and the Pattern of Tariffs." *Journal of Political Economy* 83:4 (August 1975): 757-778.

The U.S. Tariff Act of 1824 is analyzed to determine whether geographically concentrated interest groups or groups represented in many different states were more effective pressure groups in the early United States. Industries that were present in a number of different states but which had their plant locations concentrated within those states tended to be more effective in receiving protection.

* 6.116 *
Ray, Edward John. "The Determinants of Tariff and Nontariff Trade Restrictions in the United States." *Journal of Political Economy* 89:1 (February 1981): 105-121.

An analysis of U.S. protectionism finds that protection is highest in industries that do not have a comparative advantage in world trade and that these industries do not include the most labor intensive ones. Tariff protection exists in industries with different characteristics than those that have non-tariff protection.

* 6.117 *
Rousslang, Donald J., and John W. Suomela. "The Trade Effects of a U.S. Import Surcharge." *Journal of World Trade Law* 19:5 (September/October 1985): 441-450.

The authors supply estimates of the effects of a general import surcharge and a surcharge only on Japanese imports for 64 different U.S. industries. They also consider the possible effects of retaliation on trade. U.S. imports and exports would drop in all cases, but there would be an improvement in the balance of trade.

* 6.118 *
Stone, Joe A. "A Comment on Tariffs, Nontariff Barriers, and Labor Protection in the United States Manufacturing Industries." *Journal of Political Economy* 86:5 (October 1978): 959-962.

Stone finds some support for the idea that in the United States there is an association between labor intensity and protectionism. This association is particularly present when, as a measure of protection, effective tariff rates are used in conjunction with non-tariff barriers instead of the nominal tariff rates.

* 6.119 *
Travis, William P. "Production, Trade, and Protection When There Are Many Commodities and Two Factors." *American Economic Review* 62:1 (March 1972): 87-106.

Travis finds that U.S. tariffs often tend to be prohibitive to imports. Tariffs lead to wage increases in protected industries, while declines in tariffs do not lead to wage decreases, thus necessitating continued protection for the industry.

* 6.120 *
Waters, W. G., II. "Transport Costs, Tariffs, and the Pattern of Industrial Protection." *American Economic Review* 60:5 (December 1970): 1013-1020.

For the United States, ignoring transport costs understates the level of protection offered. The effective protection offered for processed goods by the U.S. tariff structure is weakened somewhat by lower transport costs. U.S. tariffs on processed products likely to be exported by developing countries are higher than tariffs on such goods from other areas.

* 6.121 *
Witthans, Fred. "Estimates of Effective Rates of Protection for United States Industries in 1967." *Review of Economics and Statistics* 55:3 (August 1973): 362-364.

An analysis of the effective rates of protection for 135 U.S. manufacturing industries indicates that neglecting substitution effects biases the level of effective protection rate upward. The U.S. tariff structure provides strong incentives for firms to concentrate on domestic sales rather than on export activity.

Non-Tariff Barriers

* 6.122 *
Adams, Walter, and Joel B. Dirlam. "Unfair Competition in International Trade." In: *Tariffs, Quotas, & Trade: The Politics of Protectionism*, edited by the Institute for Contemporary Studies. San Francisco: The Institute, 1979. ISBN 0-917-616-34-0.

The authors discuss the various measures that have been attempted in the United States under domestic political pressure from the steel industry to preserve domestic production. These efforts have been partially successful with concomitant costs for the U.S. economy. The authors conclude that ultimately the problems of the industry are self-inflicted.

* 6.123 *

Aggarwal, Vinod K., with Stephan Haggard. "The Politics of Protection in the U.S. Textile and Apparel Industries." In: *American Industry in International Competition: Government Policies and Corporate Strategies*, edited by John Zysman and Laura Tyson. Ithaca, NY: Cornell University Press, 1983. ISBN 0-8014-1577-2

Protection has been the only U.S. government policy enacted to deal with the decline in the textile and apparel industries. U.S. protectionism has had compound repercussions. Protection for cotton led to higher textile costs and lessened competitiveness. Quotas on imports from developing countries led to pressure on European markets and increased protectionism there.

* 6.124 *

Aw, Bee Yan, and Mark J. Roberts. "Measuring Quality Change in Quota-Constrained Import Markets: The Case of U.S. Footwear." *Journal of International Economics* 21:1-2 (August 1986): 45-60.

U.S. orderly marketing arrangements for footwear with Korea and Taiwan have led to an upgrading of the quality of the imports. Approximately twelve percent of the increased price of footwear was due to the importing of higher quality items in the period from 1977 to 1981.

* 6.125 *

Brody, David S. "The Domestic Shoe Industry's Attempt for Relief from Imports: Going the Section 201 Route Is for Suckers." *Law and Policy in International Business* 17:4 (1985): 815-845.

Seeking import quotas as allowed by Section 201 of the Trade Act of 1974 has been ineffective. Quotas provide little incentive for industries to modernize. Tariff quotas with tariffs being applied only after a certain level of imports have entered would be better since pressure would be placed on the domestic industry to remain competitive.

* 6.126 *

Borrus, Michael. "The Politics of Competitive Erosion in the U.S. Steel Industry." In: *American Industry in International Competition: Government Policies and Corporate Strategies*, edited by John Zysman and Laura Tyson. Ithaca, NY: Cornell University Press, 1983. ISBN 0-8014-1577-2.

When the U.S. steel industry failed to catch up to the Japanese steel industry, it resorted to political means to defend its position. The U.S. government has provided protection to the steel industry, against "unfair competition," to permit modernization while still maintaining a commitment to an open trading system.

* 6.127 *

Caine, Wesley K. "A Case for Repealing the Antidumping Provisions of the Tariff Act of 1930." *Law and Policy in International Business* 13:3 (1981): 681-726.

While U.S. anti-dumping laws are designed to promote fair trade, the provisions are so complex and their application so uncertain that they constitute an important obstacle to trade. The author prefers to deal with import problems by the use of escape clauses that exist in other legislation.

* 6.128 *

Cameron, Laurie A., and Gerald C. Berg. "The U.S. Countervailing Duty Law and the Principle of General Availability." *Journal of World Trade Law* 19:5 (September/October 1985): 497-507.

Currently countervailing duties are not applied when a foreign government provides a general subsidy available to all industries. The authors argue that some general subsidies in reality only help a few industries, and exports of products from these industries should be subject to countervailing duties.

* 6.129 *

Canto, Victor A., J. Kimball Dietrich, Adish Jain, and Vishwa Mudaliar. "The Determinants and Consequences of Across-the-Board Trade Restrictions in the U.S. Economy." *International Trade Journal* 1:1 (Fall 1986): 65-78.

Policy interventions by the U.S. government such as the Trade Act of 1974 that provided safeguards for domestic industries are often a result of balance of trade difficulties. The protection provided has led to declines in employment and in the stock market.

* 6.130 *

Canto, Victor A., Arthur B. Laffo, and Richard B. Eastin. "Failure of Protectionism: A Study of the Steel Industry." *Columbia Journal of World Business* 17:4 (Winter 1982): 43-57.

The U.S. steel industry, as well as the global steel industry, has been weakened by protectionist measures in the United States. Limits on European and Japanese exports have encouraged other countries to begin to export to the U.S. market. The authors conclude that present measures and other import barriers will not greatly aid the domestic industry.

* 6.131 *

Dam, Kenneth W. "Implementation of Import Quotas: The Case of Oil." *Journal of Law and Economics* 14:1 (April 1971): 1-60.

An analysis of the U.S. import quota on oil indicates that groups will be able to surmount governmental regulations. There is also continuous political pressure to expand the groups or areas of the country that benefit from the quota system.

* 6.132 *
Dielmann, Heinz J. "U.S. Response to Foreign Steel: Returning to Trigger Prices." *Columbia Journal of World Business* 16:3 (Fall 1981): 32-42.

If a foreign competitor sells steel below the trigger price, an investigation ensues in which the exporter has to demonstrate that the price reflects fair value. The trigger price mechanism could be challenged in U.S. courts, but a disallowal of the law could lead to new protectionist measures that would be even more disadvantageous.

* 6.133 *
Ehrenhaft, Peter D. "What the Antidumping and Countervailing Duty Provisions of the Trade Agreements Act [Can] [Will] [Should] Mean for U.S. Trade Policy." *Law and Policy in International Business* 11:4 (1979): 1361-1404.

U.S. anti-dumping laws are unrealistic because they ignore the fact that many firms, including domestic ones, often sell below cost for a variety of reasons. There is also no evidence that such provisions have helped domestic industries, although consumer prices have increased. Ehrenhaft concludes that new provisions under the 1979 Trade Agreements Act are often unworkable and provide only marginal improvements over the previous laws.

* 6.134 *
Eichengreen, Barry, and Hans van der Ven. "U.S. Antidumping Policies: The Case of Steel." In: *The Structure and Evolution of Recent U.S. Trade Policy*, edited by Robert E. Baldwin and Anne O. Krueger. Chicago: University of Chicago Press, 1984. ISBN 0-226-03604-9.

Charges of dumping in the U.S. market have ranged from basic products, including agricultural commodities, to high technology items. U.S. anti-dumping policy has increasingly moved towards legalistic procedures, emphasizing adversarial proceedings and limiting administrative discretion, as typified in the trigger price mechanism for steel. The authors also model the occurrence of dumping, including the effects of the number of firms in each national market, costs, market shares, and recognition of mutual interaction among firms.

* 6.135 *
Feenstra, Robert C. "Voluntary Export Restraint in U.S. Autos, 1980-81: Quality, Employment, and Welfare Effects." In: *The Structure and Evolution of Recent U.S. Trade Policy*, edited by Robert E.

Baldwin and Anne O. Krueger. Chicago: University of Chicago Press, 1984. ISBN 0-226-03604-9.

The 1981 VER on imports of Japanese autos led to price increases of the vehicles in 1981. Two-thirds of the increase was due to quality improvements in the types imported and one-third was from higher prices. The impact of the VER on U.S. employment was apparently small.

* 6.136 *
Finger, J. M. "The Industry-Country of Incidence of 'Less than Fair Value' Cases in U.S. Import Trade." In: *Export Diversification and the New Protectionism: The Experiences of Latin America*, edited by Werner Baer and Malcolm Gillis. Champaign: Bureau of Economic and Business Research, College of Commerce and Business Administration, University of Illinois at Urbana-Champaign, 1981. LC 81-67370.

Charges of unfair trade practices by exporters to the United States seem to be related to domestic events other than the increasing pressure for protectionism. Developed countries have more often been the targets of such charges by U.S. manufacturers, although findings against exporters in developing countries have a slightly higher rate of affirmation.

* 6.137 *
Finger, J. Michael. "Trade and the Structure of American Industry." *Annals of the American Academy of Political and Social Sciences* 460 (March 1982): 45-53.

Competition from imports has lowered the profit rates in some U.S. industries. The administrative mechanisms present, such as dumping and countervailing duty procedures, favor those groups seeking protection rather than the users of imports or consumers.

* 6.138 *
Finger, J. M., H. Keith Hall, and Douglas R. Nelson. "The Political Economy of Administered Protection." *American Economic Review* 72:3 (June 1982): 452-466.

The authors develop and operationalize a model for the effects of administered protection in the United States in the form of countervailing duties, escape clauses, and anti-dumping regulations. The administration of these regulations has had a bias towards protectionism, but it has not been a major one.

* 6.139 *
Fisher, Bart S. "The Antidumping Law of the United States: A Legal and Economic Analysis." *Law and Policy in International Business* 5:1 (1973): 85-154.

Protectionists have favored using U.S. anti-dumping provisions to limit imports. Fisher argues that such provisions should be used against continuous dumping by countries underpricing goods and predatory dumping that hurts U.S. industries, but not against sporadic dumping that is used to eliminate temporary oversupply problems. He also argues that vigorous enforcement of the provisions to placate domestic groups will permit more effective U.S. negotiations for trade liberalization.

* 6.140 *
Gerber, David J. "The United States Sugar Quota Program: A Study in the Direct Congressional Control of Imports." *Journal of Law and Economics* 19:1 (April 1976): 103-147.

Gerber analyzes the U.S. sugar quota from 1934 to 1974. The initial quota was a simple response to a problem but over the years came to be used for many policy purposes, as is the case with many quotas. Local groups favored by the quota controlled the allocation machinery and gained influence with the legislative and executive decision makers.

* 6.141 *
Godek, Paul E. "Industry Structure and Redistribution through Trade Restrictions." *Journal of Law and Economics* 28:3 (October 1985): 687-703.

Quotas are a distinctive type of U.S. trade barrier that is associated with geographically concentrated industries. Tariffs are higher in industries where political influence is an important factor in the types of protection that can be gained.

* 6.142 *
Goldstein, Judith. "The Political Economy of Trade: Institutions of Protection." *American Political Science Review* 80:1 (March 1986): 161-184.

Protectionist institutions in the United States have been designed to guard against unfair trade practices, such as dumping, and have provided for the implementation of countervailing duties. They have not become more protectionist with increases in import competition. Although a free trade orientation persists, large U.S. industries have been able to gain protection through voluntary export restraints or through subsidies.

* 6.143 *
Gray, H. Peter. "Structural Consequences of Changing International Trade Patterns and Possible Alternative Policies." In: *Western Economies in Transition: Structural Change and Adjustment Policies in Industrial Countries*, edited by Irving Leveson and Jimmy W. Wheeler. Boulder, CO: Westview, 1980. ISBN 0-891-58589-3.

Labor intensive imports from developing countries create unemployment among low skilled workers in industrialized countries. Subsidies to industries using this type of labor are the appropriate form of adjustment. The existing protective measures used by the United States are ineffective in maintaining levels of employment.

* 6.144 *
Grossman, Gene M. "Imports as a Cause of Injury: The Case of the U.S. Steel Industry." *Journal of International Economics* 20:3-4 (May 1986): 201-223.

The author develops a model for ascertaining whether import competition has injured a U.S. industry, thus justifying relief under the escape clause of the Trade Act of 1974. In the case of domestic steel production, he finds that relief is not justified.

* 6.145 *
Hartigan, James C., Philip R. Perry, and Sreenivas Kamma. "The Value of Administered Protection: A Capital Market Approach." *Review of Economics and Statistics* 68:4 (November 1986): 610-617.

Use of escape clauses has provided some aid to distressed U.S. industries, but the benefits of protection are not great. Other attributes of the firms in difficulty are more important, and protection is not the solution to difficulties its proponents claim.

* 6.146 *
Hay, Keith A. J., and B. Andrei Sulzenko. "U.S. Trade Policy and 'Reciprocity'." *Journal of World Trade Law* 16:6 (November/December 1982): 471-479.

The U.S. Reciprocal Trade and Investment Act of 1982 is designed to force other countries to liberalize trade by threatening retaliation. The law does infringe on the sovereignity of other countries by utilizing U.S. definitions of non-tariff barriers. Implementation would be costly for Canada, Japan, and Europe, and for the U.S. as well.

* 6.147 *
Hufbauer, Gary Clyde, Diane T. Berliner, and Kimberly Ann Elliott. *Trade Protection in the United States: 31 Case Studies*. Washington, DC: Institute for International Economics, 1986. ISBN 0-88132-040-4.

The authors examine the protection offered to 31 industries in the United States in the form of both high tariffs and quantitative restrictions. They provide brief summaries of the methods used in the cases and comparative data on the effects of protection on domestic production, imports, employment levels, consumption, estimates of welfare costs to the United States, and other variables.

* 6.148 *
Hufbauer, Gary Clyde, and Howard R. Rosen. *Trade Policy for Troubled Industries*. Policy Analyses in International Economics 15. Washington, DC: Institute for International Economics, March 1986. ISBN 0-88132-020-x.

Special protection for industries facing difficulties has usually failed as the protection offered lasts longer than anticipated and does not lead to industry revivals, although in a few cases industry consolidation and effective modernization have occurred. A survey of the types of special protection used in the United States in 31 cases leads the authors to suggest levels of protection that will decline over time combined with the dedication of revenues from the protection to adjustments in the industry in question.

* 6.149 *

Jackson, John H. "Perspectives on the Jurisprudence of International Trade." *American Economic Review* 74:2 (May 1984): 277-281.

Jackson notes that the U.S. system of controlling imports is legalistic in its application, but he considers that the benefits of the system outweigh the costs. He prefers the present U.S. system to one that would give greater discretion to government officials, as is the situation in other major industrial countries.

* 6.150 *

Kawahito, Kiyoshi. "Steel and the U.S. Antidumping Statutes." *Journal of World Trade Law* 16:2 (March/April 1982): 152-164.

U.S. anti-dumping regulations may be legally logical, but they violate reasonable economic theories and business practices in their definitions of dumping. The U.S. laws need to be eliminated or changed so as to encourage free trade, not limit it.

* 6.151 *

Komarow, Gary. "Effective Enforcement of U.S. Antidumping Laws: The Development and Legal Implications of Trigger Pricing." *Law and Policy in International Business* 10:3 (1978): 969-1000.

Komarow discusses the background leading up to the trigger price mechanism used to defend the domestic steel industry, as well as domestic and foreign reactions to it. Trigger pricing did avoid a more general move toward greater protectionism in the United States. Komarow notes that the adoption of this mechanism was primarily a political decision made as a result of pressure from an important domestic industry.

* 6.152 *

Krueger, Anne O. "Quotas on American Imports Would Reduce Employment in American Industry." *Public Policy* 19:4 (Fall 1971): 653-659.

Quotas, which are generally inefficient policy devices for governments, will not usually increase U.S. employment in the aggregate. Retaliation by foreign countries would lead to losses of high wage jobs in return for preserving low wage positions.

* 6.153 *

Kyle, Reuben, and Lawrence T. Phillips. "Cargo Reservation for Bulk Commodity Shipments: An Economic Analysis." *Columbia Journal of World Business* 18:3 (Fall 1983): 42-49.

Guaranteeing cargos for U.S. merchant ships is another manifestation of protectionist pressures in the United States. Costs will increase for U.S. consumers, but more importantly, a precedent will be set for a new type of protectionist practice that can be used by other countries.

* 6.154 *

Marvel, Howard P., and Edward J. Ray. "The Kennedy Round: Evidence on the Regulation of International Trade in the United States." *American Economic Review* 73:1 (March 1983): 190-197.

The tariff reductions of the Kennedy Round were ineffective as U.S. industries facing import competition were able to substitute non-tariff barriers for tariffs. Domestic political pressures were important in undermining the efforts at trade liberalization.

* 6.155 *

McMullen, Neil. "North America and the NICs." In: *The Newly Industrializing Countries: Trade and Adjustment*, edited by Louis Turner and Neil McMullen. London: George Allen & Unwin, 1982. ISBN 0-04-382036-0.

The U.S. tariffs have generally been higher in areas such as textiles where NIC exports have been concentrated, and non-tariff barriers have also come to be concentrated in these areas. McMullen also discusses the GATT Codes for Major Non-Tariff Barriers, to which the United States subscribes, which are designed to eliminate use of these measures among the signatory countries.

* 6.156 *

Mendez, Jose A. "The Short-Run Trade and Employment Effects of Steel Import Restrictions." *Journal of World Trade Law* 20:5 (September/ October 1986): 554-566.

Mendez supplies estimates of the allocation of costs and benefits from limits on steel imports. Both exports and imports have declined and non-steel sectors have had declines in employment that offset any employment gains in the steel industry. The trade barriers redistribute resources to the steel sector from other sectors of the economy.

* 6.157 *

Mintz, Ilse. *U.S. Import Quotas: Costs and Consequences*. Washington, DC: American Enterprise Institute, 1973. ISBN 0-8447-3095-5.

Mintz argues that even rough estimates of the costs of import quotas impose heavy costs on U.S. consumers, particularly low income consumers. Quotas work less well than tariffs, their principal advantage being that their use circumvents GATT rules. Mintz also discusses the effects of quotas for sugar, textiles, and a variety of other commodities.

* 6.158 *
Morici, Peter. "Trends in U.S. Trade Policy and Non-Tariff Barriers." In: *Canada-United States Free Trade*, edited by John Whalley with Roderick Hill. Toronto: University of Toronto Press, 1985. ISBN 0820-7253-4.

Morici discusses the various barriers to trade that have been used in the United States, including quotas, special tariffs, marketing arrangements, export restraints, antitrust exemptions, and subsidies. Greater use of these devices has been justified in part by the failure of other countries to adequately support a system of free trade.

* 6.159 *
Nehmer, Stanley, and Mark W. Love. "Textiles and Apparel: A Negotiated Approach to International Competition." In: *U.S. Competitiveness in the World Economy*, edited by Bruce R. Scott and George C. Lodge. Boston: Harvard Business School Press, 1985. ISBN 0-87584-173-2.

The Multi-Fibre Arrangements have improved the domestic competitiveness of U.S. firms by stabilizing world markets and encouraging investments. Similar arrangements would be worthwhile in other product areas where there is a large volume of trade and where there are significant trade conflicts with little likelihood of solution.

* 6.160 *
Palmeter, N. David. "Injury Determinations in Antidumping and Countervailing Duty Cases--A Commentary on U.S. Practice." *Journal of World Trade Law* 21:1 (February 1987): 7-45.

Palmeter reviews U.S. anti-dumping and countervailing duty practices. While generally fair, there is a procedural bias favoring those petitioning for relief. The applications do make it difficult for new producers, typically from developing countries, to enter the U.S. market and thus do provide effective protection to some U.S. industries.

* 6.161 *
Pearson, Charles. "Protection by Tariff Quota: Case Study of Stainless Steel Flatware." *Journal of World Trade Law* 13:4 (July/August 1979): 311-321.

In his case study of the application of a tariff quota in the United States, Pearson concludes that the measure was costly and ineffective.

* 6.162 *
Pellegrini, Valerie J. "GSP: A System of Preferences, Not a Bargaining Lever." *Law and Policy in International Business* 17:4 (1985): 879-906.

The United States has used its GSP schedule to attempt to extract concessions from other countries, particularly the NICs, and to provide protection. Pellegrini argues that such activities should be separated from the GSP and dealt with in bilateral negotiations.

* 6.163 *
Pelzman, Joseph. "The Multifiber Arrangement and Its Effect on the Profit Performance of the U.S. Textile Industry." In: *The Structure and Evolution of Recent U.S. Trade Policy*, edited by Robert E. Baldwin and Anne O. Krueger. Chicago: University of Chicago Press, 1984. ISBN 0-226-03604-9.

The MFA did lead to some restructuring in the U.S. textile and apparel industries, although other factors also played a role. It also offered effective protection to the industries by controlling imports, but the author notes that the cost of this success has yet to be calculated.

* 6.164 *
Pelzman, Joseph. "The Textile Industry." *Annals of the Academy of Political and Social Sciences* 460 (March 1982): 92-100.

Foreign competition has led to a revitalization and modernization of the U.S. textile industry. Further protection is not justified for this industry (unlike the apparel industry).

* 6.165 *
Pindyck, Robert S., and Julio J. Rotemberg. "Are Imports to Blame? Attribution of Injury under the 1974 Trade Act." *Journal of Law and Economics* 30:1 (April 1987): 101-122.

The authors present a model for determining whether industry declines are due to imports or other factors such as shifts in domestic demand and supply. In the case of the U.S. copper industry they found that the problems being experienced were not a consequence of imports.

* 6.166 *
Ray, Edward John. "Tariff and Nontariff Barriers to Trade in the United States and Abroad." *Review of Economics and Statistics* 63: 2 (May 1981): 161-168.

Non-tariff barriers in the United States occur in areas where high tariffs already exist, suggesting that they are used to reinforce existing protection. U.S. export levels are positively related to foreign tariff and non-tariff barriers, indicating that such protection may hurt other countries more than the United States. It might also indicate that such barriers are more likely to appear in sectors where the U.S. firms are more competitive, although the author does not note this possibility.

* 6.167 *
Reich, Robert B. "Beyond Free Trade." *Foreign Affairs* 61:4 (Spring 1983): 773-804.

The U.S. commitment to free trade has hurt the country economically. Other countries with government involvement and selective protectionist practices have undertaken a more productive approach to industrial adjustment to the present world situation. The United States already supplies substantial subsidies to domestic firms and has raised significant barriers to imports.

* 6.168 *
Rosenthal, Paul C. "Industrial Policy and Competitiveness: The Emergence of the Escape Clauses." *Law and Policy in International Business* 18:4 (1986): 749-793.

Rosenthal reviews the use of escape clauses in the face of import competition with particular reference to the U.S. steel industry. He believes that the use of the escape clause will increasingly be tied to improving the competitiveness of U.S. industries.

* 6.169 *
Soltysinski, Stanislaw. "U.S. Antidumping Laws and State-Controlled Economies." *Journal of World Trade Law* 15:3 (May/June 1981): 251-265.

U.S. regulations pertaining to dumping need to be strengthened in their application to imports from Eastern Europe, given the unique aspects of the trade mechanisms of the centrally planned economies. The present laws also tend to restrain potential importers who can easily be forced to defend their importing in an administrative hearing.

* 6.170 *
Thompson, Earl A. "An Economic Basis for the 'National Defense Argument' for Aiding Certain Industries." *Journal of Political Economy* 87:1 (February 1979): 1-36.

Thompson develops a model to test the argument that interests of national defense require protectionist practices. His model supports the argument that some industries are regulated during wartime to avoid excess profits, and they, therefore, can claim protection during peacetime. An analysis of U.S. practices during World War II is supportive of this conclusion.

* 6.171 *
Tyson, Laura, and John Zysman. "American Industry in International Competition." In: *American Industry in International Competition: Government Policies and Corporate Strategies*, edited by John Zysman and Laura Tyson. Ithaca, NY: Cornell University Press, 1983. ISBN 0-8014-1577-2.

The United States has responded to increasing international competition with protectionist policies, especially as a result of political necessity when powerful industries are affected. Orderly marketing arrangements have often been used in an effort to reconcile the demands for protection with a commitment to free trade. The authors conclude that government decisions for individual industries or sectors do not follow the implicit objectives of the national industrial policy.

* 6.172 *
Warnecke, Steven J. "The American Steel Industry and International Competition." In: *The International Politics of Surplus Capacity*, edited by Susan Strange and Roger Tooze. London: Allen & Unwin, 1981. ISBN 0-04-382034-4.

Warnecke discusses the trigger price mechanism that was instituted in the United States as a protectionist measure. He also discusses the various domestic groups that sought such protection.

* 6.173 *
Williams, Harold R. "U.S. Measures to Relieve Injury Caused by Import Competition: The Eligibility Test." *Journal of World Trade Law* 12: 1 (January/February 1978): 27-35.

The possibilities for relief from import competition are so general that protection is easy to attain. The escape clause provision should have a more demanding test. There should also be a mechanism by which such protection can be denied if it conflicts with broader U.S. economic or political interests.

* 6.174 *
Yoffie, David B. "Orderly Marketing Agreements as an Industrial Policy: The Case of the Footwear Industry." *Public Policy* 29:1 (Winter 1981): 93-119.

Orderly marketing arrangements are one of the least effective economic tools to use, yet the United States relies on them in many cases. The use of this mechanism, as demonstrated in the case of footwear, provides little protection, nor do they facilitate the necessary economic adjustments in the domestic industry.

PROTECTIONISM AND THE OTHER INDUSTRIALIZED STATES

Protectionism has increased in virtually all other developed countries, just as it has in the United States. The justifications for the increased use of obstacles to imports in these countries are similar to those that are invoked in the United States. In Europe and Japan, pressure from interest groups for relief from economic distress has usually been effective and governments have responded with increased measures of protection.

Approximately three-quarters of the world exports of all goods originate in the developed countries, and much of this trade occurs between these industrialized states. There is also trade between the developing countries and the developed ones as well as between the centrally planned economies in Eastern Europe and the free market economies of the West. These trade links combine to give the industrialized states, as a group, a central place in the international trade regime; thus, the other industrialized countries in the world--Canada, Japan, Australia, New Zealand, and the various European nations--are very significant participants in the international economy. Therefore, their activities are important for the future levels of protectionism in the world economy. These countries have faced many of the same problems and political pressures that have been present in the United States, and many of the same responses have been made to import competition and the threat of higher levels of unemployment and job losses. Increases in protectionism in these states, as a consequence of these factors, have had impacts on the other countries involved in international trade. Japan, Canada, and the West European countries have also been important participants in the various multilateral negotiations on trade liberalization, as well as many of the important bilateral negotiations.

The Increase in Protectionism

Protectionism has increased in virtually all other developed countries, just as it has in the United States. The reasons for the increased use of obstacles to imports in these countries are similar to the ones that affected the United States. The governments in these countries still generally favor free trade in principle, but domestic considerations have limited their ability to avoid supplying protection. The recessions of the 1970s put pressure on governments in these countries to preserve jobs in threatened industries at a time when the total world market for particular goods was remaining static or declining. The result was greater political efforts to save the domestic market for domestic firms and their workers, particularly as the unemployment levels started to rise.

Protection has been utilized as a solution for a number of reasons. There are exaggerated public fears of job losses, the popularity of protection, fear of the effects of cheap foreign wages, the geographical or sectoral impacts of imports, and the belief that other states are using unfair trade practices. Trade restrictions also can be more quickly put into place than can other policy alternatives. In addition, once one industry receives protection, other industries find it easier to gain similar benefits.[1] Governments in democratic countries are likely to be responsive to such pressures, particularly in election years. In the past, changes in business cycles have corresponded to changes in the levels of protection present in different countries. When business activity has declined, protection has increased while upsurges in business in a country have often been matched by declines in protection, at least for some countries in some time periods.[2]

Pressures from interest groups in various countries have usually been effective in one fashion or the other. Governments have either responded with higher tariffs or have provided subsidies and other transfer payments to the groups being adversely affected by import penetration.[3] The fact that unions are stronger in Europe than in the United States and that they are often directly or indirectly affiliated with labor, social democratic, or socialist parties has allowed the unions to enter directly into government decision-making processes. Since 1945, these parties have been represented in government cabinets, either alone or in coalition, in virtually all the European countries, Australia, and New Zealand, for at least part of the time. While their influence has varied depending upon the size of their legislative representation, their opportunity to present union objectives has been clear. Since preservation of the voting bases of these parties in forthcoming elections is a major goal of their leaders, demands for limits on import competition are more likely to lead to protectionist programs. Political parties may be responsive to particular industries, agricultural interests, or particular regions. Just as individual members of Congress in the United States may lose votes by favoring free trade and gain virtually none by doing so because of the diffuse nature of the benefits of free trade, so may individual parties in other countries suffer a loss

of voting support if they fail to protect certain industries or regions without any counterbalancing electoral gains from other segments of the society.

The democratic settings in the developed countries have provided a situation in which interest groups have become increasingly effective in eliciting protectionist responses from governments. With respect to some declining industries, such as steel, textiles, and shipbuilding, the pressure has increased because the industries are primarily owned by nation states rather than by multinational corporations. The domestic implications of potential plant closings and job losses in national industries are felt acutely in the individual countries. The level of trade obstacles that are erected as a result depends to some extent upon the political strength of the affected industries vis-a-vis other sectors.

In complex economies, different industries take differing views on protection as a consequence of their particular product lines. Those that have retained a comparative advantage over firms in other countries will be opposed to protection while those losing their comparative advantage will push for limits on imports. The increase in the levels of protection in the industrialized states has often been directed against Japan and the NICs. Exports from these countries have threatened national industries, such as steel, textiles, and shipbuilding, in many cases. A potentially more important long-term result of protectionist measures directed against these states is that the obstacles, which were created and formerly applied to protect specific industries, have increasingly become general impediments to trade from these countries as they are seen to be displacing other states as major exporters in many and varied product lines.[4] Viewing the threat as a total one rather than a sectoral one indicates that there may be an increasing reliance on protection that will continue even in times of expansion in the world economy.

Comparisons of Developed Countries

There have been a number of comparisons of the levels of protection applied by particular developed states. These comparisons have included the United States, Japan, individual European countries, and the EC as a body. They have usually been comparisons of the relative tariff levels, but they have included at times NTBs and other policies undertaken to deal with import competition. The United States has often had lower levels of tariffs and NTBs than most other countries. This tendency towards lower barriers to trade, as well as fewer programs such as adjustment policies for industries affected by import competition, holds true across a variety of industrial sectors. Evidence of the relatively low levels of protection for the United

States is not surprising given the U.S. advocacy of freer trade in the years after World War II. Among other states, the United Kingdom and Canada have also followed relatively liberal trade policies in comparison with other industrialized states.

Japan has been found to have relatively high barriers in such comparisons; in fact they have often been among the highest. In the European states the barriers to protection vary, usually being higher than those for the United States and lower than those found for Japan. France has had some of the higher levels relative to other countries and has even approached the Japanese levels in some instances. Germany and the Netherlands have usually been more favorable to the idea of trade liberalization, and the smaller European countries have generally had fewer barriers to trade than the larger ones. Many of the European states have been particularly concerned about the steel, shipbuilding, and textile industries; they have been more prone than the United States to use adjustment assistance, subsidies, cartels, and market-sharing, and other NTBs to prevent or cushion declines in these industries. Even though different countries have had different levels of effective protection, in many cases the studies have found that there have been great similarities in the types of responses to import competition that have been made. The same industries are often protected, and many of the same mechanisms are used. In many respects, the differences between the various industrialized states are often a matter of degree rather than of kind in many situations.

Canada

Canada is a relatively small economy in the world, having a smaller population than most other developed countries. Its small economic size has influenced attitudes towards protection in a number of ways. Industries have often had to compete for markets in other countries to reach productive economies of scale. To the extent that particular firms or industries are involved in production for foreign markets, increases in protectionism in other states constitute a very real economic threat. As a result, if Canada institutes protectionist barriers in areas unrelated to these firms or industries, there is still concern about the possibility of retaliation abroad.

The development over time of Canadian manufacturing, however, has led to the emergence of many industries that produce only for the domestic market behind the protection of relatively high tariff walls. Canadian trade liberalization and tariff reductions would lead to a situation in which they would be non-competitive in the face of imports originating in countries where there was a larger domestic market base. The various industries that would be hurt by such freer trade have been effective in lobbying for protection in many cases, as has been reflected in the national tariff schedules. As in other industrialized states, Canada's labor intensive industries facing import competition have often received the greatest protection. Also, even though Canadian barriers to trade have not been generally high, as a consequence of the existence of some protected domestic sectors, Canada has not been a major proponent of multilateral tariff reductions. There has been some government efforts to rationalize and concentrate firms in such sectors to make them more competitive domestically and internationally. Even with these efforts, however, the overall Canadian view towards trade liberalization remains ambivalent given the fact that any change distributes important costs to some sectors of the economy and grants benefits to other parts.

An issue particularly important to Canada has been trade relations with the United States, which is the largest single market for Canadian exports. Higher protection in the United States would have major repercussions on the Canadian economy. Because of its size, Canada is not as important a market for U.S. exports, even though it is still an important market for American products. Thus, the economic size of Canada is a disadvantage in trade negotiations with its larger neighbor in many situations. The two countries have established some agreements for the relatively free flow of goods between them, and this free trade appears to have been beneficial. There have been discussions of creating a free trade area between the United States and Canada. In the mid-1980s, the Canadian government announced its intention to bilaterally seek to reduce trade barriers between the two countries, and early in 1988 a preliminary agreement for creating a free trade area was reached.

Not every analyst believes that such trade would be beneficial to Canada. Even those who think that such free trade could benefit both economies still project more difficulties for Canada since it is the smaller economy and would face proportionally greater impacts. A number of government programs would be necessary to lessen the negative effects of free trade and to deal with the problems of the smaller manufacturing sectors. Such policies could involve the use of non-tariff forms of protection, but these have already been a cause of disagreement between the two countries, and U.S. retaliation against Canadian exports in selected areas has occurred. While interaction and trade between the two countries is too high to render large increases in protection directed at each other likely, movement toward freer trade will be slow even if the agreement on a free-trade area is ratified. If both countries do increase their obstacles to imports, it will more likely be directed toward third countries rather than each other.

Japan

Since Japan has become one of the major economic powers in the world, many of the issues involving protectionist practices have centered on it. Japanese exports have faced many barriers in other developed states during the course of Japan's rise to the status of a major exporter. Japanese firms have captured markets from exporters in other developed countries, and they have penetrated the domestic markets of many industrialized states. The VERs that the United States has imposed on Japanese automobiles and electronics have been matched by similar actions in many European states. Japanese efforts to reduce these obstacles to their exports have been one of the major points of contention in international negotiations.

Japan has also had charges of unfair trading practices leveled against it by other states. The Ministry of International Trade and Industry (MITI) has been responsible for putting together economic plans for Japanese industry. It designates industries that will be developed so that they may become internationally competitive in certain product lines. Firms in the selected industries are given government assistance in the form of subsidies, low interest loans, guaranteed shares of exports, preferential access to foreign supplies, and other types of assistance. These types of activities have caused concern in those states facing competition from the resulting exports. The management of trade by the government has been seen in other countries as constituting an unfair trade practice since competing firms in those countries have difficulties in matching the resources available to MITI and the Japanese government.

The presence of an overall planning agency for industry, MITI, has also permitted the government to apportion export shares among firms effectively when quotas and export restraints are put into place. This apportionment permits all the relevant firms to maintain economies of scale and productivity.

The challenges that Japan has presented to other developed countries have been exacerbated by the fact that Japan has been able to continue to export during the recession of the 1970s. There have been fewer domestic pressures as a result, although they have not been totally absent. Japan has also introduced fewer new barriers to trade since existing mechanisms were already in place to limit access to the domestic market. Japan has normally been seen as having a highly protected domestic market. While tariffs have been progressively lowered through time as a result of multi-lateral negotiations, they have been generally high in comparison with other countries. There have been a significant number of NTBs to imports in Japan. In the 1960s, a great many such obstacles were imposed as Japan was making a concerted effort to build up selected industries that would be capable of exporting to world markets. The protection of the domestic market was necessary to give the firms the opportunity to develop products within the framework of a guaranteed domestic market. Similar types of protection have been accorded the new high technology industries that have appeared in recent years. Other industries have benefited from NTBs, even when they have not been oriented toward foreign markets. As in other industrialized states, labor intensive industries have often been protected to avoid higher levels of unemployment, although the Japanese pattern has often been to provide protection within a framework of gradual reductions of the levels of production in these areas for domestic consumption and slowly permitting penetration by imports.

There are a variety of obstacles to imports that exist in Japan. Labeling and marketing requirements often prevent or discourage foreign firms from exporting to Japan. Japanese firms often follow a policy of buying only from certain other domestic firms that they have connections with, effectively discriminating against foreign suppliers as well as other domestic companies.[5] These obstacles may not prevent a major effort on the part of foreign firms to capture part of the Japanese market, but they do make a gradual penetration much more difficult given the high costs involved. Government purchasing policies and the preference of government and quasi-government firms for domestic goods instead of foreign products also limit imports significantly. The United States has used direct government-to-government negotiations to attempt to gain shares of purchases for U.S. firms from such corporations.[6] The economic planning of MITI that facilitates exports can also provide guaranteed shares of the domestic market to indigenous firms, at the expense of imports.

MITI has opened the domestic market to imports in areas where the Japanese comparative advantage has clearly been disappearing. These product areas, however, are ones in which the NICs and the other developing countries are competitive, not the other industrialized countries. While this type of openness belies the picture of a closed domestic market, it has its limitations. It does not provide much of an opportunity for exports from the other developed countries. Areas in which these states might be competitive with domestic Japanese firms are the ones in which obstacles to imports remain. The developed countries gain advantages only in those areas where the government has decided to permit import penetration. As in other developed states, Japan's tariff structure and other barriers to trade often tend to discriminate against products with higher degrees of processing to the disadvantage of many of the new industries present in the developing countries.

The United Kingdom

The United Kingdom has generally favored free trade through the years. To some extent this preference could be a carry-over of attitudes from the past when it was one of the premier economic powers in the world, a time when free trade was to its benefit. Even though it is no longer the leading economic power in the international economy, trade does remain important to the United Kingdom. It must import agricultural goods and raw materials and export manufactured products in exchange. As a consequence, the liberalization of trade and its maintenance has often been important for the country, even if its ability to compete for markets internationally has diminished. The decline of the United Kingdom as a trader became obvious in the years after World War II when it lost markets elsewhere in the world and when its domestic industries faced greater import competition with the resultant loss of productive capacity and jobs. Still, in many respects, the freer movement of goods is more important economically to the United Kingdom than to the United States given the limited British capacity for economic self-sufficiency. The decision to enter the EC is another indication of the country's need to have access to markets and materials outside its borders.

Notwithstanding the general free trade orientation that has been present in the United Kingdom, concerns over declining industries and unemployment have led to increasing domestic demands for protection. Some efforts have been made on behalf of particular industries and greater protectionism has indeed appeared in the country. NTBs have been of increasing importance as in other countries. Regional development policies, export subsidies, and quotas have been among the mechanisms that have provided some aid to domestic firms. Arguments have also been made for the broader application of protectionist measures. A group of economists at Cambridge University, the Cambridge Economic Policy Group or CEPG, has been particularly active in arguing for the greater use of protection to benefit the British industrial position. Admission to the EC has not really changed this group's position on the need for protection. There has been little evidence, however, that when such protection has been applied that it has been effective in preventing continued industrial decline and job losses.

France

Among the European countries, France has traditionally followed a more protectionist approach towards trade. Because French industry often lagged behind Great Britain, the government sought to protect domestic industries from British imports. French farmers were also successful in gaining protection in many cases in these years. As a consequence, a pattern of state intervention to help domestic sectors facing import competition developed. This pattern has resulted in the continuation of active state involvement in favor of domestic interests into the present time. An associated pattern of accommodating various domestic interests threatened by import competition also developed. If one group received benefits, other groups would be granted similar protection. More recently, French interest in protectionism has been fueled by competition not only in old industries such as textiles where competition from new states such as the NICs has appeared, but by competition, from some of the same countries, in more advanced industries where a developed state was expected to have been able to maintain its comparative advantage.

France has often been compared to Japan with respect to the types of state management and intervention used to provide at least some relief for domestic producers facing import competition. Although the cultural settings have been quite different, there are similarities between the two countries in the role of the state and the operation of key bureaucratic agencies and experts. France like Japan has been particularly active in the use of a variety of non-tariff obstacles such as subsidies, cartels, and bilateral trade arrangements. The increasing number of nationally owned companies in the state has also facilitated the indirect limitation of imports that threaten domestic interests. France has also been one of the major proponents of creating European industries that could compete effectively with U.S. and Japanese firms in the same product lines. These efforts have often included preferential purchases by the French government. As a member of the EC, France has been one of the members that has sought to maintain greater obstacles to outside imports into the Community. It has been the country most supportive of the Common Agricultural Policy (to be discussed in Chapter 9). It also raised questions concerning the admission of Greece into full membership in the EC since Greek membership would set a precedent for Spanish and Portuguese membership. While Greece presented no major threat to French domestic interests, potential Spanish and Portuguese competition would create difficulties for local producers.[7]

Other Industrialized Countries

The other developed countries have shown a mixed pattern of attitudes toward protectionism. All of them have made some efforts to protect threatened domestic industries, and such efforts have increased in the face of the economic recession of the 1970s. Germany has generally favored and supported trade liberalization in many areas and has often been a proponent of lowering trade barriers in the EC. The German view is congruent with the fact that German products are internationally competitive in many industries. Greater restrictions on global trade would undoubtedly hurt German export industries more than it would help those sectors threatened by import competition. Even so, in the later 1970s there was some movement towards greater protectionism in those industries facing increased import competition.

Italy, on the other hand, has taken a more protectionist stance within the EC. It is an exporter of many goods to the other EC countries, such as footwear, luggage, textiles, and apparel, where there is increasing competition from the NICs and other developing countries. The Italian comparative advantage within the EC would be lost if that common market were opened to imports from other countries. Similarly, concern for existing advantages within the EC also led to an ambivalent Italian attitude toward the enlargement of the EC to include Spain, Portugal, and Greece since these countries could provide competition for domestic producers in agricultural and some manufacturing areas.

The other, smaller European countries have generally been less protectionist. They have followed more liberal trade policies since international trade is particularly important to their overall economies. It is more important for them than for many larger states that produce more of their needs domestically. Greater protectionism in the world is likely to hurt them more than other countries given their reliance on trade. They have normally been in favor of reducing tariffs and of limiting the impacts of NTBs as well.[8] They have also been rather consistent supporters of the GATT efforts at trade liberalization. GATT is important for these smaller countries since they are not normally in a position to win in a disagreement with larger countries should protectionist conflicts develop. The smaller states are likely to need the larger country's market much more than the larger country is likely to need theirs. The smaller European economies also have relatively low levels of protection and even government policies such as

purchasing preferences and regional programs that could normally constitute significant NTBs seem not to have constituted major obstacles in most cases.

The Costs of Protectionism

Although various developed states have relied on protectionist barriers in different degrees, there has been a general increase in their use in recent years with concomitant costs to consumers. The costs of protection, however, are only one factor to be considered in making national policies for complex economies. It has to be recognized that some of the costs are borne in order to accomplish other policy objectives in the countries in question. The present costs of protection, however, are highlighted by the fact that trade liberalization in earlier periods facilitated growth in many European countries. In the case of Japan, the economy could not have grown as rapidly as it did without access to the markets in other countries. Into the early 1970s, the country seen as most likely to gain from freer trade was still Japan. The United States and many of the smaller European countries would also gain from trade liberalization, although there would be adjustment costs that would have to be met.

The United Kingdom and New Zealand were among the states that would face the need for greater adjustments.[9] These adjustment costs resulting from freer trade in the case of the United Kingdom no doubt played a role in that country's lessened commitment to trade liberalization. More recent analyses have suggested that trade liberalization would still benefit the industrialized states and that the increasing resort to protectionist practices has direct costs that do not offset the benefits. There are also indications that in the other developed countries, as in the United States, the industries receiving the protection are not likely to recover. Thus, there are not only higher costs involved, but the efforts to preserve particular sectors of the domestic economy from the effects of import competition are not likely to succeed. Import penetration has often continued, although sometimes at a lower level.

End Notes

1. Blackhurst, Richard, Nicolas Marian, and Jan Tumlir. *Adjustment, Trade and Growth in Developed and Developing Countries*. GATT Studies in International Trade no.6. Geneva: General Agreement on Tariffs and Trade, September 1978: pp.63-64.

2. Gallaroti, Guido M. "Toward a Business-Cycle

Model of Tariffs," *International Organization* 39:1 (Winter 1985): pp.155-187.

3. Blais, Andre. "The Political Economy of Public Subsidies," *Comparative Political Studies* 19:2 (July 1986): pp. 201-216.

4. Kahler, Miles. "European Protectionism in Theory and Practice," *World Politics* 37:4 (July 1985): p.493.

5. Bergsten, C. Fred, and William R. Cline. *The United States-Japan Economic Problem.* Policy Analyses in International Economics no.13. Washington, DC: Institute for International Economics, 1985: p.9.

6. Curran, Timothy J. "Politics and High Technology: The NTT Case," In: *Coping with U.S.-Japanese Economic Conflicts*, edited by I. M. Destler and Hideo Sato. Lexington, MA: Lexington Books, 1982: pp.185-241.

7. Wallace, William. "Grand Gestures and Second Thoughts: The Response of Member Countries to Greece's Application." In: *Greece and the European Community*, edited by Loukas Tsoukalis. Westmead, England: Saxon House, 1979: pp.21-38.

8. Katzenstein, Peter J. "The Small European States in the International Economy: Economic Dependence and Corporatist Politics." In: *The Antinomies of Interdependence: National Welfare and the International Division of Labor*, edited by John Gerard Ruggie. New York: Columbia University Press, 1983: pp.91-130.

9. Hawkins, Robert G. and Rita M. Rodriguez. "Potential Economic Benefits and Costs of Adjustments in Trade Liberalization," In: *The United States and International Markets: Commercial Policy Options in an Age of Controls*, edited by Robert G. Hawkins and Ingo Walter. Lexington, MA: Lexington Books, 1972: p. 193-227.

Chapter 7: Annotated Bibliography

General Works

* 7.1 *

Aharoni, Yair. *The No-Risk Society*. Chatham, NJ: Chatham House, 1981. ISBN 0-934-54007-1.

Aharoni's basic theme is that in developed countries efforts are increasingly made to eliminate threats to the economic livelihood of individuals--in effect, the creation of a no-risk society. Protectionism is considered, particularly in Chapter 6, in the context of this broader perspective in which risk and incentive are seen to be reduced.

* 7.2 *

Costa, Antonio Maria. "The Pressure Towards Protectionism: Is It Systemic? A Legacy of the Recession? The Result of Policy to Promote Recovery?" *World Development* 12:10 (October 1984): 1051-1061.

The pressure for protectionism in the developed countries is partially structural, resulting from difficulties in their economies. Global recession has contributed to this pressure. New protectionist efforts have the effect of often discriminating against smaller traders such as the developing countries.

* 7.3 *

Cuddington, John. "Import Substitution Policies: A Two-Sector, Fix-Price Model." *Review of Economic Studies* 48 (April 1981): 327-342.

Cuddington's model analyzes the effect of import substitution policies via protection on employment. The impact of such protection varies, depending upon the cause of such unemployment, and these causes must be taken into account before import substitution policies are applied as a possible corrective.

* 7.4 *

Cuddington, John T., and Ronald I. McKinnon. "Free Trade versus Protectionism: A Perspective." In: *Tariffs, Quotas, and Trade: The Politics of Protectionism*, edited by the Institute for Contemporary Studies. San Francisco: The Institute, 1979. ISBN 0-917-616-34-0.

The authors provide a useful overview of the arguments for free trade and protectionism. They discuss the domestic factors leading to governmental decisions favoring either free trade or protectionism with particular reference to the United Kingdom in the mid-nineteenth century and the United States in the twentieth century.

* 7.5 *

Hieronymi, Otto. "The New Economic Nationalism."
In: *The New Economic Nationalism*, edited by Otto
Hieronymi. London: Macmillan, 1980. ISBN
0-333-26173-9.

Floating exchange rates and protectionism
are both manifestations of governmental efforts
to isolate national economies from external occur-
rences. The return to economic nationalism can
only be prevented by establishing a new consensus
among the leading industrialized states.

* 7.6 *

Keesing, Donald B., and Martin Wolf. *Textile
Quotas against Developing Countries*. Thames Essay
no. 23. London: Trade Policy Research Centre,
1980. ISBN 0-900-84249-0.

The authors discuss both tariff and non-tariff
barriers that have been instituted to limit imports
of textiles from developing countries. They review
the arguments for protection and the consequences
of protection, concluding that the threats of imports are exaggerated, that the preservation of
the industries cannot be completely identified with
national interests, and that the protectionist measures used are not efficient, appropriate, or justified.

* 7.7 *

Olson, Mancur. *The Rise and Decline of Nations:
Economic Growth, Stagflation, and Social Rigidities*.
New Haven: Yale University Press, 1982. ISBN
0-300-03079-7.

In his discussion of the influence of interest
groups on economic decisions in nations, Olson
considers a number of issues relevant to trade.
He notes that the creation of nation-states was
very important in ensuring intra-national trade
in integrated markets. While protectionism between
nations is less important than national integration,
freer trade does facilitate growth for states prac-
ticing it, though the operation of interest groups
can lead to protection.

* 7.8 *

Page, S. A. B. "The Revival of Protectionism and
Its Consequences for Europe." *Journal of Common
Market Studies* 20:1 (September 1981): 17-40.

Page details the increasing use of a wide variety of non-tariff barriers in Europe to limit imports, with food, textiles and clothing, and later
steel having been the products most protected.
She provides calculations of the percentage of the
trade of various countries that was controlled in
some fashion in 1974, and proposes several reasons
for the growth of protectionism.

* 7.9 *

Sohn, Ira, and Nicola Mandarino. "Unemployment
or Protectionism: Some Choices for the USA and
Western Europe to the Year 2000." *Economic Mod-
elling* 1:2 (April 1984): 252-261.

Input-output analysis is used to determine
and predict the tradeoffs between protectionism,
employment levels, consumption, and balance of
payments for the United States, Western Europe,
Japan, and the non-resource rich developing countries.
The results have to be considered as tentative given
the high level of aggregation and the use of the
input-output coefficients from the United States
for the other countries or groups of countries.
The model does predict that protectionism will
lead to at least initial declines in levels of employment.

* 7.10 *

Witte, Willard E. "Protectionism and the Case for
Flexible Exchange Rates: A Reexamination." *International Trade Journal* 1:3 (Spring 1987): 251-275.

Efforts to maintain flexible exchange rates
are one contributing factor to the use of protectionism. Fixed rates, on the other hand, will help
offset movement toward protectionism.

The Increase in Protectionism

* 7.11 *

Arndt, Sven W. "Issues in U.S. Economic Relations
with Western Europe." *Annals of the Academy of
Political and Social Sciences* 460 (March 1982):
101-110.

Although the United States and Western Europe
have gained from trade liberalization, recent policies
including the use of non-tariff barriers and state
companies, have hindered trade. Domestic political
pressures leading to protectionism have introduced
structural rigidities in the economies on both sides
of the Atlantic.

* 7.12 *

Bhagwati, Jagdish N. "Shifting Comparative Advantage, Protectionist Demands, and Policy Responses."
In: *Import Competition and Response: A Conference
Report of the National Bureau of Economic Research*,
edited by Jagdish N. Bhagwati. Chicago: University
of Chicago Press, 1982. ISBN 0-226-04538-2.

In an intriguing essay, Bhagwati suggests two
types of industries that might lobby for protection-
-traditional, labor intensive industries such as textiles
facing competition from developing states and advanced industries threatened by technological change
that gives a competitive edge to other nations.
He presents a model of labor immigration as one
method of dealing with the first case instead of

tariff protection. In the second case he details some of the factors that have led to protectionism.

* 7.13 *
Blackhurst, Richard, Nicolas Marian, and Jan Tumlir. *Adjustment, Trade and Growth in Developed and Developing Countries*. GATT Studies in International Trade no. 6. Geneva: General Agreement on Tariffs and Trade, 1978.

In considering the various adjustment policies in the developed states, the authors note several reasons why protection against imports has been adopted. Among the reasons are public exaggeration of the effects of imports on worker displacement, the speed with which trade restrictions can be put into place compared to other policies, the popularity of protectionism, the belief that other countries use unfair trade practices, the spread of demands for protectionism after one industry receives it, fear of cheap foreign wages in the developing countries, and the geographical or sectoral concentration of problems resulting from import competition.

* 7.14 *
Blais, Andre. "The Political Economy of Public Subsidies." *Comparative Political Studies* 19: 2 (July 1986): 201-216.

One factor leading to increased government subsidies in eighteen developed nations was the presence of a low tariff structure. The analysis indicates that in democratic countries political pressure for protection will lead to response in some area, be it higher tariffs or transfer payments.

* 7.15 *
Carliner, Geoffrey. "Industrial Policies for Emerging Industries." In: *Strategic Trade Policy and the New International Economics*, edited by Paul R. Krugman. Cambridge, MA: MIT Press, 1987. ISBN 0-262-11112-8.

There are valid reasons for supporting emerging, high technology industries in the developed countries. Choosing the appropriate industries to protect, the costs to consumers and other industry sectors of the industries' products, the possible elimination of competition, and the creation of industries before the economy can support them are possible pitfalls of such a policy.

* 7.16 *
Diebold, William, Jr. "Adapting Economics to Structural Change: The International Aspect." *International Affairs* (London) 54:4 (October 1978): 573-588.

Diebold analyzes the industrial structure of developed states in the context of a changing global economy. He pinpoints a number of areas where problems have led to increased protectionist pressure.

* 7.17 *
Dymsza, William A. "Trends in Multinational Business and Global Environments: A Perspective." *Journal of International Business Studies* 15:3 (Winter 1984): 25-46.

Protectionism, particularly non-tariff barriers, has threatened the liberal trading system, led to problems for developing countries in debt service, and limited further economic integration in the European Community. U.S. labor unions have pressured multinational firms for more investment in manufacturing facilities in the United States and have sought protection as well.

* 7.18 *
Gallaroti, Giulio M. "Toward a Business-Cycle Model of Tariffs." *International Organization* 39:1 (Winter 1985): 155-187.

An analysis of tariff structures in the United States, and Germany between 1800 and 1914 finds that increases or reductions in tariffs corresponded to changes in the business cycle in the United States and Germany quite well but somewhat less so in the United Kingdom. A business cycle model would be perhaps most predictive of tariff changes in a democracy in an election year, but such a model for the present day would have to take into account the impact of non-tariff barriers.

* 7.19 *
Hindley, Brian, and Eri Nicolaides. *Taking the New Protectionism Seriously*. Thames Essay no. 34. London: Trade Policy Research Centre, 1983. ISBN 0-900842-63-6.

The weakening of GATT and the rise of the new protectionism threatens the international trading system. Politicians in the developed states are under greater domestic pressures to serve their constituents by limiting import competition. Protectionism in one country inevitably leads to protection in others.

* 7.20 *
Jones, Kent Albert. *Politics versus Economics in World Steel Trade*. Winchester, MA: Allen and Unwin, 1986. ISBN 0-04-338118-9.

Jones analyzes the background to the crisis in the world steel industry and the protectionist policies adopted in the industrialized states. The economic and political causes leading to protectionism are also detailed, although such protectionism has generally failed to prevent declines in the various national industries.

* 7.21 *

Kahler, Miles. "European Protectionism in Theory and Practice." *World Politics* 37:4 (July 1985): 457-502.

Kahler analyzes the differences and similarities of various European countries in their views toward protectionism. He notes that there is movement towards general protection and away from measures designed to deal with the problems of particular industries or economic sectors. Japan and the NICs have often been the stimulus for this movement towards generalized protection.

* 7.22 *

Kimbrough, Kent. "Commercial Policy and Aggregate Employment under Rational Expectations." *Quarterly Journal of Economics* 99:3 (August 1984): 567-585.

Protectionism as a part of commercial policy can have an effect on employment and workers' attitudes. Protection is unlikely to be effective in gaining time for industrial readjustment since workers will seek wage protection and its positive effect on wage levels. The author cautions that because commercial policy can be used to affect employment levels is not an argument that it should be so used.

* 7.23 *

Krueger, Anne O. "LDC Manufacturing Production and Implications for OECD Comparative Advantage." In: *Western Economies in Transition: Structural Change and Adjustment Policies in Industrial Countries*, edited by Irving Leveson and Jimmy W. Wheeler. Boulder, CO: Westview, 1980. ISBN 0-891-58589-3.

Krueger discusses the shifts in comparative advantage that have led to increased exports of manufactures from developing countries. She argues that pressure for protectionism in the developed states is overstated. Periods in which there are higher growth rates made adjustments to these imports easier to achieve than is the case in times of stagnation.

* 7.24 *

Kurth, James R. "The Political Consequences of the Product Cycle: Industrial History and Political Outcomes." *International Organization* 33:1 (Winter 1979): 1-34.

In the past when most industries in a country were at the same production stage, government could more easily influence the product cycle by domestic action. Today such government activities are variable, depending on the relative political strengths of industries at various stages of the cycle. Those in early stages will have distinctly different demands than those in later stages. The

outcome of the resulting domestic political conflicts will determine to what extent government interventions such as tariffs, quotas, and subsidies will occur in attempts to retard the effects of changing production patterns.

* 7.25 *

Lowe, Anthony. "Responses of a Multinational Corporation to the Problem of Surplus Capacity." In: *The International Politics of Surplus Capacity*, edited by Susan Strange and Roger Tooze. London: Allen & Unwin, 1981. ISBN 0-04-382034-4.

Multinational corporations with their global perspective often oppose protectionism since it interferes with rational utilization of multi-country facilities. National firms are more likely to favor protectionism, particularly in times of surplus capacity.

* 7.26 *

Malmgren, Harald B. "Trade Policies of the Developed Countries for the Next Decade." In: *The New International Economic Order: The North-South Debate*, edited by Jagdish N. Bhagwati. Cambridge, MA: MIT Press, 1977. ISBN 0-262-52042-7.

Non-tariff barriers and export assistance programs in the developed states have created major market distortions. Uncertainty about the future level of trade liberalization contributes to market distortions. Malmgren argues not so much for an open trading system but for one where there is greater order and certainty.

* 7.27 *

Norbye, Ole David Koht. "Industrial Policies of Rich Countries and Market Access for LDC Manufactures." In: *Commodities, Finance and Trade: Issues in North-South Negotiations*, edited by Arjun Sengupta. Contributions in Economics and Economic History no. 30. Westport, CT: Greenwood Press, 1980. ISBN 0-313-21468-7.

The developed countries are more likely to give favorable market access to manufactures from the developing countries in times of rapid economic growth. During periods of economic difficulties, democratic governments in the developed states will not be able to permit the free entry of imports. Both the developed and developing states will have to compromise on trade issues in the face of these difficulties.

* 7.28 *

Stein, Leslie. "General Measures to Assist Workers and Firms in Adjusting to Injury from Freer Trade: Issues Raised by Various European Approaches and Some ad hoc Industry Measures Adopted Elsewhere." *American Journal of Economics and Sociology* 42:3 (July 1983): 315-327.

Schemes in Europe, North America, and Oceania that help workers in industries adversely affected by imports have had varying degrees of success. Some have, in effect, been clearly protectionist. Such programs have not even been necessarily successful in easing domestic pressure for further protectionist measures.

* 7.29 *
Strange, Susan. "The Management of Surplus Capacity: Or How Does Theory Stand Up to Protectionism 1970s Style?" *International Organization* 33:3 (Summer 1979): 303-334.

The appearance of surplus production capacity, particularly in the steel, textiles, and shipbuilding industries, has produced conflicts among states and generated protectionist responses in the affected countries. The state-to-state conflict is exacerbated because these three industries, as opposed to the automobile industry for example, are primarily national industries rather than multinational ones. Market sharing arrangements have been tried, but they are inherently unstable and have not stood the test of time.

* 7.30 *
Tumlir, Jan. "The New Protectionism, Cartels, and the International Order." In: *Challenges to a Liberal International Order; A Conference Sponsored by the American Enterprise Institute for Public Policy Research*, edited by Ryan C. Amacher, Gottfried Haberler, and Thomas D. Willett. Washington, DC: American Enterprise Institute for Public Policy Research, 1979. ISBN 0-8447-2152-2.

The new protectionism has arisen in part because political life in democracies consists largely of politicians making promises to organized groups. Among the proponents of protectionist policies in the developed states have been cartels, particularly in the steel and shipbuilding industries, that are threatened by competitors in Japan and the developing countries. Although cartels in these sectors have often been only marginally effective in providing protection, they have raised the final costs to consumers.

* 7.31 *
Wetter, Theresa. "Trade Policy Developments in the Steel Sector." *Journal of World Trade Law* 19:5 (September/October 1985): 485-496.

The rise of protectionism in the steel industries of the industrialized states reflects problems present in the world trading system. Managed trade has come to be the norm, with decreasing regard for the comparative advantages of different states. Bilateral arrangements have also been on the increase.

* 7.32 *
Williamson, Peter J. "Multinational Enterprise Behavior and Domestic Industry Adjustment under Import Threat." *Review of Economics and Statistics* 68:3 (August 1986): 359-368.

Data on subsidiaries of multinational firms in the United States and Australia indicate that they adapt more readily to import competition than domestic firms. Such multinationals are also more likely to favor free trade as a result.

Comparisons of Developed Countries

* 7.33 *
Anthony, David V., and Carol K. Hagerty. "Cautious Optimism as a Guide to Foreign Government Procurement." *Law and Policy in International Business* 11:4 (1979): 1301-1343.

The authors analyze GATT's Code on Government Procurement and conclude that it will provide opportunities for U.S. firms. They also provide a useful comparison of some of the purchasing practices often used in various developed states.

* 7.34 *
Arpan, Jeffrey S., Jose de la Torre, and Brian Toyne. "International Developments and the U.S. Apparel Industry." *Journal of International Business Studies* 12:3 (Winter 1981): 49-64.

The U.S. apparel industry had had difficulties in exporting to other countries in part due to the presence of significant tariff and non-tariff barriers. The United States has offered less protection, as well as fewer incentives and less assistance, than many foreign governments.

* 7.35 *
Bollino, C. Andrea. "Industrial Policy: A Review of European Approaches." In: *Industrial Policies for Growth and Competitiveness: An Economic Perspective*, edited by F. Gerard Adams and Lawrence R. Klein. Lexington, MA: Lexington Books, 1983. ISBN 0-669-05412-7.

The instruments available for industrial policy in Europe are quite varied. They do include protectionist measures, such as tariffs, quotas, subsidies and grants, and other non-tariff barriers.

* 7.36 *
Borrus, Michael, James E. Millstein, and John Zysman with Aton Arbisser and Daniel O'Neill. "Trade and Development in the Semiconductor Industry: Japanese Challenge and American Response." In: *American Industry in International Competition: Government Policies and Corporate Strategies*, edited by John Zysman and Laura Tyson. Ithaca, NY: Cornell University Press, 1983. ISBN 0-226-03604-9.

The government should support competitiveness in the U.S. semiconductor industry since this industry is important to other sectors and overall national comparative advantage. The Japanese government has supported its industry in a variety of ways, including protection limiting the entrance of imports and investments in the Japanese domestic market.

* 7.37 *
Conlon, R. M. "Transport Cost and Tariff Protection of Australian and Canadian Manufacturing: A Comparative Study." *Canadian Journal of Economics* 14:4 (November 1981): 700-707.

Conlon establishes that Australian industries derive greater protection from higher transport costs than Canadian firms and that they also have higher effective tariff protection. Even with these differences, however, the same industries that are relatively highly protected in Australia are also relatively highly protected in Canada.

* 7.38 *
De la Torre, Jose. "Public Intervention Strategies in the European Clothing Industries." *Journal of World Trade Law* 15:2 (March/April 1981): 124-148.

The author compares various adjustment policies of the European countries for the clothing industry. Efforts at job preservation have clearly failed. Market protection has been adopted as the easiest policy to implement, even though there are long-range disadvantages.

* 7.39 *
De la Torre, Jose, and Michel Bacchetta. "The Uncommon Market: European Policies Towards the Clothing Industry." *Journal of Common Market Studies* 19:2 (December 1980): 95-122.

The authors review various measures, including protectionist ones, taken to deal with declines in the clothing industry in European states. They argue that aid to a declining sector is a necessary social and economic function of governments and that the effort should be directed toward transferring resources to new economic areas.

* 7.40 *
Franko, Lawrence G. "Current Trends in Protectionism in Industrialized Countries: Focus on Western Europe." In: *Protectionism or Industrial Adjustment?* Atlantic Papers no. 39. Paris: Atlantic Institute for International Affairs, 1980.

Protectionism, already present in the mid-1970s, accelerated in Europe in the late 1970s. The new obstacles appeared to be directed more against other developed states and the socialist countries than the developing states. Subsidies are used in a variety of European states, in some cases in conjunction with other adjustment policies.

* 7.41 *
Godek, Paul E. "The Politically Optimal Tariff: Levels of Trade Restrictions across Developed Countries." *Economic Inquiry* 24:4 (October 1986): 587-593.

The level of trade restrictions present in developed countries is affected by the size of the country, level of government spending as a portion of GNP, and per capita income. Other government activities can substitute for tariffs but not for quotas.

* 7.42 *
Gourevitch, Peter Alexis. "International Trade, Domestic Coalitions, and Liberty: Comparative Responses to the Crisis of 1873-1896." *Journal of Interdisciplinary History* 8:2 (Autumn 1977): 281-313.

The author ascribes the responses of various major countries to the Great Depression of 1873-1896 to the goals of domestic interest groups. Economic characteristics of the countries and characteristics of their political systems combine to explain the actions taken. A state's position in the international system and economic ideology had little to add in explanatory power.

* 7.43 *
Hamilton, Carl. "Voluntary Export Restraints and Trade Diversion." *Journal of Common Market Studies* 23:4 (June 1985): 345-355.

The effects of voluntary export restraints on trade are compared for a number of European countries. Trade diversion in textiles and clothing was very evident for France and Sweden, somewhat evident for Italy and Germany, and not present for the United Kingdom.

* 7.44 *
Hughes, Helen. "The Political Economy of Protection in Eleven Industrial Countries." In: *Issues in World Trade Policy: GATT at the Crossroads*, edited by R. H. Snape. New York: St. Martin's, 1986. ISBN 0-312-43724-2.

Hughes considers the factors leading to a growth of protection in various developed countries and the types of measures used. The rise in protectionism has been particularly directed toward imports from the developing countries. She concludes that domestic lobbying for additional protection from import competition has been largely ineffective.

* 7.45 *
Katzenstein, Peter J. "Conclusion: Domestic Structures and Strategies of Foreign Economic Policy." *International Organization* 31:4 (Autumn 1977): 879-920.

Katzenstein compares the domestic structures and resulting foreign economic policies of the United States, Great Britain, France, Italy, Germany, and Japan. The historical development of the six states affected their domestic politics and institutions and the resultant economic policies. Japan is the most neo-mercantilist with protectionist policies, with the United States and Britain the least so, and the other European countries in the middle, although France is the closest to the Japanese case.

* 7.46 *

Mahon, Rianne, and Lynn Krieger Mytelka. "Industry, the State, and the New Protectionism: Textiles in Canada and France." *International Organization* 37:4 (Autumn 1983): 551-581.

The authors compare the governmental responses of Canada, a state favoring a liberal international economy, and France, a state that has been more oriented toward protectionism, to increasing competition to their domestic textile industries. Both countries followed mixed patterns of adjustment, increased efficiency in the sector, and some protectionist policies, notwithstanding different ownership patterns and the different previous state attitudes and industrial policies.

* 7.47 *

Mauer, Laurence Jay, and A. J. W. van de Gevel. "Non-Tariff Distortions in International Trade: A Methodological Review." In: *Prospects for Eliminating Non-Tariff Distortions*, edited by Anthony E. Scaperlanda. Leiden: A. W. Sijthoff, 1973. ISBN 90-286-0063-9.

Non-tariff barriers have increased as an alternative form of protection and as a flexible means of easing balance of payments difficulties. These barriers affect the exports of developing states more than the exports of developed ones. Japan and France had the highest levels of such barriers while the United States and the United Kingdom had the lowest among the developed countries.

* 7.48 *

McAleese, Dermot. "Do Tariffs Matter? Industrial Specialization and Trade in a Small Economy." *Oxford Economic Papers* n.s.29:1 (March 1977): 117-127.

A comparison of the trade of Northern Ireland and the Republic of Ireland, which had higher levels of protection, indicates that intra-industry specialization was much higher in Northern Ireland. The overall trade of the Republic did increase in the 1964-71 period after tariffs had been reduced.

* 7.49 *

McMullen, Neil, and Laura L. Megna. "Automobiles." In: *The Newly Industrializing Countries: Trade and Adjustment*, edited by Louis Turner and Neil McMullen. London: Allen & Unwin, 1982. ISBN 0-04-382036-0.

Trade in automobiles will decrease somewhat in the future as market saturation is reached, creating difficulties for the auto industries in the industrialized states. The United States and West European countries have tried a variety of adjustment policies and have also used protectionist measures. Except for Germany, European firms have received more government support in the form of subsidies and protection than U.S. firms.

* 7.50 *

Morici, Peter, and Laura L. Megna, with Sara N. Krulwich. *U.S. Economic Policies Affecting Industrial Trade: A Quantitative Assessment.* Washington, DC: National Planning Association, 1983. ISBN 0-89068-068.

The authors discuss the various non-tariff barriers used in the United States and compare the levels with those in other developed states. They find that U.S. non-tariff barriers provide less protection overall than those used in other countries, particularly Japan, France, and the United Kingdom.

* 7.51 *

Olechowski, Andrzej, and Gary Sampson. "Current Trade Restrictions in the EEC, the United States and Japan." *Journal of World Trade Law* 14:3 (May/June 1980): 220-231.

The authors compare the protection offered in Japan, the United States, and the EC. Tariffs are of declining importance, but non-tariff barriers provide real obstacles. Of those countries included by the authors, Japan has a lower incidence of non-tariff barriers. The developing countries are particularly affected by the obstacles that exist.

* 7.52 *

Organisation for Economic Co-Operation and Development. *Textile and Clothing Industries: Structural Problems and Policies in OECD Countries.* Paris: OECD, 1983.

The OECD countries face severe problems in their domestic textile and clothing industries. This volume contains useful comparisons of the trade policies relating to protection in nine of the countries of the OECD group.

* 7.53 *

Ray, Edward J., and Howard P. Marvel. "The Pattern of Protection in the Industrialized World." *Review* of *Economics and Statistics* 66:3 (August 1984): 452-458.

The authors compare the protection offered in the United States, Japan, Canada, and the EC from 1975 on for both tariffs and non-tariff barriers. Nominal tariff rates understate the protection offered in all cases, and non-tariff barriers have limited the effects of tariff cuts, particularly for exports from developing states.

* 7.54 *

Sampson, Gary P. "On the Use of Belgium-Netherlands Coefficients for Effective Protection Analysis." *Oxford Economic Papers* n.s.31:3 (November 1979): 496-507.

The authors find that Benelux tariffs and other import limitations provide high effective rates of protection compared to other industrial countries. The industrial patterns of these states as a result cannot be used to approximate a free trade situation.

* 7.55 *

Schultz, Siegfried, and Dieter Schumacher. "The Re-Liberalization of World Trade." *Journal of World Trade Law* 18:3 (May/June 1984): 206-223.

The authors analyze both tariff and non-tariff barriers to trade in the industrialized states. They argue that adjustment policies in these countries for displaced workers would limit the need for protection.

* 7.56 *

Toyne, Brian, Jeffrey S. Arpan, Andy H. Barnett, David A. Ricks, and Terence A. Shimp. "The International Competitiveness of the U.S. Textile Mill Products Industry: Corporate Strategies for the Future." *Journal of International Business Studies* 15:3 (Winter 1984): 145-165.

U.S. firms, faced with declining competitiveness in the world market, have undertaken commercial adjustment policies and reacted defensively by seeking protection. Industries in other countries have reacted similarly, resulting in a situation in which all their governments use tariff and non-tariff protection. The industries in the other states have generally proceeded further in the rationalization of production, a policy the authors recommend for the U.S. industry.

* 7.57 *

Woolcock, Stephen. "The International Politics of Trade and Protection in the Steel Industry." In: *National Industrial Strategies and the World Economy*, edited by John Pinder. Totowa, NJ: Allanheld, Osmun, 1982. ISBN 0-86598-040-3.

The industrialized countries have avoided long-term protection in their steel industries, be-

cause of the loss of competitiveness in their steel consuming industries that would occur. Measures have been taken to avert the crisis and provide protection for restructuring. The United States lacks the governmental structures to implement major industrial readjustment.

* 7.58 *

Woolcock, Stephen. "Iron and Steel." In: *The Newly Industrializing Countries: Trade and Adjustment*, edited by Louis Turner and Neil McMullen. London: Allen & Unwin, 1982. ISBN 0-04-382036-0.

Problems in the steel industries of the industrialized countries have led to efforts to deal with declining markets. The governments of the countries involved have sought multilateral arrangements to limit damage, but they have also adopted protectionist measures and utilized government adjustment programs. To date, such protectionist measures have been largely directed against other advanced states, but increasing production in the NICs may make them targets in the future.

* 7.59 *

Yeats, A.J. "Effective Tariff Protection in the United States, the European Economic Community, and Japan." *Quarterly Review of Economics and Business* 14:2 (Summer 1974): 41-50.

Effective tariff rates are much higher than nominal ones for the countries analyzed. The effective protection is graduated by stage of processing, hindering the creation and extension of manufacturing industries in developing countries. The United States has lower nominal and effective rates than either Japan or the EC.

Canada

* 7.60 *

Aho, C. Michael, and Marc Levinson. "A Canadian Opportunity." *Foreign Policy* 66 (Spring 1987): 143-155.

The authors argue that a bilateral agreement to reduce trade barriers between the United States and Canada is possible and would be beneficial to both countries. It would also indicate that trade liberalization is still possible in the global economy. A successful agreement would serve as a deterrent to protectionist sentiment.

* 7.61 *

Bloch, Harry. "Prices, Costs, and Profits in Canadian Manufacturing: The Influence of Tariffs and Concentration." *Canadian Journal of Economics* 7:4 (November 1974): 594-610.

Concentration of sales among relatively few firms in Canadian industries leads to higher profits in general. Higher tariffs are also associated with higher profits. Concentrated industries have higher profits even with lower tariffs, while industries with little concentration and low tariffs have lower profit levels. Bloch does not directly analyze the possibility that concentrated industries are better able to achieve higher levels of tariff protection.

* 7.62 *
Boyd, Roy, and Kerry Krutilla. "The Welfare Impacts of U.S. Trade Restrictions against the Canadian Softwood Lumber Industry: A Spatial Equilibrium Analysis." *Canadian Journal of Economics* 20:1 (February 1987): 17-35.

U.S. tariffs on Canadian lumber could result in a substantial loss to Canadian producers. A voluntary restraint on exports could lead to increased profits for Canadian firms.

* 7.63 *
Britton, John N. H. "Locational Perspectives on Free Trade for Canada." *Canadian Public Policy* 4:1 (Winter 1978): 4-19.

Free trade between Canada and the United States would probably have negative effects for Canada. The shift that has occurred of U.S. industries to the southern portion of the country suggests that Canada would suffer as have the northern portions of the United States.

* 7.64 *
Caves, Richard E. "Economic Models of Political Choice: Canada's Tariff Structure." *Canadian Journal of Economics* 9:2 (May 1976): 278-300.

Caves finds that an interest group model provides the best explanation of the protection offered by the structure of Canadian tariffs. The political process involving activity by industries is important to bargaining over the effective tariff rates rather than the nominal rates imposed.

* 7.65 *
Cox, David, and Richard G. Harris. "A Quantitative Assessment of the Economic Impact on Canada of Sectoral Free Trade with the United States." *Canadian Journal of Economics* 19:3 (August 1986): 377-394.

The authors estimate the gains to Canada from free trade in selected manufacturing sectors. Although the gains are not as great as would occur with a bilateral free trade arrangement, they are substantial.

* 7.66 *
Cox, David, and Richard Harris. "Trade Liberalization and Industrial Organization: Some Estimates for Canada." *Journal of Political Economy* 93:1 (February 1985): 115-145.

The authors model the effects of both unilateral and multilateral tariff reductions on Canad-

ian industry and find a welfare gain of eight percent to ten percent of GNP for the Canadian economy with multilateral reductions and smaller gains from unilateral reductions. They conclude that the nature of industrial organization, few firms or many, in a small open economy is important in analyzing the costs of protectionism.

* 7.67 *
Daly, Donald J. "The Continuing Debate about Freer Trade and Its Effects: A Comment." *Canadian Public Policy* 8 (Supplement 1982): 444-450.

Daly comments on many of the issues involved in the debate over reducing tariffs and non-tariff barriers between Canada and the United States. He generally believes that freer trade would benefit Canadian industries.

* 7.68 *
Drummond, Ian M. "On Disbelieving the Commissioners' Free Trade Case." *Canadian Public Policy* 12 (Supplement February 1986): 59-67.

Drummond critically analyzes a government commission's arguments for free trade, either multilateral or bilateral. He suggests that such a policy requires many correct adjustment and assistance policies to be enacted by the national and provincial governments.

* 7.69 *
Eastman, H. C. "Canada in an Interdependent North Atlantic Economy." In: *North American and Western European Economic Policies*. Proceedings of a Conference Held by the International Economic Association, edited by Charles P. Kindleberger and Andrew Shonfield. London: Macmillan, 1971. ISBN 0-312-57890-3.

Canada is dependent on foreign markets given its own small domestic market, and tariffs reduce these foreign opportunities. As is the case for other industrialized nations, Canada protects its more labor intensive sectors through a variety of measures. Canada's low profile in multilateral tariff negotiations is due in part to the fact that many of its commodity exports have a fixed market that will not be noticeably increased by tariff reductions.

* 7.70 *
English, H. Edward. "Canada." In: *Economic Foreign Policies of Industrial States*, edited by Wilfrid L. Kohl. Lexington, MA: Lexington Books, 1977. ISBN 0-669-00958.

In the 1960s, Canadian efforts to liberalize trade were hampered by the presence of too many domestic plants in a number of industries that had been built as a result of previous protection. Canada consequently has not been a strong supporter of multilateral tariff reductions and has negotiated voluntary export restraints with suppliers of labor intensive products.

* 7.71 *

Gordon, Myron J. "A World Scale National Corporation Industrial Strategy." *Canadian Public Policy* 4:1 (Winter 1978): 46-56.

Gordon argues that the Canadian government should use its policy power, including protection, to create world scale corporations in certain industries. Reciprocal free trade with the United States, a suggested alternative, would have severe negative consequences for Canada.

* 7.72 *

Grey, Rodney de C. "Some Issues in Canada-U.S. Trade Relations." *Canadian Public Policy* 8: (Supplement 1982): 451-456.

Both Canada and the United States rely on administrative procedures to guard against unfair trade practices that limit their trade. Issues such as subsidies, dumping regulations, or the Canadian requirement of local purchases of some goods by foreign companies, are involved. National and provincial government purchasing policies, favoring Canadian producers, have resulted in retaliation by some U.S. states.

* 7.73 *

Hara, Izumi. "Canadian Customs Valuation: Moving Toward Compliance with the MTN Code." *Law and Policy in International Business* 16:3 (1984): 1051-1082.

In 1979, Canada agreed to adopt the code on customs valuation previously accepted by other industrialized states in multilateral negotiations. The implementation of this system removed protection from a number of Canadian industries. The changes in the system demonstrate how tariff schedules can be used to provide protection.

* 7.74 *

Helleiner, G. K. "The Political Economy of Canada's Tariff Structure." *Canadian Journal of Economics* 10:2 (May 1977): 318-326.

Helleiner finds that the intensity of unskilled labor in an industry is easily the most significant variable in explaining the structure of Canadian tariffs. Changes in effective tariff protection, however, were not positively associated with labor intensity, indicating that the political influence of firms, including transnational firms, in concentrated industries with larger natural resource inputs was more effective in achieving protection.

* 7.75 *

Hill, Roderick, and John Whalley. "Introduction: Canada-U.S. Free Trade." In: *Canada-United States*

Free Trade, edited by John Whalley with Roderick Hill. Toronto: University of Toronto Press, 1985. ISBN 0820-7253-4.

The authors state the arguments for, and issues surrounding, the idea of free trade between Canada and the United States. They also provide an appendix summarizing previous analyses of the costs and benefits that would occur, all of which consistently find that benefits would be greater than costs for both countries.

* 7.76 *

Lea, Sperry, and John Volpe. "Conflict over Industrial Incentive Policies." *Proceedings of the Academy of Political Science* 32:2 (1976): 137-148.

Industrial incentive policies or subsidies have generated tensions between the United States and Canada. These non-tariff distortions have had a minor influence on trade and the balance of payments of the two countries, but they have had greater effects on particular industrial sectors and the role of exports of manufactured goods compared to exports of raw materials.

* 7.77 *

Loken, Mark K. "The Effective Protection of Canadian Exporting Industry." *Quarterly Review of Economics and Business* 15:1 (Spring 1975): 65-76.

The effective rates of protection for Canadian exporting industries, taking into account foreign tariff structures, are usually lower than the effective rates when only Canadian tariffs are considered. Effective protection concepts may be more relevant to a small trader such as Canada than to larger traders.

* 7.78 *

Mahant, E. E. "Canada and the European Community: The New Policy." *International Affairs* (London) 52:4 (October 1976): 551-564.

Economic factors have led Canada to attempt to improve relations with the EC. Not only has there been a desire to limit U.S. economic influence, but the protectionism inherent in the EC's Mediterranean policy and the formation of economic blocs has led to concern. There was some fear in the EC that an accommodation with Canada would lead to increased protectionism in the United States as a countermeasure.

* 7.79 *

Markusen, James R. "Canadian Gains from Trade in the Presence of Scale Economies and Imperfect Competition." In: *Canada-United States Free Trade*, edited by John Whalley with Roderick Hill. Toronto: University of Toronto Press, 1985. ISBN 0820-7253-4.

Free trade between Canada and the United States would increase benefits for both states due to economies of scale possible in various industries. Bilateral trade liberalization would generate greater benefits than unilateral free trade. Markusen finds no evidence that there would be contraction in Canadian manufacturing industries.

* 7.80 *
Moroz, Andrew R. "Some Observations on Non-Tariff Barriers and Their Use in Canada." In: *Canada-United States Free Trade*, edited by John Whalley with Roderick Hill. Toronto: University of Toronto Press, 1985. ISBN 0820-7253-4.

Non-tariff barriers have increased as tariff levels have been reduced through multilateral negotiations. Canada has had a long history of using a wide variety of such measures. Even so, Canada has a more open economy than Japan or many West European countries.

* 7.81 *
Rugman, Alan M., and Andrew Anderson. "U.S.-Canadian Trade Liberalization and Adjustment Mechanisms: A Survey." *International Trade Journal* 1:3 (Spring 1987): 219-250.

The authors review previous studies of trade between the United States and Canada, as well as the effects of freer trade and protectionism in Canada. They argue that it is necessary to include the effects of non-tariff barriers and intra-firm trade within multinational enterprises in future research given the importance of these factors.

* 7.82 *
Sarna, A.J. "The Canada-U.S. Free Trade Option." *Journal of World Trade Law* 13:4 (July/August 1979): 303-310.

Sarna summarizes the arguments both for and against a free trade area comprising Canada and the United States and discusses the advantages of sectoral arrangements between the two countries. The value of such an agreement would be affected by the extent of multilateral tariff reductions.

* 7.83 *
Sarna, A.J. "Safeguards against Market Disruption --The Canadian View." *Journal of World Trade Law* 10:4 (July/August 1976): 355-370.

The author presents the arguments of the Canadian government for protection. Short-term safeguard measures have been used to deal with problems of high unemployment. Canada with its smaller domestic market is particularly susceptible to sudden increases in imports.

* 7.84 *
Saunders, Ronald S. "The Political Economy of Effective Tariff Protection in Canada's Manufacturing Sector." *Canadian Journal of Economics* 13:2 (May 1980): 340-348.

The Canadian industries best able to lobby and achieve higher effective tariff protection are those that are largely domestically owned, are not major exporters, and have lower labor productivity than their American counterparts. Industries with greater seller concentration also generally have higher levels of protection. The negative association with foreign ownership could either reflect less domestic pressure achievable by foreign owners or the foreign ownership's preference for lower tariffs to facilitate intra-firm trade.

* 7.85 *
Shearer, Ronald A. "Regionalism and International Trade Policy." In: *Canada-United States Free Trade*, edited by John Whalley with Roderick Hill. Toronto: University of Toronto Press, 1985. ISBN 0820-7253-4.

Canadian support for free trade would require consensus among the provinces, but different areas have different interests. If the provinces support their local economic interests, a free trade strategy is unlikely to appear in Canada.

* 7.86 *
Stegemann, Klaus. "Special Import Measures Legislation: Deterring Dumping of Capital Goods." *Canadian Public Policy* 8:4 (Autumn 1982): 573-585.

Stegemann discusses the new laws that will limit dumping. The legislation will be an effective deterrent and aid domestic capital goods producers, but the ultimate national cost could be high.

* 7.87 *
Stegemann, Klaus, and Keith Acheson. "Canadian Government Purchasing Policy." *Journal of World Trade Law* 6:4 (July/August 1986): 442-478.

Government purchasing policies in Canada have had a multitude of objectives, some of which are protectionist and some of which are not. Multiple objectives may not be an effective mechanism for attaining results, and they limit the accountability of various government agencies.

* 7.88 *
Watkins, Mel. "Reservations Concerning a Free Trade Area." In: *Canada-United States Free Trade*, edited by John Whalley with Roderick Hill. Toronto: University of Toronto Press, 1985. ISBN 0820-7253-4.

A free trade area between Canada and the U.S. could threaten Canadian national sovereignity. The Canadian government might be unable to initiate the appropriate adjustment policies brought about by such an arrangement due to U.S. pressure.

* 7.89 *

Wilkinson, Bruce W. "Canada-U.S. Free Trade and Some Options." *Canadian Public Policy* 8: (Supplement 1982): 428-439.

Free trade with the United States will not be a solution to problems in domestic manufacturing industries. Other policies are needed, with or without trade, to solve these problems.

* 7.90 *

Wilkinson, Bruce W. "Some Comments on Canada-U.S. Free Trade." In: *Canada-United States Free Trade*, edited by John Whalley with Roderick Hill. Toronto: University of Toronto Press, 1985. ISBN 0820-7253-4.

The gains from free trade between Canada and the United States have been overstated. Any free trade agreements must also provide protection for the smaller state in case of the reimposition of trade barriers by the larger one. Although free trade in specific sectors might be useful, it also creates problems, particularly when unemployment levels are high in both countries.

* 7.91 *

Williams, Glen. "The National Policy Tariffs: Industrial Underdevelopment Through Import Substitution." *Canadian Journal of Political Science* 12:2 (June 1979): 333-368.

The structure of Canadian industry today, and its weaknesses, results in part from decisions in the nineteenth and twentieth centuries to protect the home market in some areas and to seek international competitiveness in other specialized areas. The protective tariff led to inefficient import substitution in some sectors.

* 7.92 *

Wonnacott, Paul, and Ronald J. Wonnacott. "Free Trade Between the United States and Canada: Fifteen Years Later." *Canadian Public Policy* 8: (Supplement 1982): 412-427.

Free trade between Canada and the United States would still produce many benefits for Canada. Canadian trade policy has been focused too narrowly on what jobs in specific industries would be affected. The appropriate perspective should be the overall effect of free trade on the economy.

* 7.93 *

Wonnacott, R. J. "Canada's Future in a World of Trade Blocs: A Proposal." *Canadian Public Policy* 1:1 (Winter 1975): 118-130.

In a world of trading blocs, Canada suffers since it lacks special access to any large market. Canada should support GATT negotiations to reduce tariffs and also attempt to secure agreements with the United States and Europe for reciprocal reductions.

* 7.94 *

Wonnacott, Ronald J. "The Canadian Content Proposals of the Task Force on the Automobile Industry." *Canadian Public Policy* 10:1 (March 1984): 1-9.

Proposals to require domestic content in auto imports are essentially protectionist. They would raise prices for Canadian consumers. Other risks include Japanese retaliation, possible impairment of the agreement on automobiles between the United States and Canada, and a weakening of efforts to achieve a liberal trading system.

* 7.95 *

Wonnacott, Ronald J. "Industrial Strategy: A Canadian Substitute for Trade Liberalization." *Canadian Journal of Economics* 8:4 (November 1975): 536-547.

The author analyzes proposals put forward for a government industrial policy to coordinate and cartelize Canadian industry to maximize returns. The analysis concludes that such an effort will be effective only if Canadian industries become more export oriented and involved in international trade. The industrial policy approach would be less effective than trade liberalization in any event.

* 7.96 *

Wonnacott, Ronald J. "On the Employment Effects of Free Trade with the United States." *Canadian Public Policy* 12:1 (March 1986): 258-263.

Free trade between Canada and the United States would be likely to increase employment levels in Canada as a result of access to the U.S. market. A free trade arrangement would also prevent unemployment that would result from U.S. protection.

* 7.97 *

Wonnacott, Ronald J. "Potential Economic Effects of a Canada-U.S. Free Trade Agreement." In: *Canada-United States Free Trade*, edited by John Whalley with Roderick Hill. Toronto: University of Toronto Press, 1985. ISBN 0820-7253-4.

Canada would gain from a free trade arrangement with the United States in the long term as a result of access to the larger market, but there would be short-run costs. While many Canadian manufacturers realize that there would eventually be benefits, they have not supported such a free trade arrangement due to the immediate difficulties that would be faced.

Japan

* 7.98 *

Abegglen, James C., and Thomas M. Hout. "Facing

up to the Trade Gap with Japan." *Foreign Affairs* 57:1 (Fall 1978): 146-168.

Japan has liberalized its trade system and uses many fewer import restrictions than before, but there is a residual perceptual effect on U.S. businessmen and government officials. Except in food products, U.S. exports of raw materials to Japan have declined in some areas due to cost factors rather than import barriers. Some trade barriers to imports of U.S. manufactures exist, including limitations on foreign sales to Japanese public corporations.

* 7.99 *

Calder, Kent E. "Opening Japan." *Foreign Policy* 47 (Summer 1982): 82-97.

Japan has become less protectionist over time. Multilateral tariff reductions have decreased Japanese duties from the highest among developed nations to the lowest, although complex non-tariff barriers remain important. Unlike other developed countries, Japan has not attempted to shield labor intensive industries like textiles from import competition from the developing states.

* 7.100 *

Drucker, Peter F. "Japan: The Problems of Success." *Foreign Affairs* 56:3 (April 1978): 564-578.

In his wider survey of Japanese society, Drucker notes that protectionist practices are also designed to protect cultural values, such as the ideal of the small farming sector, as well as economic interests. In the agricultural areas the higher Japanese consumer costs are a significant burden for the economy.

* 7.101 *

Dunn, James A., Jr. "Automobiles in International Trade: Regime Change or Persistence." *International Organization* 41:2 (Spring 1987): 225-252.

Trade in automobiles was never very free. In the 1950s and 1960s it was liberal within different regions, with limits on outside penetration. Recent restraints on Japanese automobiles reflect less the appearance of new protectionism than a continuation of the old trading system.

* 7.102 *

Fukui, Haruhiro. "The GATT Tokyo Round: The Bureaucratic Politics of Multilateral Diplomacy." In: *The Politics of Trade: U.S. and Japanese Policymaking for the GATT Negotiations*, edited by Michael Blaker. Occasional Papers of the East Asian Institute. New York: Columbia University Press, 1978. ISBN 0-317-17100-3.

Fukui analyzes the differing views of important ministries in arriving at the Japanese negotiating position during the Tokyo Round. The desire

to achieve consensus hindered bureaucratic negotiations and eliminated some topics from consideration, particularly in areas where one of the ministries had an important domestic clientele.

* 7.103 *

Fukushima, Kiyohiko. "Japan's Real Trade Policy." *Foreign Policy* 59 (Summer 1985): 22-39.

The author argues that Japan has a greater commitment to free trade than is often recognized. Within Japan there are, however, many trends that encourage protectionism. The Japanese often see their country as being treated unfairly by the United States and the Europeans in trade matters.

* 7.104 *

Hills, Jill. "Foreign Policy and Technology: The Japan-U.S., Japan-Britain and Japan-EEC Technology Agreements." *Political Studies* 31:2 (June 1983): 205-223.

Japan has attempted to create technological interdependence with the United States, particularly in areas of defense applications, as one means of defusing protectionist sentiment in the United States. While Japan is still vulnerable to protectionism in the West, its technological advances will provide political power in the future.

* 7.105 *

Johnson, Chalmers. "MITI and Japanese International Economic Policy." In: *The Foreign Policy of Modern Japan*, edited by Robert A. Scalapino. Berkeley: University of California Press, 1977. ISBN 0-520-03499-6.

The governmental bureaucracy is divided in its views on protectionism with some agencies favoring trade liberalization and others protection. The Ministry of International Trade and Industry (MITI), the most important economic agency, has been protectionist, but for the purpose of promoting Japan's international competitiveness. Japan's protectionist attitude may be changing toward a more internationalist position.

* 7.106 *

Kanemitsu, Hideo. "Change in the International Economic Environment." In: *Japan's Economy: Coping with Change in the International Environment*, edited by Daniel Okimoto. Boulder, CO: Westview, 1982. ISBN 0-86531-3504.

Protectionism and violation of GATT rules increased in the 1970s, as a result of the politicization of economic issues by protectionist advocates who gained influence in many countries. Kanemitsu argues that Japan should develop a foreign economy policy stressing free trade and opposed to protectionism, particularly since Japan's role in the international system has increased with the decline of the United States as a hegemon.

* 7.107 *
Kojima, Kiyoshi. "Hidden Trade Barriers in Japan." *Journal of World Trade Law* 7:2 (March/April 1973): 137-168.

Kojima surveys Japanese non-tariff barriers. He argues that they are relatively few in number and that their repercussions are overemphasized in other countries.

* 7.108 *
Komiya, Ryutaro. "The U.S.-Japan Trade Conflict: An Economist's View from Japan." In: *Japan's Economy: Coping with Change in the International Environment*, edited by Daniel Okimoto. Boulder, CO: Westview, 1982. ISBN 0-86531-350-4.

Komiya discusses the economic conflicts between Japan and the United States, arguing that neither of these two leaders of GATT should engage in protectionism nor be so concerned about the bilateral trade accounts. He suggests other policies to deal with the trade imbalance. He further argues that, contrary to general belief, Japan has not been particularly protectionist nor resorted to major non-tariff barriers and that the Japanese economy is as open as that of the United States or Western European countries.

* 7.109 *
Kosaka, Masataka. "The International Economic Policy of Japan." In: *The Foreign Policy of Modern Japan*, edited by Robert A. Scalapino. Berkeley: University of California Press, 1977. ISBN 0-520-03499-6.

Japan's economic policy is nationalistic and defensive due to the country's lack of raw materials and its history as a late industrializer. Japan's tariff structure protects infant industries and industries that employ large numbers of workers, even if they are stagnating or declining. Japan also relies on many non-tariff barriers, although Kosaka argues that these barriers are not as extensive as often claimed.

* 7.110 *
Krause, Lawrence B., and Sueo Sekiguchi. "Japan and the World Economy." In: *Asia's New Giant: How the Japanese Economy Works*, edited by Hugh Patrick and Henry Rosovsky. Washington, DC: Brookings Institution, 1976. ISBN 0-8157-6933-4.

In their review of the Japanese economy, the authors note that tariff liberalization exposed the other barriers to imports that exist. Effective protection rates in Japan also increase rapidly as processing increases, giving much greater levels of protection to manufactures.

* 7.111 *
Magaziner, Ira C., and Thomas M. Hout. *Japanese Industrial Policy*. London: Policy Studies Institute, 1980. ISBN 0-85374-176-x.

Japanese industrial policy is discussed, in both general and specific aspects. Such policies have included a variety of measures to protect the home market and to promote exports.

* 7.112 *
Ozaki, Robert S. *The Control of Imports and Foreign Capital in Japan*. New York: Praeger, 1972. LC 79-181697.

Ozaki offers a comprehensive survey of the protectionist measures used to restrict imports into the Japanese market in the 1960s. He notes that these controls were designed to facilitate industrialization, but he does not attempt to measure the costs and benefits or the appropriateness of the Japanese experience for other countries.

* 7.113 *
Patrick, Hugh T. "The Economic Dimensions of the U.S.-Japan Alliance: An Overview." In: *Japan's Economy: Coping with Change in the International Environment*, edited by Daniel Okimoto. Boulder, CO: Westview, 1982. ISBN 0-86531-350-4.

Patrick discusses various aspects of economic linkages between Japan and the United States, including the reasons for the rise of protectionist practices and the consequences of such policies in Japan and the United States.

* 7.114 *
Pempel, T.J. "Japanese Foreign Economic Policy: The Domestic Bases for International Behavior." *International Organization* 31:4 (Autumn 1977): 723-773.

Pempel provides a useful overview of the political and bureaucratic structures that have permitted Japan to implement a variety of protectionist practices. These structures have also permitted the government to resist domestic pressures relatively easily and to negotiate with other countries on such issues as voluntary export restraints.

* 7.115 *
Saxonhouse, Gary G. "The World Economy and Japanese Foreign Economic Policy." In: *The Foreign Policy of Modern Japan*, edited by Robert A. Scalapino. Berkeley: University of California Press, 1977. ISBN 0-520-03499-6.

U.S. diplomatic pressure led to some Japanese trade liberalization in the early 1970s as well as fewer European restrictions on imports from Japan. Japan reacted to the U.S. soybean embargo in 1973 by seeking to achieve greater self-sufficiency in food through the protection of domestic agriculture.

Saxonhouse concludes by arguing that the Japanese type of governmental involvement in international economic decisions with trade-restricting effects will become more prevalent in other countries in the future.

* 7.116 *

Shinkai, Yoichi. "Elasticities of Substitution for the Japanese Imports." *Review of Economics and Statistics* 54:2 (May 1972): 198-202.

Trade liberalization by Japan has permitted greater substitution of goods in production processes. The effect, as expected, is greater for finished goods than for intermediate ones or crude materials.

* 7.117 *

Weil, Frank A., and Norman D. Glick. "Japan--Is the Market Open? A View of the Japanese Market Drawn from U.S. Corporate Experience." *Law and Policy in International Business* 11:3 (1979): 845-902.

While Japan has reduced official import obstacles, there are many informal practices in the government that continue to severely limit import competition. The co-operation between industry and government agencies in industrial planning also handicaps foreign producers. The potential for U.S. imports, however, is increasing.

* 7.118 *

Wheeler, Jimmy W., Merit E. Janow, and Thomas Pepper, with Midori Yamamoto. *Japanese Industrial Development Policies in the 1980s: Implications for U.S. Trade and Investment*. Croton-on-Hudson, NY: Hudson Institute, October 1982.

The authors review the many aspects of Japanese industrial policy in a variety of industries. Such policies concentrate on either new industries or declining ones, which are exactly the areas where foreign competition would be greatest if protection were not available. Pressure for lower prices by consumers may lead to lessened protection for the domestic market.

The United Kingdom

* 7.119 *

Barker, T.S., and S.S. Han. "Effective Rates of Protection for United Kingdom Production." *Economic Journal* 81 (June 1971): 282-293.

The authors calculate the effective rates of protection provided to UK industries in 1963. There was a very close association between the nominal rates and the calculated effective rates.

* 7.120 *

Burn, Duncan, and Barbara Epstein. *Realities of Free Trade: Two Industry Studies*. Toronto: University of Toronto Press, 1972.

Analyses of the chemical and electrical engineering industries in Great Britain found that tariffs had little effect on the ability to compete in international trade. For chemicals, technological advantages were most important. For the electrical equipment sector, however, non-tariff barriers, particularly government procurement policies and national technical standards, were important impediments to trade.

* 7.121 *

Cable, Vincent. "British Foreign Policy to 1985, VII: Britain, the 'New Protectionism' and Trade with the Newly Industrializing Countries." *International Affairs* (London) 55:1 (January 1979): 1-17.

Mercantilism has been ever present in Great Britain and other states; it has simply taken new forms in the postwar era, such as subsidies and other forms of government assistance. The NICs' exports to industrialized states have a small cost and higher, but still small, benefits. As a result, interest groups affected by imports are able to mount effective pressure for protection.

* 7.122 *

Cable, Vincent, and Jeremy Clarke. *British Electronics and Competition with Newly Industrializing Countries*. London: Overseas Development Institute, 1981. ISBN 0-850-30765.

The future of various portions of the UK electronics industry requires innovation in new product lines in order to gain competitive advantages from countries like the NICs. The industry argues that protection against imports from the NICs is necessary for its immediate survival and ultimate ability to undertake the process of innovation.

* 7.123 *

Collyns, Charles. *Can Protection Cure Unemployment*. Thames Essay no. 31. London: Trade Policy Research Centre, 1982. ISBN 0-900-84261.

The Cambridge Economic Policy Group has suggested that protection could be a cure for British unemployment. Collyns' analysis finds that protection would alleviate unemployment marginally, but negative side effects would outweigh any benefits.

* 7.124 *

Cripps, Francis, and Wynne Godby. "Control of Imports as a Means to Full Employment and the Expansion of World Trade: The UK's Case." *Cambridge Journal of Economics* 2:3 (September 1978): 327-334.

The authors argue that limitations on imports may help a country to increase its competitiveness if the protection is not directed against weak suppliers. Such import limitations should also not provide an economic incentive for retaliation by other countries.

* 7.125 *
Denton, Geoffrey, Seamus O'Cleireacain, and Sally Ash. *Trade Effects of Public Subsidies to Private Enterprise*. London: Macmillan, 1975. ISBN 0-8419-5014-8.

The authors analyze subsidies in Great Britain to determine their effect on trade. Policies designed to aid depressed regions and efforts to maintain employment levels have led to import substitution and the subsidization of exports. The ultimate effect of such subsidies has been serious trade distortion.

* 7.126 *
Foreman-Peck, J.S. "Tariff Protection and Economies of Scale: The British Motor Industry before 1939." *Oxford Economic Papers* n.s. 31:2 (July 1979): 237-257.

The author finds that tariff protection afforded the British automobile industry was beneficial in costs and benefits. Earlier imposition of the tariff would also apparently have strengthened the industry even more.

* 7.127 *
Grampp, William D. "Economic Opinion When Britain Turned to Free Trade." *History of Political Economy* 14:4 (Winter 1982): 496-520.

Grampp outlines the debate and the protagonists in 1820 for free trade and protection. He notes that the debate was conducted on both economic and political grounds and reflected to some extent the influence of domestic pressure groups.

* 7.128 *
Hindley, Brian. *Britain's Position on Non-Tariff Protection*. Thames Essay no. 4. London: Trade Policy Research Centre, 1972. ISBN 0-900-84219-9.

Hindley reviews the major non-tariff barriers in use in the United Kingdom and some of their effects. He notes that some of these barriers lead to welfare losses for the implementing state and not for other countries; therefore, they are not a subject of international concern.

* 7.129 *
Hitiris, Theodore. "Effective Protection and Economic Performance in UK Manufacturing Industry, 1963 and 1968." *Economic Journal* 88 (March 1978): 107-120.

A number of factors are compared with profit rates for British industries for these two years. Concentration in industries is one important factor, but the level of effective protection is consistently

important, indicating that the protection from import competition permitted domestic industries to earn extra profits.

* 7.130 *
Katrak, Homi. "Foreign Competition, Tariffs, and Industrial Concentration in Britain, 1963 and 1968." In: *Current Issues in Commercial Policy and Diplomacy*, edited by John Black and Brian Hindley. New York: St. Martin's, 1980. ISBN 0-312-17926-x

Foreign competition has led to industrial concentration as defensive mergers occur among domestic firms. Tariffs have also led to concentration, higher profits, and welfare losses to consumers. Tariff cuts, however, may not solve the problem of concentration among large firms, since foreign competition would discourage new firms from being established.

* 7.131 *
Kilpatrick, Andrew, and Tony Lawson. "On the Nature of Industrial Decline in the UK." *Cambridge Journal of Economics* 4:1 (March 1980): 85-102.

Import controls are the only effective response to the declining position of the United Kingdom in the short term in some cases. Such controls should be combined with state planning in order for such efforts to be successful. Controls, however, face the problem that they may have to be self-perpetuating to avoid higher levels of unemployment at some point.

* 7.132 *
Miles, Caroline. "Protection of the British Textile Industry." In: *Public Assistance to Industry: Protection and Subsidies in Britain and Germany*, edited by W.M. Corden and Gerhard Fels. London: Macmillan, 1976. ISBN 0-333-19031-9

British textiles were protected in the 1950s, 1960s, and 1970s through a variety of mechanisms. Government protection and adjustment assistance did not prevent the decline of the industry but were useful in dealing with some aspects of the decline.

* 7.133 *
Minford, Patrick. "The New Cambridge Economic Policy: A Critique of Its Prescriptions." *Government and Opposition* 17:1 (Winter 1982): 48-60.

Minford presents the basic arguments of the Cambridge Economic Policy Group that emphasize the need for import controls in all developed states. He then argues that the protectionist approach advocated will not be productive.

* 7.134 *
Naraine, Mahindra. "Britain and the Global Economy." In: *The Global Political Economy in the 1980s*, edited

by Michael Stohl and Harry R. Targ. Cambridge, MA: Schenkman, 1982. ISBN 0-87073-236-6.

Naraine argues that Britain never favored free trade since it relied on force and imperialism rather than industrial strength to gain markets. Protectionism has traditionally been used to protect weak industries, and recent efforts by unions and the Labour Party, among others, constitute a continuation of past trends.

* 7.135 *

Oulton, Nicholas. "Effective Protection of British Industry." In: *Public Assistance to Industry: Protection and Subsidies in Britain and Germany*, edited by W. M. Corden and Gerhard Fels. London: Macmillan, 1976. ISBN 0-330-19031-9.

Effective protection in Great Britain was higher than nominal protection in 1968, but the order for the level of protection for industries was generally the same with both rates. The British tariff structure seems to reflect the historical development of tariffs rather than efforts to protect key industries or industries threatened by imports.

* 7.136 *

Scott, M. F. G., W. M. Corden, and I. M. D. Little. *The Case Against General Import Restrictions.* Thames Essay no. 24. London: Trade Policy Research Centre, 1980. ISBN 0-900-84250-4.

The authors attack the position of the Cambridge Policy Group that argues for protectionism in the United Kingdom. They demonstrate that protectionism will not solve the economic problems of the United Kingdom as claimed.

* 7.137 *

Shepherd, Geoffrey. "UK Economic Policies and Their Implications for Third World Countries: The Case of Textiles and Clothing." In: *Adjustment or Protectionism: The Challenge to Britain of Third World Industrialisation*, edited by Abby Rubin Riddell. London: Catholic Institute for International Relations, 1980. ISBN 0-904-39348-8.

Faced with increasing import penetration of textiles and clothing from developing countries, particularly those in the Mediterranean that had agreements with the EC, the United Kingdom has become the most interventionist EC state. Both direct protection and subsidies have been used. Protectionism is not a long-term solution; technological improvements and market adaptation are necessary.

France

* 7.138 *

Cohen, Stephen S. "Informed Bewilderment: French Economic Strategy and the Crisis." In: *France in the Troubled World Economy*, edited by Stephen S. Cohen and Peter A. Gourevitch. London: Butterworth Scientific, 1982. ISBN 0-408-10787-1.

The industrial adjustment strategies of the French government are unlikely to solve long-term problems. Protectionism has been used by France, particularly unofficial forms or uses of official regulations. The French auto industry is concerned that Japanese investment in plants in the United States will lead to increased Japanese exports originating in Japan to Europe at the expense of French sales.

* 7.139 *

Gourevitch, Peter A. "Making Choices in France: Industrial Structure and the Politics of Economic Policy." In: *France in the Troubled World Economy*, edited by Stephen S. Cohen and Peter A. Gourevitch. London: Butterworth Scientific, 1982. ISBN 0-408-10787-1.

France is facing the loss of markets in more advanced industries. Protectionism is one policy option that is supported by owners and employees in affected industries. The protectionist issue cuts across existing divisions among the political parties, given their bases of support in particular regions or economic sectors.

* 7.140 *

Kahler, Miles. *Decolonization in Britain and France: The Domestic Consequences of International Relations.* Princeton: Princeton University Press, 1984. ISBN 0-691-07672-3.

Kahler discusses the economics of decolonization in his fourth chapter. Businesses relying on protected colonial markets or selling colonial goods in the metropole were opposed to colonial independence. The higher levels of protectionism in France led to greater opposition to change among French firms than was the case with British firms.

* 7.141 *

Kahler, Miles. "International Response to Economic Crisis: France and the Third World in the 1970s." In: *France in the Troubled World Economy*, edited by Stephen S. Cohen and Peter A. Gourevitch. London: Butterworth Scientific, 1982. ISBN 0-408-10787-1.

French ties with former colonies have provided a protected market for some French goods, although not as protected as in the days of colonialism. The markets in Africa have permitted France to take a protectionist stance against the East Asian

NICs without fear of retaliation since they are not major markets for French goods.

* 7.142 *
Mytelka, Lynn Krieger. "The French Textile Industry: Crisis and Adjustment." In: *The Emerging International Economic Order: Dynamic Processes, Constraints and Opportunities*, edited by Harold K. Jacobson and Dusan Sidjanski. Beverly Hills, CA: Sage, 1982. ISBN 0-8039-1833-x

France has had a protectionist tradition that was applied to the domestic textile industry when it faced increasing import competition. Protection and industry consolidation have not solved the problems, and there is continuing pressure for maintaining or increasing the protection offered.

* 7.143 *
Mytelka, Lynn Krieger. "In Search of a Partner: The State and the Textile Industry in France." In: *France in the Troubled World Economy*, edited by Stephen S. Cohen and Peter A. Gourevitch. London: Butterworth Scientific, 1982. ISBN 0-408-10787-1.

The textile industry has pressed for tariff protection, even though previous protection had left the industry in a non-competitive international position. The French state has provided subsidies and other protection for modernization and reorganization of the industry.

* 7.144 *
Rehfeldt, Udo. "France." In: *Integration and Unequal Development: The Experience of the EEC*, edited by Dudley Seers and Constantine Vaitsos with Marja-Liisa Kiljunen. New York: St. Martin's, 1980. ISBN 0-312-41890-6.

France's traditional protectionist stance has limited the effects of imports from the developing countries, unlike other EC members. EC policies have also contributed greatly to France's ability to move from being a net importer of agricultural goods to becoming a net exporter.

* 7.145 *
Smith, Michael Stephen. *Tariff Reform in France, 1860-1900: The Politics of Economic Interest.* Ithaca, NY: Cornell University Press, 1980. ISBN 0-8014-1257-9.

Smith analyzed the formation of French tariff policy in the last half of the nineteenth century from the perspective of competing economic interest groups favoring protection and free trade. The controversy gradually changed from one of confrontational politics to that of accommodation of the critical interests of the groups on both sides of the issue.

* 7.146 *
Zysman, John. "The French State in the International Economy." *International Organization* 31:4 (Autumn 1977): 839-877.

Since World War II, the French government has consistently followed a neo-mercantilist policy and sought to manipulate the international economy to French advantage. The well-developed French political and economic institutional infra-structure has utilized tariffs, subsidies, cartels, and other forms of protectionism, and the government has also appeared as a state trader in some bilateral arrangements. The protection for farmers insisted upon by France in the negotiations leading to the formation of the EC is one prominent case in point.

* 7.147 *
Zysman, John. *Political Strategies for Industrial Order: State, Market, and Industry in France.* Berkeley: University of California Press, 1977. ISBN 0-520-02889-9.

Zysman discusses the relationship of business and government in France, including state efforts related to international economic activities. France has a protectionist tradition, including the highest tariffs in the EC at the time of its formation. State policy has recently shifted from protection to promotion, although promotional activities such as subsidies, government contracts, and cartels also serve protectionist purposes.

Other Industrialized Countries

* 7.148 *
Dolan, Michael. "European Restructuring and Import Policies for a Textile Industry in Crisis." *International Organization* 37:4 (Autumn 1983): 583-616.

The textile industry in the European Community has been a declining one due to foreign competitors. Over time the EC and its members have become more protectionist, including Germany, Denmark, and the Netherlands, which generally have favored a more liberal or free trade policy. A variety of adjustment policies have been tried in efforts to deal with the decline in the textile sector in the context of rising protectionist sentiment in the member states.

* 7.149 *
Fels, Gerhard. "Overall Assistance to German Industry." In: *Public Assistance to Industry: Protection and Subsidies in Britain and Germany*, edited by W.M. Corden and Gerhard Fels. London: Macmillan, 1976. ISBN 0-333-19031-9.

Fels calculates the overall effective assistance given to eleven German economic sectors, including the effects of tariffs, non-tariff barriers, and other types of government assistance. The agricultural sector receives the greatest amount of assistance. Industries suffering from import competition also receive above average assistance.

* 7.150 *
Garnaut, Ross. "Australia's Shrinking Markets." In: *Economic Interaction in the Pacific Basin*, edited by Lawrence B. Krause and Sueo Sekiguchi. Washington DC: Brookings Institution, 1980. ISBN 0-8157-5028-5.

In discussing the difficulties that Australia faced in light of the international economic problems of the 1970s, Garnaut also deals with protectionism in the Australian context. Australia's exports were hurt by the adoption of protectionist measures in other countries, while domestic political pressure led it to adopt severe import restrictions that particularly hurt some of the developing states in Southeast Asia.

* 7.151 *
Hiementz, Ulrich, and Kurt V. Rabenau. "Effective Protection of German Industry." In: *Public Assistance to Industry: Protection and Subsidies in Britain and Germany*, edited by W. M. Corden and Gerhard Fels. London: Macmillan, 1976. ISBN 0-333-19031-9.

Effective tariff rates in Germany in the early 1970s were much higher than nominal ones, particularly in product areas threatened by import competition. Preferences to developing countries exerted little effect since they were in product lines where these states were not competitive.

* 7.152 *
Hough, Jerry F. "Attack on Protectionism in the Soviet Union? A Comment." *International Organization* 40:2 (Spring 1986): 489-503.

Hough argues that the Soviet Union clearly follows protectionist practices, although the forms are different given the trade structures present in this centrally planned economy. He also argues that economic progress in the Soviet Union will require Gorbachev to dismantle some of the protectionist measures and involve the USSR in the international economy--in other words, trade liberalization is necessary.

* 7.153 *
Katzenstein, Peter J. "The Small European States in the International Economy: Economic Dependence and Corporatist Politics." In: *The Antinomies of Interdependence: National Welfare and the International Division of Labor*, edited by John Gerard Ruggie. New York: Columbia University Press, 1983. ISBN 0-231-05725-3.

The smaller European states, Norway, Sweden, Denmark, Austria, Belgium, Switzerland, and the Netherlands, have economies that depend more on trade; thus, they have favored more liberal trade and opposed protectionism, including the use of non-tariff barriers. Their own trade policies are much more liberal than those of larger industrial states. Katzenstein further argues that the successful domestic adjustments undertaken in these countries have been related to corporatist policies, the effective political representation of major economic sectors.

* 7.154 *
Kierzkowski, Henryk. "Displacement of Labor by Imports of Manufactures." *World Development* 8: 10 (October 1980): 753-762.

Kierzkowski analyzes the effects of imports of manufactures, particularly those from developing countries, on employment in Sweden from 1963 to 1977. Such imports appear to have very little influence, suggesting that protectionist measures to safeguard jobs will not be effective or necessary.

* 7.155 *
Koekkoek, K.A., and L.B.M. Mennes. "Liberalizing the Multi-Fibre Arrangement: Some Aspects for the Netherlands, the EC, and the LDCs." *Journal of World Trade Law* 20:2 (March/April 1986): 142-167.

Complete elimination of the Multi-Fibre Arrangements would provide many benefits. The developing countries could increase employment in the textile and clothing industries, and consumers in the EC states would pay lower prices. The potential gains are much higher in the clothing sector than for textiles.

* 7.156 *
Lloyd, Peter J. "Discrimination against Imports in Australian Commodity Taxes." *Journal of World Trade Law* 9:1 (January/February 1975): 89-101.

Australian sales and excise taxes provide significant protection for some commodities. They are a minor part of overall protection, but they can be an effective non-tariff barrier.

* 7.157 *
Lundgren, Nils. "International Economic Policies of a Nordic Group." In: *North American and Western European Economic Policies. Proceedings of a Conference Held by the International Economic Association*, edited by Charles P. Kindleberger and Andrew Shonfield. London: Macmillan, 1971. ISBN 0-312-57890-3.

In a discussion of many aspects of Nordic economic policies, Lundgren considers a variety of protectionist issues of importance to these states. They are supporters of GATT and trade liberalization, and they also support limitations on non-tariff barriers, particularly since they have few of their own.

* 7.158 *
McAleese, Dermot. "Intra-Industry Trade, Level of Development and Market Size." In: *On the Economics of Intra-Industry Trade: Symposium 1978*, edited by Herbert Giersch. Tubingen: J.C.B. Mohr, 1978. ISBN 0-89563-548-8.

Small countries like Ireland can benefit from the reduction of non-tariff barriers to trade within the EC. Tariffs have reduced both exports and imports within the same Irish industry, and thus trade liberalization will lead to an increase of intra-industry trade.

* 7.159 *
Monke, Eric A., Scott R. Pearson, and Jose-Paulo Silva-Carvalho. "Welfare Effects of a Processing Cartel: Flour Milling in Portugal." *Economic Development and Cultural Change* 35:2 (January 1987): 393-408.

A combination of natural trade barriers due to transport costs and the flour cartel's ability to set prices and apportion production has led to higher costs for Portuguese consumers. Government subsidies have also helped domestic producers.

* 7.160 *
Neu, Axel D. "Protection of the German Textile Industry." In: *Public Assistance to Industry: Protection and Subsidies in Britain and Germany*, edited by W.M. Corden and Gerhard Fels. London: Macmillan, 1976. ISBN 0-333-19031-9.

The German textile industry has not received special industrial assistance, but the indirect assistance received with import quotas on textiles and clothing from low wage exporters has provided important indirect assistance. In such protected product areas, prices for German products are relatively higher than in unprotected product areas.

* 7.161 *
Neu, Axel, and Hans H. Glismann. "Quantitative Aspects of Nontariff Distinctions of Trade in the Federal Republic of Germany." In: *Prospects for Eliminating Non-Tariff Distortions*, edited by Anthony E. Scaperlanda. Leiden: A. W. Sijthoff, 1973. ISBN 90-286-0063-9.

The authors provide detailed information on existing non-tariff barriers in Germany as of 1969. The effects of various barriers were considerable in some product areas. The authors suggest that tariffs would often be a preferable policy instrument for protection than quotas.

* 7.162 *
Pelkmans, Jacques. "Government Aid to Industry in the Benelux-Countries." In: *Prospects for Eliminating Non-Tariff Distortions*, edited by Anthony

E. Scaperlanda. Leiden: A. W. Sijthoff, 1973. ISBN 90-286-0063-9.

Both the Netherlands and Belgium have adopted regional policies to aid portions of the countries. While there have been some trade distortions as a result, the effects have apparently not been great.

* 7.163 *
Riedel, James. "Tariff Concessions in the Kennedy Round and the Structure of Protection in West Germany: An Economic Assessment." *Journal of International Economics* 7:2 (May 1977): 133-143.

German concessions in the Kennedy Round of tariff reductions supported the short-term interests of labor. While trade was liberalized, it was not opened greatly in areas where employment levels would be threatened.

* 7.164 *
Van Lith, Jan A. "Government Procurement in the Benelux Countries." In: *Prospects for Eliminating Non-Tariff Distortions*, edited by Anthony E. Scaperlanda. Leiden: A. W. Sijthoff, 1973. ISBN 90-286-0063-9.

Although national purchasing policies favoring domestic firms exist in Belgium and the Netherlands, they have not greatly discriminated against trade with outside states. In fact, they are probably at as minimum level of such national preferences as can be reasonably expected.

* 7.165 *
Verreydt, Eric, and Jean Waelbroeck. "European Community Protection against Manufactured Imports from Developing Countries: A Case Study in the Political Economy of Protection." In: *Import Competition and Response; a Conference Report of the National Bureau of Economic Research*, edited by Jagdish N. Bhagwati. Chicago: University of Chicago Press, 1982. ISBN 0-226-04538-2.

The authors provide an overview of the political and economic pressures for protectionism in the European Community and the interaction among Community institutions and national governments. They discuss various industries, such as textiles, clothing, footwear, steel, and shipbuilding, and the reasons for success in gaining protection. They conclude by noting that public support for protectionism may be weakening since previous measures did not lead to the hoped for results.

* 7.166 *
Wagenhals, Gerhard. "Industrial Policy in the Federal Republic of Germany: A Survey." In: *Industrial Policies for Growth and Competitiveness: An Economic Perspective*, edited by F. Gerard Adams and Lawrence R. Klein. Lexington, MA: Lexington Books, 1983. ISBN 0-669-05412-7.

West German industrial policy includes protection for some industries. Protection is often applied in cases where international competitiveness is seen to be hindered by protection in other states. *Ad hoc* measures applied in times of economic stress have tended to become permanent.

* 7.167 *
Yannopoulos, George. "The Effects of Full Membership on the Manufacturing Industries." In: *Greece and the European Community*, edited by Loukas Tsoukalis. Westmead, England: Saxon House, 1979. ISBN 0-566-00232-9.

Greek tariffs had an anti-export bias that favored firms that produced for the domestic market. The lowering of tariffs with full EC membership will lower effective protection rates against imports from third countries, but Greece is better off as a full member of the EC in a world that is increasingly mercantilist.

Costs of Protectionism

* 7.168 *
Birnberg, Thomas B. "Trade Reform Options: Economic Effects on Developing and Developed Countries." In: *Policy Alternatives for a New International Economic Order: An Economic Analysis*, edited by William R. Cline. New York: Praeger, 1979. LC 79-87553.

According to detailed results of analyses of the effects of tariff cuts and reductions in non-tariff barriers, trade liberalization by the developed countries would lead to greater benefits than losses. Such liberalization would also aid the developing countries with only limited labor displacement in the developed states.

* 7.169 *
Blackhurst, Richard. "Reluctance to Adjust and Economic Nationalism." In: *The New Economic Nationalism*, edited by Otto Hieronymi. London: Macmillan 1980. ISBN 0-333-26173-9.

The failure to make adequate economic adjustments in the industrialized nations is the source of the majority of international and domestic economic problems. Import restrictions in effect are restrictions on exports as well and will lead to employment losses.

* 7.170 *
Corden, W. Max. "Policies Towards Market Disturbances." In: *Issues in World Trade Policy: GATT at the Crossroads*, edited by R. H. Snape. New York: St. Martin's, 1986. ISBN 0-312-43724-2.

Corden considers various policies that the developed countries can use to deal with problems resulting from the global recession, including income policy, welfare programs, market operations, and protection. He argues that protectionist policies, including tariffs and quotas, cannot solve the problems.

* 7.171 *
Corden, W. Max. *Trade Policy and Economic Welfare.* Oxford: Clarendon Press, 1974. ISBN 0-19-828199-4.

Corden presents a lengthy theoretical consideration of the consequences of protection, both tariff and non-tariff, in employment, income distribution, foreign investment, and capital accumulation among others. He concludes by arguing that in most cases a policy not related to trade is the best one for dealing with various domestic economic difficulties in such areas. He does note that intervention in the trade sector may be appropriate and have advantages, including the fact that protectionism may be a helpful cosmetic policy for the government.

* 7.172 *
Deardorff, Alan V., Robert M. Stern, and Mark N. Greene. "The Implications of Alternative Trade Strategies for the United States." In: *The New International Economic Order: A U.S. Response*, edited by David B.H. Denoon. New York: New York University Press, 1979. ISBN 0-8147-1769-1.

The authors analyze the effects of multilateral tariff reductions on the developed countries. Such reductions will lead to lower prices for imports and also exports to a lesser extent. Even industries in specific states that suffer from the loss of protectionism will have some gains if the tariff reductions are multilateral. The authors also note that U.S. tariffs are generally lower than those of the other developed countries.

* 7.173 *
Edwards, Geoffrey. "Four Sectors: Textiles, Man-Made Fibers, Shipbuilding, Aircraft." In: *National Industrial Strategies and the World Economy*, edited by John Pinder. Totowa, NJ: Allanheld, Osmun, 1982. ISBN 0-86598-040-3.

Edwards analyzes a number of industries and the potential for their growth in various nations. Protection has been present in many of these industries, but it has hindered rather than prevented imports from other countries.

* 7.174 *
Hawkins, Robert G., and Rita M. Rodriguez. "Potential Economic Benefits and Costs of Adjustments in Trade Liberalization." In: *The United States and International Markets: Commercial Policy Options in an Age of Controls*, edited by Robert G. Hawkins and Ingo Walter. Lexington, MA: Lexington Books, 1972. ISBN 0-669-84020-3.

The authors develop a model to examine the trade possibilities of a number of industrialized states, and they find that Japan would gain with trade liberalization with small adjustment costs; Australia, Norway, Sweden, and the United States would gain with some adjustment costs; and the United Kingdom, New Zealand, and to a lesser extent Austria and Canada would have high adjustment costs if multilateral trade liberalization occurred. The authors also provide a pairwise comparison of these nations to ascertain the probable costs and benefits of bilateral reductions.

* 7.175 *

Hindley, Brian. "EC Imports of VCRs from Japan: A Costly Precedent." *Journal of World Trade Law* 20:2 (March/April 1986): 168-184.

The first voluntary export restraint (VER) imposed on Japan by the EC in 1983 was most important as a precedent for future actions of a similar type. The VER failed to help domestic producers in the EC and provided no incentive for domestic firms to improve their competitive situation.

* 7.176 *

Horstmann, Ignatius J., and James R. Markusen. "Up the Average Cost Curve: Inefficient Entry and the New Protectionism." *Journal of International Economics* 20:3-4 (May 1986): 225-247.

Protection will lead to the entry of new firms into an industry, generating inefficiency and higher costs. The authors' model corresponds closely with the actual entry and exit of Canadian firms and their responses to trade liberalization.

* 7.177 *

Maddison, Angus. "North Atlantic Trade and Payments." In: *North American and Western European Economic Policies: Proceedings of a Conference Held by the International Economic Association*, edited by Charles P. Kindleberger and Andrew Shonfield. London: Macmillan, 1971. ISBN 0-312-57890-3.

Maddison calculated the effects of trade liberalization on past economic growth in Europe and the United States, as well as probable future effects. Liberalization has made modest contributions to European growth in the past but has had virtually no effect on the U.S. performance.

* 7.178 *

Root, Franklin R. "Some Trends in the World Economy and Their Implications for International Business Strategy." *Journal of International Business Studies* 15:3 (Winter 1984): 19-23.

In his general overview of the global economy, Root argues that protection of declining industries in the industrialized states will ultimately fail since the economic imperative of shifting comparative advantage will overcome the political imperative of protection in these states. He also argues that firms must adjust to a global economy and be willing to externalize operations.

* 7.179 *

Sampson, Gary P. "Market Disturbances and the Multifibre Arrangement." In: *Issues in World Trade Policy: GATT at the Crossroads*, edited by R.H. Snape. New York: St. Martin's, 1986. ISBN 0-312-43724-2.

Sampson discusses the Multi-Fibre Arrangement and limitation on imports of textiles into the developed countries. After 20 years, the limitations remain even though they were supposed to be temporary measures to permit industrial readjustments--some of which has occurred. Such obstacles to imports have costs for the domestic economies of the developed states and actually hinder structural readjustments.

* 7.180 *

Tsoukalis, Loukas, and Robert Strauss. "Crisis and Adjustment in European Steel: Beyond Laisser-Faire." *Journal of Common Market Studies* 23:3 (March 1985): 207-228.

The authors review the problems of the steel industry in Europe and measures taken to aid it, including protection. They note that protectionism is not a long-term solution but that it is justified while the industry undergoes adjustment and reorganization.

THE DEVELOPING COUNTRIES ADRIFT IN A PROTECTIONIST SEA

The developing countries have faced some special difficulties in the world economy as a result of the rise of the new protectionism. Some of these problems have resulted from neo-mercantile policies in the developed states while other difficulties have been a consequence of their own domestic protectionist policies. The NICs of Asia and Latin America have been targets for much of the protectionist response in the world since their exporting activities have been threatening industries in the developed countries with increasing import competition.

Although the industrialized states play a larger role in international trade than the developing ones, the increase of protectionism in the developed world, as well as its continuing presence in the developing one, has created greater problems for the developing states. The industrial bases of the developing countries, even the NICs, are not as diversified as those of the industrialized nations. Thus, a quota in a developed state, or some other obstacle to imports, could adversely affect the export potential of a particular developing country. That country, lacking the requisite diplomatic and economic leverage for negotiating effectively with a larger state, may then have to acquiesce in voluntary limitations on its exports with limited options for increasing exports in other product lines.

Many of the developing states have sought to further their economic growth by exporting to the large markets in the developed countries, on the grounds that such increases in exports would not only facilitate domestic industrialization but provide the hard currency for essential foreign purchases. The rise of the new protectionism has created obvious difficulties for this approach to economic development. As noted in Chapter 5, the inability of GATT to deal with the trade problems of developing states led these countries to use UNCTAD as a forum for their international efforts. The call for the creation of Generalized Systems of Preferences (GSPs) by the developed states to the advantage of the developing ones was one of the major topics of UNCTAD conferences.

Freer Trade and the Developing Countries

Many analysts of the position of the developing states in the global economic system have agreed that these states have gained in the past from a liberal trade regime and would gain in the future from a liberalization of present trade practices. The multilateral tariff reductions negotiated under GATT led to increases of exports of manufactures and raw materials. Further reductions in tariffs and decreases in NTBs are seen as one useful mechanism for improving opportunities for economic growth in the developing states by expanding the opportunities for trade. Continued trade liberalization is seen as being more important than the granting of special market access to the developing states. This view implicitly accepts the idea that the developing states can gain from shifts in comparative advantage or that they will be permitted to gain from such shifts. Trade liberalization, of course, would facilitate shifts in comparative advantage in at least some product areas from the developed countries to the developing ones. In many cases, the resulting exports from the developing states would not initially present major problems for the industrialized nations since the volume of such exports would be small in comparison to the overall global market and particular domestic markets in the developed countries.

Effects of Protectionism in the Industrialized Countries

Existing obstacles to imports in the industrialized countries have often worked to the special disadvantage of developing states. As noted in earlier chapters, tariff schedules often favor imports of raw materials over goods that have undergone some processing. Specific tariffs are more likely to be part of the duty applied to products from the developing countries as well, with such specific tariffs increasing the overall cost of an originally low priced item. The consequence of such a situation is that the developing countries can competitively export raw materials much more readily than they can export the semi-processed goods, even though the development of the processing facilities can be an important first step in the creation of a local industrial base. Removal of tariff obstacles to imports would increase the exports of developing countries with only small costs to the industrialized nations.[1]

One of the few changes in tariffs that have been of help to developing states has been the elimination of nuisance tariffs on some goods that only they are likely to export. The removal of these small duties from imports lessens the need for paperwork and may even slightly increase their price competitiveness with substitutable goods, such as bananas for apples. Various NTBs used in the developed nations have also been more likely to protect processing industries in a developed state rather than raw materials producers, although there have been exceptions in the case of some

strategic materials considered important for national defense. As a consequence, such NTBs will hurt the developing countries in particular. Subsidies and other forms of government assistance have often been given to sectors facing import competition from the developing states. The NTBs presently used in the industrialized countries in general often do affect exports from the developing countries more than those from other developed states, a possibly unintentional bias that nonetheless makes developing countries more vulnerable to the effects of the NTBs.[2]

Other than Japan, orderly marketing arrangements and export restraints have almost exclusively been applied to the exports of the developing countries. Textile and apparel industries in the developed countries have been protected at the expense of a wide variety of developing states. The increasing protection given to these industries has removed products from the potential export mix that are very suitable for developing countries in the early stages of industrialization. A textile industry with its standardized technology has often been one of the first kinds of industries that can be created where a country will have a comparative advantage in global markets vis-a-vis established exporters. Japan's early re-industrialization after World War II followed this path, as did some of the NICs in later years. The absence of markets in other countries is particularly important for smaller developing countries since they lack a domestic market large enough to support a textile industry independent of exports. Although the protection in the industrialized states has not prevented the development of these kinds of industries, it has slowed down the pace of their creation and expansion, hurting the prospects for economic growth in some of the developing states.

The Generalized System of Preferences

The developing countries have sought to have the developed states institute GSPs for many of the products they export, particularly some manufactured items. Under such schedules, goods from the developing countries are charged lower tariffs than similar goods from industrialized nations. If all other price considerations are equal, the goods from the developing countries will then have a market advantage. The preference might also make them competitive when an industry is just developing even though the initial prices might be somewhat higher than for similar goods produced in the developed countries. In some cases, even greater tariff advantages have been suggested for exports from the very poor developing countries. The United States, the EC as a body, other European countries, and Japan have set up GSPs, which then to some extent constitute a trade barrier to imports from the countries that are not favored under the schedule.

As might be expected in a world economy where protection is on the increase, the schedules authorize many exceptions and safeguards to prevent sudden large scale inflows of imports that would threaten local industries. Many schedules contain ceilings beyond which the preference disappears. Such ceilings do not provide a great incentive for additional exports from the developing states. There are also rules of origin, designed to prevent developing countries from simply serving as assembly points for goods produced in other developed countries. The countries with the GSPs have also often excluded exactly those items that are produced locally for the domestic market by firms already experiencing import competition from the developing world. Overall, GSPs have not yet been a solution to the problems that the developing countries have had in seeking markets in the developed world. Given the limitations of and restrictions on the GSPs, it is not surprising that their effects on the export positions of the developing countries has not generally been great. The preferences do not even necessarily offset the existing tariff disabilities that are present for many developing country exports.[3] There have been some increases in their exports of certain products, but the overall volume increase has not been large. In some cases, the countries that have gained the most from GSPs have been those that were already exporting the product, and therefore were already competitive. The tariff preferences then permitted them to expand their exports.[4] While the volumes involved have not been a large portion of a particular developed nation's imports or the imports of the developed world, they have at times constituted major increases in the exports of a developing country or countries. Thus, certain states have probably gained significant benefits from the expansion of export possibilities, although the benefits have not been present for large numbers of countries. In fact, one of the arguments made by supporters of the GSP idea is that the amount of new exports will not cause major dislocations in the industrialized countries but will still be important for the economic growth of the developing states.

The creation of the GSPs has generated some controversy about their effects on efforts at trade liberalization. Technically they violate the equal treatment provisions of GATT at first, but their general, if grudging, acceptance and implementation by the industrialized states has prevented the issue from being important. There has been at least some recognition that GSPs are an appropriate way to attempt to assist economic growth in the developing states. Eventually, GATT rules were modified to permit special treatment such as the GSP for the developing countries. The schedules do, however, further the trend away from freer trade in the international economic system. The preferences for the developing countries could also make it less likely for industrialized nations to reduce their existing barriers to imports from other developed states since that would mean increased import competition for domestic firms. Also, it is politically more palatable to domestic audiences to reduce barriers to imports from poor countries than to reduce barriers to imports from other rich states. The existence of the GSPs may also make it less likely that NTBs will be reduced since the preferences make the protection they offer more important. Ultimately, there is also a fear among those favoring trade liberalization that GSPs are one additional factor that makes it much more difficult to continue supporting the principle of free trade.

The presence of GSPs may have slowed the support for trade liberalization among at least some of the developing countries. If tariffs in some product areas are dramatically reduced, then the marketing advantage for the developing states could be lost. For example, if the *ad valorum* tariff on a $5 import is ten percent, the duty would increase the cost to $5.50. If the preference system provides that the tariff on goods from developing countries is half the normal duty (in this case five percent), a $5.20 import from a developing country will be priced at $5.46 after the tariff. Thus, it will have a small price advantage over the imports from the country without the preference. If multilateral tariff negotiations reduce the tariff level to four percent, and thus two percent for developing states, the same import from another developed country will be $5.20 while the import from the developing state will be $5.304 after the duty has been assessed. Some developing countries have feared losing their price advantages if the effect of the preferences is eroded by general tariff reductions. While it has been argued that general trade liberalization will ultimately help the developing countries more than preferences, it is not clear that such overall liberalization will occur, particularly in product areas where the developing states can effectively compete, in the light of the recent history of the use of protectionist measures. In addition, while the developing countries as a group may gain from freer trade, it is quite possible that individual states could actually lose markets even though the group as a whole gains. Thus, the rational policy for many of these states would be to oppose tariff reductions if they would lose markets or if they perceive that there will be a net loss. Perceptions, of course, can be as important as facts when policy decisions are made. Present market advantages are clear and possible gains from trade liberalization are less clear, especially in a time when protectionism has been on the rise and when NTBs have often been used to re-create the obstacles to imports removed by tariff reductions.

Trade Policies of the Developing Countries

The developing countries themselves have not always supported free trade or trade liberalization by the policies that they have adopted. They have often maintained relatively high barriers to imports, at least in particular areas, either in the form of tariffs, quotas, licensing requirements, or subsidies. The resulting effective levels of protection have often been quite high. The high levels of protection have continued even though there have been indications that economic growth has been greater in countries with lower levels of tariffs,[5] although it should be noted that it is possible that countries experiencing greater growth were the ones that were more likely to reduce their levels of protection since their industries were more competitive. The products that have received the highest levels of protection have often been ones that are produced in other developing states, thus limiting the potential for self-supporting trade among the developing states and making the decisions of the industrialized countries regarding protection that much more important.

Developing states have often maintained protection in some economic sectors as part of an effort to industrialize and to build up infant industries. This approach is usually referred to as import substitution since the new domestic industries are expected to replace goods that were formerly imported. Import substitution has been effective in at least some countries in building up basic industries. Eventually, as industrialization proceeds, production for overseas markets should occur, requiring governments to change their trade policies. Such changes, however, can be difficult. Owners, management, and workers in the industries favored by an infant industry tariff or by an import substitution policy may have increased their political influence to such an extent that removal of the favorable trade policy is difficult. Also, import substitution policies have at times failed to include sufficient incentives for industries to move to a position where they will be competitive without the protection.

The protectionist barriers that are maintained by developing states, either as a consequence of import substitution policies or as a response to domestic pressures, have definite costs. As is always the case, consumers naturally pay more for the protected goods. It may also be difficult to meet long-term policy objectives. The protection applied in developing countries often discriminates against export industries, even though expansion of exports is frequently another goal of government policy. Firms may find it more profitable to produce for the domestic market rather than for overseas markets. The authoritarian forms of government that are typical of many of the developing countries have often seen the capital intensive economic sectors combine with the bureaucracy to implement policies that favor production for the domestic market at the expense of labor intensive exports.[6] The increased cost for goods that are inputs into the final product may also make goods noncompetitive in overseas markets. Even when subsidies are provided to firms in export sectors, they are often insufficient to compensate for the existing disincentives. The frequently high levels of protection thus result in limitations on both imports and exports, resulting in suggestions that the developing countries would fare better overall with lower levels of protection. The protection provided tends to discriminate against imports from other developing countries more than imports from the developed states since the developing countries are frequently attempting to create the same industries. It then becomes impossible to determine which developing country has a comparative advantage in which products.[7]

The developing states do have at least some need for the protection of their local firms. Without at least some initial protection, industries would find it extremely difficult to develop at all, and they could not hope to compete with foreign imports. Import substitution can be effective in the early stages of industrialization in a country. Export subsidies have been considered to be the best mechanism for aiding infant industries. Unlike tariffs or quotas, they encourage efficiency in production.[8] Such subsidies, however, face the danger of countervailing duties being applied in the developed countries. When more advanced products can be manufactured locally, such a policy can become counter-productive. It is necessary to change policies at the appropriate time from one favoring import substitution to one supporting global competitiveness. Some form of transition from import substitution to exporting is usually necessary. The governments of developing countries still have to be aware of domestic pressures that may limit their ability to change the policies. While many of these states do not have the open interest group competition and electoral contests found in the developed states, the wishes of the population or key groups in the society cannot be ignored. These domestic considerations will further complicate any transitional stage in trade policies.

One response to the need or demands for high barriers to imports and the associated need to promote exports has been the creation of free trade zones. Firms locate in these areas and essentially produce for overseas markets. The firms in question can take advantage of local resources that are present for manufacturing enterprises but still avoid the disincentives to exporting that the high levels of protection around the domestic market can create. The free trade zones are designed to provide employment for nationals, earn foreign exchange, and increase the skill levels of the population with some eventual spillover to the domestic economy outside the free trade zone. Free trade zones have been widely utilized in the developing countries in Asia, including the Asian NICs, as a means of increasing exports. Free trade zones, however, can create problems, such as attracting too many skilled workers to the zone at the expense of the domestic economy, attracting investment funds away from local firms not in the zone, or requiring substantial government expenditures in infrastructural support that could potentially be more profitably invested elsewhere in the country.

The Newly Industrializing Countries

The NICs are the most economically advanced developing countries. Singapore, Hong Kong, South Korea, Taiwan, Brazil, and Mexico are usually included in the group of countries considered to be NICs. Argentina, Chile, Colombia, Malaysia, Thailand, and Turkey have sometimes been included as well, but they are more frequently considered to be states nearing the NIC status. The NICs were important figures in the events leading to the rise of protectionism. The ability of their exports to penetrate the domestic markets of the developed nations was one of the factors that led these states to increase their levels of protection. The NICs had begun to export products in areas where producers in the developed states were active. Multilateral tariff reductions normally favored intra-industry trade, which aided the developed states without posing a threat to any of them. When such reductions facilitated competition from the NICs, protectionism appeared.[9] The NICs have been among the states that have faced VERs, OMAs, and quotas of various kinds, as well as other barriers to their imports. There have also been suggestions in the developed states that the GSPs only be granted to poorer developing countries, suggestions that frequently have been aimed at reducing import competition from the NICs. The NICs, however, have been able to adapt to at least some of the restrictions on their products and have continued to export. Their adaptability in turn has led to increased pressures for barriers in other countries, especially in times of higher unemployment associated with global recession. Thus, they are victims of their successful ability to export, although other developing states, as a consequence, have faced difficulties with protectionism as well.

The Asian NICs have also adopted some of the same practices that Japan has used to encourage exports, which has led to some of the same kinds of charges of unfair trading practices. Again, their successes in exporting to world markets have created problems and encouraged protection elsewhere. The fact that the NICs also protect some of their domestic industries makes it difficult for them to mount effective protests against similar practices in other states.

The NICs have not been active in supporting global trade liberalization. While they would undoubtedly gain markets if free trade were the norm, they have no reason to assume that liberalization would necessarily occur in the product areas in which they have been able to compete. The NICs, in fact, have been among the countries that have gained markets as a result of the various GSPs instituted in the industrialized countries. Further reductions of tariffs could reduce their present export opportunities by reducing their margins of preference without any offsetting gains in other product areas. The policies of the NICs in regard to their domestic markets also militates against support for trade liberalization since they have tended to have significant barriers to imports. They have generally gone through an import substitution phase and then moved to a more export oriented trade policy, facing many of the problems inherent in that transition. Their levels of protection in at least some areas have continued to effectively limit import competition long past the time justified by the import substitution policy. Like other states they have attempted to protect industries with large numbers of employees to avoid the domestic discontent that could occur with the displacement of that many workers. The protection that is maintained has often been more selective than has been the case for many other developed states, but it does increase the costs for domestic consumers in the industrial sectors in question.

End Notes

1. Golub, Stephen S. and J. M. Finger, "The Processing of Primary Commodities: Effects of Developed Country Tariff Escalation and Developing-Country Export Taxes." *Journal of Political Economy* 87:3 (June 1979): pp.559-577.

2. Walter, Ingo. "Nontariff Barriers and the Export Performance of Developing Economies." *American Economic Review* 61:2 (May 1971): pp.195-205.

3. Yeats, Alexander J. "Tariff Valuation, Transport Costs and the Establishment of Trade Preferences among Developing Countries." *World Development* 8:3 (March 1980): pp.129-136.

4. Sapir, Andre and Lars Lundberg. "The U.S. Generalized System of Preferences and Its Impacts," in: *The Structure and Evolution of Recent U.S. Trade Policy*, edited by Robert E. Baldwin and Anne O. Krueger. Chicago: University of Chicago Press, 1984: pp.195-231.

5. Cooper, Richard N. "Third World Tariff Tangle," *Foreign Policy* 4 (Fall 1971): PP.35-50.
   and
   Morrison, Thomas K. "Manufactured Exports and Protection in Developing Countries: A Cross-Country Analysis," *Economic Development and Cultural Change* 25:1 (October 1976): pp.151-158.

6. Findlay, Ronald and Stanislaw Wellisz. "Some Aspects of the Political Economy of Trade Restrictions," *Kyklos* 36:3 (1983): pp. 469-481.

7. Krause, Lawrence B. and Sueo Sekiguchi. "Dealing with Change," in: *Economic Interaction in the Pacific Basin*, edited by Lawrence B. Krause and Sueo Sekiguchi. Wahington, D.C.: Brookings Institution, 1980: p. 251.

8. Bergsman, Joel. "Commercial Policy Allocative Efficiency, and 'X-Efficiency'" *Quarterly Journal of Economics* 78:3 (August 1974: pp.424-425.

9. Ruggie, John Gerard. "Another Round, Another Requiem? Prospects for the Global Negotiations," in: *Power, Passions, and Purpose: Prospects for North-South Negotiations*, edited by Jagdish N. Bhagwati and John Gerard Ruggie. Cambridge, MA: MIT Press, 1984: pp.37-38.

Chapter 8: Annotated Bibliography

General Works

* 8.1 *
Bell, Harry H. "Trade Relations with the Third World: Preferential Aspects of Protective Structures." In: *The United States and International Markets: Commercial Policy Options in an Age of Controls*, edited by Robert G. Hawkins and Ingo Walter. Lexington, MA: Lexington Books, 1972. ISBN 0-669-84020-3.

The author discusses the wide range of protectionist practices in the industrialized states that limit the exports of the developing states and, in the developing countries, an equally wide range of protectionist practices that hinder trade. He notes with approval that in 1969 Hong Kong, with virtually no protection, exported more manufactures than the South Asian subcontinent and South America combined. He also considers various preference schemes put forward to encourage exports from the developing world.

* 8.2 *
Bishop, Vaughn F. "The New International Economic Order and Sub-Saharan Africa." In: *The Global Political Economy in the 1980s*, edited by Michael Stohl and Harry R. Targ. Cambridge, MA: Schenkman, 1982. ISBN 0-97073-236-6.

Among other difficulties, the African states face the consequences of protectionism in developed countries, particularly in agricultural products. High levels of protection of domestic markets in the African countries reduce incentives for increased productivity and efficiency.

* 8.3 *
David, Wilfred L. "Dimensions of the North-South Confrontation." In: *Issues and Prospects for the New International Economic Order*, edited by William G. Tyler. Lexington, MA: Lexington Books, 1977. ISBN 0-669-01445-1.

David suggests that trade liberalization will aid the developing countries, but he also views favorably import substitution policies in these states and some autarchic development. Industrialization in the developing world would benefit its members and the industrialized countries.

* 8.4 *
Junz, Helen B. "Adjustment Policies and Trade Relations with Developing Countries." In: *Protectionism or Industrial Adjustment?* Atlantic Papers no. 39. Paris: Atlantic Institute for International Affairs, 1980.

Protection against exports from the developing states will be counter-productive since they represent the major expanding market in the world for exports from the industrialized nations. Institutionalizing preferences for the developing countries and accepting infant industry arguments will not benefit these states in the long run. The developing countries should begin to accept all the obligations of membership in GATT.

* 8.5 *

Little, I. M. D. "The Developing Countries and the International Order." In: *Challenges to a Liberal International Order: A Conference Sponsored by the American Enterprise Institute for Public Policy Research*, edited by Ryan C. Amacher, Gottfried Haberler, and Thomas D. Willett. Washington, DC: American Enterprise Institute for Public Policy Research, 1979. ISBN 0-8447-2152-2.

Little argues that a liberal international economic order with limits on protectionism and other constraints on trade has in fact aided many developing countries to attain remarkable economic growth. Those developing countries that have followed appropriate policies, including limited protection for their own domestic industries, have fared well. Thus, a reduction of protectionism in the developed and developing states with appropriate policies in other areas should lead to continued growth and economic development in the developing states.

* 8.6 *

McCulloch, Rachel. "Gains to Latin America from Trade Liberalization in Developed and Developing Nations." In: *Export Diversification and the New Protectionism: The Experience of Latin America*, edited by Werner Baer and Malcolm Gillis. Champaign: Bureau of Economic and Business Research, College of Commerce and Business Administration, University of Illinois at Urbana-Champaign, 1981. LC 81-61370.

Exporters in other developing countries have penetrated the markets of developed countries more than have those in Latin America, even in the face of non-tariff barriers. Multilateral tariff reductions have also hurt the Latin American export performance by eliminating some of the advantages of preference schemes. Even increased trade within LAFTA seems to have resulted from increased demand rather than the reduction of protection within this free trade area.

* 8.7 *

Ruggie, John Gerard, "Political Structure and Change in the International Economic Order: The North-South Dimension." In: *The Antinomies of Interdependence: National Welfare and the International Division of Labor*, edited by John Gerard Ruggie. New York: Columbia University Press, 1983. ISBN 0-231-05725-3.

Ruggie argues that the major principles in international trade and international monetary interactions since World War II have been liberalization and domestic stabilization. Liberalization has proceeded the farthest in trade in manufactures since such trade has led to intra-industry specialization that has not greatly threatened domestic stability in the industrialized states. Stabilization, including protectionist measures, has taken precedence in agricultural trade and in industries that lack intra-industry specialization, which include those in which the NICs have been most competitive.

* 8.8 *

Uri, Pierre. *Development without Dependence*. New York: Praeger, 1976. ISBN 0-275-55830-4.

In considering problems of economic growth facing the developing countries, Uri deals with a variety of trade related issues, particularly in chapters 7, 8, and 9. He notes the limitations of special tariff preferences, the biases against developing countries in the protectionist barriers of the industrialized states, and the limited positive benefits of customs unions.

* 8.9 *

Wall, David. "Developing Countries in the Liberalisation of World Trade." In: *Towards an Open World Economy*, edited by Frank McFadzean, Sir Alec Cairncross, Sidney Golt, James Meade, W. M. Corden, Harry G. Johnson, and T. M. Rybczynski. London: Macmillan, 1972. ISBN 0-312-81060-1.

Some preferences for developing country exports have been created, although protective devices have been instituted in developed states to prevent the developing countries from taking full advantage of export opportunities. Wall offers suggestions for improving the trade position of the developing countries.

Freer Trade and the Developing Countries

* 8.10 *

Balassa, Bela, and Constantine Michalopoulos. "Liberalizing Trade between Developed and Developing Countries." *Journal of World Trade Law* 20:1 (January/February 1986): 3-28.

Present levels of protection have imposed higher costs on both the developed and developing states. Non-tariff barriers need to be removed and the developing countries need to reduce their levels of protection. GATT needs to be strengthened as part of a move for trade liberalization.

* 8.11 *

Behrman, Jere R. "Rethinking Global Negotiations: Trade." In: *Power, Passions, and Purpose: Prospects for North-South Negotiations*, edited by Jagdish N. Bhagwati and John Gerard Ruggie. Cambridge, MA: MIT Press, 1984. ISBN 0-262-02201-x.

Non-tariff barriers in the developed countries were originally used against imports from other developed states but have increasingly been aimed at imports from the developing countries. Creation of special preferences have favored the more advanced developing states and encouraged protectionism in the developed countries. While free trade is not a panacea for their problems, the developing countries would probably gain more by working to strengthen GATT and an open trading system.

* 8.12 *
Cline, William R. *Exports of Manufactures from Developing Countries: Performance and Prospects for Market Access.* Washington, DC: Brookings Institution, 1984. ISBN 0-8157-1463-7.

After an analysis of protection levels in the developed states, Cline argues that prospects for increased exports by the developing countries, particularly the NICs, are good and are not likely to lead to increased protection. Such exports will contribute greatly to economic development, but an open trading regime is essential to progress.

* 8.13 *
Finger, J. M. "Effects of the Kennedy Round Tariff Concessions on the Exports of Developing Countries." *Economic Journal* 86 (March 1976): 87-95.

Finger analyzed the effects of the Kennedy Round reductions in tariffs on the exports of manufactures from the developing countries. He found that tariff cuts did matter in that they led to substantial increases of imports from the developing countries as well as from other developed states.

* 8.14 *
Fishlow, Albert. "The Mature Neighbor Policy: A Proposal for a United States Economic Policy for Latin America." In: *Latin America and World Economy: A Changing International Order*, edited by Joseph Grunwald. Beverly Hills, CA: Sage, 1978. ISBN 0-8039-0864-4.

Although regional integration efforts such as the Central American Common Market and the Latin American Free Trade Association had some initial successes, they have foundered on disagreements over the distribution of benefits. Free trade policies would help the Latin American countries with exports, particularly of manufactures, substantially more than special tariff preferences.

* 8.15 *
Hansen, Roger D. "North-South Policy--What's the Problem." *Foreign Affairs* 58:5 (Summer 1980): 1104-1128.

Hansen's discussion of differences between the industrialized states and the developing ones includes the effects of protectionism. The Tokyo Round of GATT negotiations fell far short of the

hopes that the developing states had of greater market access to the developed countries.

* 8.16 *
Isard, Peter. "Employment Impacts of Textile Imports and Investment: A Vintage-Capital Model." *American Economic Review* 63:3 (June 1973): 402-416.

Isard argues that developing countries' exports of textiles to the United States account for a small portion of the total market, thus permitting trade liberalization. Adjustment assistance to the domestic industry will alleviate domestic problems, while liberalization will greatly aid the developing states.

* 8.17 *
Sapir, Andre, and Robert E. Baldwin. "India and the Tokyo Round." *World Development* 11:7 (July 1983): 565-574.

An analysis of the effects of the multilateral reductions of the Tokyo Round on India indicated that the gains from tariff reductions outweighed by far the losses arising from erosion of preference under the GSP. Textile exports would also increase if there were no quota limitations in the developed countries.

Effects of Protectionism in the Industrialized Countries

* 8.18 *
Bhagwati, Jagdish N. "Market Disruption, Export Market Disruption, and GATT Reform." In: *The New International Economic Order: The North-South Debate*, edited by Jagdish N. Bhagwati. Cambridge, MA: MIT Press, 1977. ISBN 0-262-52042-7.

Protectionist restrictions or even the threat of protectionist restrictions by the developed nations impose a welfare loss on developing states. Bhagwati proposes a compensation scheme within the GATT framework for the affected developing states.

* 8.19 *
Carey, Sarah C., and Sheila Avril McLean. "The United States, Countertrade and Third World Trade." *Journal of World Trade Law* 20:4 (July/August 1986): 441-473.

Countertrade is becoming increasingly prevalent in the world. The United States should take advantage of the trend to aid both itself and the developing states in Latin America. Annex 1 of the article contains a helpful recent history of the use of countertrade by sixteen Latin American countries.

* 8.20 *
Das, Dilip K. "Dismantling the Multifibre Arrangement?" *Journal of World Trade Law* 19:1 (January/February 1985): 67-80.

Ending the Multi-Fibre Arrangement on textiles and clothing would increase the exports of the developing countries at little cost to the industrialized countries. During the time that the arrangements have been in effect, world trade in these products has increased less than the growth of overall trade due to the protection offered to domestic industries in the developed states.

* 8.21 *
Finger, J. M. "GATT Tariff Concessions and the Exports of Developing Countries--United States Concessions at the Dillon Round." *Economic Journal* 84 (September 1974): 566-575.

Tariff cuts in the Dillon Round of tariff reductions in 1960-1961 had a very limited effect on U.S. imports from the developing countries. The tariff reductions involved products produced by other developed states or products from the developing countries with a fixed demand. Fixed demand meant that the lower cost and lower price to the consumer did not lead to increased imports.

* 8.22 *
Golub, Stephen S., and J.M. Finger. "The Processing of Primary Commodities: Effects of Developed Country Tariff Escalation and Developing-Country Export Taxes." *Journal of Political Economy* 87:3 (June 1979): 559-577.

The authors analyze the influence of export taxes on primary commodities in the developing countries and tariffs that discriminate against processed or semi-processed primary commodities in the developed states. They conclude that removal of these impediments to trade in eight commodity areas would greatly increase exports from the developing countries at a smaller cost to the processing industries in the developed states than the costs of the present arrangement.

* 8.23 *
Hansen, Roger D. "Trade, the Developing Countries, and North-South Relations." In: *Tariffs, Quotas & Trade: The Politics of Protectionism*, edited by the Institute for Contemporary Studies. San Francisco: The Institute, 1979. ISBN 0-917-616-34-0.

Hansen points out that exports in manufactures are very important for economic development in the developing countries as a group, yet it is these exports that are particularly threatened by protectionist measures in the industrialized states. He argues that greater exports of manufactures from the developing states will be mutually beneficial for all states and that the developed states should undertake adjustment policies rather than protectionism to deal with the dislocations of certain industries, thus permitting the general consuming public to gain from trade liberalization.

* 8.24 *
Helleiner, G. K. "The New Industrial Protectionism and the Developing Countries." In: *Protectionism or Industrial Adjustment?* Atlantic Papers no. 39. Paris: Atlantic Institute for International Affairs, 1980.

The new protectionism in industrialized states has magnified distortions of the trade patterns of developing countries, already hindered by previous barriers. It has discouraged such countries from exporting manufactured products for which they have a comparative advantage. Limiting the new protection is more important for the developing countries than tariff reductions or special preferences.

* 8.25 *
Helleiner, G. K. "Structural Aspects of Third World Trade: Some Trends and Some Prospects." *Journal of Development Studies* 15:3 (April 1979): 70-88.

The new protectionism in developed countries particularly hurts exports from the developing world, both in primary products and manufactured ones. These protectionist effects may be increased by "private nontariff barriers" used by multinational corporations.

* 8.26 *
Helleiner, G.K. "World Market Imperfections and the Developing Countries." In: *Policy Alternatives for a New International Economic Order: An Economic Analysis*, edited by William R. Cline. New York: Praeger, 1979. LC 79-87553.

The cost of market imperfections in the form of tariffs and non-tariff barriers in the developed states hurts the trade position of the developing countries. On occasion rich countries might benefit from such imperfections, but it is virtually impossible for the developing states to gain from them.

* 8.27 *
Herander, Mark G. "The Relative Impact of U.S. Specific Tariffs on Manufactured Imports from Developing and Developed Countries." *Quarterly Review of Economics and Business* 25:2 (Summer 1985): 91-108.

Exports of manufactures from developing countries face discrimination from the U.S. tariff structure. Special preferences do not overcome discrimination, and changing the tariff structure would be more valuable than preference schedules.

* 8.28 *
Hughes, Helen, and Anne O. Krueger. "Effects of Protection in Developed Countries on Developing Countries' Exports of Manufactures." In: *The Structure and Evolution of Recent U.S. Trade Policy*, edited by Robert E. Baldwin and Anne O. Krueger. Chicago: University of Chicago Press, 1984. ISBN 0-266-03604-9.

The authors argue that protection in the developed countries, particularly non-tariff barriers, did not hurt the exports from the developing countries as much as is often assumed. The rate of growth of these exports was high enough so that additional large increases in the absence of protection were unlikely.

* 8.29 *

Kaplinsky, Raphael. "The International Context for Industrialization in the Coming Decade." *Journal of Development Studies* 21:1 (October 1984): 75-96.

The author analyzes a number of problems that protectionist practices create. Particular emphasis is placed on the difficulties that developing countries face as a result of protectionism in their efforts to follow a path of export oriented industrialization.

* 8.30 *

Krause, Lawrence B., and Sueo Sekiguchi. "Dealing with Change." In: *Economic Interaction in the Pacific Basin*, edited by Lawrence B. Krause and Sueo Sekiguchi. Washington, DC: Brookings Institution, 1980. ISBN 0-8157-5028-5.

Among other issues, the authors note that freer international trade can facilitate the growth of developing countries in the Pacific Basin, although these are the countries that also often bear the costs of inappropriate commercial policies in other nations. The protection employed by developing states for their own markets make it impossible to determine relative comparative advantages and facilitate efficient trade among the Asian developing countries.

* 8.31 *

Lipton, Michael, and Peter Tulloch. "India and the Enlarged European Community." *International Affairs* (London) 50:1 (January 1974): 49-66.

The authors argue that trade liberalization would help both India and the EC since their respective economies are complementary. They also note that protectionism in the EC has hurt Indian exports.

* 8.32 *

McCulloch, Rachel. "Gains to Latin America from Trade Liberalization in Developed and Developing Countries." *Quarterly Review of Economics and Business* 21:2 (Summer 1981): 231-258.

Multilateral tariff reductions in the Tokyo Round reduced the margin of special preference received by the developing Latin American countries in some product areas in the markets of the developed countries. The discussions of non-tariff barriers failed to agree on the developed states'

safeguard procedures that constitute a significant barrier to some Latin American exports.

* 8.33 *

Mendoza, Miguel Rodriguez. "Latin America and the U.S. Trade and Tariff Act." *Journal of World Trade Law* 20:1 (January/February 1986): 47-60.

The 1984 U.S. Trade and Tariff Act provides evidence of continued movement toward managed trade in the world. Developing countries, including those in Latin America, are restricted to an insignificant share of some important U.S. markets. A variety of NTBs further limit access.

* 8.34 *

Murray, Tracy, and Ingo Walter. "Quantitative Restrictions, Developing Countries, and GATT." *Journal of World Trade Law* 11:5 (September/October 1977): 391-421.

The authors argue that in the case of quantitative restrictions on imports all alleged violations of GATT rules should be settled by GATT rather than by bilateral agreements. Exceptions to GATT rules often occur when the two states consist of a developed and a developing one.

* 8.35 *

Olechowski, Andrzej, and Alexander J. Yeats. "Hidden Preferences for Developing Countries: A Note on the U.S. Import Valuation Procedure." *Quarterly Review of Economics and Business* 19:3 (Autumn 1979): 89-96.

The U.S. method of computing tariffs favors developing countries. Japanese and European tariff levies include the costs of freight and insurance, which are generally higher for developing states. If the United States were to switch to this system, exports from developing countries would suffer.

* 8.36 *

Roemer, Michael. "Resource-Based Industrialization in the Developing Countries: A Survey." *Journal of Development Economics* 6:2 (June 1979): 163-202.

Industrialization based on natural resources runs into some difficulties due to protectionism. Shipping rates discriminate against semi-processed goods, and effective protection rates in developed countries are often substantial for processed exports from the developing countries.

* 8.37 *

Sampson, Gary P. "Contemporary Protectionism and Exports of Developing Countries." *World Development* 8:2 (February 1980): 113-127.

Sampson analyzes the types of protectionist practices in use in the developed countries and their negative effects on developing countries. Although the developing states are hurt, it is difficult for either individual developing countries or international organizations to influence policies in the developed nations.

* 8.38 *
Stein, Leslie. "The Growth and Implications of LDC Manufactured Exports to Advanced Countries." *Kyklos* 34:1 (1981): 36-59.

Tariff preferences for the developing countries are not needed. Exports from the developing states should be encouraged, particularly since the negative effects on employment in the developed nations are limited.

* 8.39 *
Stern, Robert M. "The Accommodation of Interests between Developed and Developing Countries." *Journal of World Trade Law* 10:5 (September/October 1976): 405-420.

Agreement between the developed and developing world can be reached if the developed states provide for improved access to their markets for exports from the developing countries. Various non-tariff barriers to such trade should also be diminished. Special arrangements for particular developing countries should be avoided.

* 8.40 *
Taake, Hans-Helmut, and Dieter Weiss. "The World Textile Arrangement: The Exporter's Viewpoint." *Journal of World Trade Law* 8:6 (November/December 1974): 624-654.

Limitations on textile exports from the developing countries came about from negotiations in which different states had different interests. The resultant broad and flexible agreement reflected these different interests in a compromise that protected the developing countries' access to some markets.

* 8.41 *
Walter, Ingo. "Nontariff Barriers and the Export Performance of Developing Economies." *American Economic Review* 61:2 (May 1971): 195-205.

Developing countries are particularly vulnerable to the non-tariff barriers of developed states. The structure of protection in these countries seems to be systematically biased against the developing states, though not necessarily by intent.

* 8.42 *
Whitehead, Laurence. "Britain's Economic Relations with Latin America." In: *Latin America and World Economy*, edited by Joseph Grunwald. Beverly Hills, CA: Sage, 1978. ISBN 0-8039-0864-4.

When Britain attained membership in the EC, there occurred a significant diversion of trade away from Latin America. The protectionism of the EC in areas such as textiles will also limit the potential for exports to Britain.

* 8.43 *
Yeats, Alexander J. "An Analysis of the Incidence of Specific Tariffs on Developing Country Exports." *Economic Inquiry* 14:1 (March 1976): 71-80.

The nominal and effective protection rates of U.S. tariffs are almost double for products from the developing countries, compared to similar products from developed states. This situation results from the fact that developing country exports have lower value per volume and some tariffs are based on volume and from the specific tariffs applied to particular products.

* 8.44 *
Yeats, Alexander J. "On the Analysis of Tariff Escalation: Is There a Methodological Bias against the Interest of Developing Countries?" *Journal of Development Economics* 15:1-3 (May/June/August 1984): 77-88.

Yeats analyzes the argument that as processing increases, tariff rates increase to the detriment of exports from the developing countries. His findings indicate that the disadvantages are even greater than previously thought.

The Generalized System of Preferences

* 8.45 *
Badgett, L. D. "Preferential Tariff Reductions: The Philippine Response." *Journal of International Economics* 8:1 (February 1979): 79-92.

In the case of hemp, coconut oil, and refined sugar, there are indications that U.S. preferences did aid the development of these sectors of the Philippine economy to some extent. While the gains were not major, the preferences did have some positive effects on development.

* 8.46 *
Baldwin, R. E., and T. Murray. "MFN Tariff Reductions and Developing Country Trade Benefits under the GSP." *Economic Journal* 87 (March 1977): 30-46.

The authors estimate the advantages of special preferences for the developing countries and compare them to the benefits of overall multilateral reductions in the international system. With their model, they find that beneficiaries of preference schedules gain more from the tariff reductions than is lost in preferences while non-beneficiaries of preferences gain even more from tariff reductions.

* 8.47 *
Cable, Vincent, and Ann Weston. *South Asia's Exports to the EEC--Obstacles and Opportunities.* London:

Overseas Development Institute, 1979. ISBN 0-8500-3076-5.

The gains from the GSP of the EC to the South Asian countries of India, Bangladesh, Pakistan, and Sri Lanka are limited at times by tariffs and non-tariff barriers that hinder imports and thus reduce opportunities for trade stimulation. The authors analyze the effects of both types of hindrances with particular reference to South Asian exports of textiles and apparel.

* 8.48 *

Cooper, Richard N. "The European Community's System of Generalized Tariff Preferences: A Critique." *Journal of Development Studies* 8:4 (July 1972): 379-394.

Cooper argues that the GSP of the EC will help the developing countries very little, if at all. It includes tariff quotas that are based on historical trade data, thus limiting export opportunities. The traditional levels of trade are too low to permit the GSP to have much effect.

* 8.49 *

Frank, Isaiah. *Trade Policy Issues of Interest to the Third World.* Thames Essay no. 29. London: Trade Policy Research Centre, 1981. ISBN 0-900-84253-9.

Frank analyzes trade issues important to the developing countries, of which protectionism in industrialized states is an important one. He also discusses special preferences for exports from developing states. The establishment of such preferences were finally acknowledged as allowable in the Tokyo Round of GATT negotiations.

* 8.50 *

Fried, Jerome. "How Trade Can Aid." *Foreign Policy* 4 (Fall 1971): 51-61.

Fried argues that preferences for exports from the developing countries can be important in aiding growth. The preferences must be fairly applied by the industrialized states without constant use of escape clauses and safeguards.

* 8.51 *

Golt, Sidney. *Developing Countries in the GATT System.* Thames Essay no. 13. London: Trade Policy Research Centre, 1978. ISBN 0-900-84235-0.

Golt analyzes the background of the developing countries' argument for special preferences. There are many difficulties in implementing such preferences, and an open world economy supported by the industrialized countries would probably help the developing states more.

* 8.52 *

Grossman, Gene M. "Import Competition from Developed and Developing Countries." *Review of Economics and Statistics* 64:2 (May 1982): 271-281.

Grossman contends that multilateral tariff reductions will not erode U.S. preferences for products from developing countries. Products from both developed and developing countries can compete with U.S. produced items, but they compete in different product lines and are not mutually substitutable.

* 8.53 *

Katz, Sherman E. "The Tariff Preference: A Reconsideration." *Orbis* 14:4 (Winter 1971): 829-849.

Katz reviews the costs and benefits of tariff preferences for developing countries and argues that they are one appropriate way to aid these states. He notes that effective protection rates existing in industrialized countries fall most heavily on exports from developing states.

* 8.54 *

Law, Alton D. "Preferential Tariffs for the LDCs: Some Principles and Prospects." *Kyklos* 30:3 (1977): 461-478.

The GSPs may aid the developing countries. They are a more efficient policy for industrial development than infant industry protection since markets will be more important in determining trade potential. There are, however, a number of important problems with such preferences and their use.

* 8.55 *

McCulloch, Rachel, and Jose Pinera. "Trade as Aid: The Political Economy of Tariff Preferences for Developing Countries." *American Economic Review* 67:5 (December 1977): 959-967.

The authors analyze and model various preference schemes for exports from the developing countries. The actual gains achieved by developing states vary depending on the size of the tariff reductions, the presence or absence of associated quotas, and the optimality of the original tariff.

* 8.56 *

Meltzer, Ronald I. "The U.S. Renewal of the GSP: Implications for North-South Trade." *Journal of World Trade Law* 20:5 (September/October 1986): 507-525.

The GSP of the United States, recently renewed, has many drawbacks. It is designed to apply pressure to some developing countries. It has added further uncertainty to the international trading system.

* 8.57 *

Murray, Tracy. "Tariff Preferences and Multinational Firm Exports from Developing Countries." In: *Issues and Prospects for the New International Economic Order*, edited by William G. Tyler. Lexington, MA: Lexington Books, 1977. ISBN 0-669-01445-1.

The various GSPs introduced by the developed states have had limited effects on exports from the developing world, given the exemptions and safeguards included in them. Multinational corporations in the developing states have utilized the GSPs to some advantage to expand exports, but the consequences of the GSPs have been minimal.

* 8.58 *

Murray, Tracy. *Trade Preferences for Developing Countries*. New York: Wiley, 1977. ISBN 0-470-99080-5.

Murray provides an overview of the GSP idea for advancing the trade of the developing countries, as well as the negotiations leading to its implementation. The initial preferences provided by industrialized states have had a small influence on exports from the developing countries. These minimal gains have been eroded by escape clauses, rules of origin, the enlargement of the trade area centered on the EC, and the agreements for the multilateral reduction of tariffs.

* 8.59 *

Nemmers, Barry H., and Ted Rowland. "The U.S. Generalized System of Preferences: Too Much System, Too Little Preference." *Law and Policy in International Business* 9:3 (1977): 855-911.

The U.S. GSP scheme, as initially introduced in 1976, made its effective utilization by developing countries difficult due to its administrative procedures. While the increase in imports from the favored countries is an extremely small portion of U.S. total imports, the new markets can be beneficial to the exporting nations.

* 8.60 *

Nicolaides, P. "Preferences for Developing Countries: A Critique." *Journal of World Trade Law* 19:4 (July/August 1985): 373-386.

The GSP may result in short-term benefits for some developing countries, but its long-term effects are negative. General trade liberalization would lead to better trade opportunities and permit the adjustment of their economies to changes in trade relationships.

* 8.61 *

Sapir, Andre. "European Imports of Manufactures under Trade Preferences for Developing Countries." In: *The Challenge of the New International Economic Order*, edited by Edwin P. Reubens. Boulder, CO: Westview, 1981. ISBN 0-89158-762-4.

Sapir describes the European Community's GSP system in detail. He estimates that positive benefits have resulted from this GSP, and notes that many developing countries as a consequence have opposed moves toward multilateral tariff reductions since they would erode the existing preferences.

* 8.62 *

Sapir, Andre, and Lars Lundberg. "The U.S. Generalized System of Preferences and Its Impacts." In: *The Structure and Evolution of Recent U.S. Trade Policy*, edited by Robert E. Baldwin and Anne O. Krueger. Chicago: University of Chicago Press, 1984. ISBN 0-226-03604-9.

An analysis of trade patterns from 1975 to 1979 indicates that those countries gaining the most from the U.S. preferences were those that had already been large exporters to the U.S. market in the product areas with the largest preferences. Efforts at limiting preferences to the least developed countries appear to be ultimately designed to provide protection to U.S. industries.

* 8.63 *

Walter, Ingo, and Jae W. Chung. "Non-Tariff Distortions and Trade Preferences for Developing Countries." *Kyklos* 24:4 (1971): 733-752.

Non-tariff barriers are not particularly greater in the product areas where the industrialized states have provided tariff preferences for the developing countries. Such barriers could in some cases neutralize the effects of the preferences.

* 8.64 *

Weston, Ann, Vincent Cable, and Adrian Hewitt. *The EEC's Generalised System of Preferences: Evaluation and Recommendations for Change*. London: Overseas Development Institute, 1980. ISBN 0-8500-3071-4.

With a variety of safeguards and conditions, the EC's GSP has had only a modest influence on an increase in the developing countries' exports. A few remaining high tariffs and new non-tariff barriers continue to provide protection for European industries.

* 8.65 *

Wolf, Martin. "Two-Edged Sword: Demands of Developing Countries and the Trading System." In: *Power, Passions, and Purpose: Prospects for North-South Negotiations*, edited by Jagdish N. Bhagwati and John Gerard Ruggie. Cambridge, MA: MIT Press, 1984. ISBN 0-262-02201-X.

The developing countries would profit from a liberal trading system. They have weakened such liberal trade by their demands for special preferences, many of which have been of limited value. Support by the developing states for a liberal trade regime could help prevent the continued negative effects of protectionism in the world.

* 8.66 *

Yeats, Alexander J. "Tariff Valuation, Transport Costs and the Establishment of Trade Preferences among Developing Countries." *World Development* 8:3 (March 1980): 129-136.

Trade preferences among developing countries have had only minor benefits. High tariff rates in developing countries, combined with high transport costs, which also contribute to the cost of customs payments, have limited benefits.

* 8.67 *

Young, Robert H., Jr. "The Generalized System of Preferences: Nations More Favored Than Most." *Law and Policy in International Business* 8:3 (1976): 783-798.

The U.S. schedule of preferences was expected to have a small effect on imports from the developing countries. The Trade Act of 1974, which established these preferences, also provided a framework for multilateral tariff reductions that, if successful, would minimize the effect of the U.S. GSP.

* 8.68 *

Yusuf, Abdulqawi A. "'Differential and More Favorable Treatment': The GATT Enabling Clause." *Journal of World Trade Law* 14:6 (November/December 1980): 488-507.

Yusuf discusses the GATT enabling clause that permits developed states to provide special treatment to developing states without violating GATT rules on discrimination. The special treatment has now become a norm in the trading system rather than being an exception to the rules.

Trade Policies of the Developing Countries

* 8.69 *

Akrasanee, Narongchai. "Industrialization and Trade Policies and Employment Effects in Thailand." In: *Trade and Employment in Asia and the Pacific*, edited by Narongchai Akrasanee, Seiji Naya, and Vinyu Vichit-Vadakan. Honolulu: University Press of Hawaii, 1977. ISBN 0-8248-0573-9.

The author has undertaken a detailed analysis of the effects of a variety of government policies on employment in Thailand. Tariff protection favors industries that compete with imports, and this import substitution effect is one factor that has limited employment growth in manufacturing. Akrasanee provides an estimation of nominal and effective Thai tariffs for a number of industries.

* 8.70 *

Balassa, Bela. "Reforming the System of Incentives in Developing Economies." In: *Development Strategies in Semi-Industrial Economies*, edited by Bela

Balassa. Baltimore: Johns Hopkins University Press, 1982. ISBN 0-8018-25709.

Low protection is advisable for manufacturing industries in the developing countries due to their small market size, although temporary protection is justified for infant industries, particularly when a declining rate of protection is provided. Tariffs are a more efficient form of protection than quotas or other types of restrictions. Subsidies, both for import substitution and export promotion are desirable, although countervailing duties in the developed states may effectively limit their use.

* 8.71 *

Baldwin, Robert E. "Political Economy of Industrialisation: The Philippine Case." In: *Current Issues in Commercial Policy and Diplomacy*, edited by John Black and Brian Hindley. New York: St. Martin's, 1980. ISBN 0-312-17926-x.

Industrialization by import substitution supported by tariffs and import quotas worked initially in the 1950s. In the 1960s, the import controls used in the Philippines had begun to suppress exports as producers paid higher costs for imports and turned inward to the domestic market, thus limiting the potential for industrial activity.

* 8.72 *

Bell, Robert, and Sirousse Tabriztchi. "A New Policy on Tariffs and Ownership for LDCs." *Columbia Journal of World Business* 16:3 (Fall 1981): 71-76.

Tariffs in developing countries may be essential for the development of infant industries, but they lead to demands for their continuance and offer no incentives for efficiency. The authors suggest graduated reduction of tariffs and confiscatory taxation if cost and price reductions fail to materialize.

* 8.73 *

Bergsman, Joel. "Commercial Policy, Allocative Efficiency, and 'X-Efficiency'." *Quarterly Journal of Economics* 78:3 (August 1974): 409-433.

While some protection is needed to permit industrialization in developing countries, it should not be more than an industry needs to survive. Subsidies are preferable to protection for promoting industrialization since they encourage efficiency.

* 8.74 *

Berlinski, Julio, and Daniel M. Schydlowsky, "Argentina." In: *Development Strategies in Semi-Industrial Economies*, edited by Bela Balassa. Baltimore: Johns Hopkins University Press, 1982. ISBN 0-8018-25709.

The authors recommend various incentives for Argentine industries. They derive the effective protection and subsidies rates for the country. They also note the negative effects that protected import substitution has had on the economy.

* 8.75 *
Berry, Albert, and Francisco Thoumi. "Import Substitution and Beyond: Columbia." *World Development* 5:1-2 (January/February 1977): 89-109.

Import substitution behind tariff walls was replaced by export-oriented growth efforts in the 1960s in Columbia with positive results on growth. That Columbia joined the Andean Group, however, may have created a hindrance to continued progress by limiting this export strategy.

* 8.76 *
Bertrand, Trent J. "Decision Rules for Effective Protection in Less Developed Economies." *American Economic Review* 62:4 (September 1972): 743-746.

The author proposes a number of decision rules for tariff implementation in developing countries to ascertain whether protection should be general or industry specific. The rules are indeed general and Bertrand does not suggest that they cover all possibilities.

* 8.77 *
Bhagwati, Jagdish N. and Ernesto Tironi. "Tariff Change, Foreign Capital, and Immiserization." *Journal of Development Economics* 7:1 (March 1980): 71-83.

In certain circumstances, tariff reductions approaching free trade can lead to poverty for the bulk of the population when foreign capital is present in a developing country. In cases where imports are labor intensive, autarky may be preferable to free trade. The authors call the process of impoverishment "immiserization."

* 8.78 *
Blomqvist, A. G. "Tariff Revenue and Optimal Capital Accumulation in Less Developed Countries." *Economic Journal* 84 (March 1974): 70-89.

The author develops a model to determine the optimal tariff level for revenue to finance industrialization. The model indicates that the level varies from the normal expectation of austerity and then increased consumption is often put forward as the standard policy or result.

* 8.79 *
Chenery, Hollis B. "Interactions Between Industrialization and Exports." *American Economic Review* 70:2 (May 1980): 281-287.

Import substitution is essential for the initial phases of industrialization in a developing country. Eventually exports to the world market are necessary for continued growth, and such growth requires trade liberalization.

* 8.80 *
Cooper, Richard N. "Third World Tariff Tangle." *Foreign Policy* 4 (Fall 1971): 35-50.

Protectionism in the developing countries has hurt their chances to advance economically. Countries with moderate levels of protection have fared much better than those with high levels. The industrialized states would aid the developing countries more by trade liberalization and guarantees of market access than by specialized preferences.

* 8.81 *
Deardorff, Alan V., and Robert M. Stern. "Neighborhood Effects of Developing Country Protection." *Journal of Development Economics* 21:2 (May 1986): 327-346.

Developing countries had greater protection against exports from other developing states than against exports from developed states. For the developing states as a group, however, the effect on exports from the developed states was greater. Protection provided quite small gains for the developing countries in their terms of trade, and these gains may not have outweighed the costs.

* 8.82 *
DeMelo, Jaime A. P. "Protection and Resource Allocation in a Walrasian Trade Model." *International Economic Review* 19:1 (February 1978): 25-43.

Using data from Columbia in a model, the author tests the effects of the presence of non-traded goods on the effective rate of protection offered by tariffs. Variations in the costs of different factors of production and the relative price of non-traded goods due to changes in the tariff were quite important. The author points out the resultant difficulties in determining effective rates of protection, but the results also demonstrate the indirect effects that tariffs can have on non-protected goods.

* 8.83 *
Dennis, Robert D. "The Countertrade Factor in China's Modernization Plan." *Columbia Journal of World Business* 17:1 (Spring 1982): 67-75.

Dennis describes the countertrade practices adopted by the People's Republic of China. The need for foreign imports and lack of established markets for Chinese exports has led to a barter system typical of other centrally planned economies.

* 8.84 *
Edwards, Sebastian. "Stabilization with Liberalization: An Evaluation of Ten Years of Chile's Experiment with Free-Market Policies, 1973-1983." *Economic Development and Cultural Change* 33:2 (January 1985): 223-254.

Trade liberalization of Chile's tariff structure led to a shift of resources to more competitive sectors and even removed some deterrents to local production in the agricultural sector. There were short-term increases in unemployment, although in the long term, employment increased in the expanding sectors of the economy.

* 8.85 *

Findlay, Ronald, and Stanislaw Wellisz. "Some Aspects of the Political Economy of Trade Restrictions." *Kyklos* 36:3 (1983): 469-481.

The authors' analysis indicates that in a closed polity, or authoritarian system, the bureaucracy and the capital intensive sectors are likely to form a coalition and create a tariff that discriminates against traditional labor intensive products. This situation corresponds to the experiences of a number of developing states.

* 8.86 *

Greenaway, David, and Chris Milner. "'True Protection': Concepts and Their Role in Evaluating Trade Policies in the LDCs." *Journal of Development Studies* 23:2 (January 1987): 200-219.

The developing countries have often tried both to promote exports and follow import substitution policies. Their protective structures usually favor import substitution and production for the domestic market and hinder exports, even when countries are attempting to follow an export promotion policy.

* 8.87 *

Grossman, Gene M. "International Trade, Foreign Investment, and the Formation of the Entrepreneurial Class." *American Economic Review* 74:4 (September 1984): 605-614.

Grossman attempts to determine if protectionism can be justified on the basis of accelerating the formation of a domestic entrepreneurial group in the developing countries. His model indicates that free trade does inhibit the growth of this group, but welfare gains from free trade can easily be used to ameliorate this problem.

* 8.88 *

Ho, Alfred K. *Japan's Trade Liberalization in the 1960s*. White Plains, NY: International Arts and Sciences Press, 1973. ISBN 0-87332-0395.

Japan's efforts at trade liberalization in the 1960s were found to be associated with economic development. Although the liberalization was anything but complete, Ho argues that the Japanese case is a useful model for developing countries that often retain many types of domestic protection.

* 8.89 *

Humphrey, D.B., and T. Tsukahara, Jr. "On Substitution and the Effective Rate of Protection." *International Economic Review* 11:3 (October 1970): 488-496.

The authors develop an effective rate of protection for the Argentine economy taking into account the possibility of substitution occurring with a tariff on some imports used in other sectors. Their analysis also indicates many of the difficulties in computing effective rates of protection.

* 8.90 *

Hutcheson, Thomas L., and Daniel M. Schydlowsky. "Colombia." In: *Development Strategies in Semi-Industrial Economies*, edited by Bela Balassa. Baltimore: Johns Hopkins University Press, 1982. ISBN 0-8018-25709.

The levels of protection and incentives for Colombian economic sectors are analyzed. Suggested policy recommendations include tariff reform to increase economic efficiency, reforming the taxes and regulations on goods that are inputs for the export sector, and replacing quantitative quotas with tariffs.

* 8.91 *

Jayawardena, D.L.U. "Free Trade Zones." *Journal of World Trade Law* 17:5 (September/October 1983): 427-444.

Free trade zones have helped a number of developing countries profit from trade and an increase in exports. Other developing states have used the zones to gain from trade even though there was little assistance to domestic industrialization. A final group of developing countries have attempted to use the zones to attract capital and technology while keeping the rest of the domestic economy insulated, but the free trade zones failed to fulfill these goals.

* 8.92 *

Johnson, Harry G. "Commercial Policy and Industrialization." *Economica* 39 (August 1972): 264-275.

Subsidies serve infant industries better than tariffs, in part because in a small market such industries must export, not produce for the domestic market. Small developing countries should protect, through whatever mechanism, export industries in their development stage, and not protect import substituting ones. Tariffs are better than quotas since they generate revenues for the government, while quotas allocate revenues to a few.

* 8.93 *

Kavoussi, Rostam M. "International Trade and Economic Development: The Recent Experiences of the Developing Countries." *Journal of Developing Areas* 19:3 (April 1985): 379-392.

The author disputes the argument that developing countries have failed to grow through poor trade policy choices. The growth of export oriented states was a result of global demand considerations, not a consequence of the inherent value of the policy of trade liberalization.

* 8.94 *
Keesing, Donald B. "Exports and Policy in Latin-American Countries: Prospects for the World Economy and for Latin-American Exports, 1980-90." In: *Export Diversification and the New Protectionism: The Experiences of Latin America*, edited by Werner Baer and Malcolm Gillis. Champaign: Bureau of Economic and Business Research, College of Commerce and Business Administration, University of Illinois at Urbana-Champaign, 1981. LC 81-61370.

The Latin American countries have generally had poor export performances due to a variety of domestic policies. Protectionism in the industrialized state has not particularly hurt the Latin American states, and U.S. quotas on the Asian NICs have opened up some markets for Latin American exporters. The author also argues that tariffs and quotas in the Latin American states have played a role in their poor economic performances.

* 8.95 *
Kiguel, Miguel A. "The Choice of Appropriate Technology in a General Equilibrium Model." *International Trade Journal* 1:1 (Fall 1986): 79-101.

The choice of industrial technologies will affect international trade flows for developing countries. Labor intensive technologies are more efficient and may lead to trade reversals. Tariffs, however, can affect the technology choice, and the best choice under free trade can become suboptimal when protectionism is present.

* 8.96 *
Krueger, Anne O. "Trade Policy as an Input to Development." *American Economic Review* 70:2 (May 1980): 288-292.

Import substitution policies often entail high opportunity costs of forgone options. Trade policies designed to stimulate exports probably have a higher rate of return than other policies available to a developing country, provided that protectionism in the developed states does not limit the use of this policy approach.

* 8.97 *
Krueger, Anne O., and Baran Tuncer. "An Empirical Test of the Infant Industry Argument." *American Economic Review* 72:5 (December 1982): 1142-1152.

The authors develop and test a model of the infant industry argument for protection with Turkish data. Protected Turkish industries have not increased output as rapidly as would be expected if the industries were newly developing. Either the industries being protected were not new ones or the protection provided the wrong incentives.

* 8.98 *
Lal, Deepak. "Indian Export Incentives." *Journal of Development Economics* 6:1 (March 1979): 103-107.

With limits on imports taken as a fixed constraint, Lal's analysis indicates that the available export incentives fail to achieve the welfare levels otherwise possible for India.

* 8.99 *
Lall, Sanjaya, and Rajiv Kumar. "Firm-Level Export Performance in an Inward-Looking Economy: The Indian Engineering Industry." *World Development* 9:5 (May 1981): 453-463.

Data on engineering firms in India indicate that exporting activities are marginal and unprofitable. The policies of the government that provide a protected domestic market inhibit exports and make domestic production more attractive. These policies lead to domestic inefficiencies and effectively reduce exports.

* 8.100 *
Low, Patrick. "Export Subsidies and Trade Policy: The Experience of Kenya." *World Development* 10:4 (April 1982): 293-304.

Subsidies for exporting in Kenya have not generated the results desired. In part, the subsidies are insufficient to offset the higher costs firms face as a consequence of the levels of protection offered to the domestic market.

* 8.101 *
Mantel, Rolf R., and Ana M. Martirena-Mantel. "On the Uniformity of Optimal Tariffs." *Journal of Development Economics* 21:1 (April 1986): 41-52.

The optimum tariff for a developing country such as Argentina, which has a major exporting role in a few international markets, varies. Subsidies for export sectors are required to keep the domestic price levels equal to the international prices.

* 8.102 *
Martin, John P. "X-inefficiency, Managerial Effort and Protection." *Economica* 45 (August 1978): 273-286.

Protection may lead to less effort on the part of managers to improve production and production techniques in developing states. While protection may lead to such inefficiencies, it cannot do so alone. Decreasing effort harms national welfare only if the leisure time of managers is valued less than the losses resulting from inefficiencies.

* 8.103 *

Martin, John P., and John M. Page, Jr. "The Impact of Subsidies on X-Efficiency in LDC Industry: Theory and an Empirical Test." *Review of Economics and Statistics* 65:4 (November 1983): 608-617.

The authors develop a model to test the effects of government protective subsidies on efficiency within firms. The application of the model to Ghana suggests that protection adversely affects economic performance in the private sector.

* 8.104 *

Miyagiwa, Kaz F. "A Reconsideration of the Welfare Economics of a Free-Trade Zone." *Journal of International Economics* 21:3-4 (November 1986): 337-350.

Free trade zones will increase welfare regardless of the factors of production utilized. The relative input of capital and labor will affect the level of gain.

* 8.105 *

Morrison, Thomas K. "Manufactured Exports and Protection in Developing Countries: A Cross-Country Analysis." *Economic Development and Cultural Change* 25:1 (October 1976): 151-158.

Morrison uses tariff structure data for 18 developing countries to determine the effects of protection offered to domestic manufacturers on their ability to then export products. He finds support for the idea that high tariff protection inhibits the export of manufactures.

* 8.106 *

Morrison, Thomas K. *Manufactured Exports from Developing Countries.* New York: Praeger, 1976. ISBN 0-275-56880-6.

Morrison analyzes a variety of factors that influence the export potential of developing countries. The role of the developed nations in relation to multilateral tariff reductions, GSPs, and reduction of non-tariff barriers is important. He also found that higher levels of protection in the developing countries inhibit exports.

* 8.107 *

Mytelka, Lynn Krieger. "The Limits of Export-Led Development: The Ivory Coast's Experience with Manufactures." In: *The Antinomies of Interdependence: National Welfare and the International Division of Labor*, edited by John Gerard Ruggie. New York: Columbia University Press, 1983. ISBN 0-231-05725-3.

In a generally negative evaluation of the effects of the Ivory Coast's association with the EC, Mytelka notes that European protectionism has hurt manufactured exports in exactly those areas in which the Ivory Coast could compete, such as textiles. The use of safeguard clauses by the Europeans has been made easier rather than more difficult. The use of quotas and voluntary export restraints has further damaged the fragile industrial beginnings in African states.

* 8.108 *

Nogues, Julio J. "Alternative Trade Strategies and Employment in the Argentine Manufacturing Sector." *World Development* 11:12 (December 1983): 1029-1042.

High effective protection rates in Argentina have facilitated capital intensive industries that produce substitutes for imports, rather than industries that would be more labor intensive. This protection has also hurt the export industries that are best able to compete in the world market.

* 8.109 *

Perez, Lorenzo L. "Export Subsidies in Developing Countries and the GATT." *Journal of World Trade Law* 10:6 (November/December 1976): 529-545.

Exceptions in the use of export subsidies by developing countries should be made since subsidies are an appropriate way of aiding infant industries. The developing countries, however, need to liberalize trade themselves and use export subsidies more carefully.

* 8.110 *

Prebisch, Raul. "Commercial Policy in the Underdeveloped Countries." *American Economic Review* 49:2 (May 1959): 251-273.

Prebisch argues that the structure of the international trading system has worked against the developing countries and their exports. Building up the domestic industrial base through import substitution industrialization is necessary to overcome the structural disadvantages of the international system, and such import substitution will invariably require protection to occur. He also recommends preferences for exports from the developing states.

* 8.111 *

Rondinelli, Dennis A. "Export Processing Zones and Economic Development in Asia: A Review and Reassessment of a Means of Promoting Growth and Jobs." *American Journal of Economics and Sociology* 46:1 (January 1987): 89-105.

Free trade zones in Asian developing countries have provided jobs, generated foreign exchange, and increased exports. These benefits, however, have to be weighed against some potentially high costs in other areas that occur with such zones.

* 8.112 *

Ross-Larson, Bruce, and Larry E. Westphal. "Assessing the Performance of Infant Industries." *Journal of Development Economics* 16:1-2 (September/October 1984): 101-128.

Infant industries in developing countries have often failed to achieve international competitiveness. Failure to acquire needed technological inputs as a means of increasing productivity appears to have been one significant contributory factor to this failure.

* 8.113 *

Siggel, E. "Protection, Distortions and Investment Incentives in Zaire: A Quantitative Analysis." *Journal of Development Economics* 22:2 (July/August 1986): 295-319.

Zaire provides both protection to local industries as well as incentives and subsidies. These various measures, however, have often conflicted with each other. Harmonization of policies is clearly necessary.

* 8.114 *

Sjaastad, Larry A. "The Problems of Trade Liberalization in Chile." *Journal of World Trade Law* 9:2 (March/April 1975): 160-176.

Removing domestic protection will affect the Chilean economy in many ways. Unilateral trade liberalization in general will be more advantageous than liberalization within the Andean Group.

* 8.115 *

Steel, William F. "Import Substitution and Excess Capacity in Ghana." *Oxford Economic Papers* n.s. 24:2 (July 1972): 212-240.

Import substitution and associated protectionist measures did not result in economic efficiency and rapid industrialization in Ghana. The tariff structure adopted favored final stage assembly of products with imported inputs, and import quotas increased costs and uncertainty. Foreign exchange problems were also present. While import substitution may be effective or worthwhile, negative side effects must be avoided.

* 8.116 *

Urrutia, M. Miguel. "Columbia and the Andean Group: Economic and Political Determinants of Regional Integration Policy." In: *Export Diversification and the New Protectionism: The Experience of Latin America*, edited by Werner Baer and Malcolm Gillis. Champaign: Bureau of Economic and Business Research, College of Commerce and Business Administration, University of Illinois at Urbana-Champaign, 1981. LC 81-61370.

Domestic pressure groups in Colombia have both encouraged protectionism and sought to avoid it in different areas. These groups have prevented reductions in the Colombian tariff, but they have also effectively prevented Colombian integration into the Andean Group with its high external tariff wall.

* 8.117 *

Vanek, Jaroslav. "Tariffs, Economic Welfare, and Development Potential." *Economic Journal* 81 (December 1971): 904-913.

Vanek is concerned with the effects of revenue tariffs on developing countries. He finds that the costs, due to resource mis-allocation of a tariff designed to raise revenue, are outweighted by the benefits of accumulated savings that can be used for development.

* 8.118 *

Young, Leslie. "Intermediate Goods and the Formation of Duty Free Zones." *Journal of Development Economics* 25:2 (April 1987): 369-384.

Lowering duties on intermediate goods in a free trade zone can attract enterprises. Such action, however, could increase the impact of tariff distortions in the rest of the domestic economy.

The Newly Industrializing Countries

* 8.119 *

Aspra, L. Antonio. "Import Substitution in Mexico: Past and Present." *World Development* 5:1-2 (January/February 1977): 111-123.

Import substitution in Mexico has had disappointing results. Capital intensive industries have resulted rather than labor intensive ones. Continued protection has been required for the industries that have not become self-sufficient.

* 8.120 *

Aw, Yan, and Mark J. Roberts. "The Role of Imports from the Newly-Industrializing Countries in U.S. Production." *Review of Economics and Statistics* 67:1 (February 1985): 108-117.

U.S. imports from the NICs are often inputs into other products, indicating that multilateral tariff reductions and an increase in imports would lead to a net increase in U.S. employment. Such cuts would also increase the level of imports from the NICs, notwithstanding a decrease in their preferential tariff margins.

* 8.121 *

Balassa, Bela. "Development Strategies and Economic Performance: A Comparative Analysis of Eleven Semi-Industrial Economies." In: *Development Strategies in Semi-Industrial Economies*, edited by Bela Balassa. Baltimore: Johns Hopkins University Press, 1982. ISBN 0-8018-2570-9.

A comparison of eleven advanced developing countries indicates that outward looking policies based on the expansion of exports, supported by export incentives, have contributed to development. Once the initial stages have been passed, import substitution with high protection may hinder the growth of export sectors.

* 8.122 *

Balassa, Bela. *The Newly Industrializing Countries in the World Economy*. New York: Pergamon, 1981. ISBN 0-08-026336-4.

In Balassa's analysis of the overall position of the Newly Industrializing Countries in the world economy, there are several chapters that deal with protectionism. Chapters 4 and 5 discuss the effects of protectionist measures, both tariff and non-tariff, in the developed countries, while other chapters deal with specific industrializing states, their problems and their prospects. The entire volume provides a clarifying context in which to view the position of these countries in relation to the protectionism issue.

* 8.123 *

Balassa, Bela. "The Structure of Incentives in Six Semi-Industrial Economies." In: *Development Strategies in Semi-Industrial Economies*, edited by Bela Balassa. Baltimore: Johns Hopkins University Press, 1982. ISBN 0-8018-25709.

Balassa provides estimates of the nominal protection rates, effective protection rates, and effective subsidy levels provided by incentives in Argentina, Colombia, Israel, Korea, Singapore, and Taiwan. The predictive value of nominal protection compared to effective protection was variable for the six countries and often not high. Nominal protection was less related to effective protection when effective subsidy levels were included.

* 8.124 *

Baer, Werner, and Andrea Maneschi. "Import-Substitution, Stagnation, and Structural Change: An Interpretation of the Brazilian Case." *Journal of Developing Areas* 5:2 (January 1971): 177-192.

Import substitution initially fueled industrialization but has since contributed to stagnation. The economic interest groups favored by import substitution gained political strength and have subsequently opposed any major changes in the policy.

* 8.125 *

Fishlow, Albert. "Origins and Consequences of Import Substitution in Brazil." In: *International Economics and Development: Essays in Honor of Raul Prebisch*, edited by Luis Eugenio di Marco. New York: Academic Press, 1972. ISBN 0-12-216450-4.

Fishlow analyzes the role of import substitution in the industrialization of Brazil. Import substitution was facilitated by protectionist policies including tariffs, exchange rates favoring domestic producers, and import licenses. It was successful during the Great Depression in part because of tariff protection and the rise of internal demand. World War II continued the advantage enjoyed by local industries, given the absence of many foreign imports.

* 8.126 *

Frank, Isaiah. "The 'Graduation' Issue for LDCs." *Journal of World Trade Law* 13:4 (July/August 1979): 289-302.

The trading system needs to recognize greater distinctions than that of developed and developing countries. Some developing countries such as the NICs no longer should have the privileges of developing states to contravene GATT rules, even though they are not yet ready to assume the responsibilities of developed states. A process of gradual change should be created to accommodate these states.

* 8.127 *

Haggard, Stephan, and Chung-In Moon. "The South Korean State in the International Economy: Liberal, Dependent, or Mercantile." In: *The Antinomies of Interdependence: National Welfare and the International Division of Labor*, edited by John Gerard Ruggie. New York: Columbia University Press, 1983. ISBN 0-231-05724-5.

South Korea's economic performance improved following a liberalization of tariffs and exchange rates, thus reducing the level of protectionism, a policy that generally sets off the Asian NICs from those in Latin America. The smaller trading NICs, such as Korea, have profited from a more liberal trading order but now face impediments to their trade. The NICs themselves have increasingly sought bilateral agreements and preferential arrangements whenever possible.

* 8.128 *

Hufbauer, Gary Clyde, W. N. Harrell Smith IV, and Frank G. Vukmanic. "Bilateral Trade Relations." *Proceedings of the Academy of Political Science* 34:1 (1981): 136-145.

Mexico has liberalized trade in the 1970s, although domestic critics have argued against joining GATT since it would limit the use of subsidies, domestic content requirements, and other policy devices. U.S. requirements for fair trade may present difficulties in some area of bilateral trade given the continuing use of these measures by Mexico.

* 8.129 *
Karayiannis-Bacon, Harikleia. "Tariff Protection and Import Substitution in Post-War Greece." *World Development* 4:6 (June 1976): 529-542.

Effective rates of protection were much higher than nominal rates in 1961. This tariff protection, however, had little relationship to import substitution that was occurring. Tariffs apparently were not a successful component of industrial policy.

* 8.130 *
Katz, Bernard S. "Mexico's Tariff Policies." *American Journal of Economics and Sociology* 35:3 (July 1976): 235-250.

Katz analyzed Mexican tariff policy to determine if it was used to deal with balance of payments problems, to improve terms of trade, or generate revenue. Since only case specific evidence for any of these alternatives was found, the author assumed that tariff policy was designed to further industrialization, although he did not analyze the efficacy of such tariffs on industrial activity.

* 8.131 *
Kumar, Krishna, and Kee Young Kim. "The Korean Manufacturing Multinationals." *Journal of International Business Studies* 15:1 (Spring/Summer 1984): 45-61.

Quotas established by industrialized states on imports of some products have led to multinationalization by Korean firms. The Philippines, Sri Lanka, Thailand, El Salvador, and Honduras, for example, have lower wage levels and are undersubscribed on their quotas for textile products, facilitating the location of plants on their territory.

* 8.132 *
Lee, T. H., and Kuo-Shu Liang. "Taiwan." In: *Development Strategies in Semi-Industrial Economies*, edited by Bela Balassa. Baltimore: Johns Hopkins University Press, 1982. ISBN 0-8018-25709.

After import substitution in the 1950s, Taiwan shifted to the promotion of exports. Effective protection has remained highest in industries that face import competition and lowest in export industries. Taiwan was able to survive the recession of the mid-1970s better than developing states that had followed policies of import substitution.

* 8.133 *
Linder, Staffan Burenstam. "Pacific Protagonist--Implications of the Rising Role of the Pacific." *American Economic Review* 75: 2 (May 1985): 279-284.

The rise of the Asian NICs, while generating protectionism, increased the potential benefits of economic interaction between them and other states. Western protectionism is not only costly to the NICs and the Western nations themselves, but it discourages other developing states that are considering following the same path to economic development.

* 8.134 *
Lowinger, Thomas C. "Import Substitution, Export Promotion and the Structure of Brazil's Protection." *Journal of Development Studies* 10:3-4 (April/July 1976): 430-444.

The structure of protection in Brazil in the 1960s hindered both import substitution and export activities. A reduction in the level of protection was necessary simply to neutralize previous negative effects. Brazil needs to manage the transition from a policy of import substitution to one of export promotion.

* 8.135 *
Nam, Chong Hyun. "Trade and Industrial Policies, and the Structure of Protection in Korea." In: *Trade and Growth of the Advanced Developing Countries in the Pacific Basin: Papers and Proceedings of the Eleventh Pacific Trade and Development Conference*, edited by Wontack Hong and Lawrence B. Krause. Seoul: Korea Development Institute, 1981. ISBN 0-824-80791.

Between 1968 and 1978 there has been little real change in the level of protection for the domestic market in Korea. In all industries domestic sales are favored over exports, and important protection is provided for industries that would otherwise face significant import competition.

* 8.136 *
Rousslang, Donald, and Stephen Parker. "Cross-Price Elasticities of U.S. Import Demand." *Review of Economics and Statistics* 66:3 (August 1984): 518-523.

Multilateral tariff reductions would erode the tariff preferences of the NICs to the advantage of the developed states and the other developing countries if no compensatory changes occurred in the preferential tariffs. Eliminating GSP benefits for the NICs would aid the developing countries more than it would help the developed states.

* 8.137 *
Sussman, Zvi. "Israel." In: *Development Strategies in Semi-Industrial Economies*, edited by Bela Balassa. Baltimore: Johns Hopkins University Press, 1982. ISBN 0-8018-2570-9.

Sussman discusses the protection offered to Israeli industries and compares the nominal and effective rates of protection. Subsidies have been used to protect inefficient manufacturing industries, and the overall system of protection has discriminated against exports.

* 8.138 *
Tan, Augustine H. H., and Ow Chin Hock. "Singapore." In: *Development Strategies in Semi-Industrial Economies*, edited by Bela Balassa. Baltimore: Johns Hopkins University Press, 1982. ISBN 0-8018-25709.

The authors provide estimates of effective protection and effective subsidies for Singapore. Even during the import substitution phase of the 1960s, Singapore had lower levels of protection than most developing countries. Discrimination against export sectors has been low as well.

* 8.139 *
Teitel, Simon, and Francisco Thoumi. "From Import Substitution to Exports: The Manufacturing Exports Experience of Argentina and Brazil." *Economic Development and Cultural Change* 34:3 (April 1986): 455-490.

Both Argentina and Brazil favored import substitution with a variety of government aid programs and through trade barriers. Export incentives generally failed to compensate for the bias favoring domestic production. The era of import substitution, however, does seem to have facilitated the creation of manufacturing sectors that were later able to export and compete on the world market.

* 8.140 *
Turner, Louis. "Western Europe and the NICs." In: *The Newly Industrializing Countries: Trade and Adjustment*, edited by Louis Turner and Neil McMullen. London: George Allen & Unwin, 1982. ISBN 0-04-382036-0.

Protection in the EC has been particularly directed against the more advanced NICs. The General System of Preferences (GSPs) and other forms of market access have often been structured in such a way as to inhibit imports from these countries, often justified as a way of helping the least developed countries. In addition, it is often believed in Europe that Japan and the NICs use low wages and government policies such as tariffs, non-tariff barriers, and subsidies to provide unfair advantages; hence, protection in Europe is justified.

* 8.141 *
Tyler, William G. "Effective Incentives for Domestic Market Sales and Exports: A View of Anti-Export Biases and Commercial Policy in Brazil, 1980-81." *Journal of Development Economics* 18:2-3 (August 1985): 219-242.

Effective protection levels in Brazil have led to significant costs. Industries with scope for greater import substitution have received more protection, and the protectionist policies have generally discriminated against exports.

* 8.142 *
Weiss, John. "Japan's Post-War Protection Policy: Some Implications for Less Developed Countries." *Journal of Development Studies* 22:2 (January 1986): 385-406.

Weiss argues that an internally competitive market in Japan rather than a protected domestic market contributed to Japan's ability to compete globally. Protectionism at some stages of development in certain industries, however, may have facilitated development.

* 8.143 *
Weisskoff, Richard. "Trade, Protection and Import Elasticities for Brazil." *Review of Economics and Statistics* 61:1 (February 1979): 58-66.

Brazilian industry was highly protected in the 1960s, often more by exchange rates than by tariffs. Import substitution had negative impacts on development, and by 1975 Brazilian economic growth had ceased.

* 8.144 *
Westphal, Larry E., and Kwang Suk Kim. "Korea." In: *Development Strategies in Semi-Industrial Economies*, edited by Bela Balassa. Baltimore: Johns Hopkins University Press, 1982. ISBN 0-8018-25709.

Korea has provided a variety of subsidies for exports, and high effective subsidies for domestic sales have also favored exports of some products. Quotas and high tariffs continue to protect some inefficient domestic firms. Korea has been able to circumvent export quotas by shifting to higher quality, higher value items.

* 8.145 *
Woolcock, Stephen. "Textiles and Clothing." In: *The Newly Industrializing Countries: Trade and Adjustment*, edited by Louis Turner and Neil McMullen. London: George Allen & Unwin, 1982. ISBN 0-04-382036-0.

Woolcock provides an overview of the changing trade in textiles and clothing and the rise of protection in the industrialized states as a response to increasing exports by the NICs. In the 1970s, pressures in the EC led to protectionist measures that also had an effect on EC trade agreements with countries in the Mediterranean. One result of measures such as quotas in Europe and the United States has been for NIC exporters to concentrate on higher value added, more expensive items.

* 8.146 *
Yoffie, David B. "The Newly Industrializing Countries and the Political Economy of Protectionism." *International Studies Quarterly* 25:4 (December 1981): 569-599.

Protectionism in the industrialized countries has failed to stop gains in exports by the NICs, which have been flexible in their export techniques. Trade barriers, particularly in the United States, have been porous. The NICs have used bargaining rather than confrontation to successfully defend their positions as exporters.

* 8.147 *
Yoffie, David B., and Robert O. Keohane. "Responding to the 'New Protectionism': Strategies for the Advanced Developing Countries in the Pacific Basin." In: *Trade and Growth of the Advanced Developing Countries in the Pacific Basin: Papers and Proceedings of the Eleventh Pacific Trade and Development Conference*, edited by Wontack Hong and Lawrence B. Krause. Seoul: Korea Development Institute, 1981. ISBN 0-824-80791.

Export possibilities for the Asian NICs has been hurt by the worldwide recession and the decline of U.S. leadership and ability to keep markets, including U.S. markets, open. Bilateral negotiations with industrialized states rather than multilateral ones and emphasis on long-term gains are the suggested strategies for these NICs to follow.

AGRICULTURE: THE CONTINUATION OF PROTECTIONISM

Unlike trade in other commodities, protectionism in food products does not reflect an increase but simply a continuation of previous practices. Liberalization of agricultural trade was largely excluded from the initial GATT arrangements or later multilateral negotiations. Virtually all the industrialized nations have either opposed meaningful trade liberalization in this area or have been selective in supporting it in their own self interest.

Trade in agricultural products, particularly food products, having been generally excluded from the trend toward freer trade after World War II, has faced a wide array of protectionist measures. The presence of obstacles to trade is not the result of the appearance of the new protectionism or an increasing use of neo-mercantile policies but the continuation of past policies. Multilateral negotiations have usually failed to deal with issues concerning agricultural protection, either with respect to lowering tariffs or removing NTBs. The developed countries have maintained many barriers to these imports for a variety of reasons. The developing states have frequently been disadvantaged by such protection since they export numerous agricultural goods. Since agricultural trade has never been significantly liberalized after World War II, in many ways it has remained a distinctive trade domain. It probably will continue as particularly intractable to any reduction because by tradition protection is so deeply embedded in the various national economies.

International Negotiations on Agricultural Trade

When GATT was signed, most trade in agricultural products was excluded from its provisions. Domestic supports for farmers were standard in many countries. Re-establishment of food production was a priority in many areas of the world. In the rounds of multilateral negotiations, held by GATT to liberalize trade, food products were usually excluded from consideration in deference to the wishes of important participating nations. Although food-exporting countries at times did attempt to remove barriers to the importation of their products, they were generally unsuccessful. Tariff reductions would probably not facilitate greater trade in agriculture in any significant way in any event, since the major trade obstacles are NTBs, such as quotas, subsidies, health regulations, and grading or quality requirements.

Because GATT negotiators have had greater difficulty in dealing with NTBs in general than with tariffs, liberalization of trade in food products has been correspondingly more difficult. Because disputes over agricultural trade have appeared in the international setting, they have led to some relatively short tariff wars such as those between the United States and France. Usually whatever reductions in barriers to agricultural trade there have been have resulted from bilateral agreements between states rather than from general international arrangements. Failure to reach agreements on reduction of obstacles to this trade has also hindered trade liberalization in other areas, since some countries have been unwilling to make concessions on industrial products without reciprocal concessions on the removal of obstacles to agricultural imports. Thus, while it is possible to talk about the liberal trade regime of the 1950s and 1960s, that regime never included food products and some other agricultural goods. Recent negotiations have failed to change the situation. Agriculture has continued to reflect attitudes of the 1930s when there was no regime with shared norms and values.

Reasons for the Protection of Domestic Agriculture

Governments have created obstacles to importations of food to ensure: national security in food supplies during war, state control over a large share of the agricultural sector, and a quick governmental response to national shortages.[1] The efforts of governments to ensure national sufficiency in food are directly related to defense policy so that, in the event of war, massive food shortages would not be as likely to occur. Many protectionist policies still in place have had their genesis in defensive provisions. While governments may have become less concerned with the defense aspect of agricultural protection in the nuclear age--or more so depending on their views about survivability--they have frequently been unwilling to remove protection from previously protected farmers lest unemployment and losses in the farm sector occur. Global food shortages in the early 1970s also encouraged many states to support indigenous agriculture, as a consequence of the resultant price increases on the international market. While domestic production might be more expensive in most years, it would provide a secure source of supply.

In other cases, governments have used subsidies as a means to raise the income of farmers to the level of workers in the urban areas. Such equality slows the movement of persons from rural to urban areas and eases the absorption of migrants into the urban work force. Controlling the pace in which farmers are integrated into the urban economy may be essential to social stability in a country and thus constitute an important policy objective for a government.[2] Income subsidy programs then frequently require other measures of protection to help maintain the desired income levels of farmers. During the 1970s when the global recession had led to higher levels of unemployment in industrial sectors, migrants from the rural areas would have exacerbated the existing employment difficulties.

The farming sector have often demonstrated a surprising level of political strength in a variety of forms. While they are a relatively small segment of the population in the developed states, their votes can be critical to particular parties or can affect the outcome of specific elections. The result is that politicians will attempt to win votes, or at least not to lose votes, by maintaining the subsidies and protections that already exist. Agricultural interest groups may also work with bureaucratic agencies to maintain programs that protect farmers against import competition. If farm support issues can be kept out of the political limelight and transformed into administrative questions dealt with by ministries of agriculture, continued protection is easier to maintain.

Agricultural Protection in the Developed Countries

Food-exporting developed states have frequently sought to reduce some of the obstacles to trade in foodstuffs. The United States, Canada, Australia, and New Zealand are states that are net exporters, and at times they, and particularly the United States, have sought to reduce protection in other countries. U.S. trade representatives have raised the issue in multilateral negotiations, but with little success. On the bilateral level there have been similar efforts with limited successes. Even these food-exporting countries have been inconsistent in their approaches to trade liberalization of food products. While favoring freer trade for some commodities, those in which they are internationally competitive, they have been much less willing to remove protection in other commodities that would result in import competition for their farmers. These countries protect at least some domestic production through tariffs, subsidies, quotas, or other mechanisms. Thus, there is no bloc of industrialized states that has been in a position to argue for overall trade liberalization in agricultural products.

Among the industrialized nations, Japan is clearly very dependent on food imports, yet it has protected indigenous farming in spite of, or perhaps because of, its need to import. There are important obstacles to imports and high levels of subsidization, particularly for rice production. A number of factors prescribe these Japanese efforts. Although the country can never be self-sufficient in food, its government can affect the extent of its reliance on imports. Security of supply is important for a country so dependent on food imports. Interruptions of supplies, due to the actions of exporting countries such as the United States, have enhanced the desirability of maintaining appropriate levels of domestic production.

In addition, Japanese governments have attempted to raise the incomes of farmers to levels equivalent to some industrial workers in order to limit migration to the cities and to avoid possible social instability. Japanese barriers to imports are also designed to protect the cultural values of the small farmer community. These values are considered to be important for the nation as a whole.[3]

The European countries have shown a mixed pattern in food importations. Given its need to import food, Britain's protection was generally low prior to membership in the EC although certain commodities were protected even then. Other European countries have provided at least some protection to farmers. To some extent, one common policy goal, as in Japan, has been to raise the incomes of farmers to levels closer to that of other workers. In some cases the competitiveness of an export sector has been maintained. There has also been concern over security of supply for at least some foodstuffs. France in particular has had a long history of protecting domestic agricultural interests with high barriers to imports for many products. France has even discriminated against agricultural imports from fellow members of the EC, contrary to the provisions of the Community documents and rulings from the European Court of Justice, the body that deals with legal issues arising in the EC.[4] Continued government support of protection through the years has been in part due to the fact that all the major French political parties derive some voting support from rural areas. While the reasons for the disparate farm support for different parties are historical in most cases, the situation has meant that no major party could advocate large scale reduction in the protection traditionally accorded the farm sector.

Protectionist attitudes in the various European states carried over into the EC which has been highly protective of Community farmers. The Common Agricultural Policy (CAP), provided for at the time of the formation of the EC, is essentially a subsidy for the farming sectors. Imports of many food products only enter when there is a shortfall in domestic EC production or when normal production will not meet demand. The CAP was created largely at French insistence, and EC protection of agricultural interests was one of the conditions of France's joining the Community. The

policy has been so effective in supporting French farmers that France went from being an importer of wheat to a net exporter. The large subsidies have created problems with third countries that object to the closure of the EC market to many of their products and that consider the sale of subsidized wheat or other products on the world market to be an unfair trading practice.

Other EC countries have supported the CAP in many cases either because their farmers gain directly or because it creates a large protected market in which they can compete successfully. British farmers expanded production considerably under the CAP because they became competitive in their own domestic market. The wish of the member states to protect their agricultural sectors was also apparent with the reservations over the admission of Spain and Portugal to the Community, noted in Chapter 8, since agricultural interests in France and Italy in particular might suffer from competition from the lower cost agricultural production in these two states. The agricultural sectors of the member states have also been protected in the trade treaties negotiated with the countries bordering the Mediterranean Sea, including Spain and Portugal before they all concluded membership agreements. Imports that would compete with domestic farmers were severely limited in these arrangements. Overall, it is probably the case that the EC has maintained agricultural protection at higher levels than would have been present on the average for the various members as individual states, with French views in this area of Community policy having carried such great weight.

Agricultural protection has had high costs for the developed states. Countries such as Canada and the United States raise the costs to their consumers when they protect selected sectors or when they limit imports during periods of falling prices for farm products. Even so, since farmers in these states can compete internationally in many cases, the costs to the consuming public are not as high as in other countries. The CAP in the EC has been very costly and has threatened to absorb the entire Community budget. The costs of the program have risen to such levels that the general expectation has often been that support for farmers will have to be lowered for purely financial reasons. Some changes have been made to lower the costs as a result, but they still remain high. It has been estimated that food costs in the EC are 27 percent higher, with the CAP, than they would be if there were free trade in agricultural commodities.[5] Increases in food costs in the United Kingdom have led to British opposition to continuation of the CAP at its present high levels, and recently an agreement was reached where the overall level of British contributions to the program were reduced. Japan has also faced high costs for food as a result of its protection of domestic farmers. From 1978 to 1980, Japan paid the highest costs of any nation for such protection. The combination of higher prices for consumers and of the tax money expended for subsidies from the government treasury amounted to a 140 percent surcharge over what the foodstuffs would have cost in the world market.[6] The overall costs to consumers in various industrialized nations has obviously been considerable.

Effects on the Developing Countries

Agricultural protectionism has been costly for the developing countries as well. Many of these states can competitively export food products, yet their exporting potential is directly limited by the trade obstacles in the developed world. Not only are exports of the same food goods as those produced domestically in the developed countries restricted, but there are limitations on products that might compete indirectly. Only products such as tea, coffee, and cacao, which cannot be produced in the developed states, face few barriers to imports. Thus, one of the areas where developing countries could profitably engage in trade is reduced. The impact on the developing countries becomes greater in many cases since agricultural products form a much larger percentage of their existing exports.

Limitation of foreign markets then effectively reduces the potential gains from export activity by a considerable margin. The lack of export possibilities can then limit economic growth, especially as low productivity in the agricultural sector has limited progress in many countries. The lack of market possibilities may even be increasing since some of the Asian NICs have begun to emulate the developed states by instituting programs to subsidize their domestic farmers.

Sugar provides a good example of the effects that obstacles can have on agricultural trade. Sugar is unique in one sense. Cane sugar, grown in the tropics principally in developing countries, and beet sugar, grown in temperate climates principally in developed states, are interchangeable. This interchangeability has led to the adoption of import barriers in industrialized nations. Beet growers in countries such as Germany and the United States are subsidized by their governments. Quotas then are used to limit the level of imports of cane sugar, or even other beet sugar, that can enter to compete with the domestic product. These restrictions exist even though cane sugar can normally be procured more cheaply, absent the subsidies and protection, from the developing countries.

The protected production of sugar in the in-

dustrialized states has greatly reduced the scope for the sale of sugar from the developing world. Markets in the developed world still exist, but they are small. Developing states that have been especially hurt by such import barriers have included many island states in the Caribbean, Pacific, and Indian Ocean areas, which have few alternative products to export. Even the presence of guaranteed markets for some of the production of certain developing states in the industrialized nations can be self-defeating. The developing state has a market for some of its production, but if beet crops in the developed nation are plentiful, the resulting surplus is dumped on the world market to compete with the remainder of the sugar produced in the developing state, driving world prices down.[7] Protection in this one agricultural commodity clearly demonstrates the high costs that protection can have and the problems that it creates for developing states.

End Notes
1. Feis, Herbert. "Effects of Trade Barriers on World Food Movements," *Proceedings of the Academy of Political Science* 30:3 (1971): pp. 145-146.

2. Hayami, Yujiro. "Adjustment Policies for Japanese Agriculture in a Changing World." In: *U.S.-Japanese Agricultural Trade Relations*, edited by Emery N. Castle and Kenzo Hemmi with Sally A. Skillings. Washington, DC: Resources for the Future, 1982. pp. 368-392.

3. Drucker, Peter F. "Japan: The Problems of Success." Foreign Affairs 56:3 (April 1978): pp. 564-578.

4. Keeler, John T. S. "Dreams of Green Oil, Nightmares of Inequality: French Agricultural Policy and the External Challenges of the 1980s." In: *France in the Troubled World Economy*, edited by Stephen S. Cohen and Peter A. Gourevitch. London: Butterworth Scientific, 1982. pp.97-113.

5. Hubbard, L. J. and D. R. Harvey. "Greece and the Common Agriculture Policy." In: *Greece and the EEC: Integration and Convergence*, edited by George N. Yannopoulos. New York: St. Martin's, 1986. p.128.

6. Kihl, Young Whan and James M. Lutz. *World Trade Issues: Regime, Structure, and Policy*. New York: Praeger, 1985. p. 130.

7. Mahler, Vincent A. "Britain, the European Community, and the Developing Commonwealth: Dependence, Interdependence, and the Political Economy of Sugar." *International Organization* 35:3 (Summer 1981): p. 478.

Chapter 9: Annotated Bibliography

General Works

* **9.1** *

Anderson, Kym, and Rodney Tyers. "International Effects of Agricultural Policies." In: *Issues in World Trade Policy: GATT at the Crossroads*, edited by R. H. Snape. New York: St. Martin's, 1986. ISBN 0-312-43724-2.

Domestic agricultural policies in West Europe and Japan distort trade and are being increasingly copied by the newly industrializing countries. Agricultural protectionism also encourages other countries to retain barriers to other kinds of imports. The authors supply some estimates of the costs of EC protection for domestic agriculture.

* **9.2** *

Hillman, Jimmye S. *Nontariff Agricultural Trade Barriers*. Lincoln: University of Nebraska Press, 1978. ISBN 0-8032-2301-3.

Hillman discusses the various non-tariff barriers that have come to replace direct tariffs as major impediments to trade in agricultural products. He notes that these barriers constitute administrative protectionism in many cases with officials having the resultant discretion. He then discusses the practices of various countries and provides detailed case studies, at times also indicating the magnitude of the costs involved to consumers.

* **9.3** *

Johnson, D. Gale. "What Difference Does Trade Make in World Community Welfare?" In: *U.S. Trade Policy and Agricultural Exports*, edited by the Iowa State University. Center for Agricultural and Rural Development. Ames: Iowa State University Press, 1973. ISBN 0-8138-16556.

Governments have provided protection to their agricultural sectors with subsidies, politically the most acceptable method of meeting domestic demands. Johnson considers the costs to consumers inside the protective barriers, the costs to countries that have lost export markets, as well as the profits of those who benefit from the protection.

* **9.4** *

Johnson, D. Gale. "World Food Institutions: A 'Liberal' View." In: *The Global Political Economy of Food*, edited by Raymond F. Hopkins and Donald J. Puchala. Madison: University of Wisconsin Press, 1978. ISBN 0-299-07750-0.

A liberal trade order for agricultural goods would aid the developing countries since it would require the developed nations to reduce their import obstacles and subsidies. Such liberalization would also permit better allocation of food supplies through the global market.

* **9.5** *

Josling, T. E. "Expansion of Commercial Trade in Agricultural Products." In: *Towards an Open World Economy*, edited by Frank McFadzean, Sir Alec Cairncross, Sidney Golt, James Meade, W. M. Corden, Harry G. Johnson, and T. M. Rybczynski. London: Macmillan, 1972. ISBN 0-312-81060-1.

Josling considers the chaotic state of international trade in agriculture to be a result of national support programs and subsidies. He describes in detail the practices of the European CAP and proposes possible reforms. Negotiations to reduce agricultural protectionism must be based on reciprocal advantages.

* **9.6** *

Yeutter, Clayton K. "Food and Foreign Affairs: The Role of Agricultural Trade Policy in International Commerce and Domestic Relations." In: *Food and Agricultural Policy*. Washington, DC: American Enterprise Institute for Public Policy Research, 1977. ISBN 0-8447-2109-3.

Yeutter reviews the various forms of protection offered in the developed and developing states. He concludes that reduction of agricultural protection is necessary, and that inadequate GATT rules must be strengthened.

International Negotiations on Agricultural Trade

* **9.7** *

Boger, William H., III. "The United States-European Community Agricultural Export Subsidies Dispute." *Law and Policy in International Business* 16:1 (1984): 173-238.

The United States and the EC both subsidize exports of agricultural products, giving rise to disputes over their use. Boger argues that bilateral negotiations can be used to solve the problems as long as it is realized that both sides have important interests they must protect.

* **9.8** *

Houck, James P. "Agreements and Policy in U.S.-Japanese Agricultural Trade." In: *U.S.-Japanese Agricultural Trade Relations*, edited by Emery N. Castle and Kenzo Hemmi with Sally A. Skillings. Washington, DC: Resources for the Future, 1982. ISBN 0-8018-2815-5.

The political power of Japanese farmers and farm organizations has supported continued protectionism in Japan. The Kennedy Round in the 1960s reduced agricultural tariffs in Japan moderately, leading to only approximately $8 billion in additional U.S. exports. The tariff cuts of the Tokyo Round and agreements on quota increases in Japan in the 1970s, however, were calculated to produce a $211 million increase in U.S. agricultural exports.

* 9.9 *
Houck, James P. "U.S. Agricultural Trade and the Tokyo Round." *Law and Policy in International Business* 12:1 (1980): 265-295.

Although the Tokyo Round did not make major breakthroughs in liberalizing trade in agricultural products, some gains for U.S. agricultural exports were achieved. It did set in place a general framework for dealing with other problems, including non-tariff barriers.

* 9.10 *
Patterson, Kathleen. "Keeping Them Happy Down on the Farm." *Foreign Policy* 36 (Fall 1979): 63-70.

Patterson discusses disagreements between the United States and the EC, and most particularly France, over agricultural exports to third countries. The United States considers sales of French wheat, subsidized by the EC, to be an unfair trading practice.

* 9.11 *
Sato, Hideo, and Timothy J. Curran. "Agricultural Trade: The Case of Beef and Citrus." In: *Coping with U.S.-Japanese Economic Conflict*, edited by I.M. Destler and Hideo Sato. Lexington, MA: Lexington Books, 1982. ISBN 0-669-05144-6.

The political power of Japanese farmers in the ruling Liberal Democratic Party has successfully maintained numerous import quotas on agricultural products. U.S. pressure has managed to lower some of the barriers.

* 9.12 *
Warley, T. K. "Western Trade in Agricultural Products." In: *International Economic Relations of the Western World, 1959-1971: Volume 1, Politics and Trade*, edited by Andrew Shonfield with Hermia Oliver. London: Oxford University Press, 1976. ISBN 0-19-218314-1.

Protectionism in agriculture increased during the period under study, particularly as a consequence of the actions of the EC. Multilateral negotiations for tariff reductions have generally excluded agricultural products and the increasing use of non-tariff barriers that hinder agricultural trade. Warley provides a variety of indications of

the benefits that could occur with reduced protectionism and the costs of existing measures.

Reasons for the Protection of Domestic Agriculture

* 9.13 *
Feis, Herbert. "Effects of Trade Barriers on World Food Movements." *Proceedings of the Academy of Political Science* 30:3 (1971): 143-150.

Countries create barriers to food imports because national security in war requires them, because the state controls the agricultural sector, or because national shortages require immediate action that cannot wait on international markets. Feis argues that trade barriers have become less important than national economic policies in limiting agricultural trade.

* 9.14 *
Preeg, Ernest H. "Trade Liberalization and the Agricultural Impasse." In: *The United States and International Markets: Commercial Policy Options in an Age of Controls*, edited by Robert G. Hawkins and Ingo Walter. Lexington, MA: Lexington Books, 1972. ISBN 0-669-84020-3.

Although trade liberalization in industrial products was evident in the 1960s, agriculture was largely excluded from such trends. Nations preferred some self-sufficiency in food for security reasons and also wished to maintain farming sectors with reasonable incomes. Preeg concludes that the gains possible from liberalization of agricultural trade are considerable.

* 9.15 *
Yoshioka, Yutaka. "The Personal View of a Japanese Negotiator." In: *U.S.-Japanese Agricultural Trade Relations*, edited by Emery N. Castle and Kenzo Hemmi with Sally A. Skillings. Washington, DC: Resources for the Future, 1982. ISBN 0-8018-2815-5.

Japanese agricultural protectionism is designed to protect the Japanese small farmer, as is the CAP in the EC. The policies are also designed to aid in food self-sufficiency, a concern that was exacerbated in the mid-1970s by global food shortages and the failure of U.S. policies to meet the Japanese needs in the area of food security.

Agricultural Protection in the Developed Countries

* 9.16 *
Buckwell, Allan E., David R. Harvey, Kenneth J. Thomson, and Kevin A. Parton. *The Costs of the Common Agricultural Policy*. London: Croom Helm, 1982. ISBN 0-7099-0671-4.

While the Common Agricultural Policy is costly, it affects the member states differently since not all products are covered. Consumers pay higher costs, an expected consequence of a policy whose main goal is to raise the income of farmers. The overall level of protection offered by the EC is higher than would be likely if individual member states were to administer and pay for such a policy.

* 9.17 *
Carey, Michael J. "European Food Policy." In: *Food Politics: The Regional Conflict*, edited by David N. Balaam and Michael J. Carey. Totowa, NJ: Allanheld, Osmun, 1981. ISBN 0-916672-52-2.

The formation of the EC and the construction of the Common Agricultural Policy provided the members with greater food self-sufficiency within the EC as opposed to national programs or efforts at international cooperation. The EC uses subsidies and protection to promote security of supply in food. It has resisted U.S. efforts to liberalize trade in agricultural products in the GATT multilateral negotiations.

* 9.18 *
Harvey, D.R., and K.J. Thomson. "Costs, Benefits and the Future of the Common Agricultural Policy." *Journal of Common Market Studies* 24:1 (September 1985): 1-20.

The EC's Common Agricultural Policy has faced problems in part because it has sought to fulfill multiple objectives. Support for the program is declining in the EC, particularly in the United Kingdom, due to its high costs.

* 9.19 *
Hayami, Yujiro. "Adjustment Policies for Japanese Agriculture in a Changing World." In: *U.S.-Japanese Agricultural Trade Relations*, edited by Emery N. Castle and Kenzo Hemmi with Sally A. Skillings. Washington, DC: Resources for the Future, 1982. ISBN 0-8018-2815-5.

Japan's protection of small farmers is typical of that accorded in all developed states at equivalent levels of industrialization. This protection is necessary to maintain social stability in such countries, including Japan. Hayami argues further that before such protection can be removed, the rural areas have to be integrated into the Japanese national economy through policies that are basically non-agricultural.

* 9.20 *
Hemmi, Kenzo. "Agriculture and Politics in Japan." In: *U.S.-Japanese Agricultural Trade Relations*, edited by Emery N. Castle and Kenzo Hemmi with Sally A. Skillings. Washington, DC: Resources for the Future, 1982. ISBN 0-8018-2815-5.

The ruling Liberal Democratic Party endorses agricultural protectionism in part due to its strong support among farmers and overrepresentation of rural areas in the legislature. All the political parties are protectionist, however, and Japanese consumers are tolerant of high food prices. Major changes are unlikely since government policies seem to accurately reflect public opinion.

* 9.21 *
Honma, Masayoshi, and Yujiro Hayami. "Structure of Agricultural Protection in Industrial Countries." *Journal of International Economics* 20:1-2 (February 1986): 115-129.

The authors measure nominal rates of protection in ten countries and the EC for agricultural products. The United States has the lowest levels by far and Switzerland the highest. Nominal levels of protection were related to a variety of factors, including comparative advantage, the share of agriculture in the total economy, EC membership, terms of trade between agricultural and manufactured products, and food security considerations.

* 9.22 *
Hopkins, Raymond F., and Donald J. Puchala. *Global Food Interdependence: Challenge to American Foreign Policy*. New York: Columbia University Press, 1980. ISBN 0-231-04858-0.

The authors discuss the role of the United States in international trade of foodstuffs. Chapter 2 deals with commercial policy with some emphasis on the consequences of protectionism in other parts of the world.

* 9.23 *
Houck, James P. *Elements of Agricultural Trade Policies*. New York: Macmillan, 1986. ISBN 0-02-947720-4.

Houck analyzes the various protectionist policies of industrialized countries in both exports and imports. He concentrates on the economic factors that underlie them.

* 9.24 *
Hubbard, L. J., and D. R. Harvey. "Greece and the Common Agricultural Policy." In: *Greece and the EEC: Integration and Convergence*, edited by George N. Yannopoulos. New York: St. Martin's, 1986. ISBN 0-312-34717-0.

Overall, food costs in the EC are 27 percent higher with the Common Agricultural Policy than they would be with free trade. Greece has gained increased markets for its exports from the protection supplied by this program.

* 9.25 *
Johnson, D. Gale. *World Agriculture in Disarray*. London: Macmillan, 1973. ISBN 0-850-03076-5.

Among other issues, Johnson considers the

consequences of high levels of agricultural protectionism in the developed states. These levels have led to higher costs for consumers and have particularly hurt the developing countries that could otherwise export more agricultural products. He notes that changes in attitudes in the developed countries must occur before there is any prospect of trade liberalization in agricultural commodities.

* 9.26 *
Josling, T. E. Mark Langworthy, and Scott Pearson. *Options for Farm Policy in the European Community.* Thames Essay no. 27. London: Trade Policy Research Centre, 1981. ISBN 0-900-84252-0.

The Common Agricultural Policy (CAP) of the EC is under pressure to change because of the increasingly high domestic costs of price supports. The authors provide some estimates of the budgetary costs of the CAP and projections for the future.

* 9.27 *
Keeler, John T. S. "Dreams of Green Oil, Nightmares of Inequality: French Agricultural Policy and the External Challenges of the 1980s." In: *France in the Troubled World Economy*, edited by Stephen S. Cohen and Peter A. Gourevitch. London: Butterworth Scientific, 1982. ISBN 0-408-10787-1.

French farmers are important politically, and various governments have supported the Common Agricultural Policy of the EC that protects them. Protection against imports from other EC members has even been applied, although the EC's Court of Justice ruled that the practices were not valid.

* 9.28 *
Malmgren, H.B., and D.L. Schlechty. "Rationalizing World Agricultural Trade." *Journal of World Trade Law* 4:4 (July/August 1970): 515-537.

Government, particularly in Europe, is already heavily involved in agricultural trade. Free trade is impossible, but various governments do need to restrain each other in the creation of obstacles. All the major developed areas of the world have at least some forms of protection.

* 9.29 *
Marsh, J.S. "The Common Agricultural Policy and the Mediterranean Countries." In: *The EEC and the Mediterranean Countries*, edited by Avi Shlaim and G. N. Yannopoulos. Cambridge: Cambridge University Press, 1976. ISBN 0-317-20827-6.

Marsh notes that pressure for the maintenance of the protectionist Common Agricultural Policy comes in the form of pressure by farmers on their national governments and pressure on the Community by the governments when a national interest is perceived to be at stake. The Mediter-

ranean associates are hurt by the EC agricultural policies since their agricultural products have difficulty entering European markets. The agricultural price levels used effectively keep out products that have a tariff preference since they cannot penetrate a market that is oversupplied in the most important food products.

* 9.30 *
Sanderson, Fred H. "Managing Our Agricultural Interdependence." In: *U.S.-Japanese Agricultural Trade Relations*, edited by Emery N. Castle and Hemmi Kenzo with Sally A. Skillings. Washington, DC: Resources for the Future, 1982. ISBN 0-8018-2815-5.

In his overview of U.S. and Japanese agricultural policies, Sanderson notes that while Japan has liberalized import barriers, significant ones still remain. He suggests that both governments consult and provide advance warnings of changes in practice that affect each other.

* 9.31 *
Sampson, Gary P., and Richard H. Snape. "Effects of the EEC's Variable Import Levies." *Journal of Political Economy* 88:5 (October 1980): 1026-1040.

The EC uses variable import levies and variable export subsidies for agricultural commodities under its Common Agricultural Policy that are designed to maintain domestic prices and ensure exports if world prices are low. These policies have the effects of depressing world prices further when they are low and further increasing world prices that are rising. The EC is also able to capture portions of the subsidies paid to farmers in other states through these mechanisms.

* 9.32 *
Schram, Ronald B. "International Repercussions of National Farm Policies: A Look at American Wheat Programs." *Law and Policy in International Business* 3:2 (1971): 239-265.

U.S. policies for wheat, including subsidies and supply restrictions, have provided protection for American farmers. They have hindered efforts to reduce barriers to trade in agricultural commodities and adversely affected the U.S. goal of trade liberalization.

* 9.33 *
Sorenson, Vernon L. "Contradictions in U.S. Trade Policy." In: *U.S. Trade Policy and Agricultural Exports*, edited by the Iowa State University. Center for Agricultural and Rural Development. Ames: Iowa State University Press, 1973. ISBN 0-8138-1655-6.

Exceptions to the free trade principles of GATT appeared early in agricultural products. U.S. trade policy has been contradictory in that there have been efforts to open up foreign markets to some farm exports while domestic protection has been applied to other products. Exports of competitive agricultural products from the developing countries have been particularly handicapped by this protection.

* 9.34 *
Talbot, Ross B. "Effect of Domestic Political Groups and Forces on U.S. Trade Policy." In: *U.S. Trade Policy and Agricultural Exports*, edited by the Iowa State Center for Agricultural and Rural Development. Ames: Iowa State University Press, 1973. ISBN 0-8138-1655-6.

Domestic agricultural groups supported President Kennedy's efforts at trade liberalization in the hope of gaining access to foreign markets. Through time U.S. farm organizations have had a mixed pattern of success in achieving their goals, which have included both trade liberalization and in some cases protectionism.

* 9.35 *
Talbot, Ross B., and Young W. Kihl. "The Politics of Domestic and Foreign Policy Linkages in U.S.-Japanese Agricultural Policy Making." In: *U.S.-Japanese Agricultural Trade Relations*, edited by Emery N. Castle and Kenzo Hemmi with Sally A. Skillings. Washington, DC: Resources for the Future, 1982. ISBN 0-8018-2815-5.

The authors review the political differences and similarities in the United States and Japan that have led to their respective international economic policies on agricultural trade. The U.S. free trade orientation and Japanese protectionism in this area do represent the economic interests of their domestic agricultural groups.

* 9.36 *
Tontz, Robert L. "U.S. Trade Policy: Background and Historical Trends." In: *U.S. Trade Policy and Agricultural Exports*, edited by the Iowa State University. Center for Agricultural and Rural Development. Ames: Iowa State University Press, 1973. ISBN 0-8138-1655-6.

Tontz reviews U.S. agricultural trade since World War I, including the effects of U.S. and foreign protectionism. He provides an extremely useful appendix, listing U.S. non-tariff barriers to agricultural imports frequently noted as troublesome by other countries.

* 9.37 *
Warley, Thorald K. "Issues in Canadian Agricultural Trade Policy." In: *Canada-United States Free Trade*, edited by John Whalley with Roderick Hill. Toronto: University of Toronto Press, 1985. ISBN 0820-7253-4.

Canada has supported liberalization of trade in agricultural products although little has been accomplished in this area. National and provincial subsidies to farmers, however, have created problems with other countries, including the United States. Canadian producers receive high levels of protection in some product areas.

Effects on the Developing Countries

* 9.38 *
Duncan, Ron, and Ernst Lutz. "Penetration of Industrial Country Markets by Agricultural Products from Developing Countries." *World Development* 11:9 (September 1983): 771-786.

Developing countries have been unable to increase their market shares for agricultural products in the industrialized states. In some products they have incurred losses in market shares. Increased agricultural self-sufficiency in developed states and protectionism are two important causes of this situation.

* 9.39 *
Johnson, D. Gale. *The Sugar Program: Large Costs and Small Benefits*. Washington, DC: American Enterprise Institute for Public Policy, 1974. ISBN 0-850-03076-5.

U.S. protection of domestic sugar growers through subsidies and import quotas has resulted in small net gains for the producers compared to larger costs for the country. Johnson suggests phasing out support for domestic producers with compensation for short-term losses.

* 9.40 *
Martin, Michael V., and John A. McDonald. "Food Grain Policy in the Republic of Korea: The Economic Costs of Self-Sufficiency." *Economic Development and Cultural Change* 34:2 (January 1986): 315-331.

Korea has protected domestic agriculture to attain greater food self-sufficiency and to raise the income of farmers. The policy has been successful in some areas, but at a higher cost to consumers and taxpayers. The authors caution against judging such a program only on the basis of economic costs and benefits since any government evaluates such policies on other criteria.

* 9.41 *
Smith, Ian. "EEC Sugar Policy in an International Context." *Journal of World Trade Law* 15:2 (March/April 1981): 95-110.

The EC support of sugar has led to a surplus in production and exports to the world market. These exports have created significant instability in the world market. The domestic production also makes it difficult for the EC to fulfill its commitment to provide a guaranteed market with sugar exporters that signed the Lome Convention.

* 9.42 *
Smith, Ian. "Sugar Markets in Disarray." *Journal of World Trade Law* 9:1 (January/February 1975): 41-62.

The world sugar market faces a number of crises, such as overproduction and falling prices. Protection of beet producers in the developed states is part of the problem and is not justified.

* 9.43 *
Tsadik, Tesfaye W. "The International Sugar Market: Self-Sufficiency or Free Trade." *Journal of World Trade Law* 16:2 (March/April 1982): 133-151.

Both the United States and Europe have contributed to the problems of world sugar trade and resultant difficulties for the developing states. The EC in particular has created problems. Although self-sufficiency in the EC may be justified, the generation of surpluses for export is especially disruptive.

CUSTOMS UNIONS, FREE TRADE AREAS, AND TRADING BLOCS

Customs unions and free trade areas can have a major protectionist effect on trade patterns. The European Community (EC) is the prime example of such a customs union, but there are or have been a number of other important regional groupings. There is also a possibility that such regional economic organizations could be the forerunners of a global trading community that is increasingly regionalized.

Since World War II, there have been numerous economic agreements leading to the creation of special trading areas that are limited to selected countries in the world, trading areas that have had diverse effects on international commerce. They provide producers in the member states with special access to a wider market because of a reduction of barriers to each other's trade. Non-member states, however, continue to face obstacles to markets in the member states. This access then serves to provide protection to producers within the trading areas at the expense of external competitors.

The existence of a larger domestic market in the member states does provide for the liberalization of trade, but only for a portion of the world trading community. The exact form that such trading arrangements take varies. Although the idea of reciprocity for all nations, including the most favored nation status, is a key tenet of GATT and applies to all GATT members, exceptions to this reciprocity principle are permissible under GATT rules when certain conditions are met in the creation of such trade areas. While all the conditions have not been consistently met by such trading communities, they have been formed nonetheless, and they have been accepted by other states, although not without complaint. At the simplest level of such a trade arrangement, two countries may agree to lower barriers to trade between themselves in certain products or sectors. A free trade area is more general in its effects in that it will lower or eliminate tariff barriers between member countries for all or almost all trade.

Each country in the free trade areas, however, will retain its individual national tariff schedule vis-a-vis non-members. Since the national tariff levels will vary, free trade area arrangements necessitate agreements on rules of origin for imports into the area. These rules of origin will be structured to prevent foreign producers from bypassing the high tariff in one state by shipping to another member with lower tariffs and then re-shipping the goods to the high tariff country.

A customs union carries trade unity one step further. The member states will not only eliminate barriers to trade among themselves, but they will create a common external tariff schedule for imports from external sources, thus creating a true common domestic market. The European Community is the major, present day example of such a customs union. It has liberalized trade among the member states, but it has maintained and created obstacles to trade with third countries. Other types of arrangements exist that link countries together in trade--so much so that there has been some fear that the international economic system will become regionalized into trading blocs with trade increasingly occurring within such groups rather than between countries in different blocs.

Customs Union Theory

From the perspective of trade relationships, and indirectly protection, two significant aspects of customs unions and free trade areas have been specified--trade creation and trade diversion. Trade creation occurs within the customs union when producers in the different member states begin to ship to the markets now available in the other member states rather than producing only for national domestic consumption. Since there is free or freer trade within the trade group, there are lower costs for the consumers in the member states as the comparative advantages of the different participants come into play. Such conditions can particularly help smaller firms that would not otherwise become involved in exporting activities.[1] Trade diversion, on the other hand, occurs when the members replace trade relations formerly transacted with non-members with interactions between the member states. Rather than import from a third country or export to that state, a member now trades instead with other members, at least to some extent. The absence of internal obstacles in the trade area plus barriers to external sources of imports will change the pre-existing trade patterns.

Although countries may join a customs union primarily for political reasons, when economic issues are paramount, they form or join such a trade area to gain the benefits of lower costs for some goods and wider markets for their exports. In most cases, countries have a variety of economic incentives to form such groups since there will be net benefits overall. Even if one country were to receive all the benefits from such a union, these benefits could be redistributed to the other members in a variety of forms. A customs union will provide protection against foreign competition in at least some markets, a concern for countries that have joined them. Joining might also preserve access to an especially important market that could be lost by staying outside the union. Ireland's decision to join the EC, for example, was clearly predicated on the fact that the United Kingdom was going to join. There are costs that occur with customs unions, but these costs are normally borne by non-member states that have lost markets.

The balance between trade creation and trade diversion will determine whether a customs union provides net benefits in global efficiency of production, in all countries both inside and outside of such areas. There generally are net benefits--if not, the union will not survive--, but customs unions will lead to re-distributive effects among nations. They liberalize trade for a portion of the world but very often create greater barriers against the rest of the world.

Models have been developed to consider the likelihood and the extent of trade creation and trade diversion under different sets of circumstances. In any customs union both effects will result, but the levels will vary. In some cases the removal of internal barriers may even benefit non-members as productive allocations within the trade area change. Even though some third countries might gain in certain situations, other states are still likely to suffer losses due to the circumscribing of their trade opportunities. A number of other factors can be important in the effects that customs unions can have. The level of economic development in the members can affect their relative gains and even lead to some losses among them. In addition, the relative size of the economies of the members can be a factor. The levels of present protection in the members at the time the customs union is formed can be important. If low tariffs are the norm, the effects of the customs union will be smaller in relation to changes in trade patterns. If higher barriers had previously existed, both the trade creation and trade diversion effects may be enhanced.

The European Community

The EC is clearly the most important customs union in existence in the world today. The European Common Market, as it was first generally called, came into force in 1957 with the signing of the Treaty of Rome. It built upon two earlier efforts at reducing obstacles to European trade. Belgium, the Netherlands, and Luxembourg had become members of the Benelux customs union at the end of World War II. The Benelux union had operated smoothly and provided an indication of how effective such an arrangement could be in promoting trade and economic cooperation. In 1951, the three Benelux states, Germany, France, and Italy agreed to form the European Coal and Steel Community (ECSC), which was a sectoral free trade arrangement designed to rationalize and to increase the efficiency of the national steel industries. The success of this arrangement then encouraged the six ECSC members to create a more ambitious customs union.

The EC over time has eliminated all internal tariffs among the original members and maintained a common external tariff vis-a-vis outside countries. In multilateral negotiations today, officials of the EC, not the member nations, conduct negotiations on tariff reductions for the Community as a whole. The various non-tariff barriers that previously affected trade among the members have also been largely eliminated over time as well. In some cases there has even been a common EC policy on NTBs versus outside states, and at other times the individual members have followed separate paths. The CAP is perhaps the prime example of such a common protective device, while national quotas and subsidies are examples of individual approaches.

The individual nations also still undertake many policies such as regional planning or health regulations that can inhibit imports as a by-product of other policy goals. Even in these policies, commonalities have begun to appear. Harmonization of many types of policies have occurred over time, leading to similarities in the barriers present to imports. Such harmonization can also facilitate trade flows among the members and hamper foreign competitors, who will be less familiar with the programs.

The formation of a customs union may help eliminate at least some NTBs. The creation of the Benelux union forced the members to recognize their influence and to address resultant problems. As a consequence, many such obstacles to trade were removed. Their removal or limitation also had a positive effect on trade with non-member states.[2] The same process has occurred in the EC as well, in some areas. The successive enlargements of the EC, however, have expanded its significance for world trade and magnified the consequences of the remaining tariffs and NTBs. The addition of Great Britain, Ireland, and Denmark in 1973 resulted in their eventual integration into this common framework, although special provisions were initially necessary to ease the effects that total and immediate intra-Community free trade would have had in some economic sectors of the new members. The arrangements admitting Greece and then Spain and Portugal provided similar protection in some sectors for the new members, but the interests of the existing members were also protected in some cases from immediate, unfettered competition for a transition period.

The EC, in both its initial six-member and its present enlarged form, has clearly had both trade distorting and trade creating effects. Trade creation among the members has been substantial, and the lower costs involved as a result have been credited with facilitating the significant economic growth of the original members. The common market has been especially effective in facilitating intra-industry trade among firms in the member countries with positive consequences for efficiency and competitiveness. The United States originally encouraged the European countries to form the EC to generate exactly this type of economic development. Trade diversion has also been obvious, although analyses have generally found it to be of a lower magnitude than trade creation. The increase in benefits have accrued to the member states, while the costs resulting from changes in trade linkages have been sustained by outside countries, such as the United States, which have lost markets. The CAP is a particularly clear example of these trade diverting effects since domestic agricultural production has been encouraged and third countries have either lost important European markets or found it impossible to develop them.

While the EC has been a major economic success story for its members, it has contributed to the new protectionism in a number of ways. Domestic industries are protected from import competition to an extent by the common external tariff and by the presence of Community non-tariff obstacles to imports. The EC even negotiated a voluntary export restraint agreement with Japan, a possible omen of the future use of such arrangements against other foreign competitors. The interests of the different members over trade policy may also have placed new obstacles in the way of multilateral efforts at trade liberalization since consensus on which sectors to open to import competition becomes more difficult to achieve, particularly during times of world recession.

The member countries have not been united in a common policy, even though efforts have been made to find such a common approach. Germany, the Netherlands, and Denmark generally favor free trade, while France and Italy are more protectionist, as was noted in Chapter 7. Different industrial sectors in the members also have different interests in terms of free trade versus protection debates, depending upon their orientation towards exporting to countries outside the Community or their dependence on the EC market for sales. These different interests will make consensus on a common trade policy difficult. In other cases interest group activity has crossed national boundaries in the EC, forming coalitions that place additional pressure on the EC to maintain or institute protection. In addition, the member states have had to adjust to free trade within the Community itself, which could make adjustment to outside competition more difficult if multilateral trade liberalization were to occur. Complete removal of tariffs could also weaken the unity of the EC since it would remove a common bond among the members. The common external tariff serves both economic and political purposes in creating a sense of unity among the members, and the political purposes more than the economic ones might necessitate its retention.[3] The individual member countries also have less need of global trade liberalization as a mechanism of generating economic benefits since they have achieved or are achieving such gains within the Community. To some extent, they have both the best of free trade and the best of protectionism in an increasingly neo-mercantile world. In that neo-mercantile world it is clearly better to be inside the largest custom union than to be outside of it. The protectionist effects of the EC, and the advantages of membership in it, have been heightened by the series of special trade agreements that the EC has signed with many other countries.

The EC Extended--An Emerging Trade Bloc?

In addition to the full members, the EC has negotiated a large number of preferential trade agreements with many other countries, even though some of these arrangements were contrary to GATT rules. The trade treaties can be conveniently grouped as: those with other European nations, with the former colonies of the members, and with the countries around the Mediterranean littoral. The agreements with the other European countries included early arrangements with the European Free Trade Area (EFTA), which was formed by the United Kingdom, Switzerland, Austria, Portugal, Norway, Denmark, and Sweden as a reaction to the creation of the EC. The negotiations between the two groups led to lower trade barriers between them in many areas and further facilitated intra-industry trade in Europe to the advantage of the members of both groups and to the disadvantage of many other countries. Although there was increased trade between the two trade areas, there was also trade diversion in some products as members traded more within their respective groups and less with the countries in the other trading area. Not surprisingly, agriculture was one area in which there was less trade as a consequence of the formation of the rival groups.

EFTA was weakened in 1973 when two of its members joined the EC, but the special arrangements were maintained with the other five coun-tries. Spain, before its admission to the Community, Turkey, Finland, and Yugoslavia also reached similar preferential arrangements with the EC. Turkey's agreement provided for the eventual full membership of that country in the EC. One effect of these agreements with the European countries has been to create a large, generally free, trade area encompassing virtually all of Western Europe, at least for manufactured goods, and even for some agricultural products. The result of all these agreements has been a general rise in the trade among the signatories and some declines in trade with other countries.

The original EC members also negotiated the two Yaounde Conventions with the former French, Belgian, and Italian colonies in sub-Saharan Africa. The conventions granted these developing states the status of associate members of the EC, although the term associate soon fell into disuse given its connotation of second class standing. The agreements provided the African states with some preferential access to the EC market and in some cases guaranteed minimum purchases of some of their products. The first Yaounde Convention even provided for reverse preferences for EC exports, contrary to GATT rules. These initial agreements were later extended to most of the developing countries in Africa, as well as former European colonies in the Caribbean and the Pacific--hence the designation of the countries as the ACP states--under the two Lome Conventions that followed. The inclusion of these additional developing countries in part reflected the impending admission of Great Britain into the EC and the need to include the former British colonies in some form of association with the Community, particularly since many of them were losing the Commonwealth preferences that had previously aided their exporting to British markets.

India, Pakistan, Sri Lanka, Singapore, Malaysia, and Hong Kong, however, were specifically excluded from eligibility. Both the European countries and other developing countries desired to exclude these states on the grounds that their level of industrialization and export capability threatened domestic industries in Europe, such as steel, textiles, and other manufactures, and that most of the fledgling industries in the ACP states could not hope to compete on equal terms with these Asian countries. The exclusion of these countries from any special association with the EC clearly reflected a desire to protect domestic producers in areas sensitive to imports. In effect, associate status was conferred on those developing countries that would be least able to compete with the weaker domestic industries in the member states.[4]

Although these conventions have led to some trade creation, the overall effects have been somewhat limited. The trade of the ACP countries is such a small portion of the total EC trade that it has had little significant effect on Europe, a fact that may help explain why there has been generally only muted domestic opposition to the resultant limited import competition. The trade links are of course much more important for the ACP countries given their smaller economic bases and trade totals. Many potentially important products, however, have been excluded from special consideration under the conventions. Protectionist sentiment in Europe has resulted in ACP agricultural exports being restricted. Compared to raw materials, semi-processed and processed goods are also much less likely to receive any special preferences on a scale that will make them competitive with domestic producers. In effect, domestic firms are protected in this area. Quotas in products such as textiles have even been placed on ACP exports in areas where European industries are facing difficulties due to lost exports and import competition.[5]

Other developing countries, such as those in Latin America and Asia, have argued that these preferential arrangements have placed limitations on their exports of some products to European markets and that the ACP states have benefited at their expense. NTBs, such as quotas, have particularly limited the imports of some items from these other developing states while permitting entrance of ACP exports. The GSP for the Community has also only been of limited aid to these other developing countries since it was structured in such a way that the special access for products from the ACP was not damaged or eroded. Protection of this margin of preference is one factor that may lead the EC and ACP countries to be likely opponents of further general trade liberalization since it would negate the special access provisions that now exist. Other developing countries also find it more difficult to export to the EC since the second Lome Convention contains liberal rules of origin for the ACP states. Exports utilizing components from other ACP countries or from EC members are treated as if they were produced locally in the exporter, thus qualifying for any preferences that are available. These rules of origin also have the advantage of encouraging the ACP states to purchase many products and components from EC members as a means of retaining their preferential market access for exports. In effect, the rules of origin protect European firms from competition in some markets of the ACP states.

The EC has also negotiated trade treaties with many of the countries bordering on the Mediterranean Sea, including Morocco, Algeria, Tunisia, Egypt, Cyprus, Israel, Syria, and Lebanon, arrangements that have given them some special access to European markets, although the agreements have also protected certain domestic industries from import competition. The European countries have in some cases received preferences for their exports in return. These agreements have increased trade between these countries and the EC, but at the expense of other states, including the ACP countries in some circumstances. The ACP states do have greater margins of preference for many of the products in question, but they cannot effectively compete with the more advanced developing states such as those in the Mediterranean area. The whole effort to form trade links with these countries has been part of a broader EC policy to strengthen political and economic links with the Mediterranean area.

The extended EC has come to form at least an incipient trade bloc encompassing most of Europe and Africa. The territories in the Caribbean and the Pacific that are included are mostly small island states; thus, they do not form a major component of the trading system as such. All these developing countries are directly linked with the EC markets through some type of preferential access. While direct reverse preferences for European products are no longer usually present, there is a natural tendency for reverse trade flows to occur, a tendency that is reinforced by such measures as the rules or origin requirements contained in the second Lome Convention in the case of the ACP countries. Asian and Latin American developing states have lost markets as a result of the arrangements that the ACP countries and Mediterranean states have with the EC. In effect, there has been trade diversion at their expense.

The recent enlargement of the EC proper will be likely to increase problems of protectionism inside the organization for the developing countries since Spain and Portugal export many of the same types of products as developing countries, including the ACP and Mediterranean states. Other industrialized countries such as the United States that are outside this larger system have also suffered from lost trade opportunities due to the protection that is offered within this trade group. The fact that many of the arrangements violate GATT rules had led to complaints from outside states in the past, but some of this concern has declined over time as more and more countries, including a majority of GATT members, have signed trade treaties with the EC.[6] The presence of the EC with its extended treaty network, however, has led other countries to consider closer trading relationships as a counterpoise.

Other Free Trade Areas--Developed Countries

There have been a number of other attempts to create customs unions or free trade areas among developed states. EFTA functioned well until some of its members joined the EC. While it was in operation, there were both trade creation and trade diversion effects for the members in addition to similar effects resulting from the agreements between EFTA and the EC. EFTA was also fairly effective in reducing many NTBs that otherwise would have restricted trade among the members. As noted previously, the creation of a free trade area between the United States and Canada was negotiated in October of 1987, and it awaits ratification by both governments in 1988.

The United States and Israel have signed an agreement to form a free trade area, and Australia and New Zealand are considering closer economic ties. The Council of Mutual Economic Assistance (CMEA or COMECON) unites the Soviet Union and East Europe in a customs union. This organization has led to noticeable trade creation among the members. Trade diversion, on the other hand, has been relatively limited, in part due to the lack of pre-existing economic links with outside states.[7] At times, this organization has been used to protect members from Western economic penetration, although the rationale for the protection has often been more political than economic, to the extent that the two can be separated.

Other Free Trade Areas--Developing Countries

Numerous trading groups that have been attempted among the developing countries have been formed in the expectation that they would create greater export opportunities, permit industries to be created or expanded due to the presence of a larger domestic market, and generally facilitate economic development and growth. Many of these efforts at economic union were spurred by the obvious successes of the EC, but the vast majority of them have failed to have any significant economic or trade effect. Three of them, however, are notable for having achieved at least some early successes in attaining the hoped-for goals.

The Central American Common Market (CACOM) was a full customs union that initially had a great deal of success in stimulating trade among the five members. There were also some trade diversion effects present as a result of the union. The organization has since become moribund as a result of the political disturbances in Central America and the resulting political animosities among the former members, although Honduras had withdrawn earlier from the group after failing

to receive any significant economic benefits from membership.

The Latin American Free Trade Association (LAFTA), the second of the three, joined the countries of South America and Mexico in a free trade area. Trade among the members did increase initially as the larger market permitted increases in intra-LAFTA trade, although much of the increased trade was diverted from outside sources.[8] This initial impetus for greater trade did not continue. Many of the smaller member states felt that Argentina, Brazil, and Mexico, with their much larger economies and more developed industrial bases, were gaining most of the benefits from the free trade area. As a result, the Andean Group or Andean Pact was formed within LAFTA from among most of the smaller South American members to negotiate as a group in LAFTA for the location of industrial plants and for changes in tariff schedules.

The third successful organization for freer trade is the Association of Southeast Asian Nations (ASEAN), consisting of Malaysia, Thailand, Singapore, Indonesia, the Philippines, and more recently Brunei. It is a newer grouping than CACOM or LAFTA, but it has had initial successes in terms of increasing trade and economic cooperation.

ASEAN, LAFTA, and CACOM all provided benefits to the member states, or at least most of them. Trade among the members did increase, at times at the expense of outside countries. The organizations did provide an opportunity for intra-industry trade within the groupings and the possibility for states to develop or expand industries for the larger market. Such customs unions among developing countries, however, need to avoid creating trade barriers against non-member states that are too high. Just as individual national policies of protection in developing states can discourage exports, encourage production for domestic consumption rather than exporting, and generate inefficiencies, high external tariffs or other obstacles to imports can lead to the same results in a customs union or free trade area. The force of these barriers on development potential can be seen in the fact that some of the early successes of these trade groups were due to the removal of the existing barriers to trade, obstacles that had often been formidable. In effect, the unions had corrected the problems created by the obstacles to imports from other developing countries that had previously been created.[9] Although free trade with the world might ultimately do more for the economic development of these developing states, that possibility has not really existed. These efforts to establish customs unions and free trade areas have lowered at least some barriers to trade among the members. Their ultimate utility to the member states, however, may still depend upon the level of protection that is provided against non-member countries.

Trade Blocs

Trade blocs, while not customs unions, can be a logical outgrowth of such organizations, and can perform much the same functions of protecting the domestic industries in at least some of the bloc countries from outside competition and of preserving internal markets. The former colonial empires formed such trading entities in many cases in the past. Free trade within the empire was often the rule, although revenue tariffs may have existed, but barriers against external products existed. Sometimes the barriers to outside imports were political rather than economic and were prohibitive to such trade. The system of preferences in the British Commonwealth is a more recent example of a similar though weaker trade system. The potential for outside trade was much greater and generally at the discretion of the individual national governments. The EC with its extended network of trade treaties has many of the characteristics of a trade bloc in that commercial interactions occur increasingly among the members rather than between members and outside states.

The EC has in fact played a major role in the creation of regional trading systems and has been considered the "prime exemplar" of the trade bloc.[10] EFTA was initially formed as a counterweight to this organization, and its defensive response demonstrated to some extent its concern over the EC's economic success. There has also been some discussion of creating an economic organization in the Pacific to further trade and economic cooperation. This group would be centered on Japan and the United States and include industrialized countries such as Canada and Australia, the Asian NICs, and the developing countries in the region. An alternative trade bloc, centered in North America, would result from the ratification of the US-Canadian free trade agreement. These two countries could become the core of a Western Hemisphere regional trading group or become part of a larger Asian-Pacific system. The efforts of the Soviet Union at times to limit trade between the East and the West represents another type of regional trading bloc. While trade in the world may not become increasingly regionalized, higher levels of intra-region or intra-bloc trade with provisions for special access would undoubtedly strengthen protectionism within the regions

against outsiders and make a return to a more liberal trade regime much more difficult to achieve.

End Notes

1. Hirsch, Seev and Zvi Adar. "Protected Markets and Firms' Export Distribution," *World Development* 2:8 (August 1974): pp.29-36.

2. Schneider, J.W. "Intra-Benelux NTD's." In: *Prospects of Eliminating Non-Tariff Distortions*, edited by Anthony E. Scaperlanda. Leiden: A. W. Sijthoff, 1973. pp.73-106.

3. Denton, Geoffrey, and Theo Peeters. "The European Community." In: *Economic Foreign Policies of Industrial States*, edited by Wilfrid L. Kohl. Lexington, MA: Lexington Books, 1977. pp.189-213.

4. Vaitsos, Constantine. "From the Ugly American to the Ugly European: The Role of Western Europe in North-South Relations." In: *The New International Economy*, edited by Harry Makler, Alberto Martinelli, and Neil Smelser. Sage Studies in International Sociology no.26. Beverly Hills, CA: Sage, 1982. p.186.

5. Ravenhill, John. *Collective Clientelism: The Lome Conventions and North-South Relations*. New York: Columbia University Press, 1985. pp.171-179.

6. Matthews, Jacqueline D. *Association System of the European Community*. New York: Praeger, 1977. p.105.

7. Pelzman, Joseph. "Trade Creation and Trade Diversion in the Council of Mutual Economic Assistance: 1954-1977." *American Economic Review* 67:4 (September 1977): pp.713-722.

8. George, Robert, Eldon Reiling, and Anthony Scaperlanda. "Short-Run Trade Effects of the LAFTA." *Kyklos* 30:4 (A77): pp.618-636.

9. Cochrane, James D., and John W. Sloan. "LAFTA and the CACM: A Comparative Analysis of Integration in Latin America." Journal of Developing Areas 8:1 (October 1973): pp.13-38.

10. Barraclough, Geoffrey. "The EEC and the World Economy." In: *Integration and Unequal Development: The Experience of the EEC*, edited by Dudley Seers and Constantine Vaitsos with Marja-Liisa Kiljunen. New York: St. Martin's, 1980. p.58.

Chapter 10: Annotated Bibliography

General Works

* 10.1 *

Brada, Josef C., and Jose A. Mendez. "Regional Integration and the Volume of Intra-Regional Trade: A Comparison of Developed and Developing Country Experience." *Kyklos* 36:4 (1983): 589-603.

Based on data from 1954 to 1977, the authors show that the formation of the EC, EFTA, and CACOM increased trade among members fourfold. LAFTA and the Andean Pact had little effect on such trade. Per capita income and geographic distance were two important explanatory factors.

* 10.2 *

Burnett, Robin, and Ric Lucas. "The Trade Agreement between Australia and Papua New Guinea." *Journal of World Trade Law* 12:5 (September/October 1978): 547-451.

The agreement between Australia and Papua-New Guinea may not meet all the requirements of a free trade area under GATT rules. The agreement may provide an incentive for other developing countries to seek similar agreements with Australia.

* 10.3 *

Haight, F.A. "Customs Unions and Free-Trade Areas under GATT: A Reappraisal." *Journal of World Trade Law* 6:4 (July/August 1986): 391-404.

Customs unions and free trade areas are permitted under GATT rules, but abuse has occurred. Haight argues that it would probably be better if the exceptions to normal GATT rules applied only to full customs unions rather than to free trade areas as well.

* 10.4 *

Hamilton, Bob, and John Whalley. "Geographically Discriminatory Trade Arrangements." *Review of Economics and Statistics* 67:3 (August 1985): 446-455.

This analysis of eight trade regions in the world, assuming discriminatory trading policies were adopted, suggests that gains and losses are related to initial protection levels, to the equality or inequality among regions, to the relative size of the regions, and existing trade patterns. Customs unions with a common external tariff may bring greater returns to the members than multilateral trade liberalization.

* 10.5 *

Huber, Jurgen. "The Practice of GATT in Examining Regional Arrangements under Article XXIV." *Jour-*
nal of Common Market Studies 19:3 (March 1981): 281-298.

Article XXIV allows for the formation of customs unions or free trade areas that provide special access to member states as long as certain conditions are met. Although virtually no trade grouping formed in the years since 1947 has met these conditions, GATT has accepted them.

Customs Union Theory

* 10.6 *

Arndt, Sven W. "Customs Union and the Theory of Tariffs." *American Economic Review* 59:1 (March 1969): 108-118.

A customs union will lead to trade losses for some external countries and trade gains for others, although it cannot be determined whether losses or gains will dominate overall. Customs unions often may be superior to other types of non-preferential tariff policies.

* 10.7 *

Bracewell-Milnes, Barry. *Eastern and Western European Economic Integration.* New York: St. Martin's, 1976. LC 76-6671.

The author considers various theoretical aspects of customs unions and then analyzes the EC and the Council of Mutual Economic Assistance (CMEA). While he notes that such trading areas can reduce free trade, he argues that the EC has liberalized trade by reducing barriers among the member states and the associated countries.

* 10.8 *

Collier, Paul. "The Welfare Effects of Customs Unions: An Anatomy." *Economic Journal* 89 (March 1979): 84-95.

Collier presents an expanded model of Viner's theory of customs unions, including outside countries, export and import diversion effects, and substitution occurring in the production and consumption sectors. These additions call into question some of Viner's basic theses.

* 10.9 *

Falvey, Rodney E., and Harold O. Fried. "Sectoral Trading Arrangements." *International Economic Review* 25:3 (October 1984): 671-685.

The authors note that previous research on the costs and benefits of free trade areas has been inconclusive. They propose a model for free trade by economic sectors in countries where the industry in question is already protected. Distributional questions about the ensuing benefits could not be answered by their model.

* 10.10 *
Hirsch, Seev, and Zvi Adar. "Protected Markets and Firms' Export Distribution." *World Development* 2:8 (August 1974): 29-36.

Free trade areas help small firms to export by establishing a preferential market. Exporting firms in non-member states suffer, particularly the small ones. Protection in a free trade area will induce outside small firms to export to other markets.

* 10.11 *
Krauss, Melvyn B. "Customs Union Theory: Ten Years Later." *Journal of World Trade Law* 6:3 (May/June 1972): 284-299.

Krauss provides an overview of many aspects of customs unions. Both political and economic motives underlie decisions to create or join such units. Developing states are most likely to join such unions for economic reasons.

* 10.12 *
McMillan, John, and Ewen McCann, "Welfare Effects in Customs Unions." *Economic Journal* 91 (September 1981): 697-703.

The authors present a formal model in order to determine if there are indeed welfare effects to be gained by forming customs unions. They find that the individual countries have incentives to construct bilateral arrangements with at least one other state as long as commodities imported are neither net substitutes or net complements.

* 10.13 *
O'Brien, Denis. "Customs Unions: Trade Creation and Trade Diversion in Historical Perspective." *History of Political Economy* 8:4 (Winter 1976): 540-563.

O'Brien uses a number of examples from the eighteenth and nineteenth centuries to demonstrate the background for Jacob Viner's views on customs unions. Many of the same fears of those desiring protectionist measures and the same arguments in favor of such unions were present in these periods.

* 10.14 *
Pomfret, Richard. "The Trade-Diverting Bias of Preferential Trading Arrangements." *Journal of Common Market Studies* 25:2 (December 1986): 109-117.

Preferential trading arrangements have proliferated despite GATT's rules against them. While there has been some trade creation, there has also

been much more trade diversion than normally thought.

* 10.15 *
Viner, Jacob. *The Customs Union Issue*. New York: Carnegie Endowment for Peace, 1950. ISBN 0-910136-01-7.

Viner's work on customs unions details the effects of their tariffs on trade. Trade is created among member nations, but trade diversion occurs in that there is trade among member states that would otherwise have been with external states. This trade diversion is inefficient and results from the protection offered by the customs union.

* 10.16 *
Wonnacott, Paul, and Ronald Wonnacott. "Is Unilateral Tariff Reduction Preferable to a Customs Union? The Curious Case of the Missing Foreign Tariffs." *American Economic Review* 71:4 (September 1981): 704-714.

While unilateral tariff reductions may increase benefits and expand exports due to lower costs, customs unions may increase trade even more. Previous models of unilateral reductions have ignored the fact that foreign tariffs could limit the gains of unilateral reductions.

The European Community

* 10.17 *
Bienefeld, Manfred. "Externalising Problems in a Future EEC." In: *Integration and Unequal Development: The Experience of the EEC*, edited by Dudley Seers and Constantine Vaitsos with Marja-Liisa Kiljunen. New York: St. Martin's, 1980. ISBN 0-312-41890-6.

In its relations with outside countries, the EC has selectively used protection while arguing for free trade in other areas. Such protection, largely invisible, has contributed to the EC trade imbalances with most of the rest of the world.

* 10.18 *
Chard, J.S., and M.J. Macmillen. "Sectoral Aids and Community Competition Policy: The Case of Textiles." *Journal of World Trade Law* 13:2 (March/April 1979): 132-157.

Aid to industries in the EC has often reflected the influence of interest groups in the member states. EC authorities have not been stringent enough in regulating or controlling the provision of such aid.

* 10.19 *
Corado, Cristina, and Jaime De Melo. "An Ex-Ante Model for Estimating the Impact on Trade Flows of a Country's Joining a Customs Union." *Journal*

of Development Economics 24:1 (November 1986): 153-166.

The authors applied a model on the effects of joining a customs union to Portugal and its admission to the EC. In a few sectors there was increased trade both with the EC and with outside countries. In most sectors, however, there was trade creation within the EC and trade diversion away from outside states.

* 10.20 *

Cairncross, Alec, Herbert Giersch, Alexandre Lamfalussy, Giuseppe Petrilli, and Pierre Uri. *Economic Policy for the European Community: The Way Forward*. New York: Holmes & Meier, 1974. ISBN 0-8419-0189-9.

The authors deal with the economic and political policies of the EC, devoting their seventh chapter to international economic policies. They cover tariffs, non-tariff barriers, preferences, and agricultural trade, among other topics.

* 10.21 *

Davenport, Michael. "The Economic Impact of the EEC." In: *The European Economy: Growth and Crisis*, edited by Andrea Boltho. Oxford: Oxford University Press, 1982. ISBN 0-19-877118-5.

The EC has appeared protectionist to the outside world, but it is not necessarily more protectionist than the individual states would have been. The EC as a single unit may facilitate international trade agreements but its position is of necessity a compromise among the member states. In the area of agriculture, the EC has been clearly protectionist.

* 10.22 *

Denton, Geoffrey, and Theo Peeters. "The European Community." In: *Economic Foreign Policies of Industrial States*, edited by Wilfrid L. Kohl. Lexington, MA: Lexington Books, 1977. ISBN 0-669-00958.

Complete reductions of tariffs by the European Community are not generally favored. They could dilute the unity of the member states since the common external tariff would be eliminated. The Community has attempted to harmonize tariff and non-tariff barriers among the member states rather than remove them entirely.

* 10.23 *

Hager, Wolfgang. "Protectionism and Autonomy: How to Preserve Free Trade in Europe." *International Affairs* (London) 58:3 (Summer 1982): 413-428.

The greatest threat that protectionism in Europe poses is not conflict with outside states, which can be managed. Protectionism also threatens trade within the EC, the free trade area that is critical for West European development. Hager argues for a regional policy, including protection, to replace national policies.

* 10.24 *

Hassid, Joseph. "Trade in Manufactures and Industrial Restructuring: The Effects of the First Three Years of Accession on the Manufacturing Sector of the Greek Economy." In: *Greece and the EEC: Integration and Convergence*, edited by George N. Yannopoulos. New York: St. Martin's, 1986. ISBN 0-312-34717-0.

The initial effects of Greek membership in the EC on trade were limited. Trade liberalization within the EC is only one factor affecting Greek trade performance.

* 10.25 *

Kalamotousakis, G.J. "Greece's Association with the European Community: An Evaluation of the First Ten Years." In: *The EEC and the Mediterranean Countries*, edited by Avi Shlaim and G. N. Yannopoulos. Cambridge: Cambridge University Press, 1976. ISBN 0-317-20827-6.

Kalamotousakis develops a model for the influence of a customs union on a developing country when the other members are developed countries. He tests the model with data on Greece. Greece's membership led to trade creation favorable to itself, the other EC countries, and the United States, indicating that customs unions can help a developing country. Greece's failure to join would have forced it into political isolation and a reliance on protectionist policies, given its level of trade with the EC countries.

* 10.26 *

Kreinin, Mordechai. "Effects of the EEC on Imports of Manufactures." *Economic Journal* 82 (September 1972): 897-920.

The effects of trade creation far outweighed trade diversion effects in the EC after its formation. The costs of trade diversion may even have been outweighed by the custom union's contribution to growth among the member countries.

* 10.27 *

Kreinin, Mordechai. "Static Effect of E.C. Enlargement on Trade Flows in Manufactured Products." *Kyklos* 34:1 (1981): 60-71.

The enlargement of the EC has led to both trade creation and trade diversion. The trade creation effects were substantially larger.

* 10.28 *

Lutz, James M., and Robert T. Green. "The Product Life Cycle and the Export Position of the United States." *Journal of International Business Studies* 14:3 (Winter 1983): 77-93.

A comparison of the export patterns in manufactures for the United States, United Kingdom, Japan, and West Germany found that changes in German exports did not follow expectations, although the patterns for the other three countries did. German membership in the EC was one possible explanation for continuing German competitiveness in product areas where declines were otherwise likely.

* 10.29 *
Mattera, A. "Protectionism Inside the European Community: Decisions of the European Court." *Journal of World Trade Law* 18:4 (July/August 1984): 283-308.

Various subtle forms of protection have been used within the EC to favor national firms. The number is surprising. Mattera argues that such protection is counterproductive and hinders the economic revival of the Community.

* 10.30 *
McGeehan, Robert, and Steven J. Warnecke. "Europe's Foreign Policies: Economics, Politics, or Both?" *Orbis* 17:4 (Winter 1974): 1251-1279.

The integration of the members' economies into the EC has made foreign trade liberalization more difficult since there are adjustments required in the member states as a result of the new domestic competition. The US emphasis on free trade has been seen as pursuance of a principle that is helpful to the US economic position.

* 10.31 *
Mendes, A. J. Marques. "The Contribution of the European Community to Economic Growth: An Assessment of the First 25 Years." *Journal of Common Market Studies* 24:4 (June 1986): 261-277.

The economic growth of the members of the EC has been significantly facilitated by the creation of the customs union. In the 1960s, trade liberalization supported this growth. In the 1970s, in the face of increasing global protectionism, enlargement of the EC and the association treaties with the EFTA countries supported growth.

* 10.32 *
Resnick, Stephen A., and Edwin M. Truman. "The Distribution of West European Trade under Alternative Tariff Policies." *Review of Economics and Statistics* 56:1 (February 1974): 83-91.

The authors use a simulation model to gauge the effects of the formation of the EC and EFTA on trade from 1953 to 1968. Their analyses show the relative trade creation and trade distortion effects for the formation of these two trading areas, as well as the expected consequences of further multilateral tariff reductions.

* 10.33 *
Schneider, J. W. "Intra-Benelux NTD's." In: *Prospects for Eliminating Non-Tariff Distortions*, edited by Anthony E. Scaperlanda. Leiden: A. W. Sijthoff, 1973. ISBN 90-286-0063-9.

A review of non-tariff distortions of trade in the Benelux customs union suggests that such unions contribute to a reduction of these obstacles among members. The Benelux arrangement also forced the discussion of these trade barriers into the open to the advantage of third countries.

* 10.34 *
Seers, Dudley. "Conclusions: The EEC and Unequal Development." In: *The Experience of the EEC*, edited by Dudley Seers and Constantine Vaitsos with Marja-Liisa Kiljunen. New York: St. Martin's, 1980. ISBN 0-312-41890-6.

The EC has reinforced international inequality by its protection of domestic markets, including the agricultural sector. Among the countries particularly hurt by these practices have been the NICs and countries like Uruguay and Argentina that produce temperate zone farm products.

* 10.35 *
Wallace, William. "Grand Gestures and Second Thoughts: The Response of Member Countries to Greece's Application." In: *Greece and the European Community*, edited by Loukas Tsoukalis. Westmead, England: Saxon House, 1979. ISBN 0-566-00232-9.

Greece's original application for full EC membership was favorably received initially, but later the prospect of Spain and Portugal following on the Greek example presented difficulties. Spain and Portugal's entry would threaten agricultural producers in the member states, as well as some industrial sectors such as textiles. Governments of the member states, as well as affected interest groups, became more concerned with the example that Greek entry would have.

* 10.36 *
Williamson, John, and Anthony Bottrill. "The Impact of Customs Unions on Trade in Manufactures." *Oxford Economic Papers* n.s. 23:3 (November 1971): 323-351.

Intra-EC trade was approximately 50 percent greater than it would have been without the customs union. The gains were largely from trade creation rather than trade diversion, and other positive consequences from EC trade balanced the effects of trade diversion on third countries. EFTA had a greater amount of trade diversion among its member states.

* 10.37 *

Winters, L. Alan. "British Imports of Manufactures and the Common Market." *Oxford Economic Papers* n.s. 36:1 (March 1984): 103-118.

Britain's accession to the EC led to an increase in imports at the expense of British producers. This change indicated that there had been significant trade creation but little trade diversion.

* 10.38 *

Yannopoulos, George N. "The European Community's Common External Commercial Policy: Internal Contradictions and Institutional Weaknesses." *Journal of World Trade Law* 19:5 (September/October 1985): 451-465.

The EC has not been able to develop an effective Community commercial policy for trade and other economic issues. Community institutions have been unable to cope with competing objectives of the members. The EC has moved towards greater levels of protection, but its record compares favorably with those of Japan and the United States.

* 10.39 *

Ziebura, Gilbert. "Internationalization of Capital, International Division of Labor and the Role of the European Community." *Journal of Common Market Studies* 21:1/2 (September/December 1982): 127-140.

The members of the EC are divided between support for liberal trade and 'organized' free trade. The countries that are competitive internationally in a given economic sector favor free trade while non-competitive states favor protection in that sector.

The EC Extended--An Emerging Trade Bloc?

* 10.40 *

Aitken, Norman D. "The Effect of the EEC and EFTA on European Trade: A Temporal Cross-Section Analysis." *American Economic Review* 63:5 (December 1973): 881-892.

By 1967 both the EC and EFTA had experienced larger than expected increases in trade compared to estimates of trade without the presence of either trade area. The increase was larger for the EC. There was also evidence of trade diversion for both areas at the other's expense once the trade areas had been established.

* 10.41 *

Aitken, Norman, and Robert S. Obutelewicz. "A Cross Sectional Study of EEC Trade with the Association of African Countries." *Review of Economics and Statistics* 18:4 (November 1976): 425-433.

The association of the former African colonies with the EC has had a significant trade creation effect for exports from both the EC members and the African countries from 1959 to 1971. The size of the effect increased progressively through time.

* 10.42 *

Ashoff, Guido. "The Textile Policy of the European Community Towards the Mediterranean Countries: Effects and Future Options." *Journal of Common Market Studies* 22:1 (September 1983): 17-45.

Ashoff reviews the effects of a variety of protectionist devices on exports of textiles from Mediterranean countries that have economic agreements with the EC. These states do gain since their products, even though limited in quantity, are protected from competition from other low cost exporters.

* 10.43 *

Cohen, Yaacov. "Implications of a Free Trade Area between the EEC and Israel." *Journal of World Trade Law* 10:3 (May/June 1976): 252-264.

The author describes the negotiation of the free trade area between Israel and the EC. Israel with a small domestic market needed access to a larger market for its industries and agriculture, but many domestic industries will have to become more competitive in the face of competition from European imports.

* 10.44 *

Donges, Juergen B. "The Economic Integration of Spain with the EEC: Problems and Prospects." In: *The EEC and the Mediterranean Countries*, edited by Avi Shlaim and G.N. Yannopoulos. Cambridge: Cambridge University Press, 1976. ISBN 0-317-20827-6.

The EC tariff structure discriminates most against labor intensive products or those with raw materials inputs, products in which Spain would have a comparative advantage. The tariff preferences granted to Spain in its agreement, prior to the recent decision for full membership, will constitute an export subsidy while preferences granted to the EC in return will facilitate EC exports to Spain.

* 10.45 *

Dunlap, James B., and Robert N. King. "Regional Economic Integration and GATT: The Effects of the EEC-EFTA Agreements on International Trade." *Law and Policy in International Business* 6:1 (1974): 207-235.

In 1972 the EC and five EFTA members signed agreements providing for the reduction of trade barriers in industrial products. Since the agreements were likely to hurt the trade of third countries with the signatories, they violated the spirit of

GATT in as much as the ultimate result was the creation of a trade area with preferences for a restricted number of states.

* 10.46 *
Frey-Wouters, Ellen. *The European Community and the Third World: The Lome Convention and Its Impact.* New York: Praeger, 1980. ISBN 0-275-90484-9.

The EC countries have protected declining industries against imports to the detriment of the developing states. Although there have been complaints by developing countries that lack preferential trade agreements with the EC, there appears to have been little trade diversion.

* 10.47 *
Gaines, David B., William C. Sawyer, and Richard Sprinkle. "EEC Mediterranean Policy and U.S. Trade in Citrus." *Journal of World Trade Law* 15:5 (September/October 1981): 431-439.

The EC agreements with the Mediterranean countries clearly violate GATT rules. There has been significant trade diversion at the expense of non-Mediterranean states, including the United States and Brazil. Israel and Spain have been among the major beneficiaries.

* 10.48 *
Green, Reginald H. "The EEC Enlargement and Commercial Policy Toward the Third World." In: *European Studies in Development: New Trends in European Development Studies*, edited by Jacques de Bandt, Peter Mandi, and Dudley Seers. New York: St. Martin's, 1980. ISBN 0-312-27086-0.

The addition of Spain, Portugal, and Greece to the EC will likely lead to an increase in protectionism, violation of GATT principles, and limits on imports from the developing countries, including the ACP states and the NICs. The end result will be trade diversion rather than trade creation.

* 10.49 *
Hager, Wolfgang. "The Mediterranean: A European Mare Nostrum?" *Orbis* 81:1 (Spring 1974): 231-251.

Hager analyzes the EC's trade policies and associations with Mediterranean countries in the context of other issues. He concludes that the efforts to develop economic links and to give preferences to producers in the area are not likely to succeed.

* 10.50 *
Henig, Stanley. "The Mediterranean Policy of the European Community." *Government and Opposition* 6:4 (Autumn 1971): 502-519.

Henig describes the early years of the EC's policy toward Mediterranean countries. The series of preferential agreements with non-members violated some GATT rules and contained provisions for mutual preferences. The need to protect agricultural producers in some member states limited the scope of many agreements.

* 10.51 *
Jepma, Catrinus. "An Application of the Constant Market Shares Technique on Trade Between the Associated African and Malagasy States and the European Community." *Journal of Common Market Studies* 20:2 (December 1981): 175-192.

The former colonies of the original EC members in Africa had declining exports in the first half of the 1960s in part because they lost their protected European markets. The implementation of the GSP in the EC led to further declines in the 1970s of export competitiveness.

* 10.52 *
Kebschull, Dietrich. "The Effects of EEC Preferences to Associated States on Trade Flows." In: *The EEC and the Mediterranean Countries*, edited by Avi Shlaim and G.N. Yannopoulos. Cambridge: Cambridge University Press, 1976. ISBN 0-317-20827-6.

An analysis based on four commodities indicates that the EC tariff preference granted to associate members has not discriminated against third countries in EC markets. Kebschull notes also that a system of generalized preferences will further limit the effect of the tariff preference. He does fail, however, to discuss the guaranteed quotas that exist for some products exported by the associate members.

* 10.53 *
Kreinin, Mordechai. "US Trade Interests and the EEC Mediterranean Policy." In: *The EEC and the Mediterranean Countries*, edited by Avi Shlaim and G.N. Yannopoulos. Cambridge: Cambridge University Press, 1976. ISBN 0-317-20827-6.

The United States has expressed displeasure with the extent of EC preferential agreements, particularly after the expansion of the Community and the extension of associate status to many of the Mediterranean countries. The United States, other developed countries, and the Asian Commonwealth countries have lost markets for industrial exports as a result. Reverse preferences by associated developing countries appear to have transferred resources from these countries to the European members of the Community.

* 10.54 *
Matthews, Jacqueline D. *Association System of the European Community.* New York: Praeger, 1977. ISBN 0-275-23270-0.

The wide range of EC trade agreements has provided for trade liberalization among a large group of states. Arguments that these links violate GATT principles have declined as more states, including a majority of GATT members, have signed such agreements. It does not appear that preferences within this group have hurt the trade of other countries.

* 10.55 *
McQueen, Matthew. "Lome and the Protective Effect of Rules of Origin." *Journal of World Trade Law* 16:2 (March/April 1982): 119-132.

The rules of origin in the Lome Convention have the effect of protecting EC industries and of requiring the developing countries to import from EC firms. McQueen concludes that more realistic rules of origin clearly are necessary.

* 10.56 *
McQueen, Matthew. "Some Measures of the Economic Effects of Common Market Trade Preferences for the Mediterranean Countries." In: *The EEC and the Mediterranean Countries*, edited by Avi Ahlaim and G.N. Yannopoulos, Cambridge: Cambridge University Press, 1976. ISBN 0-317-20827-6.

The Mediterranean associates of the EC have attempted to expand their exports to the Community at the same time that protectionist sentiment in Europe has been increasing. Exports from Greece, Morocco, Tunisia, and Spain to the EC were probably higher due to the preferential agreements, while Greek and Turkish imports from the EC were probably higher because of reverse preferences.

* 10.57 *
Moss, Joanna, and John Ravenhill. "Trade Developments during the First Lome Convention." *World Development* 10:10 (October 1982): 841-856.

The first Lome Convention failed to create an expanded market for exports from the developing ACP states. There were even declines. The ACP states did have better export performances than other, non-oil exporting, developing states in the EC market.

* 10.58 *
Mytelka, Lynn, and Michael Dolan. "The EEC and the ACP Countries." In: *Integration and Unequal Development: The Experience of the EEC*, edited by Dudley Seers and Constantine Vaitsos with Marja-Liisa Kiljunen. New York: St. Martin's, 1980. ISBN 0-312-41890-6.

With the exception of France, the members of the EC are moving towards a policy of limiting preferences for the ACP states. In France, the debate is between large, multi-national firms favoring liberal trade and smaller firms favoring continued protectionism.

* 10.59 *
O'Sullivan, Declan. "New Problems for Countries Outside the Trading Blocs." *Columbia Journal of World Business* 8:1 (Spring 1973): 61-65.

O'Sullivan notes that there are significant problems that countries outside the enlarged EC face if they do not have preferential trading agreements with that organization. These countries will lose potentially important markets.

* 10.60 *
Pomfret, Richard. "Trade Effects of European Community Preferences to Mediterranean Countries: The Case of Textile and Clothing Imports." *World Development* 10:10 (October 1982): 857-862.

EC preferences to Mediterranean producers of textiles have apparently expanded their export levels to the EC. Protectionist measures adopted in the EC, such as the second Multi-Fibre Agreement, have helped further since these states were largely unaffected by them.

* 10.61 *
Ravenhill, John. "Asymmetrical Interdependence: Renegotiating the Lome Convention." In: *The Political Economy of EEC Relations with African, Caribbean and Pacific States: Contributions to the Understanding of the Lome Convention on North-South Relations*, edited by Frank Long. Oxford: Pergamon, 1980. ISBN 0-080-24077-1.

The second Lome Convention reflected in part the effects of British membership in the EC and the need to replace Commonwealth preferences for the developing states that were former British colonies. The weakness of the British and French economies militated against granting liberalized access for ACP exports.

* 10.62 *
Ravenhill, John. *Collective Clientelism: The Lome Conventions and North-South Relations.* New York: Columbia University Press, 1985. ISBN 0-231-05804-7.

In a wide ranging discussion of the effects of preferential arrangements of the ACP states with the EC, Ravenhill notes that these states gain little from special preferences and lower tariffs, although the EC members have gained slightly from special market situations available to them. The ACP states have also been hurt by domestic pressures for protection in Europe, notwithstanding their special access. Ravenhill concludes that their special access has been more important in principle than in practice.

* 10.63 *
Robert, Annette. "The EEC and the Maghreb and Mashreq Countries." In: *Integration and Unequal Development: The Experience of the EEC*, edited

by Dudley Seers and Constantine Vaitsos with Marja-Liisa Kiljunen. New York: St. Martin's, 1980. ISBN 0-312-41890-6.

EC protectionist policies have been directed against exports in which the North African and Eastern Mediterranean countries have a comparative advantage. Factors other than special EC preferences have led to increased exports of these states, and the preferences contain the potential for the use of quotas and safeguards. The admission of Spain, Greece, and Portugal to the EC will lead to trade diversion effects at the expense of these countries.

* 10.64 *
Robert, Annette. "The Effects of EEC Enlargement on the Maghreb Countries." In: *European Studies in Development: New Trends in European Development Studies*, edited by Jacques de Bandt, Peter Mandi, and Dudley Seers. New York: St. Martin's, 1980. ISBN 0-312-27086-0.

The EC has shown a willingness to discriminate against products in which non-Community producers can compete with domestic ones. The enlargement of the EC will undoubtedly increase the use of protectionist measures that will hurt exports from the Maghreb (Morocco, Algeria, and Tunisia).

* 10.65 *
Scaperlanda, Anthony. "E.E.C. N.T.D.'s and Developing Countries." In: *Prospects for Eliminating Non-Tariff Distortions*, edited by Anthony E. Scaperlanda. Leiden: A. W. Sitjthoff, 1973. ISBN 90-286-0063-9.

The EC reductions of tariffs on tropical products and the establishment of a special preference for exports from the developing countries highlighted the effects of non-tariff barriers. These barriers have favored the former European colonies at the expense of the other developing countries. Quotas have been a particularly important barrier to exports from these other states.

* 10.66 *
Stordel, Harry. "Trade Cooperation: Preferences in the Lome Convention, the Generalized System of Preferences and the World Trade System." In: *The Lome Convention and a New International Order*, edited by Frans A. M. Alting von Geusau. Leyden: A. W. Sijthoff, 1977. ISBN 90-286-0217-8.

The European Community's GSP was designed to protect the existing advantages of those developing states that signed the Lome Convention. The Convention also aids the signatories by establishing more liberal rules of origin provisions than the GSP and by reducing some non-tariff barriers. The EC and the associated developing countries are not likely to support multilateral tariff reductions since it would reduce the special access portions of the Convention.

* 10.67 *
Tovias, Alfred. "The Outcome of Closer Economic Links with the EEC for LDCs' Exports Previously Dumped in World Markets: An Empirical Investigation." *Oxford Economic Papers* n.s. 31:1 (March 1979): 121-132.

One result of the agreements of states with the European Community has been the ability of inefficient producers to continue to export due to EC import barriers against other producers. Multilateral tariff reductions would have led to greater global efficiency.

* 10.68 *
Twitchett, Carol Cosgrove. "Patterns of ACP/EEC Trade." In: *The Political Economy of EEC Relations with African, Caribbean and Pacific States: Contributions to the Understanding of the Lome Convention on North-South Relations*, edited by Frank Long. Oxford: Pergamon, 1980. ISBN 0-08-024077-1.

ACP exports to the EC have been hampered by protectionist policies in that organization. Their agricultural exports have been treated more favorably than similar exports from other states, but they receive less favorable treatment than domestic EC producers, a situation that effectively limits ACP exports. Protection for European textile industries included the imposition of quotas for ACP exports of textiles for the first time in 1978.

* 10.69 *
Von Gleich, Albrecht. "The Economic Relations between Germany and Latin America and the Significance of the European Community." In: *Latin America and World Economy*, edited by Joseph Grunwald. Beverly Hills, CA: Sage, 1978. ISBN 0-8039-0864-4.

The formation of the EC eventually led to a reduction of Latin American imports. The EC is seen as a protectionist group in Latin America, and the connections of the EC and the ACP states are seen as further limiting Latin American exports to the EC.

* 10.70 *
Yannopoulos, G. N. "The Mediterranean Policy of the EEC: Its Impact on the Associated Developing Countries." *Journal of World Trade Law* 11:6 (November/December 1977): 489-500.

Yannopoulos answers the arguments of those who think that association with the EC has hurt the developing countries of the Mediterranean. While there are still EC barriers to trade, particularly in agriculture, the agreements have aided the developing states. They would have been worse off without these agreements.

* 10.71 *
Yannopoulos, George N. "Patterns of Response to EC Tariff Preferences: An Empirical Investigation of Selected Non-ACP Associates." *Journal of Common Market Studies* 25:1 (September 1986): 15-30.

EC trade preferences for various Mediterranean countries did lead to export expansion and diversification, although in a limited number of product areas. Such trade preferences can be effective.

* 10.72 *
Young, Charles. "Association with the EEC: Economic Aspects of the Trade Relationship." *Journal of Common Market Studies* 11:2 (December 1972): 120-135.

The early association of former colonies with the EC has led to trade diversion and no trade creation. The African states have gained a few advantages from association while the European states have gained somewhat more. The trade of the European members with the African associates is such a small percentage of their total trade, however, that the gain is negligible.

Other Free Trade Areas--Developed Countries

* 10.73 *
Chittle, Charles R. "Tariff Discrimination and Cyclical Trade Flows." *Journal of Common Market Studies* 10:4 (June 1972): 314-325.

Chittle used EFTA trade data to test whether tariff preferences lead to instability in trade patterns. He found no evidence for such instability among the member nations or their trade partners --both other members of states outside of EFTA. States generally continued to trade with the same partners.

* 10.74 *
Curzon, Victoria. *The Essentials of Economic Integration: Lessons of EFTA Experience.* New York: St. Martin's, 1974. ISBN 0-312-26425-9.

Curzon discusses the effects of EFTA on tariffs, non-tariff barriers, and agricultural preferences. EFTA led to trade creation among the seven members as well as trade diversion from other countries, although the effects of trade creation were larger than those of trade diversion.

* 10.75 *
Drabek, Zdenek, and David Greenaway. "Economic Integration and Intra-Industry Trade: The EEC and CMEA Compared." *Kyklos* 37:3 (1984): 444-469.

Economic integration has led to greater intra-industry trade in the EC than in the Council of Mutual Economic Assistance. The lower level of such trade in the CMEA is related to a number of possible factors characteristic of centrally planned economies such as bilateral trade balancing, less demand, and non-tariff interventions of the government in the economy.

* 10.76 *
Pelzman, Joseph. "Trade Creation and Trade Diversion in the Council of Mutual Economic Assistance: 1954-1970." *American Economic Review* 67:4 (September 1977): 713-722.

An analysis of trade patterns for the members of CMEA (or COMECON), the trading area for the European centrally planned economies, indicated that there were major trade creation effects for the members. There were only small trade diversion effects at the expense of Western countries, a not surprising result given the nature of trade links with these states.

* 10.77 *
Sawyer, W. Charles, and Richard L. Sprinkle. "U.S.-Israel Free Trade Area: Trade Expansion Effects of the Agreement." *Journal of World Trade Law* 20:5 (September/October 1986): 526-539.

Both Israel and the United States will gain from a recently negotiated free trade area agreement. Difficulties may be experienced by US firms facing the free entry of Israeli goods. If future free trade area agreements are signed, as seems possible, consideration will have to be given to providing special adjustment assistance to US firms negatively affected by such imports.

* 10.78 *
Stedman, Charles. "Canada-U.S. Automotive Agreement: The Sectoral Approach." *Journal of World Trade Law* 8:2 (March/April 1975): 176-185.

Although multilateral trade negotiations have focussed on general tariff restrictions, the US-Canadian automotive agreement used a sectoral approach. It contained various adjustment and escape clauses providing a flexibility that recommends the sectoral over the general approach.

Other Free Trade Areas--Developing Countries

* 10.79 *
Aitken, Norman D., and William R. Lowry. "A Cross-Sectional Study of the Effects of LAFTA and CACM on Latin American Trade." *Journal of Common Market Studies* 11:4 (June 1973): 326-336.

Neither LAFTA nor CACM have had trade diversion effects on the trade of other Latin American countries. Both, however, have had trade creation effects among member states.

* 10.80 *

Balassa, Bela. "Intra-Industry Trade and the Integration of Developing Countries in the World Economy." In: *On the Economics of Intra-Industry Trade: Symposium 1978*, edited by Herbert Giersch. Tubingen: J.C.B. Mohr, 1978. ISBN 0-89563-548-8.

The Central American Common Market has led to intra-industry specialization due to tariff reductions. There have been similar gains for the members of the Latin American Free Trade Association. Less protection in the developing states would also lead to increased productivity as a result of increased competition. Regional trading areas should also have a low common external tariff to increase specialization and competition.

* 10.81 *

Balassa, Bela. "Tariffs and Trade Policy in the Andean Common Market." *Journal of Common Market Studies* 12:2 (December 1973): 176-195.

Balassa suggests a common external tariff for the members of the Andean group that is lower than the individual country tariffs. This tariff in conjunction with harmonization of export subsidies, quotas, and other devices is expected to stimulate intra-regional trade and economic growth.

* 10.82 *

Cochrane, James D., and John W. Sloan. "LAFTA and the CACM: A Comparative Analysis of Integration in Latin America." *Journal of Developing Areas* 8:1 (October 1973): 13-38.

The Central American Common Market has had greater initial successes than the Latin American Free Trade Association, in part due to greater homogeneity of its members, greater external support, the small size of the states that has encouraged cooperation, and a better structural design. Both efforts have succeeded in part because the organizations removed previously existing important protectionist obstacles to trade among the members.

* 10.83 *

George, Robert, Eldon Reiling, and Anthony Scaperlanda. "Short-Run Trade Effects of the LAFTA." *Kyklos* 30:4 (1977): 618-636.

The creation of LAFTA led to greater intra-area trade for all members. Most of this additional trade, however, was diverted from third countries.

* 10.84 *

Morawetz, David. "Extra-Union Exports of Industrial Goods from Customs Unions among Developing Countries." *Journal of Development Economics* 1:3 (December 1974): 247-260.

Data from the Central American Common Market indicate that in some cases intra-industry specialization in the market did lead to increases in exports. For other goods, however, the availability of a larger, protected domestic market led to decreases in exports to other countries.

* 10.85 *

Reynolds, Clark W. "Fissures in the Volcano?: Central American Economic Prospects." In: *Latin America and World Economy*, edited by Joseph Grunwald. Beverly Hills, CA: Sage, 1978. ISBN 0-8039-0864-4.

The Central American Common Market led to an initial expansion of trade among the member states. The resulting grade diversion led to higher costs for imports of manufactures for Honduras, explaining Honduran dissatisfaction with the organization.

* 10.86 *

Willmore, L.N. "Free Trade in Manufactures Among Developing Countries: The Central American Experience." *Economic Development and Cultural Change* 20:4 (July 1972): 659-670.

One of the effects of the Central American Common Market has been increased trade, particularly in manufactures. The trade has not so much led to the creation of industries in only one country but rather intra-industry specialization with plants in the different member countries becoming more specialized and producing for a larger market. Willmore indicates that a free trade area may be more effective than protectionist practices.

* 10.87 *

Willmore, Larry N. "Trade Creation, Trade Diversion and Effective Protection in the Central American Common Market." *Journal of Development Studies* 12:4 (July 1976): 396-414.

There was both trade creation and trade diversion within CACOM. Trade creation occurred in Honduras and Costa Rica and trade diversion effects were generally present in the other three members.

Trade Blocs

* 10.88 *

Barraclough, Geoffrey. "The EEC and the World Economy." In: *Integration and Unequal Development: The Experience of the EEC*, edited by Dudley Seers and Constantine Vaitsos with Marja-Liisa Kiljunen. New York: St. Martin's, 1980. ISBN 0-312-41890-6.

The EC has become increasingly inward looking and opposed to exports from the developing world that threaten domestic industries. It is also creating a regional trading bloc in a world that is characterized by increasing regionalism.

* 10.89 *

Kihl, Young Whan, and James M. Lutz. *World Trade Issues: Regime, Structure, and Policy*. New York: Praeger, 1985. ISBN 0-03-063057-6.

The authors discuss a variety of protectionist issues including free trade and neomercantilism, protectionism in the developed countries and its impact on developing states, and the costs of agricultural protectionism. In part 3 they discuss trading blocs that have formed or have begun to form in various parts of the world.

* 10.90 *

Preeg, Ernest H. *Economic Blocs and U.S. Foreign Policy*. Washington, DC: National Planning Association, 1974. LC 73-91688.

The author analyzes the possibility that economic blocs may appear centered on Japan, North America, and Western Europe and discusses their effects on countries in the blocs and outside them. Preeg sees such blocs as leading to increased discrimination in world trade.

* 10.91 *

Robertson, David. "The European Community's Mediterranean Policy in a World Context." In: *The EEC and the Mediterranean Countries*, edited by Avi Shlaim and G. N. Yannopoulos. Cambridge: Cambridge University Press, 1976. ISBN 0-317-20827-6.

Robertson notes that the agreements reached with the Mediterranean countries constitute multiple examples of trade discrimination, and they undermine the GATT principles designed to prevent bilateralism. The EC preferential agreements with a variety of countries have thus constituted progressive discrimination. The EC Mediterranean policy is part of the broader issue of regionalism versus multilateralism in international trade.

RADICAL VIEWS ON THE INTERNATIONAL
ECONOMY AND PROTECTIONISM

The issue of protectionism can be interpreted from a more radical perspective and in the context of a broad view of the international economic system. Much of this critical concern focuses on the developing countries and their possible exploitation by the industrialized nations or capitalist classes.

A radical critique of many aspects of the international economic system as it has operated after World War II has appeared in the literature. While many of the critics are Marxist or neo-Marxist --adapting Marxist ideas by extension to new situations and concentrating on class relationships within and between states-- in their orientation, not all the critical commentary can be classified as falling into any single ideological perspective. For example, dependency and neo-colonialist theorists, who have argued that the international economic system is unfair to the developing states, have drawn on Marxist ideas at times, but their approach to the problems that they highlight is different. In fact, many of the works included in the previous chapters contain criticisms of the operation of at least some aspects of international trade relationships, but the more extensive criticisms contained in the articles and books included in this chapter can be distinguished by a broader view of the roles that trade and protectionism play as a part of a wider set of relationships in the global economy.

These critics have generally argued that international economic exchanges work to the advantage of certain states and to the disadvantage of other countries or to the advantage of particular groups in certain states and to the disadvantage of other groups in the same or different countries. In addition, this uneven distribution of benefits is not accidental. It was created by design or is, at least, perpetuated by conscious action. The developing countries as a group are usually considered to be exploited by the more industrialized nations, often, though not necessarily, to the benefit of the capitalist classes in the developed states.

Within the context of exploitative relationships, the critics have not necessarily viewed protectionism and free trade as key issues in their own right, although it is possible to extract views on protectionism from their writings, sometimes by inference. The degree of openness in the trade regime is rather a symptom of other basic conditions in the international system. If free trade is the prevailing norm in the international system, it is because the advanced states can derive advantages or profits from it. Unfettered free trade provides the developed states with the opportunity to keep the other countries from developing their own resources and benefiting from them. In this sense, the hegemony views discussed in Chapter 4 are accepted in many ways by the critics. The hegemon will maintain and support a system of free trade because it, or at least its ruling groups, gains from such a regime. It has been argued that the classic textbook example used to demonstrate the value of free trade and comparative advantage also shows the dangers of free trade for a less industrialized country.

In this example, British textiles were exchanged for Portuguese wine since the British could more efficiently produce textiles while the Portuguese had a comparative advantage in the production of wine. Early in the eighteenth century, generally free trade between Great Britain and Portugal was established, facilitating the exchange of many goods, including British textiles and Portuguese wine. One outcome of this trade relationship, however, was the demise of the fledgling Portuguese textile industry, which could not compete with the cheaper British imports. When the Portuguese textile industry was eliminated as a competitor, British firms were even able to raise the prices that were charged for their imports. The initially cheap imports also prevented the Portuguese economy from developing an important early domestic industrial base. Other Portuguese industries suffered similar fates due to their inability to compete with British imports, and Portugal was kept in a weak economic position in relation to its larger trading partner.[1]

This process has also occurred in other territories and in other time periods to the advantage of the stronger state and the disadvantage of the weaker one. Great Britain used free trade as a mechanism for dominating many parts of the world, a policy that was preferable to direct territorial occupation.[2] The US support of free trade after World War II has also been seen as part of a design to further the effective economic control of Europe and Japan by capitalist groups. The operations of US capital supported the creation and maintenance of US hegemony that had been established.

The presence of barriers to trade has also been seen as a reflection of disunity and dissension among different groups of national capitalists. The trade wars of the 1930s were an indication

of the absence of a hegemon and the presence of conflict among different national capitalist classes, a conflict that led to World War II. More recently, the rise of neo-mercantilism reflected changes in the previous hegemonic position of the United States. The US failure to preserve free trade was a consequence of the appearance of vigorous capitalist classes in Europe and Japan that were in competition with US capital. The increase in protection resulted from the conflict of capital in these different areas of the world. In addition, the formation of the EC has been seen as a defensive reaction by European capitalists to their domination by US capital. In the former hegemon, the loss of economic power led to division in the capitalist classes. Some portions of US capital favored protection and even military options to preserve their profits while others favored peace and international cooperation among capitalists as the best means of maintaining economic influence.[3]

The creation of obstacles to imports from the developing countries is seen as another example of the use of protection in the pursuance of broader goals by these critics. It is a means by which the developing states can be kept weak and subservient in the international political and economic systems. In many cases such obstacles do not reflect the fear of import competition from manufacturing industries in the developing world, since such imports are a very small portion of overall consumption and are not responsible for serious job losses or industry declines. The intent is to keep the developing countries from creating their own industrial bases. Without the industrial bases, they will be forced to rely on exports of raw materials to pay for their necessary imports. Some of these raw materials are critically needed in the industrialized states, especially in Europe, which is resource poor. Thus, it is not surprising that trade policies in Europe, both in general and with regard to the ACP states, have favored exports of raw materials and hindered exports of manufactured goods.[4]

The neo-colonialist theorists see this economic manipulation as a reflection of the desire of the industrialized states to dominate the developing world through economic means. Economic control has replaced direct political control of territory. In a similar vein, the special preferences or reduced tariffs that are offered to the developing countries are unlikely to change their relative position in the world. Almost by definition to critics, if these preferences are being offered by the developed nations, they are largely meaningless.

As a result of the manipulation of the trade regime to the disadvantage of the developing states, a special sort of protectionism has been suggested as being appropriate for the developing world. These countries should attempt to develop their economies as independently as possible from the international economic system. Greater self-reliance, particularly through the adoption of socialism as the viable road to economic development, has been one frequent suggestion.[5] Complete autarchy--no trade or economic interaction with outside states--is generally recognized as not being feasible. Trade contacts, however, should be limited as much as possible to prevent adverse effects. Since much of the existing trade presently benefits foreign investors and multinational corporations rather than the developing states, this type of trade needs to be avoided at all costs. Instead, a domestic industrial base should be developed, from indigenous resources to the extent possible. Trade among the developing countries themselves is a possible exception to this approach of non-involvement since the dangers of exploitation are less.

Even this type of trade is subject to some problems if multinational corporations are in control of the exchanges. Trade among the developing states has been relatively limited in the past in part due to the manipulation of the international economic system by the industrialized countries since such trade would weaken the ability of the industrialized states to control the economic system and to utilize the associated political power. The implicit assumption is that in at least some cases the developing states should take steps to encourage such trade, including at least the selective reduction of obstacles to imports from other developing countries, ignoring the most favored nation and reciprocity principles of GATT.

Ultimately, the radical critics argue that a complete restructuring of the international economic system is necessary to remove inequities that are present, including the adverse effects that either protection or free trade can have on the growth of the developing world. A fairer international division of labor is necessary to benefit all countries that participate in trade. Such changes are often seen as unlikely unless changes in the political structures of the industrialized countries and of some of the developing states take place. It has been further argued that the capitalist classes that dominate the economic, political, and so-

cial structures of both types of countries will need to have their influence diminished, if not eliminated, before meaningful change can occur.

While it may be doubtful that the industrialized countries, or the capitalist classes, have had the requisite ability to coordinate the effort necessary to dominate and manipulate the world economy as suggested by these critics, their arguments have raised some important issues for understanding trade relations in the international economy. While the issue of protectionism has often been considered only indirectly or as part of a much wider conceptual framework, the critics have illuminated potentially important factors that affect its absence or presence. Although the works included in this chapter are few in number as a consequence of these critics' concern with broader problems, they give an indication of some of the major characteristics of the radical perspective.

End Notes

1. Baumgartner, T., and T.R. Burns. "The Structuring of International Economic Relations," *International Studies Quarterly* 19:2 (June 1975): pp. 126-159.

2. Gallagher, John and Ronald Robinson. "The Imperialism of Free Trade," *Economic History Review* 6:1 (1953): pp.1-15.

3. Chase-Dunn, Christopher. "Interstate System and Capitalist World Economy," *International Studies Quarterly* 25:1 (March 1981): 19-42.

4. Vaitsos, Constantine V. "From the Ugly American to the Ugly European: The Role of Western Europe in North-South Relations," in: *The New International Economy*, edited by Harry Makler, Alberto Martinelli, and Neil Smelser. Sage Studies in International Sociology, no.26. Beverly Hills, CA: Sage, 1982. p.186.

5. Smith, Tony. "The Underdevelopment of Development Literature: The Case of Dependency Theory," *World Politics* 31:2 (January 1979): p. 288.

Chapter 11: Annotated Bibliography

General Works

* 11.1 *

Arrighi, Giovanni. "A Crisis of Hegemony." In: *Dynamics of Global Crisis*, by Samir Amin, Giovanni Arrighi, Andre Gunder Frank, and Immanuel Wal-

lerstein. New York: Monthly Review Press, 1982. ISBN 0-85345-606-2.

Arrighi argues that the problems in the international economy reflect problems inherent in a capitalist world system that is moving away from US hegemony. The crisis in the US imperial order is primarily restricted to the financial arena as other states have attempted to regain control of their liquidity. He argues that what is key about protectionism is that so few measures have appeared under increasing pressure for such moves and intensifying capitalist competition.

* 11.2 *
Barraclough, Geoffrey. "The EEC and the World Economy." In: *Integration and Unequal Development: The Experience of the EEC*, edited by Dudley Seers and Constantine Vaitsos with Marja-Liisa Kiljunen. New York: St. Martin's, 1980. ISBN 0-312-41890-6.

The EC's initial successes were deceptive and due to favorable economic conditions. The EC has perpetuated unequal trade relations and has discriminated against exports from developing countries despite marginal adjustments in a few mature industries. European integration will continue to further unequal development in the world.

* 11.3 *
Baumgartner, T., and T.R. Burns. "The Structuring of International Economic Relations." *International Studies Quarterly* 19:2 (June 1975): 126-159.

The authors contend that it is necessary to make a complex analysis of economic structures in the international system. To do so, they use two case studies that reflect protectionist issues. First, they argue that free trade between Portugal and England beginning in the 1700s destroyed many nascent Portuguese industries, leaving that country in an underdeveloped condition. Second, they note that US pressure on the United Kingdom after World War II to remove trade barriers and Commonwealth preferences served the interests of US exporters.

* 11.4 *
Chase-Dunn, Christopher. "Interstate System and Capitalist World Economy." *International Studies Quarterly* 25:1 (March 1981): 19-42.

Hegemonic states in a capitalist world economy do not protect their producers as much as other states. When the position of industries in the core state is threatened by competition, the capitalists split between those favoring protection and military pressure and those favoring peace and cooperation with foreign capitalists. The new mercantilism represents a return to an era of capitalist competition in the absence of a hegemonic state.

* 11.5 *
Cox, Robert W. "Production and Hegemony: Toward a Political Economy of World Order." In: *The Emerging International Economic Order: Dynamic*

Processes, Constraints and Opportunities, edited by Harold K. Jacobson and Dusan Sidjanski. Beverly Hills, CA: Sage, 1982. ISBN 0-8039-1833-X.

British and later US hegemony structured the international system in various periods and functioned through control over production processes, over relationships among classes, and over the state. Capitalist groups in the hegemonic states were in control while the hegemony lasted. The working class has been divided and manipulated.

* 11.6 *
Frobel, Folker, Jurgen Heinrichs, and Otto Kreye. *The New International Division of Labour: Structural Unemployment in Industrialised Countries and Industrialisation in Developing Countries.* Translated by Pete Burgess. Cambridge: Cambridge University Press, 1980. ISBN 0-521-28720-0.

The authors analyze the division of labor between developing countries and the industrialized states using, as a detailed case study, trade in textiles and garments from multinational firms in Germany. They argue that the process of establishing plants in the developing states has contributed little to the development of these countries and that free trade or free processing zones are counterproductive in that they provide cheap exports to the developed states while contributing little to industrial development in the developing countries.

* 11.7 *
Gallagher, John, and Ronald Robinson. "The Imperialism of Free Trade." *Economic History Review* 6:1 (1953): 1-15.

The authors argue that Britain imposed free trade as a means of economically dominating large areas of the world to gain raw materials for Britain and to secure outlets for British manufactures. Direct occupation of territory was a last resort policy to achieve these goals. By implication, protectionism would have been in the best interests of many states at this time.

* 11.8 *
Galtung, Johan. "Global Processes and the World in the 1980s." In: *World System Structure: Continuity and Change*, edited by W. Ladd Hollist and James N. Rosenau. Beverly Hills, CA: Sage, 1981. ISBN 0-8039-1629-9.

The dominance of the international economy by capitalist industrialized states has led to many problems, including exploitation of developing countries by the developed ones. As the developing countries industrialize, however, Galtung predicts that the developed states will abandon free trade, considering the costs of import competition greater than the benefits of exports.

* 11.9 *
Green, Reginold Herbold. "The Child of Lome: Messiah, Monster or Mouse." In: *The Political Economy of EEC Relations with African, Caribbean and Pacific States: Contributions to the Understanding of the Lome Convention on North-South Relations*, edited by Frank Long, Oxford: Pergamon, 1980. ISBN 0-08-024077-1.

The second Lome Convention was less neocolonial than its predecessor. The ACP states have benefited less than the EC states from the agreement. The EC has considered exports of consumer goods as a threat, although the failings of the convention result more from the rise of mercantilist attitudes in the world and protectionism in the EC rather than from shortcomings in the agreement as such.

* 11.10 *
Hudson, Michael. *Global Fracture: The New International Economic Order*. New York: Harper & Row, 1977. ISBN 0-06-012004-5.

Difficulties in the international economic system, including the rise of protectionism, reflect the inability of the United States to dominate economic transactions for its own advantage. Europe and Japan with their increasing economic strength are no longer willing to be economic satellites of the United States. The United States advocated free trade after World War II because it was in the US interest; support of free trade was very quickly abandoned when it ceased to be advantageous.

* 11.11 *
Kaldor, Mary. *The Disintegrating West*. London: Allen Lane, 1978. ISBN 0-7139-1076-3.

Protectionism is one indication of the decline of the economic power of the United States. Parochialism in the United States has led to such attitudes elsewhere in the world. The rise to economic power of multinational corporations has been one major cause of the economic weakness of the United States.

* 11.12 *
Kolko, Joyce. *America and the Crisis of World Capitalism*. Boston: Beacon Press, 1974. ISBN 0-807-04790-2.

Kolko sees the rise of protectionism as one manifestation of the conflict over world markets and the contradictions of world capitalism. She argues that efforts at integration and economic unity in the EC would be undone by protectionist pressures. US foreign trade policy has been responsive to US-based multinationals that oppose protectionism and favor free trade.

* 11.13 *
Magdoff, Harry. *The Age of Imperialism: The Economics of U.S. Foreign Policy*. New York: Monthly Review Press, 1966. LC 69-19788.

In his argument that US foreign policy is primarily designed to increase the profits of American business, Magdoff does consider trade issues. The US free trade policy was designed to permit US corporations to penetrate and dominate developing country markets. These corporations also limit exports from developing states in order not to compete with themselves, thus providing protection for the United States. Free trade, as well as foreign investment, is often detrimental to the economic development of these states.

* 11.14 *
Mandel, Ernest. *Europe vs. America: Contradictions of Imperialism*. New York: Monthly Review Press, 1970. ISBN 85345-221-0.

Mandel argues that the EC was formed to permit European capitalists to avoid absorption by US capitalists. The EC protects European capitalists and has also facilitated the division of the developing world into economic spheres of influence for the United States, Japan, and Western Europe.

* 11.15 *
Martinelli, Alberto. "The Political and Social Impact of Transnational Corporations." In: *The New International Economy*, edited by Harry Makler, Alberto Martinelli, and Neil Smelser. Sage Studies in International Sociology, no. 26. Beverly Hills, CA: Sage, 1982. ISBN 0-8039-9792-2.

In his broad analysis of transnational corporations, Martinelli notes that they oppose protectionism and can overcome domestic coalitions in host countries that favor protectionism. Protectionist pressure occurs in part because of the inherent tension between the corporations desiring profits and the nation-state with its economic goals.

* 11.16 *
Mazier, Jacques. "Growth and Crisis--A Marxist Interpretation." In: *The European Economy: Growth and Crisis*, edited by Andrea Boltho. Oxford: Oxford University Press, 1982. ISBN 0-19-877118-5.

Freer trade after World War II led to economic growth in European countries, the accumulation of capital on a multinational scale, and increased importance for multinational firms. The operations of US capital supported US hegemony until European and Japanese capital undercut that hegemony. Increasing government economic regulation, opposition to NIC exports, and conflicts among US, Japanese, and European capital have been among the results for developed states.

* 11.17 *

Rosenbaum, H. Jon, and William G. Tyler. "South-South Relations: The Economic and Political Content of Interactions among Developing Countries." In: *World Politics and International Economics*, edited by C. Fred Bergsten and Lawrence B. Krause. Washington, DC: Brookings Institution, 1975. ISBN 0-317-20637-0.

The developing countries need to achieve greater authority and a redistribution of world resources to deal with international economic problems. Greater cooperation among developing states would permit them to overcome protectionism in developed countries and ensure greater input in international negotiations.

* 11.18 *

Stohl, Michael, and Harry R. Targ. "The Global Political Economy from Bretton Woods to the 1980s." In: *The Global Political Economy in the 1980s*, edited by Michael Stohl and Harry R. Targ. Cambridge, MA: Schenkman, 1982. ISBN 0-87073-236-6.

US efforts to bring about economic recovery in Europe and Japan after World War II were designed to meet US economic needs and to permit the establishment of capitalist control in Europe. The GATT freed trade among industrial states but kept restrictions on agricultural trade from the developing countries. Recent protectionist pressure in the United States reflects the US loss of control over the international economy.

* 11.19 *

Tironi, Ernesto. "Customs Union Theory in the Presence of Foreign Firms." *Oxford Economic Papers* n.s. 34:1 (March 1982): 150-171.

Tironi's model shows that trade creation and trade diversion are not the only relevant issues for customs unions among developing countries. The presence of foreign firms or multinationals, particularly in situations of monopolistic advantage, can lead to profit creation or diversion for these firms at the expense of the member states.

* 11.20 *

Vaitsos, Constantine V. "From the Ugly American to the Ugly European: The Role of Western Europe in North-South Relations." In: *The New International Economy*, edited by Harry Makler, Alberto Martinelli, and Neil Smelser. Sage Studies in International Sociology, no. 26. Beverly Hills, CA: Sage, 1982. ISBN 0-8039-9792-2.

European protectionist practices that hinder exports of manufactures from developing countries are not due to any threat to domestic markets since the volumes in question are low. The protectionist practices are designed to prevent industrialization in the developing countries and to maintain them as sources of raw materials.

* 11.21 *

Vaitsos, Constantine V. "The Role of Europe in North-South Relations." In: *European Studies in Development: New Trends in European Development Studies*, edited by Jacques de Bandt, Peter Mandi, and Dudley Seers. New York: St. Martin's, 1980. ISBN 0-312-27086-0.

Protectionism in Europe against the exports, and particularly the manufactured exports, of the ACP states and other developing countries reflects the EC's adverse balance of trade in these products with Japan and North America. Vaitsos argues that European firms will use monopolistic structures along with protectionist practices to lock developing countries into an inferior position in the international division of labor and monopolize the returns from geographically diversified manufacturing efforts.

* 11.22 *

Wallerstein, Immanual. *The Capitalist World-Economy*. Cambridge: Cambridge University Press, 1979. ISBN 0-521-22085-8.

In this compilation of previous work, Wallerstein analyzes the effects of a capitalist world system on countries and on groups within them. While not commenting on protectionism directly, he does note that some states should reduce trade, even balanced trade, to ensure more equitable development. He also notes that Tanzania's self-reliant approach is useful. In effect, Wallerstein argues that protectionism is necessary at times to isolate countries to at least some extent from the dominant forces in the world economy.

* 11.23 *

Willoughby, John. "The Changing Role of Protection in the World Economy." *Cambridge Journal of Economics* 16:2 (June 1982): 195-211.

Willoughby offers a Marxist critique of the general view that protectionist policies were linked with the rise of imperialism and the concentration of domestic capital. He argues that such linkages were conditioned by specific historical environmental factors in the late nineteenth and early twentieth centuries.

KEY DATES RELATING TO PROTECTIONISM SINCE WORLD WAR II

14 March 1947. The Hague Protocol establishing the Benelux Customs Union was signed.

April 1947. The first round of multilateral tariff negotiations began in Geneva.

30 October 1947. General Agreement on Tariffs and Trade (GATT) created.

1 January 1948. The General Agreement on Tarriffs and Trade entered into force.

1 January 1948. The Benelux Customs Union goes into effect.

March 1948. Negotiations for the proposed International Trade Organization completed in Havana.

January 1949. The Council of Mutual Economic Assistance was established.

April 1949. The second round of GATT multilateral tariff negotiations began in Annecy, France.

9 May 1950. Robert Schuman first made the proposal that led to the establishment of the European Coal and Steel Community.

December 1950. President Truman withdrew the ITO treaty from consideration before the Senate could give it certain defeat.

18 April 1951. The European Coal and Steel Community was established.

April 1951. Third round of GATT multilateral tariff negotiations were undertaken at Torquay, France.

January 1956. Fourth round of GATT multilateral tariff negotiations takes place in Geneva, Switzerland.

25 March 1957. Treaty of Rome creating the European Economic Community was signed.

1 January 1958. The Treaty of Rome becomes effective for the six member countries of the European Economic Community.

20 November 1959. A convention establishing the European Free Trade Association was initialled in Stockholm.

February 1960. The Latin American Free Trade Association was formed.

3 May 1960. The convention establishing the European Free Trade Association entered into force.

1 September 1960. The fifth round of GATT multilateral tariff negotiations began.

December 1960. The Central American Common Market was created.

1 October 1962. The Long-Term Textile Agreement for cotton was negotiated providing for controlled marketing of textiles.

20 July 1963. First Yaounde Convention signed between the members of the European Community and their former African colonies.

23 March 1964. The first meeting of the UN Conference on Trade and Development (UNCTAD) is held.

May 1964. GATT established the International Trade Centre.

4 May 1964. Sixth round (Kennedy Round) of GATT multilateral negotiations on tariffs began.

July 1966. The Common Agricultural Policy of the EC went into effect.

8 August 1967. The Association of Southeast Asian Nations was formed.

29 July 1969. Second Yaounde Convention was signed.

30 January 1970. The Andean Group within the Latin American Free Trade Association was created.

1 January 1971. The Second Yaounde Convention entered into force.

22 January 1972. The Treaty of Accession admitting Denmark, Ireland, and the United Kingdom to the European Community was signed.

1 January 1973. Denmark, Ireland, and the United Kingdom officially became members of the EC.

September 1973. Tokyo Round of multilateral tariff reductions began.

October 1973. OPEC announced major increases in the price of oil.

1 January 1974. The first Multi-Fibre Textile Arrangement was signed.

28 February 1975. The first Lome Convention was signed by the European Community and the ACP states.

November 1975. First of the annual economic summit meetings among the leaders of the United States, Canada, Japan, United Kingdom, Germany, France, and Italy was held.

January 1976. The United States became the last major industrialized country to introduce a Generalized System of Preferences.

December 1977. Second Multi-Fibre Textile Arrangement was established.

1 January 1979. Oil prices began significant rise due to agreement among OPEC members.

April 1979. Tokyo Round of negotiations on tariff reductions was completed.

April 1979. First GATT codes on non-tariff barriers agreed to during the Tokyo Round and signed by some members.

October 1979. Second Lome Convention was signed.

1 January 1981. Greece became a member of the European Community.

May 1981. Japanese-U.S. voluntary export restraint on automobiles signed.

22 December 1981. Second Multi-Fibre Textile Arrangement extended to 1985.

1982. Volume of world trade falls for only the third time since the end of World War II.

February 1983. The European Community negotiates the first voluntary export restraint with Japan.

8 December 1984. The third Lome Convention between the EC and 66 ACP states was signed.

1 January 1986. Spain and Portugal became members of the European Community.

July 1986. Third Multi-Fibre Arrangement was agreed to.

October 1987. United States and Canada complete a draft treaty to establish a free trade area.

TECHNICAL TERMS RELATED TO PROTECTIONISM

Included in this selective glossary of economics and international relations are words and phrases whose specialized meanings differ, in varying degrees, from those of everyday language. It is designed to serve as a convenient reference to the vocabulary of the analytic introductions as well as of the annotations.

ACP - See: **African, Caribbean, and Pacific.**

ASEAN - See: **Association of Southeast Asian Nations.**

Adjustment assistance - assistance granted to industries to aid in changing or modernizing production in the face of import competition.

Ad valorum tariff - a customs duty that is levied as a percentage of the value of the import.

African, Caribbean, and Pacific (ACP) states - designation applied to the developing countries in these three areas of the world that as a group have a formal trade agreement with the European Community.

Association of Southeast Asian Nations (ASEAN) - organization for freer trade and economic cooperation among the member states in Southeast Asia.

Autarky - a policy of national economic self-sufficiency.

Benelux - customs union of Belgium, Luxembourg, and the Netherlands that went into effect after World War II.

Business cycle - term for the periodic increases and declines in economic activity within a country.

CACM or CACOM - See: **Central American Common Market.**

CAP - See: **Common Agricultural Policy.**

CMEA - See: **Council of Mutual Economic Assistance.**

COMECON - See: **Council of Mutual Economic Assistance.**

Cartels - organizations of business firms that allocate shares of domestic or international markets among themselves to avoid competing with each other for markets.

Central American Common Market (CACOM or CACM) - a now moribund customs union formed by five Central American countries.

Code of standards - a term generally used to refer to the GATT agreement that was designed to regulate some non-tariff barriers.

Common Agricultural Policy (CAP) - the European Community's protectionist support mechanism for the Community's farmers.

Common external tariff - the common tariff on imports for all members of a customs union.

Comparative advantage - the view that with free trade each country will produce those goods in which it is most productive relative to other countries, exchanging the surplus for goods that it would be more costly to produce domestically.

Council of Mutual Economic Assistance (CMEA or COMECON) - a customs union centered on the Soviet Union and the East European centrally planned economies.

Countertrade - agreement between two countries providing that at least some deliveries of goods from one state will be counterbalanced by shipments from the other.

Countervailing duties - additional charges on imports that are imposed to offset the effects of foreign export subsidies or to prevent dumping.

Domestic content legislation - requirements that industries include a specified portion of materials produced domestically in their final products.

Dumping - the selling of goods in a foreign market at prices that are less than the cost of production.

EC - See: **European Community.**

EEC - See: **European Community.**

EFTA - See: **European Free Trade Association.**

Effective protection rate - the actual level of protection that is offered to domestic industries by tariffs and non-tariff barriers when the impact of the application of these measures, including effects on intermediate goods and the availability of substitutes, are considered.

Escape clause - See: **Safeguard clause.**

European Community (EC) - a customs union originally composed of six European nations. Its membership now consists of twelve member states. A variant name is European Economic Community (EEC).

European Free Trade Association (EFTA) - free trade area that was formed in 1959 by seven European states in reaction to the creation of the European Community.

Free trade zones - factory areas created to encourage the production of export goods by eliminating or lowering tariffs on machinery or imports needed for the production processes.

GATT - See: **General Agreement on Tariffs and Trade.**

GSP - See: **Generalized System of Preferences.**

General Agreement on Tariffs and Trade (GATT) - an international convention that most countries adhere to, providing rules and guidelines for trade practices.

Generalized System of Preferences (GSP) - the application of lower tariff schedules in the industrialized states for some goods imported from the developing countries while retaining higher tariffs on the same goods imported from other countries.

Hegemon - a state that exercises hegemony.

Hegemony - economic and political dominance by one state and its ability to influence general trends in the system of international trade.

Import substitution - practice of protecting domestic industries so that they can produce goods that were formerly imported.

Infant industry argument - view that a new industry just developing should receive protection in its formative stages until it can compete with foreign producers.

International Trade Commission - a U.S. executive agency that hears cases dealing with charges of dumping, requests for countervailing duties, and requests for relief under various safeguard provisions that protect against damage resulting from import competition.

Kennedy Round - the sixth round of GATT multilateral tariff negotiations that removed or lowered many of the remaining tariff barriers to trade in manufactured goods.

LAFTA - See: Latin American Free Trade Association.

Latin American Free Trade Association (LAFTA) - free trade area formed by the countries of South America and Mexico.

Lome Conventions - agreements between the ACP countries and the European Community providing for a special trade relationship.

MFAs - See: Multi-fibre arrangements.

Most favored nation status - any trade concessions granted to one country are automatically granted to all other states holding this status with the granting country.

Multi-fibre arrangements (MFAs) - a series of agreements providing a framework in which a developed country and a developing one can negotiate orderly marketing arrangements for controlling the level of imports of textiles and apparel.

NICs - See: Newly industrializing countries.

NTBs - See: Non-tariff barriers.

Newly industrializing countries - the most economically advanced developing countries. Singapore, Hong Kong, South Korea, Taiwan, Brazil, and Mexico are now considered to be NICs.

Nominal protection rate - the posted duty that must be paid for imports when they enter a country.

Non-tariff barriers (NTBs) - various mechanisms, other than tariffs, that create obstacles to imports in order to protect domestic industries.

OMA - See: Orderly marketing arrangement.

Orderly marketing arrangement (OMA) - an agreement between an exporting and an importing country to control the increase in the rate of penetration of particular imports into a domestic market in order to ease the adjustment problems of industries in the importing country.

Quota - a numerical limit on imports of particular products that can enter a domestic market.

Rules of origin - limitations in customs unions, free trade areas, and other trade agreements that prevent the by-passing of one country's barriers by shipping to another state that is a member of the agreement. Such rules also provide preferences to goods that are produced within the countries associated by the trade treaty.

Safeguard (escape) clause - a rule in GATT and other international agreements that permits a state to impose restrictions on imports when undue disruption of the domestic market occurs.

Sectoral trade liberalization - the removal of obstacles to trade in one manufacturing area at a time rather than a general trade liberalization.

Specific tariff - a customs duty that is fixed for each item of an import regardless of value.

Tariff quota - a limited amount of imports are admitted at a low tariff rate with additional imports facing escalating customs duties.

Third countries - term used with reference to customs unions or free trade areas for countries that are not members.

Tokyo Round - the most recent GATT multilateral rounds on trade obstacles that began in 1973 and lasted until 1979.

Trade creation - term used with reference to customs unions or free trade areas for the additional production for trade, rather than the domestic market, among members that results from the removal or lowering of tariff barriers. The term has meaning only for customs union theory.

Trade diversion - term used with reference to customs unions or free trade areas for the additional trade among members at the expense of trade with non-members.

Trigger prices - protection is automatically provided if foreign imports fall below a specified price level.

UNCTAD - See: **United Nations Conference on Trade and Development.**

United Nations Conference on Trade and Development (UNCTAD) - UN agency increasingly used by the developing countries to press their demands for changes in trade policies, particularly in the developed countries.

VER - See: **Voluntary export restraint.**

Voluntary export restraint (VER) - an agreement by an exporter or exporters to limit their shipments of specified products to particular markets.

X-efficiency - a term used to denote questions of managerial practices and their effects on efficiency in industries, especially in developing states.

Yaounde Conventions - trade agreements providing the former colonies of the original members of the European Community with special access to the joint Community market.

Author Index

Moss, Joanna (10.57)
Mudaliar, Vishwa (6.129)
Mueller, Hans G. (6.94)
Murphy, Robert G. (2.55)
Murray, T. (8.46)
Murray, Tracy (3.29)
Murray, Tracy (8.34)
Murray, Tracy (8.57)
Murray, Tracy (8.58)
Mussa, Michael (3.14)
Mutti, John (2.43)
Mutti, John H. (6.14)
Mutti, John H. (6.15)
Mytelka, Lynn (10.58)
Mytelka, Lynn Krieger (7.46)
Mytelka, Lynn Krieger (7.142)
Mytelka, Lynn Krieger (7.143)
Mytelka, Lynn Krieger (8.107)
Nam, Chong Hyun (8.135)
Naraine, Mahindra (7.134)
Narbye, Ole David Koht (7.27)
Naya, Seiji (5.42)
Naya, Seiji (8.69)
Nehmer, Stanley (6.159)
Nelson, Douglas R. (6.138)
Nemmers, Barry H. (8.59)
Neu, Axel (7.161)
Neu, Axel D. (7.160)
Nicolaides, Eri (7.19)
Nicolaides, P. (8.60)
Niho, Yoshio (2.36)
Nivola, Pietro S. (6.95)
Nogues, Julio J. (8.108)
Norman, George (2.61)
Nye, Joseph S. (4.2)
Nye, Joseph S., Jr. (5.47)
O'Brien, Denis (10.13)
Obutelewicz, Robert S. (10.41)
Ochs, Jack (6.105)
O'Cleireacain, Seamus (3.46)
O'Cleireacain, Seamus (6.76)
O'Cleireacain, Seamus (7.125)
Odell, John S. (5.70)
Okimoto, Daniel (7.106)
Okimoto, Daniel (7.108)
Okimoto, Daniel (7.113)
Olechowski, Andrzej (7.51)
Olechowski, Andrzej (8.35)
Oliver, Hermia (5.10)
Oliver, Hermia (9.12)
Olson, Mancur (7.7)
O'Neill, Daniel (7.36)
Ono, Yoshiyasu (2.39)
Ono, Yoshiyasu (3.30)
Ostry, Sylvia (1.12)
O'Sullivan, Declan (10.59)
Oulton, Nicholas (7.135)
Ozaki, Robert S. (7.112)
Page, John M., Jr. (8.103)
Page, S. A. B. (7.8)
Pagoulatos, Emilio (1.28)
Palmeter, N. David (6.160)
Panagariya, Arvind (2.26)
Panagariya, Arvind (2.44)
Parker, Stephen (8.136)
Parmenter, Brian R. (3.66)
Parton, Kevin A. (9.16)
Pastor, Robert (6.66)
Pastor, Robert A. (6.65)
Patrick, Hugh (3.79)
Patrick, Hugh (7.110)
Patrick, Hugh T. (7.113)
Patterson, Eliza R. (5.18)
Patterson, Gardner (1.13)
Patterson, Kathleen (9.10)
Pearson, Charles (5.51)

Pearson, Charles (6.161)
Pearson, Scott R. (7.159)
Pease, Don J. (6.114)
Pelkmans, Jacques (7.162)
Pellegrini, Valerie J. (6.162)
Pelzman, Joseph (6.163)
Pelzman, Joseph (6.164)
Pelzman, Joseph (10.76)
Pempel, T. J. (7.114)
Pepper, Thomas (7.118)
Perez, Lorenzo L. (8.109)
Perry, Philip R. (6.145)
Petrilli, Giuseppe (10.20)
Phegan, Colin (3.57)
Phillips, Lawrence T. (6.153)
Pincus, J. J. (6.52)
Pincus, J. J. (6.115)
Pincus, Jonathan J. (6.67)
Pinder, John (5.71)
Pinder, John (6.5)
Pinder, John (7.57)
Pinder, John (7.173)
Pindyck, Robert S. (6.165)
Pinera, Jose (8.55)
Poirier, Rene (5.43)
Pomeranz, Morton (5.52)
Pomfret, Richard (2.56)
Pomfret, Richard (10.14)
Pomfret, Richard (10.60)
Prebisch, Raul (8.110)
Preeg, Ernest H. (9.14)
Preeg, Ernest H. (10.90)
Price, Victoria Curzon (4.18)
Puchala, Donald J. (9.4)
Puchala, Donald J. (9.22)
Pugel, Thomas (9.96)
Pugel, Thomas A. (6.33)
Putman, Robert D. (5.72)
Rabenau, Kurt V. (7.151)
Rajski, Jerzy (3.80)
Ramachandran, Rama (2.32)
Ramsey, James B. (2.24)
Rangarajan, L. (1.14)
Rapkin, David P. (4.10)
Rapkin, David P. (6.32)
Ravenhill, John (10.57)
Ravenhill, John (10.61)
Ravenhill, John (10.62)
Ray, Edward J. (7.53)
Ray, Edward J. (6.154)
Ray, Edward John (2.62)
Ray, Edward John (6.116)
Ray, Edward John (6.166)
Razin, Assaf (2.22)
Razin, Assaf (2.33)
Razin, Assaf (2.34)
Real, P. Lavergne (6.68)
Rehfeldt, Udo (7.144)
Reich, Robert B. (6.97)
Reich, Robert B. (6.167)
Reifman, Alfred (6.12)
Reifman, Alfred (6.55)
Reiling, Eldon (10.83)
Renner, John C. (5.104)
Resnick, Stephen A. (10.32)
Reubens, Edwin P. (6.78)
Reubens, Edwin P. (8.61)
Reynolds, Clark W. (10.85)
Richardson, J. David (6.14)
Richardson, J. David (6.15)
Richardson, J. David (6.98)
Ricks, David A. (7.56)
Riddell, Abby Rubin (7.137)
Riedel, James (7.163)
Rivers, Richard R. (5.53)
Robert, Annette (10.63)

Vernon, Raymond (5.20)
Verreydt, Eric (7.165)
Verrill, Charles Owen, Jr. (6.70)
Vichit-Vadakan, Vinyu (5.42)
Vichit-Vadakan, Vinyu (8.69)
Viner, Jacob (10.15)
Vogt, Donna (6.64)
Volpe, John (7.76)
Von Gleich, Albrecht (10.69)
Vukmanic, Frank G. (8.128)
Waelbroeck, Jean (5.88)
Waelbroeck, Jean (7.165)
Wagenhals, Gerhard (7.166)
Wall, David (8.9)
Wallace, William (10.35)
Wallerstein, Immanuel (4.22)
Wallerstein, Immanual (11.22)
Wallerstein, Immanuel (11.1)
Walsh, James A. (3.83)
Walsh, James A. (3.84)
Walter, Ingo (3.15)
Walter, Ingo (3.16)
Walter, Ingo (3.29)
Walter, Ingo (6.96)
Walter, Ingo (7.174)
Walter, Ingo (8.1)
Walter, Ingo (8.34)
Walter, Ingo (8.41)
Walter, Ingo (8.63)
Walter, Ingo (9.14)
Walters, Robert S. (6.101)
Warley, T. K. (9.12)
Warley, Thorald K. (9.37)
Warnecke, Steven J. (6.172)
Warnecke, Steven J. (10.30)
Warr, Peter G. (3.66)
Waters, W. G., II (2.63)
Waters, W. G., II (6.120)
Watkins, Mel (7.88)
Waverman, Leonard (2.64)
Weil, Frank A. (7.117)
Weintraub, Sidney (5.29)
Weiss, Dieter (8.40)
Weiss, John (8.142)
Weisskoff, Richard (8.143)
Wellenstein, Edmund (5.80)
Wellisz, Stanislaw (2.68)
Wellisz, Stanislaw (2.71)
Wellisz, Stanislaw (8.85)
Weston, Ann (8.47)
Weston, Ann (8.64)
Westphal, Larry E. (8.112)
Westphal, Larry E. (8.144)
Wetter, Thereas (7.31)
Whalley, John (1.19)
Whalley, John (2.54)
Whalley, John (5.37)
Whalley, John (6.12)
Whalley, John (6.23)
Whalley, John (6.158)
Whalley, John (7.75)
Whalley, John (7.79)
Whalley, John (7.80)
Whalley, John (7.85)
Whalley, John (7.88)
Whalley, John (7.90)
Whalley, John (7.97)
Whalley, John (9.37)
Whalley, John (10.4)
Wheeler, Jimmy W. (1.28)
Wheeler, Jimmy W. (3.5)
Wheeler, Jimmy W. (3.8)
Wheeler, Jimmy W. (6.143)
Wheeler, Jimmy W. (7.23)
Wheeler, Jimmy W. (7.118)
Whitehead, Laurence (8.42)

Whitman, Marina V. N. (4.23)
Whitman, Marina V. N. (5.57)
Wilkinson, Bruce W. (7.89)
Wilkinson, Bruce W. (7.90)
Willett, Thomas D. (1.32)
Willett, Thomas D. (6.57)
Willett, Thomas D. (8.5)
Willett, Thomas D. (6.29)
Willett, Thomas D. (6.38)
Willett, Thomas D. (7.30)
Williams, Glen (7.91)
Williams, Harold R. (6.173)
Williams, Thomas (5.39)
Williamson, John (10.36)
Williamson, Peter J. (7.32)
Willmore, L. N. (10.86)
Willmore, Larry N. (10.87)
Willougby, John (11.23)
Wilson, John D. (2.71)
Winham, Gilbert R. (5.58)
Winham, Gilbert R. (6.54)
Winham, Gilbert R. (6.71)
Winters, L. Alan (10.37)
Witte, Willard E. (7.10)
Witthans, Fred (6.121)
Wolf, Martin (5.88)
Wolf, Martin (7.6)
Wolf, Martin (8.65)
Wolff, Alan Wm. (6.11)
Wonnacott, Paul (7.92)
Wonnacott, Paul (10.16)
Wonnacott, R. J. (7.93)
Wonnacott, Ronald J. (7.92)
Wonnacott, Ronald J. (7.94)
Wonnacott, Ronald J. (7.95)
Wonnacott, Ronald J. (7.96)
Wonnacott, Ronald J. (7.97)
Wonnacott, Ronald (10.16)
Woolcock, Stephen (3.85)
Woolcock, Stephen (5.81)
Woolcock, Stephen (7.57)
Woolcock, Stephen (7.58)
Woolcock, Stephen (8.145)
Yamamoto, Midori (7.118)
Yamamura, Kozo (3.79)
Yannopoulos, G. N. (9.29)
Yannopoulos, G. N. (10.25)
Yannopoulos, G. N. (10.44)
Yannopoulos, G. N. (10.52)
Yannopoulos, G. N. (10.53)
Yannopoulos, G. N. (10.56)
Yannopoulos, G. N. (10.70)
Yannopoulos, G. N. (10.91)
Yannopoulos, George (7.167)
Yannopoulos, George N. (9.25)
Yannopoulos, George N. (10.24)
Yannopoulos, George N. (10.38)
Yannopoulos, George N. (10.71)
Yarbrough, Beth V. (4.24)
Yarbrough, Beth V. (5.82)
Yarbrough, Robert M. (4.24)
Yarbrough, Robert M. (5.82)
Yeager, Leland B. (6.36)
Yeats, A. J. (7.59)
Yeats, Alexander J. (2.28)
Yeats, Alexander J. (2.29)
Yeats, Alexander J. (8.35)
Yeats, Alexander J. (8.43)
Yeats, Alexander J. (8.44)
Yeats, Alexander J. (8.66)
Yeutter, Clayton K. (9.6)
Yoder, Amos (5.30)
Yoffie, David B. (3.34)
Yoffie, David B. (6.174)
Yoffie, David B. (8.146)
Yoffie, David B. (8.147)